ENJOY A FULL YEAR
FREE

Thank you for adding **Best Holiday Gatherings** to your kitchen library! Soon you'll be paging through 560+ festive, family-pleasing recipes from *Taste of Home*. And now you can keep the delicious, family favorites coming all year long— **FREE**! Here's how

$27.93 VALUE

149 FANTASTIC & FESTIVE RECIPES AND TIPS

REAL FOOD FROM REAL HOME COOKS   COOKING • CARING • SHARING

taste of home

#1 Cooking Magazine in the World

Your Best Ever Thanksgiving
•No-fuss appetizers
•Savory autumn sides
•Luscious pies

Have Some Scary Fun
MONSTER CUPCAKES

Bakers, Start Your Ovens!
12 WINNING HOLIDAY COOKIES

Wow! Champagne Basted Turkey

Give Thanks

DETACH HERE &
MAIL TODAY!

taste of home
FREE SUBSCRIPTION CARD

Return this card today to claim your Free Subscription (a $27.93 value) to *Taste of Home* magazine. You'll enjoy a full year of new recipes and fresh cooking ideas!

YES! PLEASE START MY FREE 1-YEAR SUBSCRIPTION TO *TASTE OF HOME* MAGAZINE!

NAME _____
(please print)

ADDRESS_____

CITY _____

STATE_____ ZIP _____

E-MAIL _____

Free subscription to *Taste of Home* magazine valid only by returning this card. Your 1-year (7-issue) subscription includes a special issue, which counts as 2 issues in your subscription. Please allow 4-6 weeks for delivery of your first FREE issue.

QL0TP27T

MAIL THIS CARD TODAY!

Now Give Your Family the Fresh Flavors They Crave!

As a *Taste of Home* subscriber, you'll look forward to:

- **Hundreds of mouth-watering recipes** from home cooks, all tested and approved by the *Taste of Home* Test Kitchen.

- Easy recipes with simple, affordable **everyday ingredients**.

- Top winners from **national recipe contests**.

- Dozens of **Clip & Keep recipes** you'll turn to again and again.

- **Color photos** for picture-perfect results.

- **Real food from real home cooks** like you!

FROM: _____

PLACE STAMP HERE

MAIL THIS CARD TODAY!

SUBSCRIPTION FULFILLMENT CENTER
PO BOX 5509
HARLAN IA 51593-1009

BEST HOLIDAY Gatherings

taste of home

taste of home BOOKS

REIMAN MEDIA GROUP, INC. • GREENDALE, WISCONSIN

taste of home Reader's Digest

A TASTE OF HOME/READER'S DIGEST BOOK

© 2011 Reiman Media Group, LLC
5400 S. 60th St., Greendale WI 53129
All rights reserved.

Editor-in-Chief: Catherine Cassidy
Vice President, Executive Editor/Books:
Heidi Reuter Lloyd
North American Chief Marketing Officer:
Lisa Karpinski
Food Director: Diane Werner RD
Senior Editor/Books: Mark Hagen
Editors: Heidi Reuter Lloyd,
Julie Blume Benedict
Art Directors: Edwin Robles, Jr., Jessie Sharon
Content Production Supervisor: Julie Wagner
Design Layout Artists: Emma Acevedo,
Kathy Crawford
Proofreader: Vicki Soukup Jensen
Recipe Asset System Manager:
Coleen Martin
Recipe Testing & Editing:
Taste of Home Test Kitchen
Food Photography: Taste of Home Photo Studio
Administrative Assistant: Barb Czysz

The Reader's Digest Associaton, Inc.

President and Chief Executive Officer:
Tom Williams
**Executive Vice President, RDA, and
President, Lifestyle Communities:**
Suzanne M. Grimes

For other Taste of Home books and products,
visit **shoptasteofhome.com.**

For more Reader's Digest products and information,
visit **rd.com** (in the United States)
or see **rd.ca** (in Canada).

International Standard Book Number (10): 0-89821-946-9
International Standard Book Number (13): 978-0-89821-946-3
Library of Congress Control Number: 2010925922

Pictured on the front cover (clockwise from top):
Turkey with Apple Stuffing (p. 31), Tortilla Dressing
(p. 58), Butternut Bisque (p. 114), Flank Steak with Wine
Sauce (p. 53) and Spicy Oatmeal Cookie Mix (p. 283).

Pictured on the back cover:
Chocolate Peanut Butter Grahams (p. 262).

Printed in China
1 3 5 7 9 10 8 6 4 2

TABLE OF CONTENTS

Special Times Call for Special Recipes
561 Holiday Favorites from *Taste of Home*

Ah, the holidays. A magical time of year, to be sure, but mixed in with all the joy and excitement is a little angst. There is so much to do and so many places to go. Is there really enough time for it all?

Yes, when this book is your holiday companion. *Taste of Home Best Holiday Gatherings* will get you through the special family dinners, the neighborhood round robin, the church bring-a-dish-to-pass supper, your girlfriends' annual cookie exchange and the after-work potluck.

This cookbook will make all of your holiday events for Thanksgiving, Christmas Eve, Christmas Day, New Year's Eve, and New Year's Day a little easier and a lot tastier. Your gatherings will be memorable because the food is fabulous. And you won't be stressed because the recipes are from *Taste of Home*, the No. 1 cooking magazine in the world.

Every recipe in this cookbook came from a great home cook like you. Each recipe was double-tested in the Taste of Home Test Kitchen to make sure it tastes as delicious as was promised, plus the ingredients go together easily. Step-by-step instructions guide you through, using everyday ingredients that can readily be found in your own pantry or your local grocery store.

Taste of Home Best Holiday Gatherings is packed with more than 560 festive recipes. You'll find fresh versions of traditional holiday favorites plus new recipe ideas that will impress your family and friends. It's the blending of the comfort of the familiar with the excitement of the new that makes each holiday unique.

Inside these pages you'll find dozens of options for appetizers and beverages, breakfast and brunch dishes, entrees, side dishes, salads, soups, breads, desserts and delicious gifts from the kitchen.

Most of the recipes have beautiful full-color photos, so you can see how they will look before you make them. This comes in handy when you're planning menus for specific occasions.

We know you'll enjoy *Taste of Home Best Holiday Gatherings*. May all your holidays be filled with good food, good people and good times!

APPETIZERS & BEVERAGES

PICKLED
SHRIMP
P. 11

FLUFFY FRUIT DIP

sue pence, alexandria, virginia

We've been making this dip in my family for generations. Serve it throughout the year with whatever fresh fruits are in season.

- 1/2 cup sugar
- 2 tablespoons all-purpose flour
- 1 cup unsweetened pineapple juice
- 1 tablespoon butter
- 1 egg, lightly beaten
- 1 cup heavy whipping cream, whipped

Assorted fresh fruit

1 In a small saucepan, combine the sugar and flour. Gradually whisk in pineapple juice. Add the butter. Cook and stir until butter is melted and mixture comes to a boil. Cook and stir for 1-2 minutes or until thickened.

2 Remove from the heat. Stir a small amount of hot mixture into egg; return all to the pan, stirring constantly. Bring to a gentle boil; cook and stir for 1 minute. Remove from the heat. Cool to room temperature, stirring several times.

3 Fold in whipped cream. Cover and refrigerate for at least 1 hour. Serve with fruit.

Yield: about 2-1/2 cups.

WARM PERCOLATOR PUNCH

net crawford, ashland, kentucky

smells like Christmas all through my house when serve up this pleasantly spicy punch. It can also be ade in a Dutch oven.

- 6 cups unsweetened apple juice
- 6 cups cranberry juice
- 3 cups water
- 2/3 cup packed brown sugar
- 1/4 teaspoon salt
- 1 tablespoon whole cloves
- 2 cinnamon sticks (3 inches)

1 In a 24-cup percolator, combine the juices, water, brown sugar and salt. Place cloves and cinnamon sticks in the percolator basket; cover and begin perking. When cycle is complete, discard spices.

Yield: 15 servings (about 3-1/2 quarts).

Brown Sugar Facts

When a recipe calls for brown sugar, it should always be firmly packed. The moisture in brown sugar tends to trap air between the crystals, so firmly pack it when measuring. Taste of Home recipes specify packed brown sugar in the ingredients. Both light and dark brown sugar are a mixture of granulated sugars and molasses, with dark brown sugar containing more molasses than light brown sugar. Light brown sugar has a delicate flavor while dark brown sugar has a stronger more intense molasses flavor. They can be used interchangeably depending on your personal preference.—Taste of Home Test Kitchen

FETA ARTICHOKE BITES

louise leach, chino, california

You can prepare the flavorful topping for this appetizer ahead of time. Then spread onto slices of bread and broil for a fast, festive snack.

- 1 jar (7-1/2 ounces) marinated artichoke hearts
- 1 cup diced seeded tomatoes
- 1 cup (4 ounces) crumbled feta cheese
- 1/3 cup grated Parmesan cheese
- 2 green onions, thinly sliced
- 1 loaf sourdough baguette (about 20 inches long)

1 Drain the artichokes, reserving 2 tablespoons marinade. Chop artichokes and place in a large bowl. Stir in the tomatoes, cheeses, onions and reserved marinade. Cover and refrigerate for 1 hour.

2 Cut baguette into 1/2-in. slices. Spread with the artichoke mixture. Place on an ungreased baking sheet. Broil 4-6 in. from the heat for 4-5 minutes or until the edges of bread are browned. Serve immediately.

Yield: about 12 servings.

Seeding Tomatoes

To remove seeds from a tomato, cut it in half horizontally and remove the stem. Holding a tomato half over a bowl or sink, scrape out seeds with a small spoon or squeeze the tomato to force out the seeds. Then slice or dice as directed in the recipe.—Taste of Home Test Kitchen

BANANA NOG

jennae lefebvre, aurora, illinois

During my family's annual cookie exchange, we r out of our beloved eggnog—much to everyone's horror! So into the kitchen I went to create this c creamy concoction. It was a hit.

- 3 cups milk, *divided*
- 3 cups half-and-half cream, *divided*
- 3 egg yolks
- 3/4 cup sugar
- 3 large ripe bananas
- 1/2 cup light rum
- 1/3 cup creme de cacao
- 1-1/2 teaspoons vanilla extract

Whipped cream and baking cocoa, optional

1 In a large heavy saucepan, combine 1-1/2 cu milk, 1-1/2 cups cream, egg yolks and sugar. Co and stir over medium-low heat until mixtu reaches 160° and is thick enough to coat the ba of a metal spoon.

2 Place bananas in a food processor; cover ar process until blended. Pour milk mixture into pitcher; stir in the banana puree, rum, creme c cacao, vanilla, and remaining milk and crear Cover and refrigerate for at least 3 hours befo serving.

3 Pour into chilled glasses. Garnish with whippe cream and sprinkle with cocoa if desired.

Yield: 11 servings (about 2 quarts).

CINNAMON MOCHA COFFEE

bernice morris, marshfield, missouri

One snowy day, my neighbor called and invited me over to try a new drink she'd made. It was delicious! This spiced coffee is a lovely treat any time of year.

    1/2 cup ground dark roast coffee
      1 tablespoon ground cinnamon
    1/4 teaspoon ground nutmeg
      5 cups water
      1 cup milk
    1/3 cup chocolate syrup
    1/4 cup packed brown sugar
      1 teaspoon vanilla extract

Whipped cream, optional

1 In a small bowl, combine the ground coffee, cinnamon and nutmeg; pour into a coffee filter of a drip coffeemaker. Add water; brew according to manufacturer's directions.

2 In a large saucepan, combine milk, chocolate syrup and brown sugar. Cook over low heat until sugar is dissolved, stirring occasionally. Stir in the vanilla and brewed coffee. Ladle into the mugs; garnish with whipped cream if desired.

Yield: 6 servings.

CRISPY SHRIMP POPPERS

jacquelynne stine, las vegas, nevada

A crisp, golden coating surrounds these butterflied shrimp stuffed with bacon and cream cheese. You'll want to make a meal of these!

     20 uncooked medium shrimp, peeled and
         deveined
      4 ounces cream cheese, softened
     10 bacon strips
      1 cup all-purpose flour
      2 eggs, lightly beaten
      2 cups panko (Japanese) bread crumbs

Oil for deep-fat frying

1 Butterfly the shrimp along the outside curves. Spread about 1 teaspoon cream cheese inside each shrimp. Cut bacon strips in half lengthwise; wrap a piece around each shrimp and secure with toothpicks.

2 In three separate shallow bowls, place the flour, eggs and bread crumbs. Coat the shrimp with flour; dip into eggs, then coat with bread crumbs.

3 In an electric skillet or deep-fat fryer, heat the oil to 375°. Fry shrimp, a few at a time, for 3-4 minutes or until golden brown. Drain on paper towels. Discard toothpicks before serving.

Yield: 20 appetizers.

POTATO SALAD BITES

stephanie sheridan, plainfield, vermont

These salad-filled potato skins are packed with the kind of down-home goodness everyone loves. Let them chill for a few hours to enhance the flavor.

 10 small red potatoes
1/4 cup chopped pimiento-stuffed olives
  2 teaspoons minced fresh parsley
  1 teaspoon finely chopped onion
1/2 cup mayonnaise
1-3/4 teaspoons Dijon mustard
1/8 teaspoon pepper
1/4 teaspoon salt
Paprika
Parsley sprigs, optional

1 Place potatoes in a large saucepan and cover with water. Bring to a boil. Reduce heat; cover and cook for 12-15 minutes or until tender. Drain and immediately place potatoes in ice water; drain and pat dry.

2 Peel two potatoes; finely dice and place in a small bowl. Cut the remaining potatoes in half. With a melon baller, scoop out the pulp, leaving a 3/8-in. shell; set shells aside. Dice pulp and add to the bowl. Stir in the olives, parsley and onion. Combine the mayonnaise, mustard and pepper; gently stir into potato mixture.

3 Sprinkle potato shells with salt; stuff with potato salad. Sprinkle with paprika. Chill for at least 1 hour before serving. Garnish with parsley if desired.

Yield: 16 appetizers.

SALSA CHEESECAKE

glory windham, grand cane, louisiana

After receiving this recipe from a friend several years ago, I made it for our family Christmas party. It's now one of our traditional foods. It's a new spin on taco dip.

  2 packages (8 ounces *each*) cream cheese, softened
  2 cups (8 ounces) shredded Monterey Jack cheese
  2 cups (16 ounces) sour cream, *divided*
  3 eggs, lightly beaten
  1 cup salsa
  1 can (4 ounces) chopped green chilies, drained
Guacamole
  1 medium tomato, diced
Tortilla chips *or* crackers

1 In a small bowl, beat the cream cheese and Monterey Jack cheese until light and fluffy. Beat in 1 cup sour cream just until combined. Add eggs; beat on low speed just until combined. Stir in the salsa and chilies.

2 Pour into a greased 9-in. springform pan. Place pan on a baking sheet. Bake at 350° for 40-45 minutes or until center is almost set.

3 Remove from the oven; immediately spread with remaining sour cream. Cool on a wire rack for 10 minutes. Carefully run a knife around edge of pan to loosen; cool 1 hour longer. Refrigerate for at least 5 hours or overnight.

4 To serve, remove sides of pan. Garnish with the guacamole and diced tomato. Serve with tortilla chips or crackers. Refrigerate leftovers.

Yield: 20-24 slices.

HOT BUTTERED RUM MIX

carol beyerl, east wenatchee, washington

I offered this comforting, hot drink to guests at one of my "Bunco" gatherings. Everyone wanted the recipe. I like to keep a batch in the freezer for easy entertaining.

- 1 cup butter, softened
- 2 cups confectioners' sugar
- 1 cup plus 2 tablespoons packed brown sugar
- 2 cups vanilla ice cream, softened
- 1-1/2 teaspoons ground cinnamon
- 1/2 teaspoon ground nutmeg
- 1 teaspoon rum extract

ADDITIONAL INGREDIENT (for each serving):
- 3/4 cup boiling water

1 In a large bowl, cream the butter and sugars until light and fluffy. Add ice cream, cinnamon, nutmeg and the extract. Transfer to a freezer container; freeze overnight.

2 To prepare hot drink: Dissolve 3-4 tablespoons of mix in boiling water; stir well.

Yield: 3-1/2 cups mix (14-18 servings).

Avoid Shattering Beverage Cups

When serving hot beverages, make sure the cups are heat-resistant. Heat glass cups with warm water before adding the hot drink. If you use disposable cups that aren't heat-resistant, they'll fall apart when the hot beverage is added.—Taste of Home Test Kitchen

VEGGIE WONTON QUICHES

taste of home test kitchen

With green broccoli and red pepper, these mini quiches from our home economists are a fitting finger food for the holidays. Crispy wonton cups make a tasty crust.

- 24 wonton wrappers
- 1 cup finely chopped fresh broccoli
- 3/4 cup diced fresh mushrooms
- 1/2 cup diced sweet red pepper
- 1/4 cup finely chopped onion
- 2 teaspoons canola oil
- 3 eggs
- 1 tablespoon water
- 2 teaspoons dried parsley flakes
- 1/4 teaspoon salt
- 1/4 teaspoon dried thyme
- 1/4 teaspoon white pepper

Dash cayenne pepper
- 3/4 cup shredded cheddar cheese

1 Gently press wonton wrappers into miniature muffin cups coated with cooking spray. Lightly coat wontons with cooking spray.

2 Bake at 350° for 5 minutes. Remove wontons from cups; place upside down on baking sheets. Lightly coat with cooking spray. Bake 5 minutes longer or until light golden brown.

3 Meanwhile, in a nonstick skillet, cook broccoli, mushrooms, red pepper and onion in oil over medium heat for 4-5 minutes or until crisp-tender.

4 In a small bowl, whisk eggs and water; stir in the parsley, salt, thyme, white pepper and cayenne. Add to vegetable mixture; cook over medium heat for 4-5 minutes or until eggs are completely set.

5 Remove from the heat; stir in cheese. Spoon about 1 tablespoonful into each wonton cup. Bake for 5 minutes or until filling is heated through. Serve warm.

Yield: 2 dozen.

CINNAMON TOASTED ALMONDS

janice thompson, stacy, minnesota

Crunchy cinnamon-glazed almonds are a spectacular treat to bring to a party or gathering. They taste just like the ones you get at the fair.

- 2 egg whites
- 6 teaspoons vanilla extract
- 4 cups unblanched almonds
- 1/3 cup sugar
- 1/3 cup packed brown sugar
- 1 teaspoon salt
- 1/2 teaspoon ground cinnamon

1 In a large bowl, beat egg whites until frothy; beat in vanilla. Add almonds; stir gently to coat. Combine the sugars, salt and cinnamon; add to nut mixture and stir gently to coat.

2 Spread evenly into two greased 15-in. x 10-in. x 1-in. baking pans. Bake at 300° for 25-30 minutes or until almonds are crisp, stirring once. Cool. Store in an airtight container.

Yield: about 4 cups.

Soften Brown Sugar

To soften brown sugar, place a slice of bread or an apple wedge with the brown sugar in a covered container for a few days. Or, if you're in a hurry, microwave the brown sugar on high for 20-30 seconds. Always store brown sugar in an airtight container.
—Taste of Home Test Kitchen

PEPPERONI PINWHEELS

vikki rebholz, west chester, ohio

These golden brown rounds have lots of pepperoni flavor. They're easy to make and really good!

- 1/2 cup diced pepperoni
- 1/2 cup shredded part-skim mozzarella cheese
- 1/4 teaspoon dried oregano
- 1 egg, *separated*
- 1 tube (8 ounces) refrigerated crescent rolls

1 In a small bowl, combine the pepperoni, cheese, oregano and egg yolk. In another small bowl, whisk egg white until foamy; set aside. Separate the crescent dough into four rectangles; seal perforations.

2 Spread pepperoni mixture over each rectangle to within 1/4 in. of edges. Roll up jelly-roll style, starting with a short side; pinch seams to seal. Cut each into six slices.

3 Place cut side down on greased baking sheets; brush the tops with egg white. Bake at 375° for 12-15 minutes or until golden brown. Serve warm. Refrigerate leftovers.

Yield: 2 dozen.

PICKLED SHRIMP

kathi nelson, yorba linda, california

I appreciate this appetizer's ease of preparation, especially during the hectic holiday season. The recipe can easily be doubled for a crowd.

- 1/3 cup olive oil
- 1/4 cup red wine vinegar
- 1 tablespoon tomato paste
- 1-1/2 teaspoons sugar
- 1-1/2 teaspoons celery seed
- 1 garlic clove, minced
- 1/2 teaspoon coarsely ground pepper
- 1/4 teaspoon salt
- 1/4 teaspoon ground mustard
- 1/8 teaspoon crushed red pepper flakes
- 1/8 teaspoon hot pepper sauce
- 1 pound cooked large shrimp, peeled and deveined
- 1 small onion, thinly sliced and separated into rings
- 2 bay leaves

1 In a large resealable plastic bag, combine the first 11 ingredients; add the shrimp, onion and bay leaves. Seal bag and turn to coat; refrigerate for up to 24 hours.

2 Drain and discard marinade, onion and bay leaves. Serve shrimp with toothpicks.

Yield: about 1-1/2 dozen.

SWEET-AND-SOUR SAUSAGES

dorothy anderson, langley, british columbia

A perfect buffet item, these zesty links also make a great main course. I've prepared them so often that I can recite the recipe from memory.

- 2 packages (16 ounces *each*) miniature smoked sausages
- 2 tablespoons butter
- 1 can (15-1/4 ounces) sliced peaches, drained and halved
- 1 cup chili sauce
- 3/4 cup sugar
- 1/2 cup ketchup
- 1 teaspoon dried minced onion
- 1 teaspoon curry powder

1 In a large skillet, brown the sausages in butter. In a large bowl, combine remaining ingredients; stir in the sausages. Transfer to a greased 2-qt. baking dish.

2 Bake, uncovered, at 350° for 30 minutes. Stir; bake 15 minutes longer or until bubbly.

Yield: 18 servings.

SMOKED SALMON TOMATO PIZZA

natalie bremson, plantation, florida

This easy pizza comes in handy when you find yourself in a time crunch.

- 1 prebaked thin Italian bread shell crust (10 ounces)
- 1 cup whipped cream cheese
- 4 ounces smoked salmon *or* lox, cut into thin strips
- 1 cup chopped tomato
- 1/4 cup chopped red onion
- 2 tablespoons capers, drained
- 2 tablespoons minced fresh parsley

Pepper to taste

1 Place the crust on an ungreased 12-in. pizza pan. Bake at 450° for 8-10 minutes or until heated through. Spread with cream cheese.

2 Sprinkle with the salmon, tomato, onion, capers, parsley and pepper. Cut into slices.

Yield: 8 slices.

BAKED BRIE WITH ROASTED GARLIC

lara pennell, mauldin, south carolina

The garlic is mellow and sweet in this recipe. I never fail to get compliments when I serve this as a first course—even those who say they don't like Brie are converted!

- 1 whole garlic bulb
- 1-1/2 teaspoons plus 1 tablespoon olive oil, *divided*
- 1 tablespoon minced fresh rosemary *or* 1 teaspoon dried rosemary, crushed

- 1 round loaf (1 pound) sourdough bread
- 1 round (8 ounces) Brie *or* Camembert cheese
- 1 loaf (10-1/2 ounces) French bread baguette, sliced and toasted

Red and green grapes

1 Remove papery outer skin from garlic (do not peel or separate cloves). Cut top off bulb. Brush with 1-1/2 teaspoons oil; sprinkle with rosemary. Wrap in heavy-duty foil. Bake at 425° for 30-35 minutes or until softened.

2 Meanwhile, cut the top fourth off the loaf of bread; carefully hollow out enough of the bottom of the bread so cheese will fit. Cube removed bread; set aside. Place cheese in bread.

3 Cool garlic for 10-15 minutes. Reduce heat to 375°. Squeeze softened garlic into a bowl and mash with a fork; spread over cheese. Replace the bread top; brush outside of bread with the remaining oil. Wrap in heavy-duty foil.

4 Bake for 45-50 minutes or until cheese is melted. Serve with toasted baguette, grapes and the reserved bread cubes.

Yield: 8 servings.

CRANBERRY PARTY PUNCH

taste of home test kitchen

Cute cranberry-filled ice molds shaped like candy canes float in this refreshing five-ingredient fruit punch. It's quick to stir up and serve right away.

- 1 cup cranberries
- 1 cup crushed ice
- 4 cups cranberry juice, chilled
- 4 cups pineapple juice, chilled
- 1-1/2 cups sugar
- 1 tablespoon almond extract
- 2 liters ginger ale, chilled

1 Using three 4-in. candy cane molds or shape of your choice, arrange cranberries and the crushed ice alternately in a striped pattern. Add cold water to fill molds. Freeze for 2 hours.

2 To unmold, wrap a hot damp cloth around the bottom of the mold; invert onto a baking sheet.

3 In a punch bowl, combine the juices, sugar and extract; stir until sugar is dissolved. Add ginger ale. Place ice molds in bowl, rounded side up. Serve immediately.

Yield: 4 quarts.

JAMAICAN SHRIMP

mary lou wayman, salt lake city, utah

Zesty jerk seasoning is a nice complement to sweet mango in this crowd-pleasing appetizer. Although this delicious dish takes time to prepare, it's conveniently made ahead and refrigerated until ready to serve.

- 3 quarts water
- 1 teaspoon salt
- 2 pounds uncooked medium shrimp, peeled and deveined
- 1/3 cup olive oil
- 1/4 cup white wine vinegar
- 3 tablespoons lime juice
- 1 jalapeno pepper, seeded and finely chopped
- 4 teaspoons honey
- 3 teaspoons Caribbean jerk seasoning
- 1 medium mango *or* 2 medium peaches, peeled and cubed
- 1 small red onion, thinly sliced and separated into rings
- 1 medium lime, quartered and sliced

1 In a large saucepan, bring water and salt to a boil. Add shrimp; boil for 3 minutes or until the shrimp turn pink, stirring occasionally. Drain shrimp and rinse with cold water; transfer to a large resealable plastic bag.

2 In a jar with a tight-fitting lid, combine the oil, vinegar, lime juice, jalapeno, honey and the jerk seasoning; shake well. Pour 3/4 cup marinade over shrimp. Seal bag and turn to coat; refrigerate for 1-2 hours. Refrigerate remaining marinade.

3 Just before serving, drain and discard marinade from shrimp. On a large serving platter, layer the shrimp, mango, onion and lime. Drizzle with remaining marinade.

Yield: 15-20 servings.

Editor's Note: When cutting hot peppers, disposable gloves are recommended. Avoid touching your face.

3. Fill bread shell with spinach dip; replace top. Place any dip that doesn't fit in shell in a greased baking dish. Wrap bread in heavy-duty foil; place on a baking sheet. Bake at 350° for 1 hour or until dip is heated through. Cover and bake additional dip for 40-45 minutes or until heated through. Open foil carefully. Serve dip warm with vegetables and reserved bread cubes.

Yield: 4 cups.

Editor's Note: Fat-free cream cheese and mayonnaise are not recommended for this recipe.

CRANBERRY CAMEMBERT PIZZA

heidi mellon, waukesha, wisconsin
After I'd tasted this quick, yummy pizza at a party, I just knew I had to have the recipe. I've been serving it in my household for years, and it always disappears in minutes.

  1 **tube (13.8 ounces) refrigerated pizza crust**
  8 **ounces Camembert *or* Brie cheese, rind removed and cut into 1/2-inch cubes**
3/4 **cup whole-berry cranberry sauce**
1/2 **cup chopped pecans**

1. Unroll crust onto a lightly greased 12-in. pizza pan; flatten dough and build up edges slightly. Bake at 425° for 10-12 minutes or until light golden brown.

2. Sprinkle cheese over crust. Spoon cranberry sauce evenly over crust; sprinkle with pecans. Bake 8-10 minutes longer or until cheese is melted and crust is golden brown. Cool for 5 minutes before cutting.

Yield: 12-14 slices.

BAKED SPINACH DIP IN BREAD

shauna dittrick, leduc, alberta
This is the only way my kids will eat spinach! The dip can be made ahead and chilled. Place in the bread shell and bake just before company arrives.

  2 **packages (8 ounces *each*) cream cheese, softened**
  1 **cup mayonnaise**
  1 **package (10 ounces) frozen chopped spinach, thawed and squeezed dry**
  1 **cup (4 ounces) shredded cheddar cheese**
  1 **pound sliced bacon, cooked and crumbled**
1/4 **cup chopped onion**
  1 **tablespoon dill weed**
  1 **to 2 garlic cloves, minced**
  1 **round loaf (1 pound) unsliced sourdough bread**
Assorted fresh vegetables

1. In a large bowl, beat cream cheese and mayonnaise until blended. Stir in the spinach, cheese, bacon, onion, dill and garlic; set aside.

2. Cut a 1-1/2-in. slice off top of bread; set aside. Carefully hollow out bottom, leaving a 1/2-in. shell. Cube removed bread and place on a baking sheet. Broil 3-4 in. from the heat for 1-2 minutes or until golden brown; set aside.

CHICKEN SATAY

taste of home test kitchen

This Asian-style dish features a simple-to-prepare peanut sauce. It's a hearty addition to an appetizer buffet.

- 2 pounds boneless skinless chicken breasts
- 1/3 cup soy sauce
- 1 green onion, sliced
- 2 tablespoons sesame oil
- 1 tablespoon brown sugar
- 1 tablespoon honey
- 2 garlic cloves, minced
- 1/2 teaspoon ground ginger

PEANUT SAUCE:
- 1/2 cup salted peanuts
- 1/4 cup chopped green onions
- 1 garlic clove, minced
- 3 tablespoons chicken broth
- 3 tablespoons butter, melted
- 2 tablespoons soy sauce
- 1 tablespoon lemon juice
- 1 tablespoon honey
- 1/2 teaspoon ground ginger
- 1/4 to 1/2 teaspoon crushed red pepper flakes

1 Flatten chicken to 1/4-in. thickness; cut lengthwise into 1-in.-wide strips. In a large resealable plastic bag, combine the soy sauce, onion, sesame oil, brown sugar, honey, garlic and ginger; add chicken. Seal bag and turn to coat; refrigerate for 4 hours.

2 In a food processor, combine the peanuts, onions and garlic; cover and process until mixture forms a paste. Add the broth, butter, soy sauce, lemon juice, honey, ginger and pepper flakes; cover and process until smooth. Transfer to a serving bowl. Refrigerate until serving.

3 Drain and discard marinade. Thread chicken strips onto soaked wooden skewers. Broil 6 in. from the heat for 2-4 minutes on each side or until chicken is no longer pink. Serve with peanut sauce.

Yield: 10-12 servings.

MULLED POMEGRANATE SIPPER

lisa renshaw, kansas city, missouri

This warm, comforting cider fills the entire house with a wonderful aroma.

- 1 bottle (64 ounces) cranberry-apple juice
- 2 cups unsweetened apple juice
- 1 cup pomegranate juice
- 2/3 cup honey
- 1/2 cup orange juice
- 3 cinnamon sticks (3 inches)
- 10 whole cloves
- 2 tablespoons grated orange peel

1 In a 5-qt. slow cooker, combine first five ingredients. Place the cinnamon sticks, cloves and orange peel on a double thickness of cheesecloth; bring up corners of cloth and tie with string to form a bag. Add to slow cooker. Cover and cook on low for 1-2 hours. Discard spice bag.

Yield: 16 servings (about 3 quarts).

WINTER'S WARMTH HOT CHOCOLATE

janine johnson, minooka, illinois

I discovered this recipe as a newlywed when I was looking for something to warm us up during the season's first snowfall. We make it every year when we get our first snow—and on any other blustery days—that's why my husband gave it this name!

- 4 squares (1 ounce *each*) semisweet chocolate, coarsely chopped
- 1/4 cup light corn syrup
- 1/2 teaspoon vanilla extract
- 1/4 teaspoon ground cinnamon
- 4 cups milk
- 1 cup heavy whipping cream

White chocolate curls, optional

1 In a small heavy saucepan, melt chocolate with corn syrup over low heat, stirring occasionally until smooth. Remove from the heat; stir in vanilla and cinnamon. Cover and set aside until cool. In a large saucepan, heat milk until small bubbles form around edge. (Do not boil.)

2 Meanwhile, in a small bowl, beat cream and cooled chocolate mixture on medium-low speed until soft peaks form. To serve, spoon chocolate cream into mugs; add hot milk and stir gently. Garnish with chocolate curls if desired.

Yield: 4-6 servings.

FRUIT AND CARAMEL BRIE

tracy schuhmacher, penfield, new york

I'm a stay-at-home mother with two boys and I enjoy cooking—especially appetizers. It must run in the family because my mom served appetizers and desserts exclusively for several Christmas Eve celebrations. Brie is one of my favorite cheeses, and this sweet-savory recipe is party-special but especially easy to throw together.

- 1 round (8 ounces) Brie cheese, rind removed
- 1/3 cup caramel ice cream topping
- 1/4 cup dried cranberries
- 1/4 cup chopped dried apples
- 1/4 cup chopped walnuts
- 1 loaf (1 pound) French bread baguette, sliced and toasted

1 Place Brie in a microwave-safe bowl. In a small bowl, combine the caramel topping, cranberries apples and walnuts. Spread over Brie.

2 Microwave, uncovered, on high for 60-90 seconds or until cheese is heated through and slightly melted. Serve with toasted baguette slices.

Yield: 8 servings.

Editor's Note: This recipe was tested in a 1,100-watt microwave.

BLACK FOREST HAM PINWHEELS

kate dampier, quail valley, california

My popular pinwheels wow guests at holiday parties I attend. People like the smokiness of the ham and the sweet surprise of the cherries. I also appreciate the make-ahead convenience the recipe provides.

   1 package (8 ounces) cream cheese, softened
   4 teaspoons minced fresh dill
   1 tablespoon lemon juice
   2 teaspoons Dijon mustard

Dash salt and pepper

   1/2 cup dried cherries, chopped
   1/4 cup chopped green onions
     5 flour tortillas (10 inches), room temperature
   1/2 pound sliced deli Black Forest ham
   1/2 pound sliced Swiss cheese

1 In a small bowl, beat the cream cheese, dill, lemon juice, mustard, salt and pepper until blended. Stir in the cherries and onions. Spread over each tortilla; layer with ham and cheese. Roll up tightly; wrap in plastic wrap. Refrigerate for at least 2 hours. Cut into 1/2-in. slices.

Yield: about 3-1/2 dozen.

ANTIPASTO KABOBS

denise hazen, cincinnati, ohio

My husband and I met at a cooking class and have loved creating menus and entertaining ever since. These do-ahead appetizers are always a hit.

   1 package (9 ounces) refrigerated cheese tortellini
  40 pimiento-stuffed olives
  40 large pitted ripe olives
   3/4 cup Italian salad dressing
  40 thin slices pepperoni
  20 thin slices hard salami, halved

Fresh parsley sprigs, optional

1 Cook tortellini according to package directions; drain and rinse in cold water. In a large resealable plastic bag, combine the tortellini, olives and salad dressing. Seal bag and turn to coat; refrigerate for 4 hours or overnight.

2 Drain and discard marinade. For each appetizer, thread a stuffed olive, folded pepperoni slice, tortellini, folded salami piece, ripe olive and parsley sprig if desired on a toothpick or short skewer.

Yield: 40 appetizers.

3   Meanwhile, in a small bowl, combine the mayonnaise, lime juice and peel. Thinly slice the pork; serve on toasted bread with a dollop of lime mayonnaise. Sprinkle with additional lime peel if desired.

Yield: 20-24 appetizers.

SHRIMP TARTLETS

gina hutchison, smithville, missouri

Mini tart shells are filled with a cream cheese mixture, then topped with seafood sauce and shrimp for a beautiful look and delightful taste. This recipe makes a great appetizer, but you can also serve several with soup or salad for a fast, light meal.

  1 package (8 ounces) cream cheese, softened
1-1/2 teaspoons Worcestershire sauce
  1 to 2 teaspoons grated onion
  1 teaspoon garlic salt
1/8 teaspoon lemon juice
  2 packages (1.9 ounces *each*) frozen miniature phyllo tart shells
1/2 cup seafood cocktail sauce
 30 cooked medium shrimp, peeled and deveined

1   In a small mixing bowl, combine the first five ingredients. Spoon into tart shells. Top with seafood sauce and shrimp. Refrigerate until serving.

Yield: 2-1/2 dozen.

SPICY PORK BAGUETTE BITES

virginia anthony, jacksonville, florida

Here's an interesting twist on mini cocktail sandwiches. Lime mayonnaise provides a cool counterpoint to the nicely spiced pork, and toasted baguette slices contribute to the pleasant crunch.

  1 teaspoon paprika
1/2 teaspoon salt
1/2 teaspoon dried oregano
1/2 teaspoon ground cumin
1/4 teaspoon garlic powder
1/4 teaspoon cayenne pepper
1/4 teaspoon pepper
  1 pork tenderloin (1 pound)

LIME MAYONNAISE:
1/2 cup mayonnaise
  1 tablespoon lime juice
1/2 teaspoon grated lime peel
  1 French bread baguette (1 pound), sliced and toasted

Additional grated lime peel, optional

1   In a small bowl, combine the first seven ingredients; rub over tenderloin. Place in a large resealable plastic bag; seal and refrigerate overnight.

2   Place tenderloin on a rack in a foil-lined shallow roasting pan. Bake, uncovered, at 425° for 30-35 minutes or until a meat thermometer reads 160°. Let stand for 5 minutes.

beat just until combined. Pour into crust. Sprinkle with reserved crumb mixture.

3 Place pan on a baking sheet. Bake at 325° for 60-70 minutes or until filling is almost set. Turn oven off. Leave cheesecake in oven with door ajar for 30 minutes.

4 Cool on a wire rack for 10 minutes. Carefully run a knife around edge of pan to loosen; cool 1 hour longer. Refrigerate overnight. Remove sides of pan. Serve chilled or at room temperature with crackers.

Yield: 24-30 servings.

EGGNOG COFFEE

taste of home test kitchen
A classic Christmas drink gets a coffee kick in this luscious combination. With just two ingredients, it makes a perfect last-second entertaining option.

   1-1/3 cups eggnog
   2-2/3 cups hot strong brewed coffee (French *or* other dark roast)
Whipped cream and ground nutmeg, optional

1 Place eggnog in a large saucepan. Cook and stir until heated through. (Do not boil.) Stir in coffee. Pour into cups or mugs; serve immediately. Garnish with whipped cream and nutmeg if desired.

Yield: 4 servings.

Editor's Note: This recipe was tested with commercially prepared eggnog.

SAVORY HAM CHEESECAKE

shannon soper, west bend, wisconsin
My mom was the best cook—everything she made was special. She served this elegant cheesecake on Sunday following a Saturday ham dinner. Now I serve it and my family loves it, too!

   3 cups oyster crackers, crushed
   1 cup grated Parmesan cheese
  1/3 cup butter, melted
FILLING:
   4 packages (8 ounces *each*) cream cheese, softened
   4 eggs, lightly beaten
   2 cups finely chopped fully cooked ham
   2 cups (8 ounces) shredded Swiss cheese
  1/3 cup snipped chives
  1/4 cup minced fresh basil
  1/4 teaspoon salt
  1/4 teaspoon white pepper
Assorted crackers

1 In a large bowl, combine the cracker crumbs, Parmesan cheese and butter. Set aside 1/4 cup for topping. Press remaining crumb mixture onto the bottom and 2 in. up the sides of a greased 9-in. springform pan. Cover and refrigerate for at least 30 minutes.

2 In a large bowl, beat cream cheese until smooth. Add eggs; beat on low speed just until combined (mixture will be thick). Add the ham, Swiss cheese, chives, basil, salt and pepper;

RASPBERRY FONDUE DIP

edna hoffman, hebron, indiana

Delight your guests with this fun, non-traditional fondue. Creamy apple butter and cinnamon Red Hots add tangy flair to the richly colored dip!

- 1 package (10 ounces) frozen sweetened raspberries
- 1 cup apple butter
- 1 tablespoon red-hot candies
- 2 teaspoons cornstarch

Assorted fresh fruit

1 Place raspberries in a small bowl; set aside to thaw. Strain raspberries, reserving 1 tablespoon juice; discard seeds.

2 In a small saucepan, combine the strained berries, apple butter and Red-Hots; cook over medium heat until candies are dissolved, stirring occasionally.

3 In a small bowl, combine cornstarch and reserved juice until smooth; stir into berry mixture. Bring to a boil; cook and stir over medium heat for 1-2 minutes or until thickened. Transfer to a serving dish, fondue pot or 1-1/2-qt. slow cooker. Serve warm or cold with fruit.

Yield: 1 cup.

SUGAR 'N' SPICE NUTS

joan klinefelter, utica, illinois

My daughters, grandkids and everyone look forward to this mouth-watering mix of crunchy nuts, spices and fruit when they're home. And tucked in colorful tins, it makes a handy last-minute gift idea for busy hostesses or drop-in visitors.

- 1/4 cup packed brown sugar
- 1/2 teaspoon ground cinnamon
- 1/4 teaspoon cayenne pepper
- 1 egg white
- 1 cup salted cashews
- 1 cup pecan halves
- 1 cup dry roasted peanuts
- 1/2 cup dried cranberries

1 In a small bowl, combine the brown sugar, cinnamon and cayenne; set aside. In a large bowl, whisk the egg white; add nuts and cranberries. Sprinkle with sugar mixture and toss to coat. Spread in a single layer on a greased baking sheet.

2 Bake at 300° for 18-20 minutes or until golden brown, stirring once. Cool. Store in an airtight container.

Yield: 3-1/2 cups.

PIMIENTO-OLIVE CHEESE LOG

linda norton, sonora, california

Pimientos give great color to this soft-textured cheese log. I make it for many occasions throughout the year.

- 1 package (8 ounces) cream cheese, softened
- 1 jar (2 ounces) diced pimientos, drained
- 2 tablespoons finely chopped ripe olives
- 1-1/2 teaspoons grated onion
- 1 teaspoon lemon juice
- 1 garlic clove, minced
- 1/4 teaspoon salt
- 1/8 teaspoon dried thyme
- 1/8 teaspoon ground mustard
- 1/8 teaspoon hot pepper sauce

Assorted crackers

1 In a small bowl, beat cream cheese until smooth. Stir in the next nine ingredients. Cover and refrigerate for 1 hour or until firm. Shape into a log. Cover and refrigerate for 4 hours or overnight. Serve with crackers.

Yield: 1-1/4 cups.

BACON WATER CHESTNUT WRAPS

laura mahaffey, annapolis, maryland

The holidays around the house just wouldn't be the same without these classic wraps. Through the years, Christmas Eve guests have proven it's impossible to eat just one.

- 1 pound sliced bacon
- 2 cans (8 ounces *each*) whole water chestnuts, drained
- 1/2 cup packed brown sugar
- 1/2 cup mayonnaise
- 1/4 cup chili sauce

1 Cut bacon strips in half. In a large skillet over medium heat, cook bacon until almost crisp; drain. Wrap each bacon piece around a water chestnut and secure with a toothpick. Place in an ungreased 13-in. x 9-in. x 2-in. baking dish.

2 In a small bowl, combine the brown sugar, mayonnaise and chili sauce; pour over water chestnuts. Bake, uncovered, at 350° for 30 minutes or until hot and bubbly.

Yield: about 2-1/2 dozen.

minutes or until a meat thermometer reads 145°. Cool on a wire rack for 1 hour. Cover and refrigerate.

3 Transfer yogurt from strainer to another bowl (discard yogurt liquid). Add the cucumber, onion, garlic and remaining salt and white pepper. In a small bowl, whisk the vinegar and remaining oil; stir into yogurt mixture.

4 Thinly slice the tenderloin. Spread yogurt mixture over bread slices; top with beef, arugula and tomato slices if desired. Serve immediately or cover and refrigerate until serving.

Yield: 3 dozen.

JALAPENO CHEESE SPREAD

patricia kitts, dickinson, texas

I keep the ingredients for this wonderful cheese spread on hand so that I can assemble it at any time. The combination of jalapenos, cream cheese and pecans is always a hit at parties.

   1 package (8 ounces) cream cheese, softened
   3 tablespoons canned jalapeno slices, drained and chopped
   3 tablespoons chopped pecans, toasted

Bagel chips *or* assorted crackers

1 Place block of cream cheese on a serving plate; sprinkle with jalapenos and pecans. Serve with bagel chips or crackers.

Yield: 8 servings.

BEEF CANAPES WITH CUCUMBER SAUCE

taste of home test kitchen

A homemade cucumber yogurt sauce complements tender slices of beef in this recipe from our Test Kitchen. Both the meat and sauce are conveniently made in advance.

   4 cups (32 ounces) plain yogurt
   1 whole beef tenderloin (1-1/2 pounds)
   2 tablespoons olive oil, *divided*
   1 teaspoon salt, *divided*
 1/4 teaspoon plus 1/8 teaspoon white pepper, *divided*
   1 medium cucumber, peeled, seeded and diced
   1 tablespoon finely chopped onion
   1 garlic clove, minced
   1 tablespoon white vinegar
   1 French bread baguette (1 pound), cut into 36 thin slices
   1 cup fresh arugula

Sliced grape tomatoes, optional

1 Line a fine mesh strainer with two layers of cheesecloth; place over a bowl. Place yogurt in strainer. Cover and refrigerate for at least 4 hours or overnight.

2 Rub tenderloin with 1 tablespoon oil. Sprinkle with 1/2 teaspoon salt and 1/4 teaspoon white pepper. In a large skillet, cook tenderloin over medium-high heat until browned on all sides. Transfer to a shallow roasting pan. Bake at 400° for 25-30

3 In an electric skillet or deep-fat fryer, heat oil to 375°. Fry mozzarella sticks, a few at a time, for 1 minute or until golden brown, turning occasionally. Discard bay leaf from marinara sauce. Serve with the mozzarella sticks.

Yield: 2 dozen (3 cups sauce).

CHEERY CRANBERRY NOG

nella parker, hersey, michigan

Tangy cranberry flavors this frothy, foamy beverage that's as refreshing as a yogurt smoothie. It always brings a blush of Christmas to my holiday buffets ...and lots of compliments from guests of all ages.

- 2 cups half-and-half cream
- 6 eggs
- 1 cup sugar
- 3 cups heavy whipping cream
- 2 cans (11-1/2 ounces *each*) cranberry juice concentrate, undiluted
- 2 cups water

1 In a Dutch oven, combine the half-and-half, eggs and sugar. Cook and stir over medium heat until mixture reaches 160° or is thick enough to coat the back of a metal spoon. Remove from the heat; cool slightly. Stir in the remaining ingredients. Cover and refrigerate until chilled.

Yield: 3 quarts.

MOZZARELLA MARINARA

ellen borst, genoa city, wisconsin

My husband and I enjoy mozzarella marinara at our state fair and thought we'd try to make our own version at home. Our recipe calls for convenient egg roll wrappers instead of messy batter. The homemade marinara sauce is fast and so tasty.

- 1 small onion, chopped
- 1 garlic clove, minced
- 3 tablespoons olive oil
- 1 can (14-1/2 ounces) diced tomatoes, undrained
- 1 can (6 ounces) tomato paste
- 1 cup water
- 2 teaspoons sugar
- 1/2 teaspoon salt
- 1 bay leaf
- 24 egg roll wrappers
- 24 pieces string cheese

Oil for deep-fat frying

1 In a large saucepan, saute onion and garlic in oil. Add the tomatoes, tomato paste, water, sugar, salt and bay leaf. Bring to a boil. Reduce heat; simmer, uncovered, for 20-30 minutes or until thickened.

2 Meanwhile, place an egg roll wrapper on a work surface with a point facing you. Place a piece of cheese near the bottom corner. Fold bottom corner of wrapper over cheese; roll up just until cheese is enclosed. Fold sides of wrapper over top. Using a pastry brush, wet the top corner with water. Roll up tightly to seal, forming a tube. Repeat.

CRUNCHY ONION STICKS

leora muellerleile, turtle lake, wisconsin

Although I've been collecting recipes for more than 50 years, I never tire of tried-and-true ones like this.

- 2 eggs, lightly beaten
- 2 tablespoons butter, melted
- 1 teaspoon all-purpose flour
- 1/2 teaspoon garlic salt
- 1/2 teaspoon dried parsley flakes
- 1/4 teaspoon onion salt
- 2 cans (2.8 ounces *each*) french-fried onions, crushed
- 1 tube (8 ounces) refrigerated crescent rolls

1 In a shallow bowl, combine the first six ingredients. Place the onions in another shallow bowl. Separate crescent dough into four rectangles; seal perforations. Cut each rectangle into eight strips. Dip each strip in egg mixture, then roll in onions.

2 Place 2 in. apart on ungreased baking sheets. Bake at 375° for 10-12 minutes or until golden brown. Immediately remove from pans to wire racks. Serve warm.

Yield: 32 appetizers.

PROSCIUTTO PHYLLO ROLL-UPS

michaela rosenthal, woodland hills, california

These elegant finger foods use delicate phyllo dough. With artichoke sauce on the side, the cheesy rolls make extra-special hors d'oeuvres.

- 24 sheets phyllo dough (14 inches x 9 inches)
- 1/4 cup butter, melted
- 8 thin slices prosciutto, cut into 1-inch strips
- 24 fresh asparagus spears, trimmed
- 24 fresh green beans, trimmed

ARTICHOKE SAUCE:

- 1/4 cup sour cream
- 1/2 teaspoon lemon juice
- 1 jar (6 ounces) marinated artichoke hearts, drained
- 2 ounces cream cheese, softened
- 1/4 cup chopped roasted sweet red peppers, drained
- 3 tablespoons grated Parmesan cheese
- 2 green onions, chopped
- 1 garlic clove, peeled
- 1/4 teaspoon white pepper
- 1/4 teaspoon cayenne pepper

1 Line baking sheets with parchment paper; set aside. Place one sheet of phyllo dough on a work surface (keep remaining dough covered with plastic wrap and a damp towel to avoid drying out). Brush with butter; fold in half lengthwise. Brush with butter; fold in half widthwise.

2 Brush with butter; top with a prosciutto strip. Place an asparagus spear and a green bean at a diagonal on bottom right corner; roll up. Repeat with remaining dough, butter, prosciutto and vegetables.

3 Place roll-ups on prepared baking sheets. Bake at 400° for 6-8 minutes or until golden brown. Meanwhile, in a blender, combine the sauce ingredients; cover and process until smooth. Transfer to a small bowl; serve with roll-ups.

Yield: 2 dozen (1 cup sauce).

GREEK SALSA

heidi mitchell, cornwall, prince edward island

This salsa has a unique color, texture and a fantastic blend of flavors. It's easy to adapt to the taste preferences of your family or guests. I've made it dozens of times, and it's foolproof! Serve with hearty toasted pita wedges.

- 1 tablespoon white balsamic vinegar
- 2 tablespoons olive oil, *divided*
- 2-1/2 teaspoons Greek seasoning, *divided*
- 1 garlic clove, minced
- 1 cup grape tomatoes, quartered
- 3/4 cup chopped cucumber
- 1/2 cup crumbled feta cheese
- 1/2 cup chopped red onion
- 1 can (2-1/4 ounces) sliced ripe olives, drained
- 1 package (12 ounces) whole wheat pita breads

1 In a small bowl, combine the vinegar, 1 tablespoon oil, 1-1/2 teaspoons Greek seasoning and garlic; set aside.

2 In a large bowl, combine the tomatoes, cucumber, feta cheese, onion and olives. Drizzle with vinegar mixture and toss to coat. Chill until serving.

3 Cut each pita bread into eight wedges. Place on an ungreased baking sheet. Brush with remaining oil; sprinkle with remaining Greek seasoning. Bake at 400° for 6-8 minutes or until crisp. Serve with salsa.

Yield: 2-3/4 cups salsa and 40 pita chips.

CHRISTMAS GLOW PUNCH

marge hodel, roanoke, illinois

With a pretty crimson color, this sweet tropical beverage is perfect for the holidays. To save time, have the punch base chilling in the refrigerator, then add the ginger ale and sherbet just before serving.

- 4-1/2 cups tropical punch
- 1 cup cranberry juice
- 1 can (6 ounces) pineapple juice
- 1/3 cup lemon juice
- 2 to 3 cups chilled ginger ale
- 1 pint raspberry sherbet

1 In a 2-qt. container, combine the punch and juices. Cover and refrigerate until chilled. Just before serving, transfer to a small punch bowl. Stir in ginger ale; top with scoops of sherbet.

Yield: About 2 quarts.

WARM CHOCOLATE EGGNOG

diane hixon, niceville, florida

Serve up eggnog for a rich, smooth sipper and enjoy a holiday treat that's sure to please the adults at your party as well as the children.

> 4 cups eggnog
> 1/2 cup chocolate syrup
> 1/8 to 1/4 teaspoon ground nutmeg
> 3 teaspoons vanilla extract

Whipped cream and additional ground nutmeg

1 In a large saucepan, combine the eggnog, chocolate syrup and nutmeg; heat through over low heat, about 15 minutes (do not boil). Remove from the heat; stir in vanilla.

2 Pour into mugs. Top with a dollop of whipped cream and sprinkle of nutmeg.

Yield: 4 servings.

Editor's Note: This recipe was tested with commercially prepared eggnog.

CAJUN CANAPES

jerri peachee, gentry, arkansas

I came across these pleasantly spicy filled biscuits at a party. Now they're a family-favorite snack.

> 2 tubes (12 ounces *each*) refrigerated buttermilk biscuits
> 1/2 pound bulk pork sausage, cooked and drained
> 1-1/2 cups (6 ounces) shredded cheddar cheese
> 1/4 cup chopped green pepper
> 1/4 cup mayonnaise
> 2 green onions, chopped
> 2 teaspoons lemon juice
> 1/2 teaspoon salt
> 1/2 teaspoon paprika
> 1/4 teaspoon garlic powder
> 1/4 teaspoon dried thyme
> 1/8 to 1/4 teaspoon cayenne pepper

1 Bake biscuits according to package directions, except turn the biscuits over halfway through the baking. Remove from pans to wire racks to cool completely.

2 Using a melon baller, scoop out the center of each biscuit, leaving a 3/8-in. shell (discard biscuit center or save for another use). In a small bowl, combine the remaining ingredients. Spoon about 1 tablespoonful into the center of each biscuit.

3 Place on an ungreased baking sheet. Bake at 400° for 8-10 minutes or until heated through. Serve warm.

Yield: 20 appetizers.

SWEET CHEESE BALL

melissa friend, oakland, maryland

You'll need only a few items for this unique cheese ball. Coconut comes through in the cherry-flecked mixture that's coated in pecans. It looks pretty and tastes delicious served with apple slices, pineapple wedges, berries and other fresh fruit.

     2 packages (8 ounces *each*) cream cheese, softened
   1/2 cup confectioners' sugar
   2/3 cup flaked coconut
     8 maraschino cherries, finely chopped
   3/4 cup finely chopped pecans

Assorted fresh fruit

1 In a small bowl, beat cream cheese and the confectioners' sugar until smooth. Beat in the coconut and cherries. Shape into a ball; roll in pecans. Cover and refrigerate until serving. Serve with fruit.

Yield: 1 cheese ball (3-1/2 cups).

RANCH-SAUSAGE WONTON CUPS

betty huddleston, liberty, indiana

To dress up these tasty appetizers, use small cookie cutters to cut shapes out of additional wonton wrappers. Bake until lightly browned and serve with the wonton cups.

    32 wonton wrappers
   1/2 pound bulk Italian sausage
   1/2 pound ground beef
     3 cups (12 ounces) shredded Colby-Monterey Jack cheese
     1 cup mayonnaise
   1/2 cup sour cream
   1/2 cup milk
     2 to 3 teaspoons ranch salad dressing mix
     1 can (2-1/4 ounces) sliced ripe olives, drained

1 Press wonton wrappers into muffin cups. Bake at 350° for 5 minutes or until lightly browned.

2 Meanwhile, in a large skillet, cook sausage and beef over medium heat until no longer pink; drain. In a large bowl, combine the cheese, mayonnaise, sour cream, milk, salad dressing mix and meat mixture.

3 Spoon 2 tablespoonfuls into each wonton cup; top with olives. Bake for 5-7 minutes or until heated through. Serve warm. Refrigerate leftovers.

Yield: 32 appetizers.

SESAME SALMON SPREAD

sandy sanford, anchorage, alaska

This is one of our favorite appetizers. I pack the spread and crackers in our picnic lunch when my husband and I head out to harvest wood, which we do several times a year. We look forward to getting wood just to have this special treat!

- 1 package (8 ounces) cream cheese, softened
- 2 tablespoons lemon juice
- 1 can (14-3/4 ounces) salmon, drained, bones and skin removed
- 1/4 cup sour cream
- 1 garlic clove, minced
- 2 tablespoons sesame seeds
- 2 teaspoons Liquid Smoke, optional
- 1 teaspoon minced fresh cilantro
- 1 teaspoon minced fresh parsley
- 1/4 teaspoon dill weed
- 1/4 teaspoon salt
- 1/8 teaspoon pepper

Assorted crackers

1 In a small bowl, beat cream cheese and lemon juice until fluffy. Add the salmon, sour cream, garlic, sesame seeds, Liquid Smoke if desired, cilantro, parsley, dill, salt and pepper; beat until combined. Cover and refrigerate for at least 2 hours. Serve with assorted crackers. Refrigerate any leftovers.

Yield: 2-1/2 cups.

HAM ASPARAGUS SPIRALS

rosie huffer, westminster, california

Just three ingredients are needed to prepare these impressive-looking hors d'oeuvres. They are a welcome addition to the table.

- 20 fresh asparagus spears, trimmed
- 20 thin slices deli ham
- 1 package (10.6 ounces) refrigerated Italian breadsticks and garlic spread

1 In a large skillet, bring 1/2 in. of water to a boil; add the asparagus. Reduce the heat; cover pan and simmer for 2 minutes. Drain and immediately place asparagus in ice water; drain and pat dry.

2 Wrap a slice of ham around each asparagus spear. Unroll breadstick dough; spread with garlic spread. Cut each breadstick in half lengthwise. Wrap one piece of dough, garlic spread side out, around each ham-wrapped asparagus spear.

3 Place on an ungreased baking sheet. Bake at 375° for 13-15 minutes or until golden brown. Serve immediately.

Yield: 20 appetizers.

CINNAMON ORANGE CIDER

mark morgan, waterford, wisconsin

The warm color along with the flavor of oranges, apples and cinnamon, makes this cider a sure hit! You might want to double this, filling the punch bowl with one batch and keeping more servings simmering on the stove just for the unforgettable aroma. Your guests will be pleased!

> 4 cups apple cider *or* juice
> 2 cups orange juice
> 3 tablespoons red-hot candies
> 1-1/2 teaspoons whole allspice
> 4-1/2 teaspoons honey

1 In a large saucepan, combine the cider, juice and candies. Place the allspice on a double thickness of cheesecloth; bring up corners of cloth and tie with string to form a bag. Add to pan. Bring to a boil. Reduce heat; cover and simmer for 5 minutes or until flavors are blended.

2 Discard spice bag; stir in honey. Transfer to a small slow cooker; keep warm over low heat.

Yield: 1-1/2 quarts.

SHRIMP TOAST CUPS

awynne thurstenson, siloam springs, arkansas

These appetizers always disappear quick as a flash. The pretty toast cups lend themselves to other favorite fillings, too!

> 24 slices white bread, crusts removed
> 1 cup butter, melted
> 2 packages (8 ounces *each*) cream cheese, softened
> 1/2 cup mayonnaise
> 3 tablespoons sour cream
> 3 tablespoons prepared horseradish
> 3 cans (6 ounces *each*) small shrimp, rinsed and drained
> 16 green onions, sliced

Fresh dill sprigs, optional

1 Flatten bread with a rolling pin; cut each slice into four pieces. Place butter in a shallow dish; dip both sides of bread in butter; press into miniature muffin cups. Bake at 325° for 14 minutes or until golden brown. Remove from pans to wire racks to cool.

2 In a large bowl, beat cream cheese, mayonnaise, sour cream and horseradish until blended. Just before serving, stir in shrimp and onions; spoon into cups. Garnish with dill if desired. Refrigerate leftovers.

Yield: 8 dozen.

HOT WINGS

coralie begin, fairfield, maine

These wings are hearty for a party—with just the right amount of heat. But my family enjoys them so much I often serve them as a main course!

- 7 to 8 pounds fresh *or* frozen chicken wingettes, thawed
- 4 cups ketchup
- 2-1/2 cups packed brown sugar
- 1-1/3 cups water
- 1 cup Louisiana-style hot sauce
- 1/3 cup Worcestershire sauce
- 2-1/2 teaspoons chili powder
- 2 teaspoons garlic powder
- 1/2 teaspoon onion powder

1 Place the chicken wingettes in two greased 15-in. x 10-in. x 1-in. baking pans. In a large bowl, combine the remaining ingredients. Pour over wings.

2 Bake, uncovered, at 350° for 1 hour or until chicken juices run clear. Spoon sauce from pans over wings if desired.

Yield: about 6 dozen.

TANGY CHEESE BITES

patricia ward, fullerton, california

These hot cheese bites were brought to an election-night party I attended years ago. Sharp cheddar and blue cheese give them a slightly tangy flavor that makes them a star on an appetizer buffet.

- 1 loaf (1 pound) unsliced Italian bread
- 3/4 cup butter, cubed
- 4 ounces cream cheese, cubed
- 1-1/2 cups (6 ounces) shredded cheddar cheese
- 1-1/2 cups (6 ounces) crumbled blue cheese
- 3 egg whites
- 1 teaspoon paprika

1 Cut the crust off all sides of bread. Cut into 1-1/2-in. cubes; set the cubes aside. In a large saucepan, melt butter. Stir in cream cheese until melted. Remove from the heat; stir in the cheddar cheese and blue cheese until melted.

2 In a small bowl, beat egg whites until stiff peaks form. Fold into cheese mixture. Dip bread cubes into cheese mixture, turning to coat.

3 Place on greased baking sheets; sprinkle with paprika. Bake at 375° for 12-15 minutes or until bottoms are golden brown. Serve warm.

Yield: about 4-1/2 dozen.

ENTERTAINING ENTREES

CREAMY
SEAFOOD-
STUFFED
SHELLS
P. 37

TURKEY WITH APPLE STUFFING

nancy zimmerman, cape may court house, new jersey

Complementing your golden bird, the well-seasoned bread stuffing is sparked with a sweetness from apples and raisins.

- 1-1/2 cups chopped celery
- 3/4 cup chopped onion
- 3/4 cup butter, cubed
- 9 cups day-old cubed whole wheat bread
- 3 cups finely chopped apples
- 3/4 cup raisins
- 1-1/2 teaspoons salt
- 1-1/2 teaspoons dried thyme
- 1/2 teaspoon rubbed sage
- 1/4 teaspoon pepper
- 1 turkey (14 to 16 pounds)

Additional butter, melted

1. In a Dutch oven, saute celery and onion in butter until tender. Remove from heat; stir in bread cubes, apples, raisins and seasonings.

2. Just before baking, loosely stuff the turkey with 4 cups stuffing. Place remaining stuffing in a greased 2-qt. baking dish; refrigerate until ready to bake. Skewer turkey openings; tie drumsticks together. Place breast side up on a rack in a roasting pan. Brush with melted butter.

3. Bake, uncovered, at 325° for 3-3/4 to 4 hours or until a meat thermometer reads 180° for the turkey thigh and 165° for the stuffing, basting occasionally with pan drippings. (Cover loosely with foil if turkey browns too quickly.)

4. Bake additional stuffing, covered, for 20-30 minutes. Uncover; bake 10 minutes longer or until lightly browned. Cover turkey and let stand for 20 minutes before removing stuffing and carving. If desired, thicken pan drippings for gravy.

Yield: 10-12 servings.

ROAST PORK WITH CHERRY-ALMOND GLAZE

joan laurenzo, johnstown, ohio

Your pork roast will never dry out during cooking with this sweet cherry glaze. You can also spoon the sauce over slices of baked ham.

- 1 boneless whole pork loin roast (3-1/2 pounds)
- 1 teaspoon salt
- 1 jar (12 ounces) cherry preserves
- 1/4 cup cider vinegar
- 2 tablespoons light corn syrup
- 1/4 teaspoon *each* ground cinnamon, nutmeg and cloves
- 1/4 cup slivered almonds

1. Sprinkle roast with salt; place on a rack in a shallow roasting pan. Bake, uncovered, at 350° for 30 minutes.

2. In a small saucepan, bring the preserves, vinegar, corn syrup and spices to a boil. Reduce heat; simmer, uncovered, for 2 minutes. Set aside 3/4 cup for serving. Stir almonds into remaining mixture.

3. Brush roast with some of the glaze. Bake 35-50 minutes longer or until a meat thermometer reads 160°, brushing frequently with remaining glaze. Let stand for 10 minutes before slicing. Serve with reserved cherry mixture.

Yield: 10 servings.

CHERRY-STUFFED PORK LOIN

jim korzenowski, dearborn, michigan

This easy pork roast is moist and has a wonderful stuffing. It looks and tastes impressive, and the gravy is a great complement.

    1   cup dried cherries
  1/2   cup water
  2/3   cup chopped onion
  1/2   cup chopped celery
  1/2   cup minced fresh parsley
  1/4   cup shredded carrot
    1   tablespoon rubbed sage
    1   teaspoon minced fresh rosemary
  1/2   teaspoon minced garlic
    3   tablespoons butter
2-1/2   cups salad croutons
    1   cup chicken broth
  1/2   teaspoon pepper, *divided*
  1/4   teaspoon ground nutmeg
  1/4   teaspoon almond extract
    1   boneless whole pork loin roast
        (about 3 pounds)
GRAVY:
1-3/4   cups chicken broth
  1/2   cup water
  1/2   cup heavy whipping cream
  1/2   teaspoon minced fresh rosemary

1   In a small saucepan, bring cherries and water to a boil. Remove from the heat; set aside (do not drain).

2   In a large skillet, saute the onion, celery, parsley, carrot, sage, rosemary and garlic in butter until tender. Remove from the heat. Stir in the croutons, broth, 1/4 teaspoon pepper, nutmeg, extract and cherries. Let stand until liquid is absorbed.

3   Cut a lengthwise slit down the center of the roast to within 1/2 in. of bottom. Open roast so it lies flat;

cover with plastic wrap. Flatten to 3/4-in. thickness. Remove plastic; spread stuffing over meat to within 1 in. of edges. Close roast; tie several times with kitchen string and secure ends with toothpicks. Place fat side up on a rack in a shallow roasting pan. Sprinkle with remaining pepper.

4   Bake, uncovered, at 350° for 1-1/2 to 2 hours or until a meat thermometer reads 160°. Let stand for 10-15 minutes before slicing. Meanwhile, add broth and water to roasting pan; stir to loosen browned bits. Pour into a small saucepan. Bring to a boil over medium-high heat; cook until reduced by half. Stir in cream and rosemary. Bring to a boil. Reduce heat; simmer, uncovered, until thickened. Serve with roast.

Yield: 10-12 servings.

SEASONED RIB ROAST

evelyn gebhardt, kasilof, alaska

Gravy made from the drippings of this boneless beef rib roast is exceptional. You can also use a rib eye roast with excellent results.

1-1/2   teaspoons lemon-pepper seasoning
1-1/2   teaspoons paprika
  3/4   teaspoon garlic salt
  1/2   teaspoon dried rosemary, crushed
  1/4   teaspoon cayenne pepper
    1   beef ribeye roast (3 to 4 pounds)

1   In a small bowl, combine the seasonings; rub over roast. Place the roast fat side up on a rack in a shallow roasting pan. Bake, uncovered, at 350° for 1-3/4 to 2-1/2 hours or until meat reaches desired doneness (for medium-rare, a meat thermometer should read 145°; medium, 160°; well-done, 170°). Remove to a warm serving platter. Let stand for 10-15 minutes before carving.

Yield: 6-8 servings.

AUTUMN TURKEY TENDERLOINS

brenda sabot-lion, warren, pennsylvania

This out-of-the-ordinary meal is perfect for cool nights with family, friends or company. With cinnamon and brown sugar, it's slightly sweet, and the toasted walnuts add a toasty-nutty crunch.

- 1-1/4 pounds turkey breast tenderloins
- 1 tablespoon butter
- 1 cup unsweetened apple juice
- 1 medium apple, sliced
- 1 tablespoon brown sugar
- 2 teaspoons chicken bouillon granules
- 1/4 teaspoon ground cinnamon
- 1/4 teaspoon ground nutmeg
- 1 tablespoon cornstarch
- 2 tablespoons cold water
- 1/2 cup chopped walnuts, toasted

1 In a large skillet, brown turkey in butter. Add the apple juice, apple, brown sugar, bouillon, cinnamon and nutmeg. Bring to a boil. Reduce heat; cover and simmer for 10-12 minutes or until turkey juices run clear.

2 Using a slotted spoon, remove turkey and apple slices to a serving platter; keep warm. Combine cornstarch and water until smooth; stir into pan juices. Bring to a boil; cook and stir for 2 minutes or until thickened. Spoon over turkey and apple. Sprinkle with walnuts.

Yield: 5 servings.

CITRUS-ROSEMARY RUBBED TURKEY

della stamp, long beach, california

While recovering from hip surgery, I wrote my family for some of their favorite recipes to compile into a cookbook. This seasoned turkey is timeless.

- 2 tablespoons minced fresh rosemary *or*
- 2 teaspoons dried rosemary, crushed
- 1-1/2 teaspoons grated fresh *or* dried orange peel
- 1-1/2 teaspoons grated fresh *or* dried lemon peel
- 1 teaspoon salt
- 1 teaspoon onion powder
- 1 teaspoon garlic powder
- 1 teaspoon pepper
- 1 turkey (13 to 15 pounds)
- 1/4 cup olive oil

1 In a small bowl, combine the first seven ingredients. Place turkey, breast side up, on a rack in a roasting pan; pat dry. Brush with oil; rub rosemary mixture over turkey.

2 Bake, uncovered, at 325° for 2-3/4 to 3-1/4 hours or until a meat thermometer reads 180°, basting occasionally with pan drippings. (Cover loosely with foil if turkey browns too quickly.) Cover and let stand for 20 minutes before carving.

Yield: 13-15 servings.

Editor's Note: This turkey is shown with Corn-Bread Dressing from page 36. If stuffing the turkey, increase the baking time to 3-1/4 to 4 hours.

CRAB-STUFFED BEEF TENDERLOIN

gloria warczak, cedarburg, wisconsin

Here's a deliciously different way to serve surf and turf. It's an elegant entree that often appears on my Christmas dinner table.

- 8 bacon strips
- 1 beef tenderloin roast (3 pounds)
- 3 pouches (6 ounces *each*) lump crabmeat
- 1 cup water, *divided*
- 1/2 cup burgundy wine *or* beef broth
- 2 teaspoons lemon juice
- 2 tablespoons minced green onion
- 1 tablespoon butter
- 1 tablespoon steak sauce
- 1 teaspoon soy sauce
- 1 teaspoon browning sauce, optional
- 1 teaspoon sugar
- 1-1/2 teaspoons minced fresh parsley *or* 1/2 teaspoon dried parsley flakes

1 In a large skillet, cook bacon over medium heat until cooked but not crisp. Remove to paper towels to drain.

2 Make a lengthwise slit down the center of the tenderloin to within 1/2 in. of bottom. Open meat so it lies flat. Mound crab over the center. Close tenderloin; tie at 2-in. intervals with kitchen string.

3 Place on a rack in a shallow roasting pan. Wrap bacon around meat. Combine 1/2 cup water, wine or broth and lemon juice; pour over beef.

4 Bake, uncovered, at 425° for 45-60 minutes or until meat reaches desired doneness (for medium-rare, a meat thermometer should read 145°; medium, 160°; well-done, 170°). Remove meat to a serving platter. Cover and let stand for 10 minutes.

5 Pour pan drippings and loosened brown bits into a saucepan. Skim fat. Stir in the onion, butter, steak sauce, soy sauce, browning sauce if desired, sugar and remaining water. Bring to a boil. Reduce heat; simmer, uncovered, for 5 minutes. Stir in parsley. Slice tenderloin; serve with sauce.

Yield: 10 servings.

HOLIDAY GLAZED HAM

tammy harris, deltona, florida

This easy glaze is sure to complement any holiday ham. I serve the remaining glaze on the side.

- 1 boneless fully cooked ham (5 pounds)
- 1/2 cup butter
- 2 tablespoons all-purpose flour
- 1 cup apple jelly
- 2/3 cup packed brown sugar
- 1/2 cup orange juice
- 1/4 cup sugar
- 1/2 teaspoon *each* ground cinnamon, ground nutmeg and ground cloves

1 Place ham on a rack in a large roasting pan. Bake uncovered, at 325° for 1-1/4 hours.

2 For glaze, melt butter in a saucepan; stir in flour until smooth. Stir in the jelly, brown sugar, orange juice, sugar, cinnamon, nutmeg and cloves. Cook and stir over medium heat until smooth.

3 Brush some of the glaze over ham. Bake 30-35 minutes longer or until a meat thermometer reads 140°. Let stand for 5-10 minutes before slicing. Simmer the remaining glaze and serve with ham.

Yield: 15 servings.

ARTICHOKE SPINACH LASAGNA

carole rago, altoona, pennsylvania

We were served this meatless entree while visiting friends in Maryland. We took the recipe with us when we left and have since added a few more ingredients which make it even better.

> 1/2   cup chopped onion
> 4   garlic cloves, minced
> 1   tablespoon olive oil
> 1   can (14-1/2 ounces) vegetable *or* chicken broth
> 1   teaspoon dried rosemary, crushed
> 1/4   teaspoon *each* ground nutmeg and pepper
> 1   can (14 ounces) water-packed artichoke hearts, rinsed, drained and quartered
> 1   package (10 ounces) frozen chopped spinach, thawed and squeezed dry
> 1/2   cup sliced fresh mushrooms
> 1   jar (16 ounces) roasted garlic Alfredo *or* Parmesan and mozzarella pasta sauce
> 12   no-cook lasagna noodles
> 3   cups (12 ounces) shredded part-skim mozzarella cheese, *divided*
> 1   cup crumbled tomato and basil feta cheese *or* feta cheese
> 1/8   teaspoon garlic powder
> 1/8   teaspoon *each* dried oregano, parsley flakes and basil

1   In a large saucepan, saute onion and garlic in oil for 2-3 minutes or until tender. Stir in the broth, rosemary, nutmeg and pepper. Bring to a boil. Add the artichokes, spinach and mushrooms. Reduce heat; cover and simmer for 5 minutes. Stir in pasta sauce.

2   Spread 1 cup sauce mixture into a greased 13-in. x 9-in. baking dish. Top with three noodles and 3/4 cup mozzarella cheese. Repeat layers three times. Top with remaining sauce mixture and mozzarella cheese. Sprinkle with feta cheese, garlic powder, oregano, parsley and basil.

3   Cover and bake at 350° for 40 minutes. Uncover; bake 15 minutes longer or until heated through. Let stand for 10 minutes before cutting.

Yield: 12 servings.

RED-EYE BEEF ROAST

carol stevens, basye, virginia

The addition of hot sauce zips up this cut of meat. It takes me back to spicy dinners I enjoyed as a child in the Southwest. I like to use the leftovers in different dishes including barbecued beef sandwiches, quesadillas and burritos.

> 1   boneless beef eye of round roast (about 3 pounds)
> 1   tablespoon canola oil
> 2-1/2   cups water, *divided*
> 1   envelope onion soup mix
> 3   tablespoons cider vinegar
> 2   tablespoons Louisiana hot sauce
> 2   tablespoons all-purpose flour

1   In a Dutch oven, brown roast on all sides in oil over medium-high heat; drain. Combine 3/4 cup water, soup mix, vinegar and hot sauce; pour over roast.

2   Cover and bake at 325° for 2-3 hours or until tender. Transfer to a serving platter and keep warm. Let stand for 10-15 minutes before slicing.

3   For gravy, combine flour and remaining water until smooth; stir into meat juices. Bring to a boil; cook and stir for 2 minutes or until thickened. Serve with meat.

Yield: 10-12 servings.

TURKEY WITH CORN-BREAD DRESSING

fae fisher, callao, virginia
The dressing was always my favorite part of the meal. I can still smell the wonderful aroma that filled the house while the turkey roasted in our wood stove. We could hardly wait to sit down and eat!

CORN BREAD:
- 3 cups cornmeal
- 1 cup self-rising flour
- 4-1/2 teaspoons baking powder
- 1-1/2 teaspoons salt
- 1-1/4 cups chopped celery
- 1/3 cup chopped onion
- 1/2 teaspoon celery seed
- 2 cups milk
- 1/4 cup canola oil
- 1 egg

DRESSING:
- 1/2 cup chopped fresh parsley
- 1 to 2 tablespoons poultry seasoning
- 3/4 teaspoon pepper
- 3/4 cup egg substitute
- 1 cup butter, melted, *divided*
- 1 turkey (13 to 15 pounds)

1 In a large bowl, combine the first seven ingredients. In a small bowl, combine the milk, oil and egg; pour over cornmeal mixture and mix well. Pour into a greased 13-in. x 9-in. baking pan.

2 Bake at 350° for 50 minutes or until a toothpick inserted near the center comes out clean. Cool on a wire rack.

3 Crumble corn bread into a large bowl. Add the parsley, poultry seasoning and pepper; toss. Combine egg substitute and 3/4 cup butter; add to the corn bread mixture, stirring just until blended.

4 Just before baking, stuff the turkey with dressing. Skewer or fasten openings. Tie the drumsticks together. Place on a rack in a roasting pan. Brush with remaining butter. Place remaining dressing in a greased baking dish; cover and refrigerate until ready to bake.

5 Bake turkey at 325° for 3-1/2 to 4-1/2 hours or until a meat thermometer reads 180° for the turkey and 165° for the stuffing. When the turkey begins to brown, cover lightly with a tent of aluminum foil.

6 Bake extra dressing at 325° for 1 hour. When turkey is done, let stand for 20 minutes before carving. Remove all dressing to a serving bowl.

Yield: 8-10 servings (10 cups dressing).

Editor's Note: As a substitute for 1 cup of self-rising flour, place 1-1/2 teaspoons baking powder and 1/2 teaspoon salt in a measuring cup. Add all-purpose flour to measure 1 cup.

BEEF RIB ROAST

betty abel jellencich, utica, new york
Our mom topped beef roast with bacon and onion. Whenever I prepare it, I can't help but reminisce about the happy life she gave me and my brothers.

- 1 bone-in beef rib roast (4 to 5 pounds)
- 1 garlic clove, minced
- 1 teaspoon salt
- 1/2 teaspoon pepper
- 1 small onion, sliced
- 6 to 8 bacon strips

1 Place roast, fat side up, on a rack in a shallow roasting pan. Rub with garlic, salt and pepper; top with onion and bacon.

2 Bake, uncovered, at 325° for 2-3 hours or until meat reaches desired doneness (for medium-rare, a meat thermometer should read 145°; medium, 160°; well-done, 170°). Transfer to warm serving platter. Let stand for 10-15 minutes before slicing.

Yield: 10-12 servings.

CREAMY SEAFOOD-STUFFED SHELLS

katie sloan, charlotte, north carolina

Inspired by my love of lasagna, pasta shells and seafood, I created this recipe that's easy to make but special enough to serve company. I serve it with garlic bread and a salad.

- 24 uncooked jumbo pasta shells
- 1 tablespoon finely chopped green pepper
- 1 tablespoon chopped red onion
- 1 teaspoon plus 1/4 cup butter, *divided*
- 2 cans (6 ounces *each*) lump crabmeat, drained
- 1 package (5 ounces) frozen cooked salad shrimp, thawed
- 1 egg, lightly beaten
- 1/2 cup shredded part-skim mozzarella cheese
- 1/4 cup mayonnaise
- 2 tablespoons plus 4 cups milk, *divided*
- 1-1/2 teaspoons seafood seasoning, *divided*
- 1/4 teaspoon pepper
- 1/4 cup all-purpose flour
- 1/4 teaspoon coarsely ground pepper
- 1-1/2 cups grated Parmesan cheese

1 Cook pasta according to package directions. Meanwhile, in a small skillet, saute green pepper and onion in 1 teaspoon butter until tender; set aside.

2 In a large bowl, combine the crab, shrimp, egg, mozzarella cheese, mayonnaise, 2 tablespoons milk, 1 teaspoon seafood seasoning, pepper and green pepper mixture.

3 Drain and rinse pasta; stuff each shell with 1 rounded tablespoon of seafood mixture. Place in a greased 13-in. x 9-in. baking dish.

4 In a small saucepan, melt remaining butter over medium heat. Whisk in flour and coarsely ground pepper; gradually whisk in remaining milk. Bring to a boil; cook and stir for 2 minutes or until thickened. Stir in Parmesan cheese.

5 Pour over stuffed shells. Sprinkle with remaining seafood seasoning. Bake, uncovered, at 350° for 30-35 minutes or until bubbly.

Yield: 8 servings.

Editor's Note: Reduced-fat or fat-free mayonnaise is not recommended for this recipe.

GRILLED MARINATED SIRLOIN

taste of home test kitchen

A tasty marinade laced with lime juice is the secret behind this moist and elegant sirloin recipe. You'll enjoy warm-weather entertaining and stay out of a hot kitchen with this grilled summer standout.

- 1/4 cup lime juice
- 1 green onion, finely chopped
- 2 tablespoons paprika
- 2 tablespoons canola oil
- 1 tablespoon finely chopped jalapeno pepper
- 1-1/2 teaspoons sugar
- 2 garlic cloves, minced
- 1 teaspoon dried oregano
- 1 teaspoon grated lime peel
- 1/2 teaspoon salt
- 1 boneless beef sirloin steak (about 1-1/2 pounds)

1 In a small bowl, combine the first 10 ingredients. Pour half of the marinade into a large resealable plastic bag; add steak. Seal bag and turn to coat; refrigerate for up to 4 hours. Cover and refrigerate remaining marinade for basting.

2 Coat grill rack with cooking spray before starting the grill. Grill steak, covered, over medium heat for 8-10 minutes on each side or until meat reaches desired doneness (for medium-rare, a meat thermometer should read 145°; medium, 160°; well-done, 170°). Baste with reserved marinade during the last 2 minutes of cooking.

Yield: 6 servings.

Editor's Note: When cutting hot peppers, disposable gloves are recommended. Avoid touching your face.

SEAFOOD LASAGNA ALFREDO

dolores jensen, arnold, missouri

Once when expecting a visit from a college friend, I wanted to serve something a little different. So I came up with this lasagna. It's perfect for company because it can be assembled in advance.

      2 cans (6 ounces *each*) lump crabmeat, drained
      1 package (5 ounces) frozen cooked salad shrimp, thawed and patted dry
      1 carton (15 ounces) ricotta cheese
      2 eggs, lightly beaten
      1 tablespoon Italian seasoning
      1 pound sliced fresh mushrooms
      1 large onion, chopped
      2 garlic cloves, minced
      6 tablespoons butter
    1/2 cup all-purpose flour
      2 cans (12 ounces *each*) evaporated milk
      1 cup milk
      1 cup grated Parmesan cheese, *divided*
Salt and pepper to taste
      9 lasagna noodles, cooked and drained
      1 package (10 ounces) frozen chopped spinach, thawed and squeezed dry
      4 cups (16 ounces) shredded part-skim mozzarella cheese
      3 cups frozen chopped broccoli, thawed

1   In a small bowl, combine crab and shrimp; set aside. In another bowl, combine the ricotta cheese, eggs and Italian seasoning until smooth; set aside.

2   In a large skillet, saute the mushrooms, onion and garlic in butter until tender. Stir in flour until blended. Gradually add evaporated milk and milk. Bring to a boil; cook and stir for 2 minutes or until thickened. Reduce heat; stir in 1/2 cup Parmesan cheese, salt and pepper until cheese is melted.

3   In a greased shallow 4-qt. baking dish, layer three noodles, spinach, a third of the ricotta mixture, 1-1/3 cups mozzarella cheese and a third of the mushroom sauce. Top with three noodles, crab mixture, a third of the ricotta mixture, 1-1/3 cups mozzarella cheese, a third of the mushroom sauce and remaining noodles. Top with broccoli and the remaining ricotta mixture, mozzarella and mushroom sauce. Sprinkle with the remaining Parmesan.

4   Bake, uncovered, at 350° for 45-55 minutes or until heated through. Let stand for 10 minutes before cutting.

Yield: 12 servings.

ORANGE-PECAN PORK ROAST

yvonne novak, silver spring, maryland

Family and friends will ooh and aah when you bring out this roast with its beautiful orange glaze and nutty topping. Moist and delicious, it's a showstopper!

      1 whole boneless pork loin roast (2-1/2 to 3 pounds)
    1/2 cup finely chopped onion
      1 garlic clove, minced
      2 tablespoons canola oil
    1/2 cup orange marmalade
    1/4 cup chopped pecans
    1/4 teaspoon ground cinnamon

1   Place roast on a rack in a shallow roasting pan. In a skillet, saute onion and garlic in oil until tender. Add the marmalade, pecans and cinnamon; cook and stir until marmalade is melted. Spoon over roast.

2   Bake, uncovered, at 325° for 1-3/4 hours or until meat thermometer reads 160°. Let stand for 10 minutes before slicing.

Yield: 6-8 servings.

STUFFED CROWN ROAST OF PORK

mary ann balam, tujunga, california

Folks may be intimidated to prepare an elegant crown roast of pork, but it's actually an easy entree. Our four grown sons and their families expect this every Christmas.

- 1 pork crown roast (16 ribs and about 10 pounds)
- 2 garlic cloves, slivered
- 2 tablespoons olive oil

Salt and pepper to taste

- 2 cups apple juice *or* cider

APPLE RAISIN STUFFING:

- 1 cup raisins
- 1 cup boiling water
- 1 cup chopped onion
- 1 cup chopped celery
- 1 garlic clove, minced
- 3/4 cup butter
- 5 cups soft bread crumbs
- 3 cups chopped peeled tart apples
- 1/4 cup minced fresh parsley
- 1 teaspoon salt
- 1/4 teaspoon paprika

1 Cut slits in the bottom of each rib; insert garlic slivers. Rub oil over entire roast; sprinkle with salt and pepper. Place in a shallow roasting pan. Cover rib ends with foil. Pour apple juice into pan. Bake, uncovered, at 350° for 1 hour, basting occasionally.

2 Meanwhile, for stuffing, place the raisins in a small bowl; pour boiling water over raisins. Let stand for 2 minutes; drain and set aside. In a large skillet, saute the onion, celery and garlic in butter until tender. Add the bread crumbs, apples, parsley, salt, paprika and raisins; mix well.

3 Carefully spoon stuffing into center of roast. Bake 1 to 1-1/2 hours longer or until a meat thermometer reads 160°-170° and juices run clear. Let stand for 10 minutes. Remove foil and stuffing. Cut pork between the ribs.

Yield: 12-16 servings.

APPLE TURKEY POTPIE

georgia macdonald, dover, new hampshire

I like to take leftover holiday turkey and turn it into this hearty potpie. Apples and raisins add sweetness.

- 1/4 cup chopped onion
- 1 tablespoon butter
- 2 cans (10-3/4 ounces *each*) condensed cream of chicken soup, undiluted
- 3 cups cubed cooked turkey
- 1 large unpeeled tart apple, cubed
- 1/3 cup golden raisins
- 1 teaspoon lemon juice
- 1/4 teaspoon ground nutmeg

Pastry for a single-crust pie (9 inches)

1 In a large saucepan, saute onion in butter until tender. Add the soup, turkey, apple, raisins, lemon juice and nutmeg. Spoon into an ungreased 11-in. x 7-in. x 2-in. baking dish.

2 On a lightly floured surface, roll out pastry to fit top of dish. Place over filling; flute edges and cut slits in top. Bake at 425° for 25-30 minutes or until crust is golden brown and filling is bubbly.

Yield: 6 servings.

STUFFED STEAK SPIRALS

margaret pache, mesa, arizona

When looking for an extra-special entree to serve guests, you can rely on this impressive and appealing recipe. Tender and swirled with tangy tomato stuffing, it's a sensational way to showcase flank steak.

- 1/4 cup chopped sun-dried tomatoes (not packed in oil)
- 1/2 cup boiling water
- 1/2 cup grated Parmesan cheese
- 1/4 cup minced fresh parsley
- 1 tablespoon prepared horseradish, drained
- 1 to 1-1/2 teaspoons coarsely ground pepper
- 1 beef flank steak (1-1/2 pounds)
- 2 teaspoons canola oil

1 Place the tomatoes in a small bowl; add water. Cover and let stand for 5 minutes; drain. Stir in the Parmesan cheese, parsley, horseradish and pepper; set aside.

2 Cut steak horizontally from a long side to within 1/2 in. of opposite side. Open meat so it lies flat; cover with plastic wrap. Flatten to 1/4-in. thickness. Remove plastic; spoon tomato mixture over meat to within 1/2 in. of edges. Roll up tightly jelly-roll style, starting with a long side. Tie with kitchen string.

3 Line a shallow roasting pan with heavy-duty foil; coat the foil with cooking spray. In a large nonstick skillet coated with cooking spray, brown meat in oil on all sides. Place in prepared pan.

4 Bake, uncovered, at 400° for 30-40 minutes or until meat reaches desired doneness (for medium-rare, a meat thermometer should read 145°; medium, 160°; well-done, 170°). Let stand for 10-15 minutes. Remove string and cut into slices.

Yield: 6 servings.

MAPLE-BUTTER TURKEY WITH GRAVY

taste of home test kitchen

Thyme, sage and marjoram blend beautifully with apple cider and maple syrup in this recipe. The maple butter can be prepared 1 to 2 days in advance.

- 2 cups apple cider *or* juice
- 1/3 cup maple syrup
- 3/4 cup butter, cubed
- 2 tablespoons minced fresh thyme *or* 2 teaspoons dried thyme
- 1 tablespoon minced fresh sage *or* 1 teaspoon dried sage leaves
- 2 teaspoons dried marjoram
- 1 teaspoon salt
- 1 teaspoon pepper
- 1 turkey (14 to 16 pounds)
- 2 to 2-1/2 cups chicken broth
- 3 tablespoons all-purpose flour

1 For maple butter, in a small heavy saucepan, bring cider and syrup to a boil. Cook until reduced to 1/2 cup, about 20 minutes. Remove from the heat; stir in the butter, thyme, sage, marjoram, salt and pepper. Transfer to a bowl; cover and refrigerate until set.

2 With fingers, carefully loosen the skin from both sides of turkey breast. Rub 1/2 cup maple butter under turkey skin. Refrigerate remaining maple butter. Skewer turkey openings; tie drumsticks together. Place on a rack in a roasting pan.

3 Cover with foil and bake at 325° for 2 hours. Brush top with 1/3 cup maple butter. Bake, uncovered, 1 to 1-1/2 hours longer or until a meat thermometer reads 180°, basting occasionally with pan drippings. (Cover loosely with foil if turkey browns too

quickly.) Remove turkey to a serving platter and keep warm. Cover and let stand for 20 minutes before carving.

4   Pour drippings and loosened brown bits into a 4-cup measuring cup. Skim and discard fat. Add enough broth to drippings to measure 3 cups. In a large saucepan, combine flour and broth mixture until smooth. Stir in remaining maple butter. Bring to a boil; cook and stir for 2 minutes or until thickened. Serve with turkey.

Yield: 14-16 servings (3-1/3 cups gravy).

WALDORF STUFFED HAM

colleen vrooman, waukesha, wisconsin

I couldn't resist trying something new to enter a contest, and this recipe just popped into my head. I served it to my husband, and he said it's a keeper.

    1-1/2   cups unsweetened apple juice
      1/4   cup butter, cubed
        1   package (6 ounces) pork stuffing mix
        1   medium tart apple, finely chopped
      1/4   cup chopped sweet onion
      1/4   cup chopped celery
      1/4   cup chopped walnuts
        1   fully cooked spiral-sliced ham (8 pounds)
        1   can (21 ounces) apple pie filling
      1/4   teaspoon ground cinnamon

1   In a large saucepan, bring apple juice and butter to a boil. Remove from the heat; stir in the stuffing mix, apple, onion, celery and walnuts.

2   Place ham on a rack in a shallow roasting pan. Spoon stuffing by tablespoonfuls between ham slices. Spoon pie filling over ham; sprinkle with cinnamon.

3   Bake, uncovered, at 325° for 1-1/4 to 1-3/4 hours or until a meat thermometer reads 140°. Let stand for 10 minutes before serving.

Yield: 14-16 servings.

ASPARAGUS VEAL CORDON BLEU

jeanne molloy, feeding hills, massachusetts

I try to make varied meals for two that are both appetizing and interesting. I sometimes double this recipe so we can have the leftovers for lunch the next day because it reheats so well in the microwave.

        8   fresh asparagus spears, trimmed
        2   tablespoons water
        2   veal cutlets (6 ounces *each*)
      1/4   teaspoon salt
      1/8   teaspoon pepper
        2   garlic cloves, minced
        1   tablespoon olive oil
        4   large fresh mushrooms, sliced
        2   thin slices prosciutto *or* deli ham
      1/2   cup shredded Italian cheese blend

1   Place asparagus and water in an 11-in. x 7-in. x 2-in. microwave-safe dish. Cover and microwave on high for 2-3 minutes or until crisp-tender; drain and set aside.

2   Flatten veal to 1/4-in. thickness; sprinkle with salt and pepper. In a small skillet, saute garlic in oil. Add veal; brown for 2-3 minutes on each side.

3   Transfer to an ungreased 11-in. x 7-in. x 2-in. baking dish. In the pan drippings, saute mushrooms until tender; spoon over veal. Top each with four asparagus spears and a slice of prosciutto. Sprinkle with cheese. Bake, uncovered, at 350° for 5-10 minutes or until juices run clear.

Yield: 2 servings.

CHERRY-STUFFED PORK CHOPS

taste of home test kitchen

Grilled pork chops have a lovely stuffing of couscous, cherries and seasonings in this quick and elegant main dish. Served with a salad, it's perfect for holidays, but speedy enough for everyday family suppers.

- 1 package (5.6 ounces) couscous with toasted pine nuts
- 6 boneless pork loin chops (1 inch thick and 6 ounces *each*)
- 1/2 cup dried cherries
- 1 tablespoon brown sugar
- 1 tablespoon butter, melted
- 1/2 teaspoon minced fresh gingerroot
- 1/2 teaspoon garlic powder
- 1/2 teaspoon pepper

1 Prepare couscous according to package directions. Meanwhile, cut a deep slit in each pork chop, forming a pocket. Stir the cherries, brown sugar, butter and ginger into prepared couscous. Stuff 1/3 cup into each chop; secure with toothpicks. Sprinkle with garlic powder and pepper.

2 Grill pork chops, covered, over medium heat for 10-12 minutes on each side or until a meat thermometer reads 160°. Discard toothpicks.

Yield: 6 servings.

PEAR-STUFFED PORK LOIN

mary shivers, ada, oklahoma

From just two trees, we get an abundance of pears. So I'm always looking for new ideas on how to use them. This elegant roast offers a delicious way to incorporate pears into a main-dish stuffing and glaze.

- 1 boneless whole pork loin roast (3 to 4 pounds)
- 1/2 cup chopped peeled ripe pears
- 1/2 cup chopped dried pears
- 1/2 cup chopped walnuts
- 1/4 cup minced fresh cilantro
- 3 tablespoons honey
- 2 garlic cloves, minced
- 1/4 teaspoon crushed red pepper flakes

GLAZE:

- 1 cup finely chopped peeled ripe pears
- 1/2 cup finely chopped onion
- 1/4 cup maple syrup
- 2 tablespoons Worcestershire sauce
- 2 tablespoons chili sauce
- 1 jalapeno pepper, seeded and finely chopped
- 1/8 teaspoon cayenne pepper

1 Cut a lengthwise slit down the center of roast to within 1/2 in. of bottom. Open roast so it lies flat. On each half, make another lengthwise slit down the center to within 1/2 in. of bottom; open roast and cover with plastic wrap. Flatten to 3/4-in. thickness. Remove plastic wrap.

2 In a small bowl, combine the ripe pears, dried pears, walnuts, cilantro, honey, garlic and pepper flakes; spread over roast to within 1 in. of edges. Roll up from a long side; tie with kitchen string at 2-in. intervals. Place in a shallow roasting pan lined with heavy-duty foil.

3 Combine the glaze ingredients; spoon over roast. Bake, uncovered, at 350° for 1-1/4 to 1-1/2 hours or until a meat thermometer reads 160°, basting occasionally with pan drippings. Let stand for 10-15 minutes before slicing.

Yield: 12 servings.

Editor's Note: When cutting hot peppers, disposable gloves are recommended. Avoid touching your face.

FLANK STEAK WITH CRANBERRY SAUCE

ellen de munnik, chesterfield, michigan

This tasty and tender steak, served with a mild sweet-tart cranberry sauce, makes a pretty presentation for a special-occasion dinner.

    2 **teaspoons grated orange peel**
1/2 **teaspoon salt**
1/2 **teaspoon ground cinnamon**
    1 **beef flank steak (1-1/2 pounds)**

CRANBERRY SAUCE:
1/4 **cup chopped green onions**
    1 **garlic clove, minced**
3/4 **cup dried cranberries**
1/2 **cup reduced-sodium beef broth**
1/2 **cup dry red wine *or* additional reduced-sodium beef broth**
1/2 **cup cranberry juice**
    2 **teaspoons cornstarch**
    2 **tablespoons cold water**
1/4 **teaspoon salt**
1/4 **teaspoon pepper**

1   Combine the orange peel, salt and cinnamon; rub over the flank steak. Cover and refrigerate for 1 hour.

2   In a large saucepan coated with cooking spray, saute onions and garlic until tender. Add the cranberries, broth, wine or additional broth and cranberry juice. Bring to a boil. Reduce heat; simmer, uncovered, for 10 minutes.

3   Combine the cornstarch and water; stir into the cranberry mixture. Bring to a boil; cook and stir for 2 minutes or until thickened. Stir in salt and pepper. Reduce heat to low; keep warm.

4   Place steak on a broiler pan. Broil 3-4 in. from the heat for 7-9 minutes on each side or until meat reaches desired doneness (for medium-rare, a meat thermometer should read 145°; medium, 160°; well-done, 170°). Slice steak across the grain; serve with cranberry sauce.

Yield: 6 servings.

ROAST CHRISTMAS GOOSE

rosemarie forcum, white stone, virginia

I have such fond childhood memories of my mother serving this golden-brown Christmas goose. To flavor the meat, Mom stuffed the bird with peeled and quartered fruit that's discarded after baking.

    1 **domestic goose (10 to 12 pounds)**
Salt and pepper
    1 **medium apple, peeled and quartered**
    1 **medium navel orange, peeled and quartered**
    1 **medium lemon, peeled and quartered**
    1 **cup hot water**

1   Sprinkle the goose cavity with salt and pepper. Place the apple, orange and lemon in the cavity. Place goose breast side up on a rack in a large shallow roasting pan. Prick skin well with a fork. Pour water into pan.

2   Bake, uncovered, at 350° for 2-1/4 to 3 hours or until a meat thermometer reads 185°. If necessary, drain fat from pan as it accumulates. Cover goose with foil and let stand for 20 minutes before carving. Discard fruit.

Yield: 8 servings.

CHICKEN SALTIMBOCCA

carol mccollough, missoula, montana

White wine dresses up cream of chicken soup to make a lovely sauce for chicken, ham and Swiss cheese roll-ups. The tried-and-true recipe comes from my mother.

- 6 boneless skinless chicken breast halves (4 ounces *each*)
- 6 thin slices deli ham
- 6 slices Swiss cheese
- 1/4 cup all-purpose flour
- 1/4 cup grated Parmesan cheese
- 1/2 teaspoon salt
- 1/4 teaspoon pepper
- 2 tablespoons canola oil
- 1 can (10-3/4 ounces) condensed cream of chicken soup, undiluted
- 1/2 cup dry white wine *or* chicken broth

Hot cooked rice

1. Flatten chicken to 1/4-in. thickness. Top each piece with a slice of ham and cheese. Roll up tightly; secure with toothpicks. In a shallow bowl, combine the flour, Parmesan cheese, salt and pepper. Roll chicken in the flour mixture; refrigerate for 1 hour.

2. In a large skillet, brown roll-ups in oil on all sides; transfer to a 3-qt. slow cooker. Combine the soup and wine or broth; pour over chicken.

3. Cover and cook on low for 4-5 hours or until a meat thermometer reads 170°. Remove roll-ups and stir sauce. Discard toothpicks. Serve with rice.

Yield: 6 servings.

PRIME RIB WITH HORSERADISH SAUCE

paula zsiray, logan, utah

To ring in the New Year, we invite friends for dinner. A menu featuring tender prime rib is festive yet simple to prepare. A pepper rub and mild horseradish sauce complement the beef's great flavor.

- 1 semi-boneless beef rib roast (4 to 6 pounds)
- 1 tablespoon olive oil
- 1 to 2 teaspoons coarsely ground pepper

HORSERADISH SAUCE:
- 1 cup (8 ounces) sour cream
- 3 to 4 tablespoons prepared horseradish
- 1 teaspoon coarsely ground pepper
- 1/8 teaspoon Worcestershire sauce

1. Brush roast with oil; rub with pepper. Place roast, fat side up, on a rack in a shallow roasting pan. Bake, uncovered, at 450° for 15 minutes.

2. Reduce heat to 325°. Bake for 2-3/4 hours or until meat reaches desired doneness (for medium-rare, a meat thermometer should read 145°; medium, 160°; well-done, 170°), basting with pan drippings every 30 minutes.

3. Let stand for 10-15 minutes before slicing. Meanwhile, in a small bowl, combine the sauce ingredients. Serve with beef.

Yield: 6-8 servings.

HENS WITH APRICOT RICE STUFFING

jodi grable, springfield, missouri

When you want to impress guests, you can't beat these lovely Cornish game hens. Apricots and apricot preserves give the meat and moist wild rice stuffing a fruity flavor that everyone in our family loves.

- 1 cup sliced fresh mushrooms
- 3/4 cup chopped pecans
- 1/2 cup chopped onion
- 6 tablespoons butter, *divided*
- 1 cup cooked wild rice
- 1/2 cup chopped dried apricots
- 1 tablespoon minced fresh parsley
- 1/2 teaspoon salt
- 1/4 teaspoon pepper
- 1/8 teaspoon cayenne pepper
- 4 Cornish game hens (20 ounces *each*)
- 1/2 cup apricot preserves
- 1 tablespoon white vinegar

1 In a large skillet, saute the mushrooms, pecans and onion in 4 tablespoons butter until tender. Stir in the rice, apricots, parsley, salt, pepper and cayenne.

2 Spoon about 3/4 cup rice mixture into each hen; tie legs together. Place hens, breast side up, on a rack in a shallow roasting pan. Melt remaining butter; drizzle over hens.

3 Bake, uncovered, at 350° for 1-3/4 to 2 hours or until a meat thermometer reads 180° for hens and 165° for stuffing. In a small saucepan, warm preserves and vinegar; spoon over hens. Bake 15 minutes longer.

Yield: 4 servings.

RASPBERRY ROAST PORK

taste of home test kitchen

Our home economists pair a sage- and pepper-seasoned pork roast with raspberry sauce for an easy, yet elegant entree.

- 4-1/2 cups fresh *or* frozen raspberries
- 3 tablespoons sugar
- 1/2 cup unsweetened apple juice
- 1/4 cup red wine vinegar
- 2 garlic cloves, minced
- 3/4 teaspoon rubbed sage, *divided*
- 1 tablespoon cornstarch
- 1 tablespoon water
- 1/2 teaspoon salt
- 1/2 teaspoon pepper
- 1 boneless whole pork loin roast (3-1/2 to 4 pounds)

1 Place raspberries in a bowl; sprinkle with sugar and mash. Let stand for 15 minutes; mash again. Strain, reserving juice; discard pulp and seeds.

2 In a small saucepan, combine the raspberry juice, apple juice, vinegar, garlic and 1/4 teaspoon sage. Simmer, uncovered, for 5 minutes. In a small bowl, combine cornstarch and water until smooth; stir into raspberry juice mixture until smooth. Bring to a boil; cook and stir for 1 minute or until thickened.

3 Combine the salt, pepper and remaining sage; rub over roast. Place fat side up on a rack in a shallow roasting pan. Spread with 1/2 cup raspberry sauce.

4 Bake, uncovered, at 350° for 1-3/4 to 2 hours or until a meat thermometer reads 160°. Let stand for 10-15 minutes before slicing. Meanwhile, reheat the remaining raspberry sauce; serve with pork.

Yield: 8-10 servings.

INDIVIDUAL BEEF WELLINGTONS

taste of home test kitchen

A savory mushroom-wine sauce is draped over the golden pastry in this recipe from our Test Kitchen. The impressive entree is perfect to present to guests on Christmas.

- 6 beef tenderloin steaks (1-1/2 to 2 inches thick and 8 ounces *each*)
- 4 tablespoons butter, *divided*
- 3 sheets frozen puff pastry, thawed
- 1 egg, lightly beaten
- 1/2 pound sliced fresh mushrooms
- 1/4 cup chopped shallots
- 2 tablespoons all-purpose flour
- 1 can (10-1/2 ounces) condensed beef consomme, undiluted
- 3 tablespoons port wine
- 2 teaspoons minced fresh thyme

1 In a large skillet, brown steaks in 2 tablespoons butter for 2-3 minutes on each side. Remove and keep warm.

2 On a lightly floured surface, roll each puff pastry sheet into a 14-in. x 9-1/2-in. rectangle. Cut into two 7-in. squares (discard scraps). Place a steak in the center of each square. Lightly brush pastry edges with water. Bring opposite corners of pastry over steak; pinch seams to seal tightly. Cut four small slits in top of pastry.

3 Place in a greased 15-in. x 10-in. x 1-in. baking pan. Brush with egg. Bake at 400° for 25-30 minutes or until pastry is golden brown and meat reaches desired doneness (for medium-rare, a meat thermometer should read 145°; medium, 160°; well-done, 170°).

4 Meanwhile, in the same skillet, saute mushrooms and shallots in remaining butter for 3-5 minutes or until tender. Combine flour and consomme until smooth; stir into mushroom mixture. Bring to a boil; cook and stir for 2 minutes or until thickened. Stir in wine and thyme. Cook and stir 2 minutes longer. Serve with beef.

Yield: 6 servings.

CRANBERRY CATCH OF THE DAY

linda patrick, houston, texas

Most folks may not think of serving fish for Christmas. But a colorful cranberry sauce and pleasant pecan dressing make this entree elegant.

- 1-1/2 cups chopped celery
- 1/2 cup chopped onion
- 9 tablespoons butter, *divided*
- 6 cups cubed bread
- 3/4 cup chopped pecans
- 1/3 cup orange juice
- 1-1/2 teaspoons grated orange peel
- 1 teaspoon salt, *divided*
- 6 haddock, cod *or* halibut fillets (6 ounces *each*)

ORANGE-CRANBERRY SAUCE:
- 1/2 cup sugar
- 2 teaspoons cornstarch
- 1/2 cup water
- 1/2 cup orange juice
- 1 cup fresh *or* frozen cranberries
- 2 teaspoons grated orange peel

1 In a large skillet over medium heat, cook and stir celery and onion in 6 tablespoons butter until tender. Stir in the bread cubes, pecans, orange juice, orange peel and 1/2 teaspoon salt. Transfer to a greased 13-in. x 9-in. x 2-in. baking dish. Arrange fillets over stuffing.

2 Melt remaining butter; drizzle over fillets. Sprinkle with remaining salt. Bake, uncovered, at 350° for 25-28 minutes or until fish flakes easily with a fork.

3 In a small saucepan, combine sugar and cornstarch; whisk in water and orange juice until smooth. Bring to a boil, stirring constantly. Add cranberries; cook for 5 minutes or until berries pop. Stir in peel. Serve with fish and stuffing.

Yield: 6 servings.

RACK OF LAMB WITH FIGS

sylvia castanon, long beach, california

I got this recipe from my grandmother and I get lots of requests for it. I have my butcher use a French-cut of rack of lamb.

- 2 racks of lamb (2 pounds *each*)
- 1 teaspoon salt, *divided*
- 1 cup water
- 1 small onion, finely chopped
- 1 garlic clove, minced
- 1 tablespoon canola oil
- 2 tablespoons cornstarch
- 1 cup port wine *or* 1/2 cup grape juice plus 1/2 cup reduced-sodium beef broth
- 10 dried figs, halved
- 1/4 teaspoon pepper
- 1/2 cup coarsely chopped walnuts, toasted

1 Rub lamb with 1/2 teaspoon salt. Place meat side up on a rack in a greased roasting pan. Bake, uncovered, at 375° for 25-30 minutes or until meat reaches desired doneness (for medium-rare, a meat thermometer should read 145°; medium, 160°; well-done, 170°).

2 Remove to a serving platter; cover loosely with foil. Add 1 cup water to roasting pan; stir to loosen browned bits from pan. Using a fine sieve, strain mixture; set drippings aside.

3 In a small saucepan, saute onion and garlic in oil until tender. Stir in cornstarch until blended; gradually add the wine, drippings, figs, pepper and remaining salt. Bring to a boil. Reduce heat to medium-low; cook, uncovered, until figs are tender and sauce is thickened, about 10 minutes.

4 Sprinkle walnuts over lamb; serve with fig sauce.

Yield: 6-8 servings.

HOLIDAY SPIRAL HAM

p. lauren fay-neri, syracuse, new york

With its tangy cranberry-apple relish and the pineapple wedges on the side, this moist, festive ham makes a striking centerpiece for any special-occasion meal.

- 1 fully cooked spiral-sliced ham (8 pounds)
- 1 fresh pineapple, peeled, cored and cut into four wedges
- 1 package (12 ounces) fresh *or* frozen cranberries
- 3 medium apples, peeled and cubed
- 1-1/4 cups sugar
- 1 medium navel orange, peeled and cut into chunks
- 3 tablespoons lemon juice

1 Place ham on a rack in a shallow roasting pan. Arrange pineapple wedges around ham. Cover and bake at 325° for 1 to 1-1/2 hours.

2 Meanwhile, in a large saucepan, combine cranberries and apples. Cook over medium heat until the berries pop, about 15 minutes. Add the sugar, orange chunks and lemon juice. Cook and stir until sugar is dissolved. Remove from the heat.

3 Spoon half of the cranberry relish over ham. Bake 30 minutes longer or until a meat thermometer reads 140°. Let stand for 10 minutes before serving. Cut pineapple wedges into large chunks; serve with ham and remaining relish.

Yield: 12-16 servings.

PEPPERY ROAST BEEF

maureen brand, somers, iowa

With its spicy coating and creamy horseradish sauce, this tender roast is sure to be the star of any meal, whether it's a sit-down dinner or serve-yourself potluck.

- 1 tablespoon olive oil
- 1 tablespoon seasoned pepper
- 2 garlic cloves, minced
- 1/2 teaspoon dried thyme
- 1/4 teaspoon salt
- 1 boneless beef eye round roast (4 to 5 pounds)

HORSERADISH SAUCE:

- 1 cup (8 ounces) sour cream
- 2 tablespoons lemon juice
- 2 tablespoons milk
- 2 tablespoons prepared horseradish
- 1 tablespoon Dijon mustard
- 1/4 teaspoon salt
- 1/8 teaspoon pepper

1 In a small bowl, combine the oil, seasoned pepper, garlic, thyme and salt; rub over roast. Place fat side up on a rack in a shallow roasting pan.

2 Bake, uncovered, at 325° for 2-1/2 to 3 hours or until meat reaches desired doneness (for medium-rare, a meat thermometer should read 145°; medium, 160°; well-done, 170°). Let stand for 10 minutes before slicing.

3 In a small bowl, combine the sauce ingredients. Serve with roast.

Yield: 10-12 servings.

CHICKEN ROLLS WITH PESTO PASTA

pat stevens, granbury, texas

Fresh basil (which is available in grocery stores year-round) lends terrific flavor to these tasty chicken rolls. As the finishing touch, toss the pasta with purchased or homemade pesto just before serving.

- 4 boneless skinless chicken breast halves (6 ounces *each*)

Salt and pepper

- 1/4 cup chopped fresh basil
- 1/4 cup crumbled feta cheese
- 2 garlic cloves, peeled and halved
- 3 tablespoons olive oil, *divided*
- 1/2 pound sliced fresh mushrooms
- 2 green onions, thinly sliced
- 2 tablespoons chopped red onion
- 1 tablespoon chicken broth
- 8 ounces uncooked angel hair pasta
- 3/4 cup prepared pesto sauce

1 Flatten chicken to 1/4-in. thickness; sprinkle with salt and pepper. Place 1 tablespoon basil, 1 tablespoon feta cheese and a garlic clove half down the center of each chicken breast. Roll up and secure with toothpicks.

2 In a large skillet, brown chicken in 2 tablespoons oil on all sides. Place in an 8-in. square baking dish. In the same skillet, saute mushrooms and onions in remaining oil until tender. Add broth; cook and stir until bubbly. Pour over chicken.

3 Cover and bake at 325° for 20-30 minutes or until juices run clear. Meanwhile, cook pasta according to package directions; drain. Toss with pesto sauce. Discard toothpicks. Serve chicken with pasta and mushroom mixture.

Yield: 4 servings.

CHRISTMAS DAY CHICKEN

marcia larson, batavia, illinois

I've been fixing this delectable entree for Christmas dinner for over 10 years, but you don't have to wait for the holidays to serve it. Marinate the chicken breasts overnight for easy preparation, then simply coat with crumbs and bake.

- 16 boneless skinless chicken breast halves (4 ounces *each*)
- 2 cups (16 ounces) sour cream
- 1/4 cup lemon juice
- 4 teaspoons Worcestershire sauce
- 2 teaspoons celery salt
- 2 teaspoons pepper
- 2 teaspoons paprika
- 1 teaspoon seasoned salt
- 1 teaspoon garlic salt
- 1-1/2 to 2 cups crushed butter-flavored crackers
- 1/2 cup canola oil
- 1/2 cup butter, melted

1 Place the chicken in two large resealable plastic bags. In a bowl, combine the sour cream, lemon juice, Worcestershire sauce and seasonings. Pour over chicken; seal bags and toss to coat. Refrigerate overnight.

2 Drain and discard marinade. Coat chicken with cracker crumbs; place in two greased 13-in. x 9-in. x 2-in. baking dishes.

3 Combine oil and butter; drizzle over chicken. Bake, uncovered, at 350° for 50-60 minutes or until juices run clear.

Yield: 16 servings.

SHRIMP IN CREAM SAUCE

jane birch, edison, new jersey

This rich shrimp dish is wonderful over golden egg noodles, but you can also serve it over hot cooked rice.

- 2 tablespoons butter, melted
- 1/3 cup all-purpose flour
- 1-1/2 cups chicken broth
- 4 garlic cloves, minced
- 1 cup heavy whipping cream
- 1/2 cup minced fresh parsley
- 2 teaspoons paprika

Salt and pepper to taste

- 2 pounds large uncooked shrimp, peeled and deveined

Hot cooked noodles *or* rice

1 In a small saucepan, melt butter; stir in flour until smooth. Gradually add broth and garlic. Bring to a boil; cook and stir for 2 minutes or until thickened. Remove from the heat. Stir in the cream, parsley, paprika, salt and pepper.

2 Butterfly shrimp by cutting lengthwise almost in half, but leaving shrimp attached at opposite side. Spread to butterfly. Place cut side down in a greased 13-in. x 9-in. x 2-in. baking dish. Pour cream sauce over shrimp. Bake, uncovered, at 400° for 15-18 minutes or until shrimp turn pink. Serve over noodles or rice.

Yield: 8 servings.

TURKEY ROULADES

kari wheaton, beloit, wisconsin

The filling in this recipe goes so well with turkey.
I love the hint of lemon and the savory combo of
apples, mushrooms and spinach. The bread-crumb
coating adds a nice crunch.

- 1 cup diced peeled tart apple
- 1 cup diced fresh mushrooms
- 1/2 cup finely chopped onion
- 2 teaspoons olive oil
- 5 ounces frozen chopped spinach, thawed and squeezed dry
- 2 tablespoons lemon juice
- 2 teaspoons grated lemon peel
- 3/4 teaspoon salt, *divided*

Pinch ground nutmeg

- 4 turkey breast tenderloins (8 ounces *each*)
- 1/4 teaspoon pepper
- 1 egg, lightly beaten
- 1/2 cup seasoned bread crumbs

1 In a large nonstick skillet coated with cooking spray, saute the apple, mushrooms and onion in oil until tender. Remove from the heat; stir in the spinach, lemon juice, lemon peel, 1/4 teaspoon salt and nutmeg.

2 Make a lengthwise slit down the center of each tenderloin to within 1/2 in. of bottom. Open tenderloins so they lie flat; cover with plastic wrap. Flatten to 1/4-in. thickness. Remove plastic; sprinkle turkey with pepper and remaining salt.

3 Spread spinach mixture over tenderloins to within 1 in. of edges. Roll up jelly-roll style, starting with a short side; tie with kitchen string. Place egg and bread crumbs in separate shallow bowls. Dip roulades in egg, then roll in crumbs.

4 Place in an 11-in. x 7-in. baking pan coated with cooking spray. Bake, uncovered, at 375° for 40-45 minutes or until a meat thermometer reads 170°. Let stand for 5 minutes before slicing.

Yield: 8 servings.

PLUM-GLAZED CORNISH HENS

annie tompkins, deltona, florida

The homemade plum sauce that's baked onto these tender Cornish hens is wonderful. Save this recipe for your best company. I often sprinkle the hens with toasted coconut for a different taste sensation.

- 4 large navel oranges, sliced
- 4 Cornish game hens (20 ounces *each*), split lengthwise
- 1/4 teaspoon pepper
- 1 can (15 ounces) plums, pitted, drained
- 1/4 cup finely chopped onion
- 1/4 cup butter, cubed
- 3/4 cup lemonade concentrate
- 1/3 cup chili sauce
- 1/4 cup soy sauce
- 1-1/2 teaspoons prepared mustard
- 1 teaspoon ground ginger
- 1 teaspoon Worcestershire sauce
- 1/4 cup flaked coconut, toasted, optional

1 Arrange orange slices in two greased 13-in. x 9-in. baking dishes. Top with game hens; sprinkle with pepper. Bake, uncovered, at 350° for 45 minutes.

2 Meanwhile, place the plums in a food processor; cover and process until smooth. Set aside. In a large skillet, saute onion in butter until tender; stir in lemonade concentrate, chili sauce, soy sauce, mustard, ginger, Worcestershire sauce and plums. Bring to a boil. Reduce heat; simmer, uncovered, for 15 minutes, stirring occasionally. Set 1 cup of sauce aside. Spoon remaining sauce over hens.

3 Bake 30-45 minutes longer or until juices run clear and a meat thermometer reads 180°, basting occasionally with pan drippings. Sprinkle with coconut if desired. Serve with reserved plum sauce.

Yield: 4-6 servings.

HERB-CRUSTED PORK ROAST

mary ann lee, clifton park, new york

There is nothing like a well-seasoned pork roast, pan-seared and baked to perfection. The moist meat gets a flavor boost from a cheesy herbal crust and simple reduction sauce.

- 1 teaspoon ground mustard
- 1 teaspoon lemon-herb seasoning
- 1 teaspoon salt
- 1/2 teaspoon pepper
- 1 bone-in pork loin roast (4 pounds)
- 2 tablespoons plus 1/4 cup olive oil, *divided*
- 1 tablespoon Dijon mustard
- 1-1/2 cups soft bread crumbs
- 1/2 cup grated Parmesan cheese
- 1/4 cup minced fresh basil *or* 4 teaspoons dried basil
- 2 teaspoons *each* minced fresh thyme and minced fresh rosemary
- 2 garlic cloves, minced
- 1 cup white wine *or* chicken broth

1 In a small bowl, combine the ground mustard, herb seasoning, salt and pepper; rub over roast. In a large skillet, brown roast in 2 tablespoons oil. Place roast fat side up on a rack in a shallow roasting pan. Brush top with Dijon mustard. Combine the bread crumbs, Parmesan cheese, basil, thyme, rosemary, garlic and remaining oil; press onto roast.

2 Bake, uncovered, at 350° for 2 to 2-1/4 hours or until a meat thermometer reads 160°. Place on a warm serving platter. Let stand for 10-15 minutes before slicing.

3 Stir wine or broth into roasting pan, scraping to loosen browned bits. Pour into a saucepan.

Bring to a boil over medium-high heat; cook until reduced by half. Serve with roast.

Yield: 12-14 servings.

SPIRAL HAM WITH CRANBERRY GLAZE

pattie prescott, manchester, new hampshire

The sweet, tangy glaze that complements this ham looks so pretty, and the cranberry pairs well with it. It's been a tradition in my home for as long as I can remember.

- 1 fully cooked spiral-sliced ham (8 pounds)
- 1 can (16 ounces) whole-berry cranberry sauce
- 1 package (12 ounces) fresh *or* frozen cranberries
- 1 jar (12 ounces) red currant jelly
- 1 cup light corn syrup
- 1/2 teaspoon ground ginger

1 Place ham on a rack in a shallow roasting pan. Cover and bake at 325° for 2-1/2 hours.

2 Meanwhile, for glaze, combine the remaining ingredients in a saucepan. Bring to a boil. Reduce heat; simmer, uncovered, until cranberries pop, stirring occasionally. Remove from the heat; set aside.

3 Uncover ham; bake 30 minutes longer or until a meat thermometer reads 140°, basting twice with 1-1/2 cups glaze. Serve remaining glaze with ham.

Yield: 12-16 servings.

SEAFOOD EN CROUTE

alexandra armitage, nottingham, new hampshire

I'm a busy mom with little time to spend in the kitchen. So when I'm given a recipe like this that's impressive, easy and tasty, I know I have a winner!

- 1 package (17.3 ounces) frozen puff pastry, thawed
- 4 salmon fillets (6 ounces *each*)
- 1/2 pound fresh sea *or* bay scallops, finely chopped
- 1/3 cup heavy whipping cream
- 2 green onions, chopped
- 1 tablespoon minced fresh parsley
- 1/2 teaspoon minced fresh dill
- 1/4 teaspoon salt
- 1/8 teaspoon pepper
- 1 egg white
- 1 egg, lightly beaten

1 On a lightly floured surface, roll each pastry sheet into a 12-in. x 10-in. rectangle. Cut each sheet into four 6-in. x 5-in. rectangles. Place a salmon fillet in the center of four rectangles.

2 In a small bowl, combine the scallops, cream, onions, parsley, dill, salt and pepper. In a small bowl, beat egg white on medium speed until soft peaks form; fold into scallop mixture. Spoon about 1/2 cup over each salmon fillet.

3 Top each with a pastry rectangle and crimp to seal. With a small sharp knife, cut several slits in the top. Place in a greased 15-in. x 10-in. x 1-in. baking pan; brush with egg. Bake at 400° for 20-25 minutes or until a thermometer reads 160°.

Yield: 4 servings.

HERBED STANDING RIB ROAST

carol stevens, basye, virginia

We're a meat-and-potatoes family, so this roast is right up our alley. It really is the highlight of an elegant dinner for special guests. Leftovers are great for sandwiches, too.

- 3 tablespoons grated onion
- 2 tablespoons olive oil
- 4 garlic cloves, minced
- 2 teaspoons celery seed
- 1 teaspoon coarsely ground pepper
- 1 teaspoon paprika
- 1/4 teaspoon dried thyme
- 1 bone-in beef rib roast (6 to 7 pounds)
- 2 large onions, cut into wedges
- 2 large carrots, cut into 2-inch pieces
- 2 celery ribs, cut into 2-inch pieces
- 1/4 cup red wine *or* beef broth

Assorted herbs and fruit, optional

1 In a bowl, combine the first seven ingredients; rub over roast. Place the onions, carrots and celery in a large roasting pan; put roast over vegetables.

2 Bake, uncovered, at 325° for 1-3/4 to 2-1/2 hours or until meat reaches desired doneness (for medium-rare, a meat thermometer should read 145°; medium, 160°; well-done, 170°).

3 Remove roast to a serving platter and keep warm; let stand for 15 minutes before slicing.

4 Meanwhile, for au jus, strain and discard vegetables. Pour drippings into a measuring cup; skim fat. Add wine or broth to roasting pan, stirring to remove any browned bits. Stir in drippings; heat through. Serve with roast. Garnish platter with herbs and fruit if desired.

Yield: 10-12 servings.

GARLIC CRAB-STUFFED CHICKEN

dorothy glaeser, naples, florida

I created this recipe as a way to make ordinary chicken something extra. To save time, you can roll up the chicken early in the day, refrigerate it, then dip in the egg, brown and bake later on.

- 6 large boneless skinless chicken breast halves (8 ounces *each*)
- 2 tablespoons minced garlic
- 2 cans (6 ounces *each*) crabmeat, drained, flaked and cartilage removed
- 8 ounces Jarlsberg *or* Gouda cheese, shredded
- 3 tablespoons minced fresh parsley
- 1 egg
- 1 tablespoon cold water
- 1-1/4 cups dry bread crumbs
- 2 tablespoons canola oil
- 1 cup unsweetened apple juice
- 1 cup white wine *or* chicken broth

Wild rice, optional

1 Flatten chicken to 1/4-in. thickness. Spread 1 teaspoon garlic on one side of each chicken breast half. Place crab, cheese and parsley down the center of each. Roll up and tuck in ends; secure with toothpicks. In a bowl, beat egg and water. Place bread crumbs in another bowl. Dip chicken in egg mixture, then roll in crumbs.

2 In a large skillet, brown chicken in oil on both sides. Transfer to a greased 13-in. x 9-in. baking dish. Add the apple juice and wine or broth. Bake, uncovered, at 350° for 35-40 minutes or until the chicken is no longer pink. Serve with wild rice if desired.

Yield: 6 servings.

FLANK STEAK WITH WINE SAUCE

warner beatty, niagara falls, ontario

For best results, I always serve this lean and tasty flank steak rare. Deglaze the pan with wine, making sure to scrape up all the savory browned bits with a wooden spoon.

- 1 whole garlic bulb
- 1-1/2 teaspoons olive oil, *divided*
- 1 beef flank steak (1-1/2 pounds)
- 1 teaspoon coarsely ground pepper
- 3/4 teaspoon salt
- 2 tablespoons butter, *divided*
- 1/2 cup reduced-sodium beef broth
- 1 cup dry red wine *or* 1/4 cup grape juice and 3/4 cup additional reduced-sodium beef broth
- 1/4 cup thinly sliced green onions

1 Remove papery outer skin from garlic bulb (do not peel or separate cloves). Cut top off of garlic bulb; brush with 1/2 teaspoon oil. Wrap bulb in heavy-duty foil. Bake at 425° for 30-35 minutes or until softened. Cool for 10-15 minutes. Squeeze softened garlic into a bowl; mash and set aside.

2 Sprinkle steak with pepper and salt. In a large nonstick skillet coated with cooking spray, cook steak over medium-high heat in remaining oil for 3-4 minutes on each side or until browned.

3 Reduce heat to medium; add 1 tablespoon butter. Cook for 4-8 minutes on each side or until meat reaches desired doneness (for medium-rare, a meat thermometer should read 145°; medium, 160°; well-done, 170°). Remove and keep warm.

4 Gradually add broth and wine or grape juice and additional broth to pan, stirring to loosen browned bits. Bring to a boil. Stir in garlic. Reduce heat; simmer, uncovered, until liquid is reduced by half.

5 Strain sauce and return to pan; stir in remaining butter until melted. Thinly slice steak across the grain. Sprinkle with onions; serve with sauce.

Yield: 6 servings (3/4 cup sauce).

SHRIMP IN HERBS

iola egle, bella vista, arkansas

Dressed up with two types of parsley and other herbs, this rich shrimp entree makes a special meal.

- 2 pounds uncooked medium shrimp, peeled and deveined
- 2 tablespoons olive oil
- 3 garlic cloves, minced
- 1-1/2 cups chopped fresh tomatoes
- 1 tablespoon minced chives
- 1 tablespoon minced fresh flat-leaf parsley
- 1 tablespoon minced fresh tarragon *or*
  1 teaspoon dried tarragon
- 1 teaspoon dried chervil
- 3/4 teaspoon salt
- 1/4 teaspoon pepper
- 2 tablespoons butter, cubed

1 In a large nonstick skillet coated with cooking spray, cook shrimp in oil for 2 minutes. Add garlic; cook 2 minutes longer. Stir in the tomatoes and seasonings. Cook 3-5 minutes longer or until shrimp turn pink. Stir in butter until melted.

Yield: 4 servings.

CHICKEN ROLLS WITH RASPBERRY SAUCE

taste of home test kitchen

Give any meal an elegant feel with this impressive (but easy!) blue cheese-stuffed chicken. The raspberry sauce is also great on grilled pork tenderloin.

- 4 boneless skinless chicken breast halves (6 ounces *each*)
- 1/2 cup crumbled blue cheese
- 4 strips ready-to-serve fully cooked bacon, crumbled
- 2 tablespoons butter, melted, *divided*

Salt and pepper to taste

- 2 cups fresh raspberries
- 1/4 cup chicken broth
- 4 teaspoons brown sugar
- 1 tablespoon balsamic vinegar
- 1/2 teaspoon minced garlic
- 1/4 teaspoon dried oregano

1 Flatten chicken to 1/4-in. thickness; sprinkle with blue cheese and bacon to within 1/2 in. of edges. Roll up each jelly-roll style, starting with a short side; secure with toothpicks.

2 Place in a greased 8-in. square baking dish. Brush with 1 tablespoon butter; sprinkle with salt and pepper. Bake, uncovered, at 375° for 35-40 minutes or until meat is no longer pink.

3 Meanwhile, in a small saucepan, combine the raspberries, broth, brown sugar, vinegar, garlic and oregano. Bring to a boil. Reduce heat; simmer, uncovered, for 5 minutes or until thickened.

4 Press through a sieve; discard seeds. Stir in remaining butter until smooth. Discard toothpicks. Serve with raspberry sauce.

Yield: 4 servings.

CHRISTMAS NIGHT LASAGNA

nancy jo helffler, depauw, indiana

I tinkered with this recipe four or five times before I got it down to what it is now. It's simple—you use only two pots—but it tastes as good as the lasagnas that are a big production.

- 3 pounds ground beef
- 1 pound bulk pork sausage
- 1 *each* medium onion, chopped and medium green pepper, chopped
- 2 jars (28 ounces *each*) meatless spaghetti sauce
- 1 can (10-3/4 ounces) condensed tomato soup, undiluted
- 1 can (4 ounces) mushroom stems and pieces, undrained
- 2 teaspoons Worcestershire sauce
- 1-1/2 teaspoons Italian seasoning
- 1-1/2 teaspoons *each* salt and pepper, *divided*
- 1 teaspoon garlic powder
- 2 eggs, lightly beaten
- 2-1/2 cups (20 ounces) 4% small-curd cottage cheese
- 1 carton (15 ounces) ricotta cheese
- 2 cups (8 ounces) shredded Parmesan cheese
- 24 lasagna noodles, cooked and drained
- 12 slices part-skim mozzarella cheese

1 In a Dutch oven or several large skillets, cook the beef, sausage, onion and green pepper over medium heat until meat is no longer pink; drain. Add the spaghetti sauce, soup, mushrooms, Worcestershire sauce, Italian seasoning, 1 teaspoon salt, 1 teaspoon pepper and garlic powder. Bring to a boil. Reduce heat; simmer, uncovered, for 30 minutes, stirring occasionally.

2 Meanwhile, in a large bowl, combine the eggs, cottage cheese, ricotta and remaining salt and pepper.

3 Spread 2 cups meat sauce each into two greased 13-in. x 9-in. baking dishes. Layer each with 1/3 cup Parmesan cheese, four noodles, 1-1/4 cups cottage cheese mixture and three slices of mozzarella cheese. Repeat layers. Top with the remaining noodles, meat sauce and Parmesan.

4 Bake, uncovered, at 350° for 45 minutes or until bubbly. Let stand for 15 minutes before cutting.

Yield: 2 casseroles (12 servings each).

HERBED ROAST TURKEY BREAST

lisa mahon fluegeman, cincinnati, ohio

I made this turkey breast for my first formal dinner party as a newlywed. It was such a success that it's become a standby on all of my entertaining menus.

- 5 teaspoons lemon juice
- 1 tablespoon olive oil
- 1 to 2 teaspoons pepper
- 1 teaspoon dried rosemary, crushed
- 1 teaspoon dried thyme
- 1 teaspoon garlic salt
- 1 bone-in turkey breast (6 to 7 pounds)
- 1 medium onion, cut into wedges
- 1 celery rib, cut into 2-inch pieces
- 1/2 cup white wine *or* chicken broth

1 In a small bowl, combine the lemon juice and oil. In another bowl, combine the pepper, rosemary, thyme and garlic salt. With fingers, carefully loosen the skin from both sides of turkey breast. Brush oil mixture under the skin; rub with herb mixture.

2 Arrange onion and celery in a 3-qt. baking dish. Place turkey breast, skin side up, on top of vegetables. Pour wine or broth into the dish.

3 Bake, uncovered, at 325° for 2 to 2-1/2 hours or until a meat thermometer reads 170°, basting every 30 minutes with pan drippings. (Cover loosely with foil if turkey browns too quickly.) Cover and let stand for 15 minutes before carving.

Yield: 6 servings.

BERRY NICE BRISKET

carol hunihan, alamosa, colorado

Cranberry juice and cranberry sauce make this brisket tender and tasty. It makes a hearty main course for a holiday meal.

- 1/4 cup all-purpose flour
- 1 can (14-1/2 ounces) beef broth
- 1 can (16 ounces) whole-berry cranberry sauce
- 1 cup cranberry juice
- 3 garlic cloves, minced
- 1 tablespoon minced fresh rosemary *or*
  1 teaspoon dried rosemary, crushed
- 1 large onion, thinly sliced
- 1 fresh beef brisket (3 to 4 pounds)
- 1/2 teaspoon salt
- 1/4 teaspoon pepper

1 In a large bowl, combine flour and broth until smooth. Stir in the cranberry sauce, cranberry juice, garlic and rosemary. Pour into a large roasting pan. Top with onion slices. Season the brisket with salt and pepper.

2 Place the brisket fat side up in the pan. Cover and bake at 350° for 3 to 3-1/2 hours or until meat is tender, basting occasionally.

3 Remove brisket to a serving platter and let stand for 15 minutes. Thinly slice meat across the grain; serve with onion and pan juices.

Yield: 10-12 servings.

Editor's Note: This is a fresh beef brisket, not corned beef.

DAD'S SWEDISH MEATBALLS

michelle lizotte, cumberland, rhode island

My father used to make these meatballs every year for Christmas when I was a kid. Now I carry on the tradition.

- 1 egg, lightly beaten
- 1/2 cup milk
- 1 cup soft bread crumbs
- 1/2 cup finely chopped onion
- 1 teaspoon salt
- 1/4 teaspoon ground nutmeg
- 1/4 teaspoon pepper
- 1 pound ground beef
- 1/2 pound ground pork
- 1/4 cup butter, cubed

DILL CREAM SAUCE:
- 2 tablespoons all-purpose flour
- 1 cup heavy whipping cream
- 1 cup beef broth
- 1 teaspoon salt
- 1/2 teaspoon dill seed

1 In a large bowl, combine the first seven ingredients. Crumble beef and pork over mixture and mix well. Shape into 1-1/2-in. balls. In a large skillet, cook meatballs in butter in batches until no longer pink. Remove and keep warm.

2 In a small bowl, combine the sauce ingredients until blended. Stir into skillet. Bring to a boil; cook and stir for 2 minutes or until thickened. Serve with the meatballs.

Yield: 6 servings.

SIDE
DISHES

BUTTERY
CARROTS &
BRUSSELS
SPROUTS
P. 58

ACORN SQUASH WITH CRANBERRY STUFFING

dorothy pritchett, wills point, texas

You just can't go wrong with this recipe if you have squash or cranberry lovers at your table. The blend of flavors is delicious, colorful and goes great with a traditional holiday dinner.

    2 medium acorn squash
  1/4 cup chopped celery
    2 tablespoons chopped onion
    2 tablespoons butter
    1 medium tart apple, peeled and diced
  1/2 teaspoon salt
  1/2 teaspoon lemon juice
  1/8 teaspoon pepper
    1 cup fresh *or* frozen cranberries
  1/2 cup sugar
    2 tablespoons water

1 Cut squash in half; discard seeds. Cut a thin slice from the bottom of squash halves so they sit flat. Place squash hollow side down in an ungreased 13-in. x 9-in. baking dish. Add 1/2 in. of water. Cover and bake at 375° for 45 minutes.

2 Meanwhile, in a small skillet, saute celery and onion in butter until tender. Add the apple, salt, lemon juice and pepper. Cook, uncovered, over medium-low heat until apple is tender, stirring occasionally. Stir in the cranberries, sugar and water. Cook and stir until the berries pop and liquid is syrupy.

3 Turn squash halves over; fill with cranberry mixture. Cover and bake 10-15 minutes longer or until squash is tender.

Yield: 4 servings.

ROASTED PEPPERS 'N' CAULIFLOWER

cheryl maczko, eglon, west virginia

Roasting really enhances the taste of this veggie dish. It goes great with nearly any main course.

    1 medium head cauliflower, broken into florets
    2 medium sweet red peppers, cut into strips
    2 small onions, cut into wedges
    2 tablespoons olive oil
  1/2 teaspoon salt
  1/2 teaspoon pepper
    1 tablespoon grated Parmesan cheese
    1 tablespoon minced fresh parsley

1 Place the cauliflower, red peppers and onions in a shallow roasting pan. Add the oil, salt and pepper; toss to coat. Bake, uncovered, at 425° for 20 minutes.

2 Stir; bake 10 minutes longer or until vegetables are tender and lightly browned. Transfer to a serving bowl; sprinkle with Parmesan cheese and parsley.

Yield: 6 servings.

BUTTERY CARROTS & BRUSSELS SPROUTS

stacy duffy, chicago, illinois

Ginger and lemon really shine in this rich veggie medley. The sugar also adds sweetness to this surprisingly tasty dish.

- 1 pound carrots, cut into 1/4-inch slices
- 3/4 pound brussels sprouts, halved
- 1/4 cup butter
- 1 tablespoon minced fresh gingerroot
  or 3/4 teaspoon ground ginger
- 1 tablespoon lemon juice
- 2 teaspoons grated lemon peel
- 1 teaspoon sugar

Salt and pepper to taste

- 1 tablespoon minced fresh parsley, optional

1 In a large saucepan over medium heat, cook the carrots and brussels sprouts in boiling water until tender, about 8-10 minutes; drain. Melt butter in a small saucepan. Add ginger; cook for 2 minutes. Add lemon juice, peel, sugar, salt and pepper; pour over vegetables. Garnish with parsley if desired.

Yield: 8 servings.

TORTILLA DRESSING

dorothy bray, adkins, texas

This is not your typical holiday stuffing. Tortillas, jalapenos, chili powder and cilantro lend to its southwestern flair.

- 8 corn tortillas (6 inches), cut into 1/4-inch strips
- 1/4 cup canola oil
- 8 flour tortillas (6 inches), cut into 1/4-inch strips
- 1 cup crushed corn bread stuffing
- 1 small onion, diced
- 1/3 cup diced sweet red pepper
- 1 jalapeno pepper, seeded and chopped
- 1 tablespoon minced fresh cilantro
- 1 tablespoon chili powder
- 1 teaspoon minced fresh sage *or 1/4 teaspoon dried sage leaves*
- 1/2 teaspoon ground coriander
- 1/2 teaspoon ground cumin
- 1/4 teaspoon salt
- 1 egg, beaten
- 1 cup chicken broth

1 In a large skillet, saute corn tortilla strips in oil in batches for 1 minute or until golden brown. Drain on paper towels.

2 In a large bowl, combine the corn tortilla strips, flour tortilla strips, stuffing, onion, red pepper, jalapeno, cilantro, chili powder, sage, coriander, cumin and salt. Stir in egg and broth.

3 Transfer to a greased 13-in. x 9-in. baking dish. Cover and bake at 325° for 35-45 minutes or until a thermometer reads 160°. This dressing is best served as a side dish, rather than stuffed into poultry.

Yield: 9 cups.

Editor's Note: When cutting hot peppers, disposable gloves are recommended. Avoid touching your face.

CRANBERRY RICE PILAF

carmel patrone, longport, new jersey

Juicy cranberries and crunchy pine nuts easily dress up rice in this special side dish. The subtle flavors make it an appropriate accompaniment to many entrees.

- 3/4 cup chopped celery
- 1/2 cup chopped onion
- 2 tablespoons butter
- 1 tablespoon olive oil
- 1 cup uncooked long grain rice
- 2-1/2 cups chicken broth
- 1/2 cup chopped fresh mushrooms
- 1/2 cup dried cranberries
- 1/2 teaspoon garlic powder
- 1/2 teaspoon curry powder

Salt and pepper to taste

- 2 tablespoons minced fresh parsley
- 3 tablespoons pine nuts, toasted

1 In a large saucepan, saute celery and onion in butter and oil until tender. Add rice; cook and stir for 5 minutes or until lightly browned.

2 Add the broth, mushrooms, cranberries, garlic powder, curry powder, salt and pepper. Bring to a boil. Reduce heat; cover and simmer for 20 minutes or until liquid is absorbed and rice is tender.

3 Remove from the heat. Stir in parsley; sprinkle with pine nuts.

Yield: 4-5 servings.

What is Candied Ginger?

Candied or crystallized ginger is the root of the ginger plant that has been cooked in a sugar syrup. It's used primarily in dips, sauces and fruit desserts. Larger grocery stores will carry candied ginger in the spice section.—Taste of Home Test Kitchen

CRUNCHY SWEET POTATO BAKE

dawn riggestad, new bern, north carolina

This is one of our all-time favorites, both for holidays and everyday. The topping gives a nice nutty texture to the smooth, sweet potatoes underneath.

- 3 pounds sweet potatoes (about 7 medium), peeled and quartered
- 2/3 cup sugar
- 1/2 cup milk
- 1/3 cup butter, softened
- 1 tablespoon candied *or* crystallized ginger
- 1 teaspoon ground cinnamon
- 1/4 teaspoon ground nutmeg

TOPPING:

- 3/4 cup cornflakes, lightly crushed
- 1/4 cup packed brown sugar
- 1/4 cup chopped pecans
- 1/4 cup butter, melted

1 Place the sweet potatoes in a large saucepan and cover with water. Bring to a boil. Reduce heat; cover and simmer for 12-18 minutes or until tender. Drain. Mash sweet potatoes with the sugar, milk, butter, ginger, cinnamon and nutmeg.

2 Transfer to a greased 2-qt. baking dish. Cover and bake at 350° for 20 minutes or until heated through.

3 Combine the topping ingredients; sprinkle over potatoes. Bake, uncovered, for 5-10 minutes or until topping is lightly browned.

Yield: 8 servings.

GOLDEN POTATO SURPRISE

karen sheets, shelton, washington

I've had this recipe forever and have tinkered with it over the years to perfect it. Now it's a family favorite. I serve it a lot during the holidays.

- 4 to 5 medium white potatoes, peeled and diced
- 2 tablespoons butter
- 2 medium red onions, chopped
- 2 tablespoons all-purpose flour
- 1/2 teaspoon dried thyme
- 1/2 teaspoon salt
- 1/2 teaspoon pepper
- 1 cup half-and-half cream
- 1/2 cup mayonnaise
- 1 teaspoon Dijon mustard
- 4 bacon strips, cooked and crumbled

1 Place potatoes in a large saucepan and cover with water. Bring to a boil. Reduce the heat; cover and cook for 10-15 minutes or until tender. Drain and set aside.

2 In large saucepan, melt butter. Saute onions until tender; stir in the flour, thyme, salt and pepper until blended. Gradually add cream. Bring to a boil. Cook and stir for 2 minutes or until thickened. Remove from the heat; let cool slightly. Stir in the mayonnaise and mustard. Pour sauce over potatoes; transfer to a 1-1/2-qt. baking dish.

3 Bake, uncovered, at 350° for 30 minutes. Just before serving, sprinkle with crumbled bacon.

Yield: 4-6 servings.

WINTER VEGETABLES

charlene augustyn, grand rapids, michigan

The flavor of thyme shines through in this recipe. The colorful array of vegetables is so appealing on the table. It's a great way to showcase often unused broccoli stalks.

- 3 medium turnips, peeled and cut into 2-inch julienne strips
- 1 large rutabaga, peeled and cut into 2-inch julienne strips
- 4 medium carrots, cut into 2-inch julienne strips
- 3 fresh broccoli spears
- 1 tablespoon butter
- 1 tablespoon minced fresh parsley
- 1/2 teaspoon salt
- 1/2 teaspoon dried thyme

Pepper to taste

1 Place the turnips, rutabaga and carrots in a large saucepan and cover with water. Bring to a boil. Reduce heat; cover and cook for 10 minutes.

2 Meanwhile, cut florets from broccoli and save for another use. Cut broccoli stalks into 2-in. julienne strips; add to saucepan. Cover and cook 5 minutes longer or until vegetables are crisp-tender; drain well.

3 In a large skillet, saute vegetables in butter. Stir in the parsley, salt, thyme and pepper.

Yield: 10-12 servings.

Choosing Root Veggies

When shopping for rutabagas and turnips, select those that are smooth-skinned, unblemished, heavy, firm and not spongy. Look for rutabagas no larger than 4 inches in diameter and turnips no larger than 2 inches in diameter. Keep unwashed rutabagas and turnips in a plastic bag in your refrigerator's crisper drawer for up to 1 week.—Taste of Home Test Kitchen

SAUSAGE CORN BREAD DRESSING

rebecca baird, salt lake city, utah

The phrases "holiday dinner" and "low-fat" are seldom used together, unless this corn bread stuffing is on the menu. Made with turkey sausage, herbs, fruit and veggies, this recipe lets you enjoy all the trimmings without the guilt.

- 1 cup all-purpose flour
- 1 cup cornmeal
- 1/4 cup sugar
- 3 teaspoons baking powder
- 1 teaspoon salt
- 1 cup buttermilk
- 1/4 cup unsweetened applesauce
- 2 egg whites

DRESSING:
- 1 pound turkey Italian sausage links, casings removed
- 4 celery ribs, chopped
- 1 medium onion, chopped
- 1 medium sweet red pepper, chopped
- 2 medium tart apples, chopped
- 1 cup chopped roasted *or* canned sweet chestnuts
- 3 tablespoons minced fresh parsley
- 2 garlic cloves, minced
- 1/2 teaspoon dried thyme
- 1/2 teaspoon pepper
- 1 cup reduced-sodium chicken broth
- 1 egg white

1 For corn bread, combine the first five ingredients in a large bowl. Combine the buttermilk, applesauce and egg whites; stir into dry ingredients just until moistened.

2 Pour into an 8-in. square baking dish coated with cooking spray. Bake at 400° for 20-25 minutes or until a toothpick inserted near the center comes out clean. Cool on a wire rack.

3 In a large nonstick skillet, cook the sausage, celery, onion and red pepper over medium heat until meat is no longer pink; drain. Transfer to a large bowl. Crumble corn bread over mixture. Add apples, chestnuts, parsley, garlic, thyme and pepper. Stir in broth and egg white.

4 Transfer to a 13-in. x 9-in. baking dish coated with cooking spray. Cover and bake at 325° for 40 minutes. Uncover; bake 10 minutes longer or until lightly browned.

Yield: 16 servings.

Editor's Note: Dressing can be prepared as directed and used to stuff a 10- to 12-pound turkey.

SQUASH-APPLE BAKE

judith hawes, chelmsford, massachusetts

This is my mother-in-law's recipe, but I've made it so often I feel as though it's my own! Squash and apples are representative of New England in the fall and taste even better when baked together.

- 1 medium buttercup *or* butternut squash (about 1-1/4 pounds), peeled and cut into 3/4-inch slices
- 2 medium apples, peeled and cut into wedges
- 1/2 cup packed brown sugar
- 1 tablespoon all-purpose flour
- 1/4 cup butter, melted
- 1/2 teaspoon *each* salt and ground mace

1 Arrange squash in a 2-qt. baking dish. Top with apple wedges. Combine the remaining ingredients; spoon over apples.

2 Bake, uncovered, at 350° for 50-60 minutes or until tender.

Yield: 4-6 servings.

CRANBERRY-WALNUT SWEET POTATOES

mary wilhelm, sparta, wisconsin
For me, the best part of Thanksgiving dinner is the sweet potatoes! You can make the sauce for these up to a day ahead. Just omit the walnuts until you're ready to serve.

- 4 large sweet potatoes
- 1/4 cup finely chopped onion
- 1 tablespoon butter
- 1 cup fresh *or* frozen cranberries
- 1/3 cup maple syrup
- 1/4 cup water
- 1/4 cup cranberry juice
- 1/4 teaspoon salt, *divided*
- 1/2 cup chopped walnuts, toasted
- 1 teaspoon Dijon mustard
- 1/4 teaspoon pepper
- 2 tablespoons minced chives

1 Scrub and pierce sweet potatoes. Bake at 400° for 1 hour or until tender.

2 In a small saucepan, saute the onion in butter until tender. Add the cranberries, syrup, water, cranberry juice and 1/8 teaspoon salt. Bring to a boil. Reduce heat; cover and simmer for 10-15 minutes or until berries pop, stirring occasionally. Stir in walnuts and mustard; heat through.

3 Cut potatoes in half lengthwise; sprinkle with the pepper and remaining salt. Top each with 2 tablespoons cranberry mixture; sprinkle with chives.

Yield: 8 servings.

ARTICHOKE STUFFING

lorie verkuyl, ridgecrest, california
This recipe is so good with turkey! I also halve the recipe and use it when I bake a chicken.

- 1 loaf (1 pound) sourdough bread, cut into 1-inch cubes
- 1/2 pound sliced fresh mushrooms
- 2 celery ribs, chopped
- 1 medium onion, chopped
- 3 to 4 garlic cloves, minced
- 2 tablespoons butter
- 2 jars (6-1/2 ounces *each*) marinated artichoke hearts, drained and chopped
- 1/2 cup grated Parmesan cheese
- 1 teaspoon poultry seasoning
- 1 egg
- 1 can (14-1/2 ounces) chicken broth

1 Place the bread cubes in two ungreased 15-in. x 10-in. x 1-in. baking pans. Bake at 350° for 15 minutes or until lightly browned.

2 In a large skillet, saute the mushrooms, celery, onion and garlic in butter until tender. Stir in the artichokes, cheese and poultry seasoning. Transfer to a large bowl; stir in bread cubes.

3 In a small bowl, whisk egg and broth until blended. Pour over bread mixture and mix well.

4 Transfer to a greased 3-qt. baking dish (dish will be full). Cover and bake at 350° for 30 minutes. Uncover; bake 5-15 minutes longer or until a thermometer reads 160°.

Yield: 14 cups.

ASPARAGUS MEDLEY

millie vickery, lena, illinois

This colorful and tasty side dish is delicious served warm or cold. I get lots of compliments on the zesty sauce. The almonds add crunch.

    1   cup water
1-1/2   pounds fresh asparagus, trimmed and cut into
          2-inch pieces
    2   small tomatoes, cut into wedges
    3   tablespoons cider vinegar
  3/4   teaspoon Worcestershire sauce
  1/3   cup sugar
    1   tablespoon grated onion
  1/2   teaspoon salt
  1/2   teaspoon paprika
  1/3   cup canola oil
  1/3   cup sliced almonds, toasted
  1/3   cup crumbled blue cheese, optional

1   In a large saucepan, bring water to a boil. Add asparagus; cover and cook for 3-5 minutes or until crisp-tender. Drain. Add tomatoes; cover and keep warm.

2   In a blender, combine the vinegar, Worcestershire sauce, sugar, onion, salt and paprika; cover and process until smooth. While processing, gradually add oil in a steady stream. Pour over asparagus mixture and toss to coat.

3   Transfer to a serving bowl; sprinkle with almonds and blue cheese if desired. Serve warm.

Yield: 8-10 servings.

GINGERED ORANGE BEETS

marion tipton, phoenix, arizona

My husband was pleasantly surprised when he tried my new twist on beets. The orange and ginger are a surprising complement, making this particular vegetable a wonderful addition to any holiday table.

1-1/2   pounds whole fresh beets (about 4 medium),
          trimmed and cleaned
    6   tablespoons olive oil, *divided*
  1/4   teaspoon salt
  1/4   teaspoon white pepper
    1   tablespoon rice vinegar
    1   tablespoon orange juice concentrate
1-1/2   teaspoons grated orange peel, *divided*
  1/2   teaspoon minced fresh gingerroot
    1   medium navel orange, peeled, sectioned and
          chopped
  1/3   cup pecan halves, toasted

1   Brush beets with 4 tablespoons oil; sprinkle with salt and pepper. Wrap loosely in foil; place on a baking sheet. Bake at 425° for 70-75 minutes or until fork-tender. Cool slightly.

2   In a small bowl, whisk the vinegar, orange juice concentrate, 1 teaspoon orange peel, ginger and remaining oil; set aside.

3   Peel beets and cut into wedges; place in a serving bowl. Add the orange sections and pecans. Drizzle with orange sauce and toss to coat. Sprinkle with remaining orange peel.

Yield: 4 servings.

WHOLESOME APPLE-HAZELNUT STUFFING

donna noel, gray, maine

Try this whole grain, fruit and nut stuffing for a delicious new slant on holiday stuffing. Herbs balance the sweetness of the apples and give this dish a wonderful flavor.

- 2 celery ribs, chopped
- 1 large onion, chopped
- 1 tablespoon olive oil
- 1 small carrot, shredded
- 2 garlic cloves, minced
- 3 tablespoons minced fresh parsley *or* 1 tablespoon dried parsley flakes
- 1 tablespoon minced fresh rosemary *or* 1 teaspoon dried rosemary, crushed
- 4 cups cubed day-old whole wheat bread
- 1-1/2 cups shredded peeled tart apples (about 2 medium)
- 1/2 cup chopped hazelnuts, toasted
- 1 egg, lightly beaten
- 3/4 cup apple cider *or* unsweetened apple juice
- 1/2 teaspoon coarsely ground pepper
- 1/4 teaspoon salt

1 In a large nonstick skillet, saute celery and onion in oil for 4 minutes. Add the carrot, garlic, parsley and rosemary; saute 2-4 minutes longer or until vegetables are tender.

2 In a large bowl, combine the vegetable mixture, bread cubes, apples and hazelnuts. In a small bowl, combine the egg, cider, pepper and salt. Add to stuffing mixture and mix well.

3 Transfer to an 8-in. square baking dish coated with cooking spray. Cover and bake at 350° for 20 minutes. Uncover; bake 10-15 minutes longer or until a thermometer reads 160°.

Yield: 6 cups.

TWICE-BAKED NEW POTATOES

susan herbert, aurora, illinois

I've used these rich potatoes as both a side dish and an appetizer. Guests seem to enjoy the distinctive taste of Monterey Jack cheese and basil. These satisfying mouthfuls are perfect for a late-afternoon or evening get-together when something a little heartier is needed.

- 1-1/2 pound small red potatoes
- 2 to 3 tablespoons canola oil
- 1 cup (4 ounces) shredded Monterey Jack cheese
- 1/2 cup sour cream
- 1 package (3 ounces) cream cheese, softened
- 1/3 cup minced green onions
- 1 teaspoon dried basil
- 1 garlic clove, minced
- 1/2 teaspoon salt
- 1/4 to 1/2 teaspoon pepper
- 1/2 pound sliced bacon, cooked and crumbled

1 Pierce the potatoes; rub skins with oil. Place in a baking pan. Bake, uncovered, at 400° for 50 minutes or until tender. Allow to cool to the touch.

2 In a bowl, combine Monterey Jack, sour cream, cream cheese, onions, basil, garlic, salt and pepper. Cut potatoes in half; carefully scoop out pulp, leaving a thin shell. Add pulp to the cheese mixture and mash; stir in the bacon. Spoon or pipe into potato shells.

3 Place on a baking sheet. Broil 4-6 in. from the heat for 7-8 minutes or until heated through.

Yield: about 2 dozen.

PINEAPPLE SWEET POTATO BOATS

phy bresse, lumberton, north carolina

Crushed pineapple adds a tasty twist to these twice-baked sweet potatoes. Mini-marshmallows can be used in place of the pineapple if you prefer.

- 8 medium sweet potatoes
- 2 cans (8 ounces *each*) unsweetened crushed pineapple, drained
- 1/2 cup butter, melted
- 1 teaspoon salt
- 1/2 teaspoon *each* ground cinnamon, ginger and allspice
- 1/4 teaspoon ground nutmeg

TOPPING:

- 2 cans (14 ounces *each*) unsweetened pineapple tidbits, drained
- 6 tablespoons brown sugar

1 Scrub and pierce sweet potatoes; place on a microwave-safe plate. Microwave, uncovered, on high for 12-14 minutes or until tender, turning once.

2 When cool enough to handle, cut a thin slice off the top of each potato and discard. Scoop out pulp, leaving a thin shell. In a large mixing bowl, mash the pulp. Add the crushed pineapple, butter, salt, cinnamon, ginger, allspice and nutmeg; mix well. Spoon into sweet potato shells.

3 Place on a baking sheet. Sprinkle with pineapple tidbits and brown sugar. Bake, uncovered, at 325° for 30-35 minutes or until heated through.

Yield: 8 servings.

Editor's Note: This recipe was tested in a 1,100-watt microwave.

BEANS WITH PARSLEY SAUCE

veronica teipel, manchester, missouri

You'll likely find the main ingredient for this side dish right in your garden! For a bit of extra color, try mixing wax beans with green beans. The flavor is definitely worth the preparation time.

- 2 pounds fresh green beans, trimmed
- 2 tablespoons butter
- 2 tablespoons all-purpose flour
- 1 teaspoon salt
- 1/8 teaspoon pepper
- 1-1/2 cups chicken broth
- 2 egg yolks
- 1/2 cup milk
- 1 cup minced fresh parsley

1 Place beans in a large saucepan and cover with water; bring to a boil. Cook, uncovered, for 8-10 minutes or until crisp tender. Meanwhile, in a large skillet, melt butter over medium heat. Stir in the flour, salt and pepper until smooth. Gradually whisk in broth. Bring to a boil; cook and stir for 1-2 minutes or until thickened. Remove from the heat.

2 In a small bowl, combine egg yolks and milk. Stir a small amount of hot broth mixture into egg mixture. Return all to the pan, stirring constantly. Bring to a gentle boil; cook and stir for 2 minutes or until thickened. Stir in parsley. Drain the beans; top with the sauce.

Yield: 8 servings.

CRANBERRY CORNMEAL DRESSING

corinne portteus, albuquerque, new mexico

This moist dressing is wonderful when paired with poultry or even pork. The sweet-tart flavor of the dried cranberries really complements the dish's turkey sausage.

- 3 cups reduced-sodium chicken broth, *divided*
- 1/2 cup yellow cornmeal
- 1/2 teaspoon salt
- 1/2 teaspoon white pepper
- 1/2 pound Italian turkey sausage links, casings removed
- 1 large onion, diced
- 1 large fennel bulb, diced (about 1 cup)
- 1 garlic clove, minced
- 1 egg yolk
- 4 cups soft French *or* Italian bread crumbs
- 3/4 cup dried cranberries
- 2 tablespoons minced fresh parsley
- 1 tablespoon balsamic vinegar
- 1 teaspoon minced fresh sage
- 1 teaspoon minced fresh savory
- 1/4 teaspoon ground nutmeg

1 In a small bowl, whisk 1 cup broth, cornmeal, salt and pepper until smooth. In a large saucepan, bring remaining broth to a boil. Add cornmeal mixture, stirring constantly. Return to a boil; cook

and stir for 3 minutes or until thickened. Remove from the heat; set aside.

2 Crumble the sausage into a large nonstick skillet; add onion, fennel and garlic. Cook over medium heat until sausage is no longer pink; drain. Stir in egg yolk and cornmeal mixture. Add the bread crumbs, cranberries, parsley, vinegar, sage, savory and nutmeg.

3 Transfer to a 1-1/2-qt. baking dish coated with cooking spray. Cover and bake at 350° for 40-45 minutes or until heated through.

Yield: 8 servings.

ROASTED ASPARAGUS WITH THYME

sharon leno, keansburg, new jersey

This good-for-you festive side dish is so easy to prepare, yet the simply seasoned spears look appealing enough to serve guests.

- 3 pounds fresh asparagus, trimmed
- 3 tablespoons olive oil
- 2 teaspoons minced fresh thyme *or* 3/4 teaspoon dried thyme
- 1/2 teaspoon salt
- 1/4 teaspoon pepper

1 Place asparagus in a roasting or baking pan lined with heavy-duty foil. Drizzle with oil and toss to coat. Sprinkle with the thyme, salt and pepper.

2 Bake, uncovered, at 425° for 10-15 minutes or until crisp-tender.

Yield: 12 servings.

FRUITED HOLIDAY VEGETABLES

paula marchesi, lenhartsville, pennsylvania

Mom and I made a great team in the kitchen, cooking and baking for hours at a time. I treasure this holiday favorite from her.

- 1 large rutabaga, peeled and cubed
- 3 small red potatoes, cubed
- 3 medium sweet potatoes, peeled and cubed
- 4 teaspoons cornstarch
- 1/2 cup cold water
- 1/2 cup orange juice
- 1 cup prepared mincemeat
- 1/4 cup butter, melted
- 1/4 cup packed dark brown sugar
- 1/4 cup dark corn syrup
- 1/4 teaspoon ground ginger
- 1/4 teaspoon ground cinnamon
- 1-3/4 cups frozen unsweetened peach slices, thawed and chopped
- 1 medium tart apple, chopped
- 1 tablespoon lemon juice
- 1/2 cup chopped pecans

1 Place rutabaga in a Dutch oven; cover with water. Bring to a boil. Reduce heat; cover and simmer for 15 minutes. Add red potatoes and enough additional water to cover. Return to a boil. Reduce heat; cover and simmer for 5 minutes.

2 Add sweet potatoes and enough additional water to cover. Bring to a boil. Reduce heat; cover and simmer 15 minutes longer or until vegetables are tender.

3 Meanwhile, in a small saucepan, combine cornstarch and cold water until smooth. Gradually stir in the orange juice. Bring to a boil; cook and stir for 1-2 minutes or until thickened. Stir in the mincemeat, butter, brown sugar, corn syrup, ginger and cinnamon; heat through.

4 In a large bowl, combine the peaches, apple and lemon juice. Drain vegetables; stir in fruit mixture. Transfer to a greased 4-qt. baking dish. Add mincemeat; stir gently. Sprinkle with pecans. Bake, uncovered, at 325° for 30-35 minutes or until fruit is tender.

Yield: 12 servings.

SOUR CREAM MASHED POTATOES

caroline sperry, shelby township, michigan

I turned an accidental overcooking of potatoes into a family mainstay by adding sour cream and flavorful seasonings to the pot. My boiled potatoes were too soft for seasoned potato bites, but they were perfect for mashed potatoes!

- 2 pounds red potatoes, quartered
- 1 cup (8 ounces) sour cream
- 2 tablespoons minced fresh parsley
- 1 teaspoon salt
- 1/2 teaspoon garlic powder
- 1/2 teaspoon pepper

1 Place potatoes in a large saucepan and cover with water. Bring to a boil. Reduce heat; cover and simmer for 15-20 minutes or until tender.

2 Drain potatoes; transfer to a large bowl. Add the remaining ingredients; beat until blended.

Yield: 5 servings.

PORTUGUESE DRESSING

jean repose, north kingstown, rhode island

With beef and smoked sausage, this meaty dressing is different from many other dressing and stuffing recipes. It's delicious alongside roasted chicken or turkey for holidays or any occasion. I like to use chourico, a Portuguese specialty sausage that's popular in our area.

- 1 pound ground beef
- 1 medium onion, chopped
- 1/2 pound smoked sausage, chopped
- 2 teaspoons poultry seasoning
- 1/2 teaspoon garlic powder
- 1/8 teaspoon ground allspice
- 1 package (12 ounces) unseasoned stuffing cubes
- 1 can (14-1/2 ounces) chicken broth
- 1 egg, lightly beaten
- 1/4 cup minced fresh parsley
- 2 tablespoons butter, melted

1 In a large skillet, cook beef and onion over medium heat until meat is no longer pink; drain. Set beef mixture aside. In the same skillet, saute the sausage, poultry seasoning, garlic powder and allspice for 2 minutes.

2 In a large bowl, toss the beef mixture, sausage mixture and stuffing cubes. Add the broth, egg and parsley; mix well. Transfer to a greased 2-1/2-qt. baking dish. Drizzle with butter.

3 Cover and bake at 325° for 45 minutes. Uncover; bake 10-15 minutes longer or until lightly browned and a thermometer reads 160°.

Yield: 8 servings.

CREAMY BRUSSELS SPROUTS BAKE

elizabeth metz, albuquerque, new mexico

Eating brussels sprouts was a ho-hum experience at our house...until I put together this cheesy bake. After one taste, my husband declared it a "keeper." It's nice alongside ham, pork or beef roasts.

- 1 package (8 ounces) cream cheese, softened
- 1 cup (8 ounces) sour cream
- 1/2 pound sliced fresh mushrooms
- 1 medium onion, chopped
- 2 tablespoons butter
- 2 packages (10 ounces *each*) frozen brussels sprouts, thawed and drained
- 3/4 cup shredded cheddar cheese

1 In a small bowl, beat cream cheese and sour cream until smooth; set aside. In a large skillet, saute mushrooms and onion in butter until tender. Stir in brussels sprouts. Remove from the heat; stir in cream cheese mixture.

2 Spoon into a greased shallow 2-qt. baking dish. Cover and bake at 350° for 25-30 minutes or until bubbly. Uncover; sprinkle with cheddar cheese. Bake 5 minutes longer or until cheese is melted.

Yield: 6-8 servings.

SWEET POTATOES AND APPLES

etta johnson, south hadley, massachusetts

For a pretty and tasty side dish, try this combination of sweet potatoes and apples sprinkled with gingersnap crumbs. It's one of my favorites to serve with turkey at Thanksgiving and Christmas.

- 6 medium sweet potatoes, peeled
- 2 medium tart apples, peeled, cored and cut into rings
- 1/2 cup packed brown sugar
- 1/4 cup butter
- 2 tablespoons unsweetened apple juice
- 2/3 cup finely crushed gingersnap cookies (about 10 cookies)

1 Place the sweet potatoes in a Dutch oven; cover with water. Cover and bring to a boil; cook for 30 minutes or just until tender. Drain; cool slightly. Peel the potatoes and cut into 1/2-in. slices. Arrange half of the slices in a greased 13-in. x 9-in. x 2-in. baking dish. Top with the apples and remaining sweet potato slices.

2 In a small saucepan, bring the brown sugar, butter and apple juice to a boil, stirring constantly. Pour over potatoes and apples. Bake, uncovered, at 325° for 30 minutes or until apples are tender. Sprinkle with gingersnap crumbs. Bake 15 minutes longer.

Yield: 8-10 servings.

BAKED CAULIFLOWER

viola cirillo, mohawk, new york

I created this recipe myself. The cheddar cheese and bread crumb topping makes it an eye-catching casserole for a holiday dinner. You can easily double the amounts if you're having a larger group.

- 1 medium onion, chopped
- 1 garlic clove, minced
- 4 tablespoons butter, *divided*
- 2 tablespoons olive oil
- 1 package (16 ounces) frozen cauliflower, thawed
- 1/2 teaspoon salt
- 1/8 teaspoon pepper
- 1/8 teaspoon ground nutmeg
- 1/4 cup dry bread crumbs
- 1/4 cup shredded cheddar cheese

1 In a large skillet, saute the onion and garlic in 2 tablespoons butter and oil until onion is tender. Add the cauliflower, salt, pepper and nutmeg; saute for 2 minutes.

2 Transfer to a greased 1-qt. baking dish. Melt the remaining butter; toss with bread crumbs. Sprinkle over cauliflower mixture.

3 Cover and bake at 350° for 15 minutes. Uncover; bake for 10 minutes or until heated through. Sprinkle with cheese; bake 3-5 minutes longer or until cheese is melted.

Yield: 4-6 servings.

WILD RICE STUFFED SQUASH

robin thompson, roseville, california

I made this recipe when we invited both families to celebrate our first Thanksgiving in our new home. There were 37 of us, and those who tried this dish raved about it.

- 1 package (6 ounces) long grain and wild rice mix
- 2-1/3 cups vegetable *or* chicken broth
- 1 teaspoon rubbed sage
- 1 teaspoon dried thyme
- 2 celery ribs, chopped
- 1 medium onion, chopped
- 1 tablespoon olive oil
- 3/4 cup dried cranberries
- 1/2 cup coarsely chopped pecan halves, toasted
- 2 tablespoons minced fresh parsley
- 4 medium acorn squash (about 22 ounces *each*)
- 3/4 cup water

1 In a large saucepan, combine the rice with contents of seasoning mix, broth, sage and thyme. Bring to a boil. Reduce heat; cover and simmer for 23-25 minutes or until rice is tender and liquid is almost absorbed. Meanwhile, in a large skillet, saute celery and onion in oil until tender. Stir in cranberries, pecans and parsley. Remove from the heat. Stir in rice mixture.

2 Cut squash in half widthwise. Remove and discard seeds and membranes. With a sharp knife, cut a thin slice from the bottom of each half so squash sits flat. Fill squash halves with about 1/2 cup rice mixture. Place in a greased 15-in. x 10-in. x 1-in. baking pan. Pour water into pan.

3 Coat one side of a large piece of heavy-duty foil with cooking spray. Cover pan tightly with foil, coated side down. Bake at 350° for 50-60 minutes or until squash is tender.

Yield: 8 servings.

CONFETTI LONG GRAIN AND WILD RICE

mary jo hopkins, hobart, indiana

Summer squash, zucchini and sweet red pepper peek out from the tender grains of rice in this colorful side dish.

- 2 packages (6 ounces *each*) long grain and wild rice
- 1 small yellow summer squash, finely diced
- 1 small zucchini, finely diced
- 1 small sweet red pepper, finely diced
- 1 medium carrot, diced
- 2 green onions, thinly sliced
- 1/4 to 1/2 teaspoon salt
- 2 teaspoons olive oil

1 Cook rice according to package directions. Meanwhile, in a skillet, saute the yellow squash, zucchini, red pepper, carrot, onions and salt in oil for 4-5 minutes or until vegetables are tender.

2 Transfer rice to a serving bowl; add vegetable mixture and toss gently.

Yield: 8 servings.

CREAMED POTATO CASSEROLES

norma harder, saskatoon, saskatchewan

This classic potato dish makes enough for two dozen hungry people. It's great with ham and other meats. Guests always remark on its rich, creamy sauce and buttery crumb topping.

- 10 pounds medium potatoes (about 30)
- 2/3 cup plus 3 tablespoons butter, *divided*
- 2/3 cup all-purpose flour
- 5 cups chicken broth
- 5 cups half-and-half cream
- 8 egg yolks, lightly beaten
- 1-1/2 cups minced fresh parsley
- 3 teaspoons salt
- 3/4 teaspoon pepper
- 1/4 teaspoon cayenne pepper
- 1 cup seasoned bread crumbs

1 Place potatoes in a large stockpot or soup kettle; cover with water. Bring to a boil. Reduce heat; cover and simmer for 20 minutes or until just tender. Drain and rinse in cold water. When cool enough to handle, peel potatoes and cut into 1/4-in. slices; set aside.

2 In a large saucepan, melt 2/3 cup butter. Stir in flour until smooth; gradually add broth and cream. Bring to a boil; cook and stir for 2 minutes or until thickened. Remove from the heat. Stir 1 cup hot cream mixture into egg yolks; return all

to the pan, stirring constantly. Add the parsley, salt, pepper and cayenne. Bring to a gentle boil; cook and stir 2 minutes longer. Remove from the heat.

3 Spread 1 cup sauce into each of two 3-qt. baking dishes. Top with a third of the potato slices. Repeat layers twice. Spread with remaining sauce. Melt remaining butter; toss with bread crumbs. Sprinkle over casseroles. Bake, uncovered, at 375° for 40-45 minutes or until bubbly.

Yield: 2 casseroles (12 servings each).

BAKED SHREDDED CARROTS

carole hartwig, horicon, wisconsin

Everyone who samples this crisp and tender carrot dish loves it. I make it often when we have fresh produce from our garden. Its bright orange color looks so pretty on our Thanksgiving table.

- 6 cups shredded carrots (about 2 pounds)
- 3/4 cup chopped green onions
- 2 tablespoons sugar
- 1/2 teaspoon salt
- 1/2 teaspoon celery salt
- 1/4 cup butter

1 In a large bowl, combine the carrots, onions, sugar, salt and celery salt. Transfer to an ungreased 1-1/2-qt. baking dish. Dot with butter.

2 Cover and bake at 325° for 45-50 minutes or until carrots are crisp-tender.

Yield: 6 servings.

WHIPPED CARROTS WITH CRANBERRIES

margie haen, menomonee falls, wisconsin

The buttery texture and tang of cranberries and brown sugar make this a great addition to Thanksgiving turkey.

- 1 pound sliced fresh carrots
- 3 tablespoons butter
- 1 tablespoon brown sugar
- 1/2 teaspoon ground ginger
- 1/4 teaspoon salt
- 1/4 cup dried cranberries

1 Place 2 in. of water in a small saucepan; add carrots. Bring to a boil. Reduce heat; cover and simmer for 15-20 minutes or until tender. Drain.

2 Place carrots in a food processor; add the butter, brown sugar, ginger and salt. Cover and process until smooth. Transfer to a serving bowl; stir in cranberries.

Yield: 4 servings.

FESTIVE BEAN 'N' PEPPER BUNDLES

judith krucki, lake orion, michigan

This is a beautiful way to prepare vegetables for Christmas brunch. The pairing goes well with a variety of entrees.

- 1 pound fresh green beans, trimmed
- 1 pound fresh wax beans, trimmed
- 2 tablespoons chicken bouillon granules
- 1/2 teaspoon garlic powder
- 3 medium zucchini
- 2 medium sweet red peppers, julienned
- 1/4 cup butter, melted

1 In a large saucepan, combine the beans, bouillon and the garlic powder; cover with water. Bring to a boil. Cook, uncovered, for 8-10 minutes or until crisp-tender; drain.

2 Cut zucchini into 1/2-in. slices. Hollow out centers, leaving 1/4-in. rings; discard the centers. Thread beans and peppers through squash rings.

3 Place in a greased 15-in. x 10-in. x 1-in. baking pan; drizzle with butter. Cover and bake at 350° for 15-20 minutes or until zucchini is crisp-tender.

Yield: 12-15 servings.

NEW ENGLAND BUTTERNUT SQUASH

linda massicotte-black, coventry, connecticut

We really love this side dish. The traditional fall treat is a favorite because it has a hint of sweetness. Even the picky little eaters at the table enjoy this one!

- 1 medium butternut squash
- 1/4 cup butter, melted
- 1/4 cup maple syrup
- 3/4 teaspoon ground cinnamon
- 1/4 teaspoon ground nutmeg

1 Cut squash in half lengthwise; discard seeds. Place cut side down in a microwave-safe dish; add 1/2 in. of water. Cover and microwave on high for 15-20 minutes or until very tender; drain.

2 When cool enough to handle, scoop out pulp and mash. Stir in the butter, syrup, cinnamon and nutmeg.

Yield: 5 servings.

Editor's Note: This recipe was tested in a 1,100-watt microwave.

BROCCOLI POTATO SUPREME

jane birch, edison, new jersey

My family insists that this two-in-one casserole makes an appearance at all of our special meals. Every bite is doubly delicious!

- 3 cups hot mashed potatoes
- 1 package (3 ounces) cream cheese, softened
- 1/4 cup milk
- 1 egg
- 2 tablespoons butter, softened
- 1/2 teaspoon salt
- 1/4 teaspoon pepper
- 1 can (2.8 ounces) french-fried onions, *divided*
- 4-1/2 cups fresh broccoli florets
- 1 cup (4 ounces) shredded cheddar cheese

1 In a bowl, combine the first seven ingredients; beat until smooth. Fold in half of the onions. Spread onto the bottom and up the sides of a greased 13-in. x 9-in. baking dish, forming a shell. Bake, uncovered, at 350° for 20-25 minutes or until edges are lightly browned.

2 Cook broccoli in a small amount of water until crisp-tender; drain. Place in the potato shell. Sprinkle with cheese and remaining onions. Bake 10 minutes longer.

Yield: 8 servings.

CRANBERRY WILD RICE DRESSING

shirley bedzis, san diego, california

Rice dressing is a tasty twist to a traditional Thanksgiving dinner. Cranberry sauce adds festive color and a touch of sweetness.

- 3 cups chicken broth
- 1 large onion, chopped
- 2 celery ribs, thinly sliced
- 1 cup uncooked brown rice
- 1/2 cup uncooked wild rice
- 1 tablespoon minced fresh rosemary *or*
  1 teaspoon dried rosemary, crushed
- 1 teaspoon chicken bouillon granules
- 1/2 teaspoon salt
- 1/4 teaspoon white pepper
- 1 bay leaf
- 1 cup whole-berry cranberry sauce

1   In a large saucepan, combine the first 10 ingredients; bring to a boil. Reduce heat; cover and simmer for 45-50 minutes or until rice is tender. Remove from the heat; let stand for 5 minutes. Discard bay leaf. Stir in cranberry sauce.

2   Spoon into a greased 2-qt. baking dish. Cover and bake at 350° for 30-35 minutes or until heated through. If dressing is stuffed into poultry, bake until a meat thermometer reads 180° for poultry and 165° for dressing.

Yield: 5 cups.

SPECIAL SWEET POTATOES

ruby williams, bogalusa, louisiana

This dish is quick to prepare. I save time by boiling the sweet potatoes in advance, then complete the recipe the next day. Orange juice and cinnamon are wonderful for enhancing the flavor of sweet potatoes.

- 2 small sweet potatoes, peeled and cut into 1/2-inch cubes
- 2 tablespoons brown sugar
- 1/4 teaspoon ground cinnamon
- 1/8 teaspoon salt
- 1/4 cup orange juice
- 2 tablespoons butter
- 1/2 cup miniature marshmallows

1   In a saucepan, cook sweet potatoes in boiling salted water for 10 minutes or until tender; drain. Transfer to a greased 1-qt. baking dish. Sprinkle with brown sugar, cinnamon and salt. Drizzle with orange juice and dot with butter. Bake, uncovered, at 450° for 15 minutes. Top with marshmallows. Bake 2 minutes longer or until marshmallows are puffed and golden brown.

Yield: 2 servings.

ASIAN GREEN BEANS

harriet stichter, milford, indiana
This is a no-stress side dish. These versatile beans go with any main course.

- 1 package (16 ounces) frozen cut green beans
- 1-1/2 teaspoons cornstarch
- 1/2 cup chicken broth
- 1 tablespoon soy sauce
- 2 tablespoons chopped onion
- 1/4 to 1/2 teaspoon ground ginger
- 1-1/2 teaspoons canola oil
- 1 jar (4-1/2 ounces) sliced mushrooms, drained
- 1/2 cup sliced water chestnuts
- 1-1/2 teaspoons sesame seeds, toasted

1   Cook green beans according to package directions. Meanwhile, in a small bowl, combine the cornstarch, broth and soy sauce until smooth; set aside.

2   In a large skillet, saute the onion and ginger in oil until tender. Stir broth mixture and add to skillet. Bring to a boil; cook and stir for 1 minute or until thickened. Drain beans; add the beans, mushrooms and water chestnuts to skillet. Stir to coat. Just before serving, sprinkle with the sesame seeds.

Yield: 4 servings.

GLAZED PEARL ONIONS

jennifer tunen, delaware, ohio
As a young girl, my mom gave me the job of making the glazed onions every year. This easy, elegant recipe is a great addition to the holiday table. Everyone in my family enjoys it.

- 6 cups water
- 2 pounds pearl onions
- 1/3 cup butter, cubed
- 1/4 cup sugar

1   In a large saucepan, bring water to a boil. Add pearl onions; boil for 3 minutes. Drain and rinse in cold water; peel.

2   In a large skillet over medium heat, melt butter. Add onions; cook for 6-8 minutes or until tender, stirring occasionally. Sprinkle with the sugar. Cook 18-20 minutes longer or until the onions are golden brown, stirring occasionally. Serve with a slotted spoon.

Yield: 6 servings.

PRETZEL-TOPPED SWEET POTATOES

sue mallory, lancaster, pennsylvania

Friends with whom I've shared this recipe say it's their favorite way to serve sweet potatoes. I like to make it for brunch as a colorful go-with dish. The mingled sweet, tart and salty tastes are an unusual treat.

- 2 cups chopped pretzel rods (about 13)
- 1 cup chopped pecans
- 1 cup fresh *or* frozen cranberries
- 1 cup packed brown sugar
- 1 cup butter, melted, *divided*
- 1 can (2-1/2 pounds) sweet potatoes, drained
- 1 can (5 ounces) evaporated milk
- 1/2 cup sugar
- 1 teaspoon vanilla extract

1 In a large bowl, combine the pretzels, pecans, cranberries, brown sugar and 1/2 cup butter; set aside.

2 In a large bowl, beat the sweet potatoes until smooth. Add the milk, sugar, vanilla and remaining butter; beat until well blended.

3 Spoon into a greased shallow 2-qt. baking dish; sprinkle with pretzel mixture. Bake, uncovered, at 350° for 25-30 minutes or until the edges are bubbly.

Yield: 10-12 servings.

WILD RICE 'N' BREAD DRESSING

marilyn paradis, woodburn, oregon

Hearty wild rice is an appealing addition to traditional bread stuffing, while chopped carrot adds pretty color.

- 3/4 cup chopped celery
- 2/3 cup chopped onion
- 2/3 cup chopped carrot
- 1/3 cup canola oil
- 3 tablespoons dried parsley flakes
- 4 teaspoons chicken bouillon granules
- 1 teaspoon garlic powder
- 1 teaspoon dried marjoram
- 1 teaspoon dried rosemary, crushed
- 1 teaspoon rubbed sage
- 1/2 teaspoon pepper
- 1/4 teaspoon poultry seasoning
- 2 cups chicken broth
- 8 cups day-old bread cubes
- 3 cups cooked wild rice

1 In a large skillet, saute the celery, onion and carrot in oil until tender. Stir in the parsley, bouillon, garlic powder, marjoram, rosemary, sage, pepper and poultry seasoning. Add the broth; heat through.

2 In a large bowl, combine bread cubes and wild rice. Stir in broth mixture; toss to coat. Transfer to a greased shallow 2-1/2-qt. baking dish. Cover and bake at 350° for 30 minutes. Uncover; bake 10-15 minutes longer or until heated through.

Yield: 8-10 servings.

CHEESE-STUFFED DOUBLE BAKERS

leeann johnson, joliet, illinois

Two types of cheese, sour cream and a little garlic powder turn these twice-baked potatoes into something special. After one bite, you'll want to make them time and again.

- 4 large baking potatoes
- 1/2 cup sour cream
- 2 tablespoons butter
- 3/4 teaspoon salt
- 1/8 teaspoon *each* garlic powder, onion powder and pepper
- 1 cup (4 ounces) shredded cheddar cheese, *divided*
- 1 cup (4 ounces) shredded part-skim mozzarella cheese, *divided*
- 1/4 cup chopped green onions

1   Scrub and pierce potatoes. Bake at 375° for 1 hour or until tender. When cool enough to handle, cut each potato in half lengthwise; scoop out pulp, leaving a thin shell.

2   In a large bowl, beat the pulp with sour cream, butter, salt and seasonings. Stir in 3/4 cup each cheddar and mozzarella. Spoon or pipe into potato shells. Sprinkle with remaining cheeses.

3   Place on a baking sheet. Bake at 375° for 15-20 minutes or until heated through. Top with green onions.

Yield: 8 servings.

AND THE BEETS GO ON

alcy thorne, los molinos, california

This is an appetizing side dish. Their ruby red color and tangy flavor make these beets an excellent choice for a holiday meal.

- 2 cans (13-1/4 ounces *each*) sliced beets, drained
- 1 can (16 ounces) whole-berry cranberry sauce
- 1/4 cup orange juice concentrate

1   In a large saucepan, combine the beets, cranberry sauce and orange juice concentrate. Cook and stir over low heat until heated through. Serve with a slotted spoon.

Yield: 8 servings.

MAPLE-GLAZED CARROTS

sharon bickett, chester, south carolina

I like to make this side dish when I want to add some color to my meal. The flavor of maple syrup is a nice surprise and so compatible with the carrots. The crunch of pecans adds a special touch.

- 1-1/2 cups baby carrots *or* sliced carrots
- 1/2 cup water
- 1 tablespoon butter
- 2 tablespoons maple syrup
- 1/4 cup chopped pecans

1   In a small saucepan, bring carrots and water to a boil. Reduce heat; cover and cook for 10 minutes or until tender. Drain. Stir in the butter, syrup and pecans until the butter is melted.

Yield: 2 servings.

CRANBERRY SWEET POTATO BAKE

isabell burrows, livermore, california

This colorful casserole is the perfect side dish for Thanksgiving, with its combination of sweet potatoes, cranberries and apples. I find it convenient to cook the sweet potatoes and assemble the dish in the morning, then bake it later.

- 2 large sweet potatoes
- 3 tablespoons butter
- 1/2 cup packed brown sugar
- 2 medium apples, peeled and cubed
- 1/2 cup dried cranberries
- 1/2 teaspoon ground cinnamon
- 1/2 teaspoon ground nutmeg

1 Place the sweet potatoes in a large saucepan and cover with water. Bring to a boil. Reduce heat; cover and cook for 30-45 minutes or just until tender. Drain; cool slightly. Peel potatoes and cut into 1/2-in. slices; set aside.

2 In a large skillet, melt butter and brown sugar over medium heat. Add apples; cook and stir until crisp-tender. Stir in the cranberries, cinnamon and nutmeg.

3 In a greased 1-1/2-qt. baking dish, layer half of the sweet potatoes and half of the apple mixture; repeat layers. Cover and bake at 375° for 30-35 minutes or until bubbly.

Yield: 8 servings.

TRIPLE-CHEESE BROCCOLI PUFF

maryellen hays, wolcottville, indiana

This rich-tasting souffle is always on our Christmas morning menu. It will settle a bit after you remove the dish from the oven, but the pretty golden top is very attractive. I often add some cubed ham.

- 1 cup sliced fresh mushrooms
- 1 tablespoon butter
- 1 package (3 ounces) cream cheese, softened
- 6 eggs
- 1 cup milk
- 3/4 cup biscuit/baking mix
- 3 cups frozen chopped broccoli, thawed
- 2 cups (8 ounces) shredded Monterey Jack cheese
- 1 cup (8 ounces) 4% cottage cheese
- 1/4 teaspoon salt

1 In a small skillet, saute mushrooms in butter until tender; set aside. In a large bowl, beat the cream cheese, eggs, milk and biscuit mix just until combined. Stir in the broccoli, cheeses, salt and mushrooms.

2 Pour into a greased round 2-1/2-qt. baking dish. Bake, uncovered, at 350° for 50-60 minutes or until a knife inserted near the center comes out clean. Let stand for 10 minutes before serving.

Yield: 6-8 servings.

SPECIAL CREAMED CORN

deb hauptmann, mohnton, pennsylvania

We rarely have the same main dish at Christmas each year, since I really enjoy trying new recipes. This corn, however, has a permanent place on our table. My whole family loves it, but my son, especially, would be so disappointed if I forgot to include this with our holiday meal.

- 1/3 cup butter
- 1/3 cup all-purpose flour
-   1 cup heavy whipping cream
-   1 cup milk
- 1/4 cup sugar
-   1 teaspoon salt

Dash white pepper

-   5 cups frozen corn, thawed
- 1/4 cup grated Parmesan cheese

1 In a saucepan, melt butter over medium heat. Stir in flour until smooth. Gradually add cream, milk, sugar, salt and pepper. Bring to a boil; boil and stir for 2 minutes. Add corn; heat through.

2 Transfer the mixture to an ungreased 1-1/2-qt. broiler-proof dish. Sprinkle with Parmesan cheese. Broil 5 in. from the heat for 3-5 minutes or until lightly browned and bubbly.

Yield: 6-8 servings.

SHREDDED POTATO CASSEROLE

paula zsiray, logan, utah

This potato dish pairs well with prime rib and many other entrees. Make it ahead and have it ready to pop into the oven for the party. The topping of cornflake crumbs and Parmesan cheese adds crunch.

-   1 can (10-3/4 ounces) condensed cream of mushroom soup, undiluted
-   1 cup (8 ounces) sour cream
- 1/2 cup milk
-   1 cup (4 ounces) shredded cheddar cheese
- 1/2 cup butter, melted, *divided*
-   1 package (30 ounces) frozen shredded hash brown potatoes, thawed
-   1 cup cornflake crumbs
- 1/4 cup grated Parmesan cheese

1 In a large bowl, combine the soup, sour cream, milk, cheddar cheese and 1/4 cup butter. Stir in the hash browns. Transfer to a greased 13-in. x 9-in. x 2-in. baking dish.

2 In a small bowl, combine the cornflake crumbs, Parmesan cheese and remaining butter; sprinkle over top. Bake, uncovered, at 325° for 45-50 minutes or until heated through.

Yield: 6-8 servings.

ARTICHOKES AU GRATIN

marjorie bowen, colorado springs, colorado
This makes a great side dish for Thanksgiving, Christmas or any dinner. My niece served this at a family gathering and was kind enough to share the recipe.

- 2 cans (14 ounces *each*) water-packed artichoke hearts, rinsed, drained and quartered
- 1 garlic clove, minced
- 1/4 cup butter, *divided*
- 2 tablespoons all-purpose flour
- 1/2 teaspoon salt
- 1/4 teaspoon pepper
- 1-1/2 cups milk
- 1 egg, lightly beaten
- 1/2 cup shredded Swiss cheese, *divided*
- 1 tablespoon dry bread crumbs
- 1/8 teaspoon paprika

1 In a small skillet, saute the artichokes and garlic in 2 tablespoons butter until tender. Transfer to a greased 1-qt. baking dish.

2 In a small saucepan, melt the remaining butter. Stir in flour, salt and pepper until smooth. Gradually add milk. Bring to a boil; cook and stir for 2 minutes or until thickened. Remove from the heat. Stir a small amount of hot mixture into egg; return all to pan, stirring constantly. Stir in 1/4 cup cheese until melted.

3 Pour over artichokes; sprinkle with remaining cheese. Combine crumbs and paprika; sprinkle over top. Bake, uncovered, at 400° for 20-25 minutes or until heated through.

Yield: 4-6 servings.

HONEY-GLAZED CARROTS

pat gardetta, osage beach, missouri
These beautifully glazed carrots are colorful and dressed up enough for Christmas dinner. They have become such a favorite side dish that I often double the easy, one-skillet recipe.

- 2 pounds baby carrots
- 1/4 cup finely chopped green onions
- 1/4 cup butter
- 1/4 cup honey
- 1 teaspoon grated orange peel
- 1/2 teaspoon salt
- 1/2 teaspoon ground cinnamon
- 1/4 teaspoon pepper
- 2 teaspoons cornstarch
- 1/2 cup orange juice
- 4 teaspoons minced fresh mint *or* minced fresh parsley

1 Place 1 in. of water in a skillet; add carrots. Bring to a boil. Reduce heat; cover and simmer for 15-20 minutes or until crisp-tender. Drain and set aside.

2 In the same skillet, saute green onions in butter until tender. Stir in the honey, orange peel, salt, cinnamon and pepper. Combine cornstarch and orange juice until smooth; stir into onion mixture. Bring to a boil; cook and stir for 1-2 minutes or until thickened.

3 Return carrots to the pan. Cook and stir for 2 minutes or until heated through. Sprinkle with mint.

Yield: 8 servings.

WHITE CHEDDAR SCALLOPED POTATOES

hope toole, muscle shoals, alabama

This recipe has evolved over the past several years. After I added the thyme, ham and sour cream, my husband declared, "This is it!" I like to serve this rich, saucy entree with a salad and homemade French bread.

- 1 medium onion, finely chopped
- 1/4 cup butter, cubed
- 1/4 cup all-purpose flour
- 1 teaspoon dried parsley flakes
- 1 teaspoon salt
- 1/2 teaspoon pepper
- 1/2 teaspoon dried thyme
- 3 cups milk
- 1 can (10-3/4 ounces) condensed cream of mushroom soup, undiluted
- 1 cup (8 ounces) sour cream
- 8 cups thinly sliced peeled potatoes
- 3-1/2 cups cubed fully cooked ham
- 2 cups (8 ounces) shredded white cheddar cheese

1 In a large saucepan, saute onion in butter until tender. Stir in the flour, parsley, salt, pepper and thyme until blended. Gradually add milk. Bring to a boil; cook and stir for 2 minutes or until thickened. Stir in the soup. Remove from the heat; stir in sour cream until blended.

2 In a large bowl, combine the potatoes and ham. In a greased 13-in. x 9-in. x 2-in. baking dish, layer half of the potato mixture, cheese and white sauce. Repeat layers. Cover and bake at 375° for 30 minutes. Uncover; bake 40-50 minutes longer or until potatoes are tender.

Yield: 6-8 servings.

SWEET POTATO STUFFED APPLES

howie wiener, spring hill, florida

I inherited this recipe for baked apples from my grandmother and make it every chance I get, especially in fall. They can be served as a side dish or dessert.

- 5 medium tart apples
- 1 can (15 ounces) cut sweet potatoes, drained and mashed
- 3 tablespoons brown sugar
- 3 tablespoons maple syrup
- 1 tablespoon butter, melted
- 1/2 teaspoon ground cinnamon
- 1/4 teaspoon salt
- 2 tablespoons slivered almonds, *divided*

1 Core apples and scoop out pulp, forming a 2-in. cavity; discard seeds. Chop pulp; place in a bowl. Add the sweet potatoes, brown sugar, syrup, butter, cinnamon, salt and 1 tablespoon almonds. Spoon into apples; sprinkle with remaining almonds.

2 Place in an ungreased 11-in. x 7-in. x 2-in. baking dish. Bake, uncovered, at 350° for 30-35 minutes or until apples are tender.

Yield: 5 servings.

MASHED POTATO ROSES

darlene brenden, salem, oregon

This clever side dish turns a garden-variety meal into dinner fit for company. To save prep time, make the roses ahead and keep them covered in the fridge. Then top them with butter and paprika, and pop them into the oven shortly before eating.

- 4 medium baking potatoes, peeled and quartered
- 1 egg
- 4 tablespoons butter, *divided*
- 2 tablespoons grated Parmesan cheese
- 1 teaspoon salt
- 1 teaspoon dried minced onion
- 1 teaspoon minced fresh parsley
- 1/8 teaspoon pepper

1 Place potatoes in a large saucepan and cover with water. Bring to a boil. Reduce heat; cover and cook for 15-20 minutes or until tender. Drain.

2 In a large bowl, mash the potatoes. Beat in the egg, 2 tablespoons butter, cheese, salt, onion, parsley and pepper.

3 Spoon into eight mounds, about 1/2 cup each, on a greased baking sheet. To form rose petals, hold a teaspoon or tablespoon upside down and press tip of spoon all around the bottom of each mound. Repeat, forming three or four more rows of petals.

4 Melt remaining butter; drizzle over potato roses. Bake at 350° for 15-18 minutes or until heated through.

Yield: 8 servings.

SWEET-AND-SOUR RED CABBAGE

leonie kenyon, narragansett, rhode island

My grandfather was German, so my grandmother prepared many dishes for him from his homeland. This is one I like best.

- 1 medium onion, chopped
- 1/4 cup butter, cubed
- 1 medium head red cabbage, chopped (about 8 cups)
- 1 teaspoon salt
- 1/4 teaspoon pepper
- 2 medium tart apples, peeled and chopped
- 1/4 cup water
- 1/2 cup white vinegar
- 1/3 cup packed brown sugar

1 In a large saucepan, saute onion in butter until tender. Stir in the cabbage, salt and pepper. Reduce heat; cover and simmer for 10 minutes. Stir in apples and water; cover and simmer 45 minutes longer or until cabbage and apples are tender.

2 Combine vinegar and brown sugar; stir into cabbage mixture. Bring to a boil. Reduce heat; simmer, uncovered, for 15 minutes or until cabbage and apples are glazed.

Yield: 8 servings.

Prepping Apples

To remove any contaminants on the skin of an apple, wash it thoroughly with soapy water and rinse it off before using. To prevent browning, dip peeled apple slices into one part citrus juice and three parts water.
—Taste of Home Test Kitchen

SOUPS
& SALADS

CHERRY
PINEAPPLE
SALAD
P. 84

ORANGE-CRANBERRY TOSSED SALAD

bernice weir, hot springs village, arkansas

Candied cranberries and mandarin oranges sparkle like jewels in this merry Christmas salad we have enjoyed for years.

- 2 cups fresh *or* frozen cranberries, thawed
- 1 cup sugar
- 3 tablespoons orange juice
- 2 tablespoons cider vinegar
- 2 tablespoons honey
- 1 teaspoon poppy seeds
- 1 teaspoon ground mustard
- Dash salt and pepper
- 3/4 cup canola oil
- 2 heads Boston *or* Bibb lettuce, torn
- 1 can (11 ounces) mandarin oranges, drained

1 For candied cranberries, place cranberries in a baking pan; sprinkle with sugar. Cover tightly with foil and bake at 350° for 30 minutes, stirring every 15 minutes.

2 Place in a single layer on a greased aluminum foil; cool for at least 30 minutes.

3 For the salad dressing, combine the orange juice, vinegar, honey, poppy seeds, mustard, salt and the pepper in a small bowl. Slowly whisk in oil. Just before serving, toss the lettuce, oranges and dressing in a large bowl. Sprinkle with the candied cranberries.

Yield: 12 servings.

CREAMY WALDORF SALAD

romaine wetzel, ronks, pennsylvania

I found this recipe in a local cookbook. The whipped cream makes it a little different than the usual Waldorf salad, but it's always good with any meal.

- 4 cups chopped apples (about 3 large)
- 1 tablespoon plus 1 teaspoon lemon juice, *divided*
- 4 celery ribs, chopped
- 1 cup chopped walnuts
- 1/2 cup mayonnaise
- 2 tablespoons sugar
- 1/4 teaspoon salt
- 1 cup heavy whipping cream, whipped

1 In a large bowl, toss apples with 1 tablespoon lemon juice. Stir in celery and walnuts.

2 In a small bowl, whisk the mayonnaise, sugar, salt and remaining lemon juice until blended. Fold in whipped cream. Gently stir into fruit mixture. Refrigerate until serving.

Yield: 12 servings.

How to Whip Cream

For best results, start with cold whipping cream. Choose a deep metal bowl, as the cream will double in volume. Place the bowl and beaters in the freezer for at least 15 minutes before using. Beat quickly, scraping the bowl occasionally. Do not overbeat. Beat only until soft or stiff peaks form, depending on what your recipe needs.
—Taste of Home Test Kitchen

EMILY'S SPINACH SALAD

emily fields, santana, california

I've always loved eating spinach—it's grown here in our area. When I saw an announcement of a spinach cooking contest, I made up this recipe to enter. I was delighted when my colorful, tangy salad took the grand prize!

- 2/3 cup canola oil
- 1/4 cup red wine vinegar
- 2 teaspoons lemon juice
- 2 teaspoons soy sauce
- 1 teaspoon sugar
- 1 teaspoon ground mustard
- 1/2 teaspoon curry powder
- 1/2 teaspoon salt
- 1/2 teaspoon seasoned pepper
- 1/4 teaspoon garlic powder
- 1 package (10 ounces) fresh spinach, torn
- 5 bacon strips, cooked and crumbled
- 2 hard-cooked eggs, sliced

1 In a small bowl, whisk the first 10 ingredients; set aside. Place spinach in a large salad bowl.

2 Just before serving, whisk dressing again and drizzle over spinach; toss gently. Garnish with bacon and egg slices.

Yield: 6-8 servings.

CHERRY PINEAPPLE SALAD

leona luecking, west burlington, iowa

This recipe makes a really pretty salad. My sister-in-law often brings it to our family get-togethers on holidays and special occasions.

- 3 packages (3 ounces *each*) cherry gelatin
- 2-1/3 cups boiling water
- 2 cans (16-1/2 ounces *each*) pitted dark sweet cherries
- 1 can (20 ounces) pineapple tidbits
- 1/3 cup lemon juice
- 1/3 cup heavy whipping cream
- 1/3 cup mayonnaise
- 2 packages (3 ounces *each*) cream cheese, softened

Dash salt

- 1/2 cup coarsely chopped nuts

1 In a large bowl, dissolve gelatin in water. Drain and reserve enough cherry and pineapple juices to measure 2-1/2 cups; add to gelatin with lemon juice. Set fruits aside.

2 Divide the gelatin in half. Set aside one portion of gelatin at room temperature; chill other portion until partially set. Fold pineapple into the chilled gelatin; pour into a 13-in. x 9-in. dish. Chill until almost firm.

3 In a small bowl, beat the cream, mayonnaise, cream cheese and salt until light and fluffy. Spread over the chilled gelatin layer. Refrigerate until firm. Chill the reserved gelatin mixture until partially set. Fold in cherries and nuts; spread over cream cheese layer. Chill for at least 3 hours.

Yield: 12-16 servings.

MUSHROOM BARLEY SOUP

darlene weise-appleby, creston, ohio

Looking for a filling meatless meal in a bowl? Ladle up this delicious soup. It's a treasured favorite with my husband, five kids and grandkids. It warms the body and soul.

- 1 medium leek (white portion only), halved and thinly sliced
- 1 cup chopped celery
- 4 garlic cloves, minced
- 2 teaspoons olive oil
- 3/4 pound sliced fresh mushrooms
- 1-1/2 cups chopped peeled turnips
- 1-1/2 cups chopped carrots
- 4 cans (14-1/2 ounces *each*) reduced-sodium beef broth *or* vegetable broth
- 1 can (14-1/2 ounces) diced tomatoes, undrained
- 1 bay leaf
- 1/2 teaspoon salt
- 1/2 teaspoon dried thyme
- 1/4 teaspoon pepper
- 1/4 teaspoon caraway seeds
- 1 cup quick-cooking barley
- 4 cups fresh baby spinach, cut into thin strips

1 In a large saucepan coated with cooking spray, cook the leek, celery and garlic in oil for 2 minutes. Add mushrooms, turnips and carrots; cook 4-5 minutes longer or until mushrooms are tender.

2 Stir in the broth, tomatoes and seasonings. Bring to a boil. Reduce heat; cover and simmer for 10-15 minutes or until turnips are tender. Add barley; simmer 10 minutes longer. Stir in spinach; cook 5 minutes more or until spinach and barley are tender. Discard bay leaf.

Yield: 10 servings (about 3 quarts).

SESAME GINGER VINAIGRETTE

taste of home test kitchen

Our home economists enliven an ordinary green salad with a vinaigrette featuring orange juice, ginger and balsamic vinegar.

- 1/3 cup orange juice
- 3 tablespoons olive oil
- 1 tablespoon sugar
- 1 tablespoon balsamic vinegar
- 2 teaspoons sesame seeds, toasted
- 1/2 teaspoon sesame oil
- 1/4 teaspoon ground ginger
- 1/4 teaspoon salt

Torn salad greens, halved cherry tomatoes and sliced cucumbers

1 In a jar with a tight-fitting lid, combine the first eight ingredients; shake well. Drizzle over salad; toss to coat.

Yield: 1/2 cup.

Homemade Salad Dressing

The shelf life of salad dressings varies somewhat. Generally, vinaigrettes can be refrigerated for up to 2 weeks. Dairy-based dressings, like buttermilk, and dressings made with fresh ingredients, like chopped onion, fresh herbs, tomato sauce and chopped hard-cooked egg, will keep up to 1 week.
—Taste of Home Test Kitchen

3 Meanwhile, in a large bowl, toss bread cubes with oil and butter. Combine the oregano, basil, salt and pepper; sprinkle over bread and toss to coat.

4 Transfer to an ungreased 15-in. x 10-in. x 1-in. baking pan. Bake at 375° for 10-12 minutes or until golden brown. Garnish soup with croutons and Swiss cheese.

Yield: 11 servings (about 2-1/2 quarts).

CRANBERRY GELATIN MOLD

june blomquist, eugene, oregon
Tangy and fruity, this festive gelatin mold is not only easy to prepare but pretty, too. Once they've tried it, your family will request it again and again.

    2 packages (3 ounces *each*) raspberry gelatin
    3 cups boiling water
    1 can (16 ounces) whole-berry cranberry sauce
    2 tablespoons lemon juice
    1 can (8 ounces) unsweetened crushed pineapple, drained
  1/2 cup finely chopped celery

1 In a large bowl, dissolve gelatin in boiling water. Stir in cranberry sauce and lemon juice until blended. Chill until partially set.

2 Stir in pineapple and celery. Pour into a 6-cup ring mold coated with cooking spray. Refrigerate until firm. Unmold onto a serving platter.

Yield: 8 servings.

Using Gelatin Molds

Before inverting a gelatin mold onto a serving plate, wet the surface of the dish. This allows the gelatin to slide and makes it easy to center on the plate.
—Elaine C., Louisville, Kentucky

FLAVORFUL FRENCH ONION SOUP

taste of home test kitchen
This satisfying soup will complement any hearty main dish. Serve it as a first course to impress your guests from the start!

  1/4 cup butter, cubed
2-1/2 pounds onions, thinly sliced
    3 tablespoons brown sugar
    1 teaspoon pepper
    3 tablespoons all-purpose flour
    8 cups beef broth
    1 cup dry red wine *or* additional beef broth
  1/4 cup A.1. steak sauce

HOMEMADE CROUTONS:
    3 cups cubed French bread
    2 tablespoons olive oil
    2 tablespoons butter, melted
  1/2 teaspoon dried oregano
  1/2 teaspoon dried basil
  1/4 teaspoon salt
  1/4 teaspoon pepper
  3/4 cup shredded Swiss cheese

1 In a Dutch oven or soup kettle, melt butter. Add the onions, brown sugar and pepper; cook over low heat until onion are lightly browned, about 1 hour.

2 Sprinkle onions with flour; stir to blended. Gradually stir in broth. Add wine or additional broth and steak sauce. Bring to a boil. Reduce heat; cover and simmer for 45 minutes.

CASHEW TOSSED SALAD

raelynne fink-mahloch, kansas city, missouri

A flavorful onion dressing tastefully tops off a tossed salad featuring cashews and dried cranberries. I'm often asked to make this for meetings at church.

- 8 **cups torn mixed salad greens**
- 1 **cup salted cashews**
- 3/4 **cup dried cranberries**
- 1/2 **cup thinly sliced red onion**

DRESSING:
- 1/4 **cup sugar**
- 1/4 **cup chopped red onion**
- 3 **tablespoons olive oil**
- 2 **tablespoons canola oil**
- 2 **tablespoons white vinegar**
- 1 **teaspoon prepared mustard**

Dash pepper
- 1/4 **teaspoon poppy seeds**

1 In a large bowl, combine the greens, cashews, cranberries and sliced onion. In a blender, combine the sugar, chopped onion, olive oil, canola oil, vinegar, mustard and pepper; cover and process until blended. Stir in the poppy seeds. Drizzle over salad and toss to coat.

Yield: 8 servings.

TOMATO CLAM CHOWDER

weda mosellie, phillipsburg, new jersey

Steaming bowls of this Manhattan-style clam chowder really warm guests when they come in from the cold on Christmas Eve.

- 5 **to 6 medium potatoes, peeled and diced**
- 6 **bacon strips, diced**
- 1 **small onion, finely chopped**
- 2 **celery ribs, chopped**
- 1 **garlic clove, minced**
- 2 **cans (6 ounces** *each***) minced clams**
- 2 **cups water**
- 1 **can (15 ounces) tomato sauce**
- 1 **can (14-1/2 ounces) diced tomatoes, undrained**
- 1/2 **to 1 teaspoon pepper**
- 1/4 **teaspoon salt**
- 2 **teaspoons minced fresh parsley**

1 Place the potatoes in a soup kettle or Dutch oven and cover with water. Bring to a boil. Reduce the heat; cover and cook for 10-15 minutes or until tender.

2 Meanwhile, in a large skillet, cook bacon over medium heat until crisp. Using a slotted spoon, remove to paper towels; drain, reserving 2 tablespoons drippings. In the drippings, saute the onion, celery and garlic until tender.

3 Drain clams, reserving liquid; set clams aside. Drain potatoes and return to the pan. Add onion mixture, bacon and reserved clam liquid. Stir in the water, tomato sauce, tomatoes, pepper and salt. Bring to a boil. Reduce heat; simmer, uncovered, for 30-35 minutes or until heated through. Add clams and parsley; simmer 5 minutes longer.

Yield: 11 servings (2-3/4 quarts).

LUNCHEON SALAD

mrs. leon schleusener, tomah, wisconsin

I live in the heart of cranberry country, and I always have the key ingredients for this salad at hand. If you can't find cranberry gelatin, raspberry or other red-colored varieties work, too.

- 2 cups orange juice, *divided*
- 1 cup water
- 2 packages (3 ounces *each*) cranberry gelatin
- 1 can (16 ounces) whole-berry cranberry sauce
- 1 can (15-1/4 ounces) sliced peaches, drained
- 3 cups cubed cooked chicken
- 2 celery ribs, chopped
- 1/2 cup mayonnaise
- 1 tablespoon cider vinegar
- 1/2 teaspoon salt
- 1/8 teaspoon pepper

Lettuce leaves

- 1/4 cup coarsely chopped pecans

1 In a small saucepan, bring 1 cup orange juice and water to a boil. Place gelatin in a large bowl; add juice mixture and stir until dissolved. Stir in the remaining orange juice. Chill until partially set, about 1-1/2 hours.

2 Stir in the cranberry sauce. Pour into a 6-cup ring mold coated with cooking spray. Cover and refrigerate for 6 hours or overnight.

3 Set aside a few peach slices for garnish; cube the remaining peaches. In a large bowl, combine

the cubed peaches, chicken, celery, mayonnaise, vinegar, salt and pepper. Cover and refrigerate for 1 hour or until chilled.

4 Invert gelatin mold onto a serving plate; line center of ring with lettuce leaves. Stir pecans into chicken salad; spoon into center of gelatin. Top with reserved peach slices.

Yield: 10 servings.

APPLE-WALNUT TOSSED SALAD

mary walton, kelso, washington

The eye-catching cranberry dressing for this fall salad is also good for gift-giving.

- 1/4 cup red wine vinegar
- 1/4 cup fresh cranberries
- 2 tablespoons honey
- 1 tablespoon sugar
- 1 tablespoon chopped red onion
- 1/4 teaspoon salt
- 1/4 teaspoon pepper
- 3/4 cup canola oil
- 2 packages (5 ounces *each*) spring mix salad greens
- 3 medium Red Delicious apples, thinly sliced
- 1 cup chopped walnuts, toasted

1 For cranberry vinaigrette, combine the first seven ingredients in a blender; cover and process until blended. While processing, gradually add oil in a steady stream.

2 Transfer to a serving dish. In a large bowl, toss the salad greens, apples and walnuts. Serve with vinaigrette.

Yield: 8 servings.

COLD PLUM SOUP

carol klein, franklin square, new york

When my husband and I were first married, we dined at an inn that served a flavorful plum soup. After experimenting with different recipes, I came up with my own wonderful version!

- 2 cans (15 ounces *each*) plums
- 1 cup water
- 1/2 cup sugar, *divided*
- 1 cinnamon stick (3 inches)
- 1/4 teaspoon white pepper

Dash salt

- 1 tablespoon cornstarch
- 1/2 cup heavy whipping cream
- 1/2 cup dry red wine *or* grape juice
- 1 cup (8 ounces) sour cream
- 1/3 cup creme de cassis *or* cranberry-raspberry juice
- 2 tablespoons lemon juice
- 1 teaspoon grated lemon peel

Sour cream, optional

1 Drain plums, reserving juice. Pit plums; puree in a blender with juice. Transfer to a Dutch oven. Stir in the water, 1/4 cup sugar, cinnamon stick, pepper and salt. Bring to a boil. Reduce heat; cover and simmer for 10 minutes.

2 In a small bowl, combine cornstarch and remaining sugar; stir in cream and wine or grape

juice until smooth. Gradually add to plum mixture until blended. Bring to a boil; cook and stir for 2 minutes or until thickened, stirring constantly. Remove from the heat; discard cinnamon stick. Stir in the sour cream, creme de cassis or cranberry-raspberry juice and lemon juice.

3 Strain half of the soup through a fine mesh strainer over a 1-1/2-qt. bowl. Repeat. Stir in lemon peel. Cover and refrigerate overnight. Garnish with sour cream if desired.

Yield: 13 servings (2-1/2 quarts).

APPLESAUCE-BERRY GELATIN MOLD

gloria coates, madison, connecticut

Want a head start on your holiday meal? Try this uncomplicated, yet pretty apple-berry mold. Fresh cranberries and mint leaves are a beautiful garnish.

- 2 packages (3 ounces *each*) strawberry gelatin
- 2 cups boiling water
- 1 can (16 ounces) whole-berry cranberry sauce
- 1-3/4 cups chunky applesauce

1 In a large bowl, dissolve gelatin in boiling water. Stir in cranberry sauce and applesauce. Pour into a 6-cup ring mold coated with cooking spray. Cover and refrigerate overnight. Unmold onto a serving platter.

Yield: 12 servings.

Freeze Lemons & Limes

Whenever lemons and limes are on sale, I throw a bag of each in the freezer. Later, when I need fresh lemon or lime juice, I just defrost a single lemon or lime in the microwave.—Joan F., Turah, Montana

APPLE WALNUT SLAW

joan halford, north richland hills, texas
A co-worker shared this recipe with me. Now it's a family favorite. Apples, walnuts and raisins are a fun way to dress up coleslaw.

6	cups shredded cabbage
1-1/2	cups shredded carrot
1	cup coarsely chopped walnuts, toasted
3/4	cup raisins
1/3	cup finely chopped red onion
3/4	cup mayonnaise
3/4	cup buttermilk
4 to 5	tablespoons sugar
4-1/2	teaspoons lemon juice
3/4	teaspoon salt
1/4 to 1/2	teaspoon pepper
2	medium apples, chopped

1 In a large salad bowl, toss the cabbage, carrots, walnuts, raisins and onion. In a small bowl, combine the mayonnaise, buttermilk, sugar, lemon juice, salt and pepper. Pour over cabbage mixture and toss to coat. Gently fold in apples. Cover and refrigerate until serving.

Yield: 12 servings.

COLORFUL CAESAR SALAD

taste of home test kitchen
We guarantee you'll enjoy this take on this classic salad. The dressing can be prepared up to three days in advance.

12	cups torn romaine
3	medium tomatoes, cut into wedges
1	medium cucumber, halved and sliced
3	hard-cooked eggs
6	anchovy fillets
1/4	cup red wine vinegar
2	tablespoons lemon juice
2	tablespoons Dijon mustard
1	tablespoon Worcestershire sauce
4	garlic cloves, minced
1	teaspoon sugar
1/2	teaspoon pepper
3/4	cup olive oil
1-1/2	cups Caesar salad croutons
3/4	cup shredded Parmesan cheese

1 In a large salad bowl, combine the romaine, tomatoes and cucumber. Slice eggs in half; remove yolks. (Refrigerate whites for another use.) In a blender, combine the anchovies, vinegar, lemon juice, mustard, Worcestershire sauce, garlic, sugar, pepper and egg yolks; cover and process until smooth. While processing, gradually add oil in a steady stream.

2 Drizzle desired amount of dressing over salad and toss to coat. Sprinkle with croutons and Parmesan cheese. Serve immediately. Refrigerate any leftover dressing for up to 3 days.

Yield: 12 servings.

CREAM OF BUTTERNUT SOUP

shelly snyder, lafayette, colorado

Ginger, turmeric, cinnamon and a little sherry do an incredible job of seasoning this slightly sweet soup. After I lightened up a recipe from a friend in South Africa, it quickly became a most-requested recipe.

- 1 cup chopped onion
- 2 celery ribs, chopped
- 2 tablespoons butter
- 2 cans (14-1/2 ounces *each*) reduced-sodium chicken broth
- 1 teaspoon sugar
- 1 bay leaf
- 1/2 teaspoon salt
- 1/2 teaspoon ground ginger
- 1/2 teaspoon ground turmeric
- 1/4 teaspoon ground cinnamon
- 1 butternut squash (2-1/2 pounds), peeled and cubed
- 3 medium potatoes, peeled and cubed
- 1-1/2 cups 1% milk
- 2 tablespoons sherry *or* additional reduced-sodium chicken broth

1 In a large saucepan coated with cooking spray, cook onion and celery in butter until tender. Stir in the broth, sugar, bay leaf, salt, ginger, turmeric and cinnamon. Add the squash and potatoes. Bring to a boil. Reduce heat; cover and simmer for 15-20 minutes or until vegetables are tender.

2 Remove from the heat; cool slightly. Discard bay leaf. In a blender, puree vegetable mixture in batches. Return to the pan. Stir in milk and sherry or broth; heat through (do not boil).

Yield: 8 servings.

BAKED GERMAN POTATO SALAD

julie myers, lexington, ohio

What makes this German potato salad so different is that it's sweet instead of tangy. During the holidays, my family has an annual ham dinner, and I always prepare it. The tastes blend very well. The first time I took my potato salad to work, people kept coming out of their offices to find out what smelled so good. By lunch, it was gone. Now, I make a double batch to take to work!

- 12 medium red potatoes (about 3 pounds)
- 8 bacon strips
- 2 medium onions, chopped
- 3/4 cup packed brown sugar
- 2/3 cup water, *divided*
- 1/3 cup white vinegar
- 1/3 cup sweet pickle juice
- 2 teaspoons dried parsley flakes
- 1 teaspoon salt
- 1/2 to 3/4 teaspoon celery seed
- 4-1/2 teaspoons all-purpose flour

1 In a saucepan, cook potatoes until just tender; drain. Peel and slice into an ungreased 2-qt. baking dish.

2 In a skillet, cook bacon until crisp; drain, reserving 2 tablespoons drippings. Crumble bacon and set aside. Saute onions in drippings until tender. Stir in brown sugar, 1/2 cup water, vinegar, pickle juice, parsley, salt and celery seed. Simmer, uncovered, for 5-10 minutes.

3 Meanwhile, combine flour and remaining water until smooth; stir into onion mixture. Bring to a boil. Cook and stir for 2 minutes or until thickened. Pour over potatoes. Add bacon; gently stir to coat. Bake, uncovered, at 350° for 30 minutes or until heated through.

Yield: 8-10 servings.

LAYERED VEGGIE TORTELLINI SALAD

dennis vitale, new preston, connecticut

When you're finished writing Christmas cards, dig into this layered pasta salad. With a cheesy dressing, it's the perfect accompaniment to any main dish.

- 1 package (16 ounces) frozen cheese tortellini
- 2 cups fresh broccoli florets
- 2 cups cherry tomatoes, quartered
- 2 celery ribs, finely chopped
- 1 can (2-1/4 ounces) sliced ripe olives, drained
- 1 cup (4 ounces) shredded cheddar cheese

PARMESAN DRESSING:
- 3/4 cup mayonnaise
- 3 tablespoons grated Parmesan cheese
- 2 tablespoons lemon juice
- 2 tablespoons heavy whipping cream
- 1 teaspoon dried thyme

1 Cook tortellini according to package directions; drain and rinse in cold water. In a large 2-1/2-qt. glass salad bowl, layer the tortellini, broccoli, tomatoes, celery, olives and cheese.

2 In a small bowl, combine the dressing ingredients; spoon over salad. Cover and refrigerate until serving.

Yield: 10 servings.

CURRIED SWEET POTATO CHOWDER

kara de la vega, santa rosa, california

The flavor of curry is subtle in this creamy, comforting chowder. For fun, I sometimes sprinkle individual servings with pumpkin or sunflower kernels.

- 3 cups cubed peeled sweet potatoes
- 2/3 cup finely chopped green onions
- 4 teaspoons butter
- 2 tablespoons all-purpose flour
- 1 teaspoon curry powder
- 1 teaspoon salt
- 1/4 teaspoon pepper
- 3 cups milk
- 2 cups frozen peas, thawed
- 1 cup half-and-half cream

1 Place 2 in. of water in a large saucepan; add sweet potatoes. Bring to a boil. Reduce heat; cover and simmer for 7-9 minutes or until tender. Drain and set aside.

2 In a skillet, saute onions in butter until tender. In another large saucepan, combine the flour, curry powder, salt and pepper. Gradually stir in the milk until smooth. Add the sweet potatoes and onions. Bring to a boil; cook and stir for 2 minutes or until thickened. Stir in peas and cream; heat through (do not boil).

Yield: 6 servings.

FANCY FROZEN FRUIT CUPS

alynce wyman, pembina, north dakota

In the summer, I make a big batch of these delicious, slushy fruit cups and store them in the freezer. They make great snacks and are wonderful to have on hand when friends stop by. We also like them with blueberries, raspberries, muskmelon and cherries.

- 2 cups water
- 3/4 cup sugar
- 3/4 cup orange juice concentrate
- 3/4 cup lemonade concentrate
- 1 can (20 ounces) pineapple tidbits, drained
- 2 medium firm bananas, cut into 1/2-inch slices
- 1-1/2 cups watermelon chunks
- 1-1/2 cups green grapes
- 1-1/2 cups quartered strawberries
- 1-1/2 cups cubed peaches
- 2 kiwifruit, peeled, quartered and sliced

1. In a small saucepan, bring water and sugar to a boil, stirring constantly. Remove from the heat; stir in orange juice and lemonade concentrates. In a large bowl, combine the pineapple, bananas, watermelon, grapes, strawberries and peaches. Add juice mixture and mix well.

2. Place about 1/2 cup fruit mixture in 5-oz. disposable plastic wine glasses with removable bottoms or 5-oz. disposable cups. Top each with four kiwi pieces. Cover and freeze until firm. May be frozen for up to 1 month. Remove from the freezer about 1-3/4 hours before serving.

Yield: 18 servings.

CITRUS AVOCADO SALAD

sonia candler, edmonton, alberta

This recipe nicely showcases grapefruit and oranges, which are at their peak around the holidays. Citrus fruits pair well with a sweet dressing.

- 12 cups torn salad greens
- 2 medium grapefruit, peeled and sectioned
- 2 medium navel oranges, peeled and sectioned
- 2 medium ripe avocados, peeled and sliced
- 1 small red onion, thinly sliced and separated into rings

DRESSING:
- 1/2 cup canola oil
- 1/4 cup sugar
- 3 tablespoons lemon juice
- 1-1/2 teaspoons poppy seeds
- 1/2 teaspoon salt
- 1/4 teaspoon ground mustard
- 1/4 teaspoon grated onion

1. In a large salad bowl, gently toss the greens, grapefruit, oranges, avocados and red onion. In a jar with a tight-fitting lid, combine the dressing ingredients; shake well. Drizzle over salad and toss to coat.

Yield: 12 servings.

HOLIDAY GELATIN MOLD

bonnie bredenberg, bemidji, minnesota
No matter where I take this attractive salad, I'm asked to share the recipe. With its red and green layers, it dresses up any holiday buffet. I'm a retired teacher who loves to cook—especially dishes I can make ahead, like this one.

> 1 can (8 ounces) sliced pineapple
> 1 package (3 ounces) lime gelatin
> 4 cups boiling water, *divided*
> 2 tablespoons lemon juice
> 1 package (3 ounces) lemon gelatin
> 2 packages (3 ounces *each*) cream cheese, softened
> 1/3 cup mayonnaise
> 1 package (3 ounces) raspberry gelatin
> 2 medium firm bananas

1 Drain pineapple, reserving juice. In a bowl, dissolve lime gelatin in 1 cup boiling water. Combine the pineapple juice, lemon juice and enough cold water to measure 1 cup; add to dissolved gelatin. Cut pineapple slices in half; arrange on the bottom of a 12-cup ring mold coated with cooking spray.

2 Pour a small amount of lime gelatin over the pineapple; refrigerate until set. Add remaining lime gelatin; refrigerate until firm. In a small bowl, dissolve lemon gelatin in 1 cup boiling water. Refrigerate until partially set. Beat until light and fluffy.

3 In another small bowl, beat cream cheese until fluffy. Stir in the mayonnaise. Fold in whipped gelatin; pour over lime layer. Refrigerate until firm.

4 Dissolve raspberry gelatin in remaining boiling water. Slice bananas; place over lemon layer. Carefully spoon the raspberry gelatin over bananas. Refrigerate until firm or overnight.

Yield: 16 servings.

ABC SALAD

joan sharp, el paso, texas
Apples, broccoli and dried cranberries combine in this fresh-tasting salad that's especially good for fall and winter. I came up with the recipe after tasting something similar at a restaurant buffet.

> 1/2 cup canola oil
> 3 tablespoons lemon juice, *divided*
> 1 teaspoon sugar
> 1/4 teaspoon salt
> 1 cup dried cranberries
> 3 large red apples, cut into 1/2-inch cubes
> 2 cups fresh broccoli florets
> 1/2 cup chopped walnuts

1 In a bowl, whisk the oil, 2 tablespoons lemon juice, sugar and salt. Add cranberries; let stand for 10 minutes. In a large bowl, toss apples with remaining lemon juice. Add the broccoli, walnuts and cranberry mixture; toss to coat. Cover and refrigerate for 2 hours or until chilled. Toss before serving.

Yield: 6-8 servings.

RASPBERRY TOSSED SALAD

kerry sullivan, longwood, florida
Red raspberries brighten this tossed green salad, making it the perfect ingredient for a festive Yuletide menu. Raspberry juice brings a special touch to the light oil and vinegar dressing.

- 9 cups torn mixed salad greens
- 3 cups fresh *or* frozen unsweetened raspberries
- 2 tablespoons olive oil
- 2 tablespoons cider vinegar
- 4 teaspoons sugar
- 1/8 teaspoon salt

Dash pepper

1 In a large salad bowl, gently combine the salad greens and 2-3/4 cups raspberries. Mash the remaining berries; strain, reserving juice and discarding seeds. In a small bowl, whisk the raspberry juice, oil, vinegar, sugar, salt and pepper. Drizzle over salad; gently toss to coat.

Yield: 12 servings.

SWISS-TOPPED CAULIFLOWER SOUP

c.c. mckie, chicago, illinois
Since I came across this recipe a few years ago, it's become my husband's favorite soup. With fresh bread, we enjoy this as a hearty supper in winter.

- 2 medium onions
- 4 whole cloves
- 4 cups water
- 2 cans (10-1/2 ounces *each*) condensed chicken broth, undiluted *or* 2 cans (14-1/2 ounces) vegetable broth
- 3 medium leeks (white portion only), sliced
- 3 medium carrots, sliced
- 1 teaspoon salt
- 1 teaspoon dried marjoram
- 1/2 teaspoon celery seed
- 1/2 teaspoon ground nutmeg
- 1/4 teaspoon white pepper
- 1 medium head cauliflower, broken into florets and thinly sliced (about 6 cups)
- 1 tablespoon cornstarch
- 1/2 cup heavy whipping cream
- 2 egg yolks, beaten
- 1/2 pound sliced Swiss cheese, cut into 4-inch x 1/2-inch strips

1 Quarter one onion; stuff the cloves into the second onion. In a large saucepan, combine water and broth; add onions, leeks, carrots and seasonings. Bring to a boil. Reduce heat; cover and simmer for 15 minutes. Add cauliflower; simmer, uncovered, for 30 minutes or until vegetables are tender. Remove from the heat.

2 In a small bowl, combine cornstarch and cream until smooth. Stir in egg yolks. Stir in a small amount of hot soup into cream mixture; return all to the pan, stirring constantly. Simmer, uncovered, for 15 minutes. Discard the whole onion.

3 Ladle soup into individual ramekins. Top with cheese strips. Broil 4-6 in. from the heat for 3-5 minutes or until cheese is bubbly. Serve immediately.

Yield: 6-8 servings.

CRANBERRY CHICKEN SALAD

debbie emrick, dundee, michigan

Tart apples and dried cranberries make this chicken salad special. It's especially nice served at luncheons, and it uses lighter ingredients, too.

- 2 teaspoons paprika
- 1 teaspoon onion powder
- 1/2 teaspoon salt
- 1-1/4 pounds boneless skinless chicken breasts
- 1/3 cup reduced-fat mayonnaise
- 2 tablespoons lemon juice
- 2 medium tart green apples, chopped
- 1 cup dried cranberries
- 1 small onion, chopped

Lettuce leaves

1 In a small bowl, combine the paprika, onion powder and salt; rub over chicken. If grilling the chicken, coat grill rack with cooking spray before starting the grill. Grill chicken, uncovered, over medium heat or broil 4 in. from the heat for 3 to 4-1/2 minutes on each side or until juices run clear. When cool enough to handle, cut chicken into cubes.

2 In a large bowl, whisk mayonnaise and lemon juice until smooth. Stir in the chicken, apples, cranberries and onion. Serve on lettuce-lined plates.

Yield: 6 servings.

CREAMY LEEK SOUP WITH BRIE

taste of home test kitchen

Bits of brie add something special to this soup from our home economists. Soup is a satisfying addition to a buffet table. Use a slow cooker to keep it warm.

- 5 cups chopped leeks (white portion only)
- 1/4 cup butter
- 5 cups chicken broth
- 4-1/2 cups half-and-half cream, *divided*
- 1/2 cup all-purpose flour
- 1 teaspoon salt
- 1/4 teaspoon white pepper
- 3 packages (8 ounces *each*) Brie or Camembert cheese, rind removed
- 3 tablespoons snipped chives

1 In a soup kettle, saute leeks in butter until tender. Add broth; bring to a boil. Reduce heat; cover and simmer for 25 minutes.

2 Strain, reserving broth in pan. Place leeks in a blender with 1/2 cup of the broth; cover and process until smooth.

3 Return to the pan. Stir in 3 cups cream. Combine the flour, salt, pepper and remaining cream until smooth; stir into soup. Bring to a boil; cook and stir for 2 minutes. Reduce heat to medium.

4 Cut Brie into small pieces; add to soup in batches, stirring until most of the cheese is melted. Garnish with chives.

Yield: 12 servings (2-1/2 quarts).

HOLIDAY RIBBON GELATIN

enny hughson, mitchell, nebraska

Layers of red and green make this festive salad a favorite during the Christmas season. Kids are sure to find it fun to eat, and adults will enjoy the combination of sweet-tart flavors.

- 2 packages (3 ounces *each*) lime gelatin
- 5 cups boiling water, *divided*
- 4 cups cold water, *divided*
- 1 package (3 ounces) lemon gelatin
- 1/2 cup miniature marshmallows
- 1 package (8 ounces) cream cheese, softened
- 1 cup mayonnaise
- 1 can (8 ounces) crushed pineapple, undrained
- 2 packages (3 ounces *each*) cherry gelatin

1 In a bowl, dissolve lime gelatin in 2 cups boiling water. Add 2 cups cold water; stir. Pour into a 13-in. x 9-in. x 2-in. dish; refrigerate until set, about 1 hour.

2 In a bowl, dissolve lemon gelatin in 1 cup boiling water. Stir in marshmallows until melted. Cool for 20 minutes. In a small mixing bowl, beat cream cheese and mayonnaise until smooth. Gradually beat in lemon gelatin. Stir in pineapple. Carefully spoon over the lime layer. Chill until set.

3 Dissolve cherry gelatin in 2 cups boiling water. Add the remaining cold water; stir. Spoon over the lemon layer. Refrigerate overnight. Cut into squares.

Yield: 12-15 servings.

HOLIDAY TOSSED SALAD

pat loeffler, grafton, wisconsin

With its colorful ingredients, this salad is perfect for Christmas meals. Local cranberries and blue cheese make a great combination with salad greens, apples, walnuts and a simple cranberry vinaigrette. It's a family favorite.

- 8 cups torn mixed salad greens
- 2 medium red apples, diced
- 1/2 cup crumbled blue cheese
- 1/3 cup dried cranberries
- 1/3 cup coarsely chopped walnuts, toasted
- 1/4 cup sliced green onions
- 2 tablespoons olive oil
- 2 tablespoons cranberry juice concentrate
- 1 tablespoon white wine vinegar

Dash salt and pepper

1 In a large salad bowl, combine the greens, apples, blue cheese, cranberries, walnuts and onions. In a small bowl, whisk the remaining ingredients. Drizzle over salad and toss gently to coat. Serve immediately.

Yield: 6-8 servings.

surface with plastic wrap; cool for 30 minutes without stirring. Fold in yogurt. Cover and refrigerate for at least 2 hours.

3 Place orange cream in a serving bowl. Place in the center of a 13-in. serving platter. Line platter with romaine leaves; tear remaining romaine and place over leaves. Top the lettuce with grapefruit and orange sections. Sprinkle the pears and avocado with lemon juice; arrange over the fruit. Garnish with walnuts.

Yield: 8-10 servings.

OYSTER CORN CHOWDER

lewy olfson, madison, wisconsin
Chock-full of mushrooms, corn and oysters, this robust soup comes together quickly with a can of cream-style corn and a little half-and-half cream.

- 2 cans (8 ounces *each*) whole oysters, undrained
- 1 can (14-3/4 ounces) cream-style corn
- 1 cup half-and-half cream
- 2 cans (4 ounces *each*) mushroom stems and pieces, drained
- 2 tablespoons butter
- 1/4 teaspoon Worcestershire sauce
- 1/8 teaspoon pepper

1 In a large saucepan, combine all ingredients. Cook, uncovered, over medium-low heat until heated through (do not boil), stirring occasionally.

Yield: 4 servings.

WINTER SALAD WITH ORANGE CREAM

jeanne spina, clearwater, florida
This easy-to-make salad has great eye-appeal, and the dressing can be prepared a day ahead for convenience. It's especially festive-looking with red grapefruit and red pears.

- 1/2 cup sugar
- 1 tablespoon cornstarch
- 1/4 teaspoon salt
- 1 cup orange juice
- 1 teaspoon grated orange peel
- 2 eggs, lightly beaten
- 1 carton (8 ounces) plain yogurt
- 1 small bunch romaine
- 2 medium grapefruit, peeled and sectioned
- 2 medium navel oranges, peeled and sectioned
- 2 medium pears, cut into thin wedges
- 2 medium ripe avocados, peeled and thinly sliced
- 1 tablespoon lemon juice
- 1/3 cup chopped walnuts, toasted

1 In a small saucepan, combine the sugar, cornstarch and salt. Stir in orange juice and peel until blended. Cook and stir over medium-high heat until thickened and bubbly. Reduce heat; cook and stir 2 minutes longer.

2 Remove from the heat. Stir a small amount of hot mixture into eggs. Return all to the pan, stirring constantly. Bring to a gentle boil; cook and stir 2 minutes longer. Remove from the heat. Cover

RED PEPPER CARROT SOUP

anna hartle, loveland, ohio

This colorful soup is a tasty way to have a serving of vegetables without a lot of fat. Even my discerning teenagers lap it up happily.

      1   medium sweet red pepper
      1   pound carrots, sliced
      1   medium onion, chopped
      2   tablespoons uncooked long grain rice
      2   tablespoons butter
      2   cans (14-1/2 ounces *each*) chicken broth
      2   cups water
    1/3   cup orange juice
  4-1/2   teaspoons snipped fresh dill
      2   teaspoons grated orange peel
    1/2   teaspoon salt
    1/2   teaspoon *each* dried marjoram, thyme
            and rosemary, crushed
    1/2   teaspoon rubbed sage
    1/4   teaspoon pepper

1   Broil red pepper 4 in. from the heat until skin is blistered, about 6 minutes. With tongs, rotate pepper a quarter turn. Broil and rotate until all sides are blistered and blackened. Immediately place pepper in a bowl; cover and let stand for 15-20 minutes. Peel and discard charred skin. Remove stem and seeds; set pepper aside.

2   In a large saucepan, cook the carrots, onion and rice in butter until onion is tender. Stir in the broth, water, orange juice, dill, orange peel, salt, marjoram, thyme, rosemary, sage and pepper. Bring to a boil. Reduce heat; cover and simmer for 20-25 minutes or until carrots and rice are tender. Cool for 10 minutes.

3   In a blender, puree carrot mixture and roasted pepper in small batches. Return to the pan; heat through.

Yield: 4 servings.

SPECIAL SPINACH SALAD

laurene hunsicker, canton, pennsylvania

I always get compliments when I serve this refreshing salad during the holidays. The creamy dressing is perfect with the colorful cranberries and crunchy nuts.

    1/3   cup olive oil
      3   tablespoons sugar
      2   tablespoons white wine vinegar
      2   tablespoons sour cream
    1/2   teaspoon ground mustard
      1   package (6 ounces) fresh baby spinach
    1/2   cup chopped walnuts, toasted
    1/2   cup dried cranberries

1   In a jar with a tight-fitting lid, combine the oil, sugar, vinegar, sour cream and mustard; shake well. Divide spinach among four salad plates; drizzle with dressing. Sprinkle with walnuts and cranberries.

Yield: 4 servings.

RASPBERRY SPINACH SALAD

lauri mills, mississauga, ontario

Sugared almonds provide fun crunch in this slightly sweet spinach salad. You can easily double the recipe when entertaining a larger group.

- 2-1/4 teaspoons sugar
- 2 tablespoons slivered almonds
- 5 cups fresh baby spinach
- 1/2 cup fresh raspberries

DRESSING:

- 2 tablespoons canola oil
- 1 tablespoon raspberry vinegar
- 1 tablespoon sugar
- 3/4 teaspoon poppy seeds
- 1/2 teaspoon finely chopped onion
- 1/4 teaspoon Worcestershire sauce

Dash paprika

1 In a small heavy skillet, melt sugar over medium heat, stirring constantly. Add almonds; stir to coat. Spread on foil to cool; break apart. In a salad bowl, gently toss the spinach and raspberries.

2 In a jar with a tight-fitting lid, combine the dressing ingredients; shake well. Pour over salad. Sprinkle with sugared almonds; toss to coat.

Yield: 4 servings.

WINTERTIME BEEF SOUP

carol tupper, joplin, missouri

Kidney beans, ground beef, green pepper and chopped cabbage make this thick soup hearty and satisfying.

- 1 pound lean ground beef
- 4 celery ribs, coarsely chopped
- 1 medium onion, coarsely chopped
- 1 medium green pepper, coarsely chopped
- 1 garlic clove, minced
- 2 cups water
- 2 cups reduced-sodium tomato juice
- 1 can (14-1/2 ounces) diced tomatoes, undrained
- 1 can (8 ounces) tomato sauce
- 2 teaspoons reduced-sodium beef bouillon granules
- 2 teaspoons chili powder
- 1/2 teaspoon salt
- 2 cans (16 ounces *each*) kidney beans, rinsed and drained
- 2 cups coarsely chopped cabbage

1 In a large saucepan or Dutch oven, cook the beef, celery, onion, green pepper and garlic over medium heat until meat is no longer pink; drain. Stir in the water, tomato juice, tomatoes, tomato sauce, bouillon, chili powder and salt. Bring to a boil. Reduce heat; cover and simmer for 30 minutes.

2 Stir in kidney beans; return to a boil. Stir in cabbage. Reduce heat; cover and cook 12 minutes longer or until cabbage is tender.

Yield: 8 servings.

ONION BEET SALAD

barbara van lanen, salinas, california

Everyone loves the tangy dressing on these baked beets. I'm always asked to bring this pretty dish to family gatherings.

- 12 whole fresh beets (about 2-1/2 pounds), peeled and halved
- 5 tablespoons olive oil, *divided*
- 1 large red onion, chopped
- 1/2 cup balsamic vinegar
- 1/3 cup red wine vinegar
- 1/4 cup sugar
- 1 teaspoon salt
- 1 teaspoon dried basil
- 1/2 teaspoon pepper

1 Place the beets in a large resealable plastic bag; add 2 tablespoons oil. Seal bag and shake to coat. Place an 18-in. x 12-in. piece of heavy-duty foil in a 15-in. x 10-in. x 1-in. baking pan. Arrange beets on foil; fold foil over beets and seal tightly. Bake at 400° for 1 to 1-1/4 hours or until tender.

2 Cool to room temperature. Cut beets into cubes; place in a large bowl. Add the onion. In a small bowl, whisk vinegars, sugar, salt, basil, pepper and remaining oil.

3 Pour over beet mixture; gently toss to coat. Cover and refrigerate for at least 1 hour, stirring several times. Serve with a slotted spoon.

Yield: 9 servings.

FRUIT COMPOTE

dorothy diehl carnine, angora, nebraska

Whether you prepare this fruit dish for brunch, offer it as an appetizer or top it with a dollop of whipped cream for a light dessert, your guests will be happy. It's brimming with color and flavor and is especially welcoming during the winter.

- 1 can (20 ounces) unsweetened pineapple tidbits
- 1 can (11 ounces) mandarin oranges
- 2 tablespoons quick-cooking tapioca
- 1/4 cup orange juice concentrate
- 1-1/2 cups seedless red grapes, halved
- 1 package (10 ounces) frozen unsweetened sliced peaches
- 1-1/2 cups fresh *or* frozen raspberries
- 1 medium firm banana, sliced

1 Drain pineapple and oranges, reserving juice; set fruit aside. In a large microwave-safe bowl, combine tapioca and reserved juices; let stand for 5 minutes. Microwave, uncovered, on high for 2-3 minutes or until clear and thickened, stirring several times. Stir in orange juice concentrate.

2 In a large bowl, combine the pineapple, oranges, grapes and peaches. Add tapioca mixture; toss to coat. Cover and refrigerate overnight. Just before serving, stir in the raspberries and banana.

Yield: 12 servings.

Editor's Note: This recipe was tested in a 1,100-watt microwave.

CREAMY CRANBERRY SALAD

alexandra lypecky, dearborn, michigan

One of my piano students shared this recipe with me many years ago. She told me it's the perfect salad for the holidays, and she was right.

> 3 cups fresh *or* frozen cranberries, thawed and coarsely chopped
> 1 can (20 ounces) unsweetened crushed pineapple, drained
> 2 cups miniature marshmallows
> 1 medium apple, chopped
> 2/3 cup sugar
> 1/8 teaspoon salt
> 2 cups heavy whipping cream
> 1/4 cup chopped walnuts

1 In a large bowl, combine the cranberries, pineapple, marshmallows, apple, sugar and salt. Cover and refrigerate overnight.

2 Just before serving, in a large chilled bowl, beat cream until stiff peaks form. Fold cream and walnuts into the cranberry mixture.

Yield: 14 servings.

BLUE CHEESE SPINACH SALAD

grace sandvigen, rochester, new york

A simple dressing made of currant jelly and balsamic vinegar coats this colorful salad that's sprinkled with crunchy pine nuts. If you like blue cheese, you'll love this refreshing toss.

> 1/2 cup red currant jelly
> 3 tablespoons balsamic vinegar
> 6 cups fresh baby spinach
> 2 pints fresh strawberries, quartered
> 1 cup mandarin oranges, drained
> 1/2 medium red onion, thinly sliced
> 1/2 cup crumbled blue cheese
> 1/2 cup pine nuts, toasted

1 For dressing, heat jelly in a small saucepan over low heat, stirring until smooth. Remove from the heat; stir in vinegar.

2 In a large bowl, combine the spinach, strawberries, oranges, onion and blue cheese. Drizzle with dressing and toss to coat. Sprinkle with pine nuts.

Yield: 12 servings.

MUSHROOM TOMATO BISQUE

connie stevens, schaefferstown, pennsylvania
After tasting a similar soup in a restaurant, I tinkered around with a few recipes at home, and this was the result. It might seem complicated, but it's really not. And I love the blend of flavors.

- 1-1/2 pounds plum tomatoes, halved lengthwise
- 5 tablespoons olive oil, *divided*
- 2 garlic cloves, minced
- 1/2 teaspoon salt
- 1/2 teaspoon *each* dried basil and dried oregano
- 1/2 teaspoon pepper
- 1/2 pound sliced fresh mushrooms
- 1/2 cup finely chopped sweet onion
- 1-1/4 cups chicken broth
- 1/3 to 1/2 cup tomato paste

Pinch sugar, optional

- 3/4 cup heavy whipping cream
- 2 tablespoons grated Parmesan cheese

1 Place tomatoes cut side down in a greased 15-in. x 10-in. x 1-in. baking pan. Brush with 3 tablespoons oil. Combine garlic, salt, basil, oregano and pepper; sprinkle over tomatoes. Bake, uncovered, at 450° for 20-25 minutes or until edges are well browned.

2 Cool slightly. Place tomatoes and pan drippings in a blender. Cover and process until blended; process 1 minute longer.

3 In a large saucepan, saute mushrooms and onion in remaining oil for 5-8 minutes or until tender. Stir in broth, tomato paste, sugar if desired and tomato puree. Bring to a boil. Remove from heat; stir in cream. Garnish with Parmesan cheese.

Yield: 4 servings.

AUTUMN FRUIT SALAD

kathryn booher, laguna hills, california
I've made this recipe for special dinners for years, and it's always been a hit. It's especially delicious when the apples are freshly picked, and it adds wonderful color to any table!

- 1-1/2 cups sugar
- 1/2 cup all-purpose flour
- 1-1/2 cups water
- 1 teaspoon butter
- 1 teaspoon vanilla extract
- 6 cups cubed unpeeled apples
- 2 cups halved red seedless grapes
- 1 cup diced celery
- 1 cup walnut halves

1 In a large saucepan, combine sugar and flour. Stir in water; bring to a boil. Cook and boil until mixture thickens. Remove from the heat; stir in butter and vanilla. Cool to room temperature.

2 In a large bowl, combine the apples, grapes, celery and walnuts. Add the dressing and toss gently. Refrigerate until serving.

Yield: 8-10 servings.

WINTER SALAD

lynn ganser, oakland, california

Everyone loves the interesting textures and tastes of the combination of pears, walnuts, greens and Gorgonzola cheese. It makes good use of ingredients grown here in California, and it's nice for winter when other fruits aren't readily available.

        1   garlic clove, peeled and halved
        2   tablespoons lemon juice
        2   tablespoons honey
      1/8   teaspoon salt
        2   medium ripe pears, thinly sliced
        8   cups torn mixed salad greens
      1/2   cup chopped walnuts, toasted
      1/3   cup crumbled Gorgonzola cheese

1   Rub garlic clove over the bottom and sides of a large salad bowl; discard garlic. In the bowl, combine the lemon juice, honey and salt. Add pears; gently toss to coat. Add the greens, walnuts and cheese; toss to coat.

Yield: 6 servings.

GARLIC SOUP

iola egle, bella vista, arkansas

While this soup simmers, the great garlicky aroma will fill your kitchen! We love the toasted garlic bread floating on top of every rich bowlful. It would be a terrific first course for most any meal.

        6   garlic cloves, minced
        1   tablespoon olive oil
        8   cups chicken broth
      1/2   teaspoon salt
      1/8   teaspoon pepper
      1/8   teaspoon dried thyme
      1/8   teaspoon dried rosemary, crushed
        3   egg yolks
      1/2   cup half-and-half cream
        8   slices frozen garlic bread, thawed and toasted

Grated Parmesan cheese

1   In a large saucepan, cook and stir the garlic in oil over low heat for 5 minutes or until lightly browned. Add the broth, salt, pepper, thyme and rosemary; simmer, uncovered, for 1 hour.

2   Strain broth and return to the pan. In a small bowl, whisk egg yolks and cream. Stir in 1/2 cup hot broth. Return all to the pan, stirring constantly. Cook and stir over medium heat until soup reaches 160° (do not boil). Top each serving with a slice of garlic bread; sprinkle with Parmesan cheese.

Yield: 8 servings.

TOMATOES WITH FETA CHEESE

ruth lee, troy, ontario

This combination makes an easy and colorful salad for any time of year. I prepare this no-fuss dish at least once a month, and my family loves it. It's a great way to use up fresh summer tomatoes, and it adds zip to winter tomatoes, too.

- 8 slices tomato
- 2 tablespoons crumbled feta cheese
- 1 tablespoon balsamic vinegar
- 2 tablespoons minced fresh basil

Pepper to taste

1 Arrange the tomato slices on a serving plate. Sprinkle with the feta cheese. Drizzle with the vinegar; sprinkle with basil and pepper.

Yield: 4 servings.

CREAMY CRANBERRY APPLE SALAD

ruth turpin, cincinnati, ohio

For more than 30 years, this recipe has been a holiday tradition in my family. With marshmallows, cranberries, crisp apples and red grapes, it's sweet-tart and has a comforting creaminess that appeals to all ages.

- 1 package (12 ounces) fresh *or* frozen cranberries, thawed
- 3 cups miniature marshmallows
- 1 cup sugar
- 2 medium apples, diced
- 1/2 cup halved seedless red grapes
- 1/2 cup chopped walnuts
- 1/4 teaspoon salt
- 1 carton (8 ounces) frozen whipped topping, thawed

1 Coarsely chop the cranberries; place in a large bowl. Stir in marshmallows and sugar. Cover and refrigerate for several hours or overnight.

2 Just before serving, stir in the apples, grapes, walnuts and salt. Fold in whipped topping.

Yield: 8-10 servings.

HOT FRUIT SALAD

barb vande voort, new sharon, iowa

This spicy fruit mixture is a breeze to make—just open the cans and empty them into the slow cooker. With its easy preparation and fantastic taste, this comforting side dish is ideal for celebrating any special occasion.

- 1 jar (25 ounces) chunky applesauce
- 1 can (21 ounces) cherry pie filling
- 1 can (20 ounces) pineapple chunks, undrained
- 1 can (15-1/4 ounces) sliced peaches, undrained
- 1 can (15-1/4 ounces) apricot halves, undrained
- 1 can (15 ounces) mandarin oranges, undrained
- 1/2 cup packed brown sugar
- 1 teaspoon ground cinnamon

1 Place the first six ingredients in a 5-qt. slow cooker and stir gently. Combine brown sugar and cinnamon; sprinkle over fruit mixture. Cover and cook on low for 3-4 hours.

Yield: 16 servings.

ANYTIME TURKEY CHILI

brad bailey, cary, north carolina

I created this dish to grab the voters' attention at a chili contest we held in our backyard. With pumpkin, brown sugar and cooked turkey, it's like an entire Thanksgiving dinner in one bowl.

- 2/3 cup chopped sweet onion
- 1/2 cup chopped green pepper
- 1-1/2 teaspoons dried oregano
- 2 garlic cloves, minced
- 1 teaspoon ground cumin
- 1 teaspoon olive oil
- 1 can (16 ounces) kidney beans, rinsed and drained
- 1 can (15-1/2 ounces) great northern beans, rinsed and drained
- 1 can (15 ounces) solid-pack pumpkin
- 1 can (15 ounces) crushed tomatoes
- 1 can (14-1/2 ounces) reduced-sodium chicken broth
- 1/2 cup water
- 2 tablespoons brown sugar
- 2 tablespoons chili powder
- 1/2 teaspoon pepper
- 3 cups cubed cooked turkey breast

1 In a large saucepan, saute the onion, green pepper, oregano, garlic and cumin in oil until vegetables are tender. Stir in the beans, pumpkin, tomatoes, broth, water, brown sugar, chili powder and pepper; bring to a boil. Reduce heat; cover and simmer for 1 hour. Add turkey; heat through.

Yield: 8 servings (2 quarts).

CHRISTMAS VEGETABLE SALAD

mary dean, eau claire, wisconsin

I received this recipe at a family gathering, and I have been making the colorful, crisp salad for get-togethers, dinner parties and potlucks ever since. It travels well and holds up beautifully on the buffet table.

- 1/4 cup canola oil
- 1 tablespoon plus 1-1/2 teaspoons lemon juice
- 1 tablespoon plus 1-1/2 teaspoons white wine vinegar
- 1 teaspoon salt
- 1/2 teaspoon sugar
- Coarsely ground pepper
- 2 cups thinly sliced cauliflower
- 1/2 cup sliced pimiento-stuffed olives
- 1/3 cup chopped green pepper
- 1/3 cup chopped red pepper

1 In a jar with a tight-fitting lid, combine the first six ingredients; shake well. In a medium salad bowl, combine the cauliflower, olives and peppers; drizzle with dressing and toss to coat. Cover and refrigerate for several hours or overnight.

Yield: 6-8 servings.

CRANBERRY SPINACH SALAD

garnet amari, fairfield, california

This recipe started out as a summer salad with raspberries. I came up with this holiday version when I was putting together the menu for my first Thanksgiving dinner. I sometimes serve it on individual salad plates instead of in a big bowl.

- 1 package (6 ounces) fresh baby spinach
- 1/2 to 3/4 cup chopped pecans, toasted
- 1/2 to 3/4 cup dried cranberries
- 1/3 cup olive oil
- 3 tablespoons sugar
- 2 tablespoons balsamic vinegar *or* red wine vinegar
- 1 tablespoon sour cream
- 1/2 teaspoon Dijon mustard

1 In a large bowl, combine the spinach, pecans and cranberries. In a jar with a tight-fitting lid, combine the remaining ingredients; shake well. Drizzle over salad and toss to coat.

Yield: 6-8 servings.

MARINATED CAULIFLOWER SALAD

stephanie hase, lyons, colorado

I often serve this alongside a meat and cheese tray, but it's also a perfect side dish. What's best is that you can make it ahead.

- 1/4 cup red wine vinegar
- 1/4 cup olive oil
- 2 tablespoons water
- 1 bay leaf
- 1 garlic clove, minced
- 1/4 teaspoon salt
- 1/4 teaspoon coarsely ground pepper
- 5 cups fresh cauliflowerets
- 1/2 cup shredded carrot
- 1/4 cup chopped red onion
- 1/4 cup minced fresh parsley
- 1/4 teaspoon dried basil

1. In a small saucepan, bring the vinegar, oil and water just to a boil. Meanwhile, place the bay leaf, garlic, salt, pepper and cauliflower in a large heat-proof bowl. Add hot oil mixture; toss to combine. Cover; refrigerate for at least 6 hours or overnight, stirring occasionally.

2. Add the carrot, onion, parsley and basil; toss to coat. Cover and refrigerate for 2 hours. Discard bay leaf. Serve with a slotted spoon.

Yield: 10-12 servings.

CRANBERRY FLUFF

lavonne hartel, williston, north dakota

This fluffy fruit salad gets its sweet-tart zing from cranberries and whipped cream. We like it because it's not as sweet as many other "fluffs." I'm often asked for the secret to this luscious, jewel-toned holiday salad.

- 4 cups fresh *or* frozen cranberries
- 3 cups miniature marshmallows
- 3/4 cup sugar
- 2 cups diced unpeeled tart apples
- 1/2 cup halved green grapes
- 1/2 cup chopped nuts
- 1/4 teaspoon salt
- 1 cup heavy whipping cream, whipped

1. Place cranberries in a food processor; cover and process until finely chopped. Transfer to a large bowl; add marshmallows and sugar. Cover and refrigerate for 4 hours or overnight.

2. Just before serving, stir in the apples, grapes, nuts and salt. Fold in whipped cream.

Yield: 10-12 servings.

CHEDDAR HAM SOUP

marty matthews, clarksville, tennessee

I knew this recipe was a keeper when my mother-in-law asked for it! The hearty soup, chock-full of leftover ham, veggies and cheese, is creamy and comforting. And even though the recipe makes enough to feed a crowd of post-holiday guests, don't look for leftovers!

    2   cups diced peeled potatoes
    2   cups water
  1/2   cup sliced carrot
  1/4   cup chopped onion
  1/4   cup butter, cubed
  1/4   cup all-purpose flour
    2   cups milk
  1/4   to 1/2 teaspoon salt
  1/4   teaspoon pepper
    2   cups (8 ounces) shredded cheddar cheese
1-1/2   cups cubed fully cooked ham
    1   cup frozen peas, thawed

1   In a large saucepan, combine the potatoes, water, carrot and onion. Bring to a boil. Reduce heat; cover and cook for 10-15 minutes or until tender.

2   Meanwhile, in another saucepan, melt the butter. Stir in flour until smooth. Gradually add the milk, salt and pepper. Bring to a boil; cook and stir for 2 minutes or until thickened. Stir in cheese until melted. Stir into undrained potato mixture. Add ham and peas; heat through.

Yield: 7 servings.

JEWELED FRUIT SALAD

pam lancaster, willis, virginia

This fresh fruit salad is a mixture of vibrant colors and delightful flavor. The creamy yogurt dressing is a luscious complement.

    1   cup (8 ounces) vanilla yogurt
    2   tablespoons orange juice
    1   tablespoon mayonnaise
  1/2   teaspoon grated orange peel
    1   pint fresh strawberries, sliced
1-1/2   cups green grapes, halved
    1   can (11 ounces) mandarin oranges, drained
    1   cup fresh *or* frozen blueberries
    1   cup fresh *or* frozen raspberries
    1   medium kiwifruit, peeled and chopped
  1/4   cup fresh *or* frozen cranberries, thawed
        and halved

1   In a small bowl, combine the yogurt, orange juice, mayonnaise and orange peel. In a large serving bowl, combine the fruit. Serve with dressing.

Yield: 12 servings.

MARVELOUS MUSHROOM SOUP

laura mahaffey, annapolis, maryland

Some mushroom soups seem to have more broth than mushrooms. That's why I love this creamy version brimming with superb "shrooms!"

    3 medium onions, chopped
    2 garlic cloves, minced
  1/4 cup butter
    2 pounds fresh mushrooms, chopped
    2 cups heavy whipping cream
    2 cups beef broth
  1/2 teaspoon salt
  1/2 teaspoon pepper

Grated Parmesan cheese and minced fresh parsley, optional

1 In a.large saucepan, cook onions and garlic in butter over medium-low heat until tender. Reduce heat to low; add the mushrooms. Cook for 8-10 minutes or until tender, stirring occasionally.

2 Add the cream, broth, salt and pepper; cook and stir over low heat until heated through. Garnish with Parmesan cheese and parsley if desired.

Yield: 9 servings (about 2 quarts).

RED-HOT GELATIN SALAD

paula ptomey, porterville, california

This is my grandma's recipe. My mother makes this salad just about every year during the holidays. It has a spicy cinnamon taste that is really good. Even my daughter, who is a picky eater, likes it.

    1 package (3 ounces) cherry gelatin
1-1/2 cups boiling water, *divided*
  1/4 cup red-hot candies
  1/4 cup plus 1-1/2 teaspoons cold water
    1 cup chopped green apples
    1 cup chopped celery
  1/2 cup chopped walnuts

1 In a small bowl, dissolve gelatin in 1 cup boiling water. In another bowl, dissolve Red-Hots in remaining water; stir into gelatin. Stir in cold water. Refrigerate until slightly thickened, about 1 hour.

2 Fold in the apples, celery and walnuts. Pour into a 4-cup mold coated lightly with cooking spray. Refrigerate for 2 hours or until firm.

Yield: 6 servings.

POTATO SOUP WITH BEANS

christine ecker, linwood, new jersey

Winter winds can blow strong here on the Jersey shore. But this rich soup featuring potatoes, beans and sour cream is sure to warm your body and soul.

- 2 medium carrots, shredded
- 1 tablespoon butter
- 4 cups chicken *or* vegetable broth
- 3 medium potatoes, peeled and cubed
- 1 garlic clove, minced
- 1-1/2 teaspoons dill weed
- 1 can (15-1/2 ounces) great northern beans, rinsed and drained
- 4-1/2 teaspoons all-purpose flour
- 3/4 cup sour cream

Pepper to taste

1 In a large saucepan, cook carrots in butter for 4 minutes or until tender. Stir in the broth, potatoes, garlic and dill. Bring to a boil. Reduce heat; cover and simmer for 25 minutes or until potatoes are tender.

2 With a slotted spoon, remove half of the potatoes to a bowl; mash with a fork. Return to pan. Stir in the beans. In a small bowl, combine the flour, sour cream and pepper; add to soup. Cook over low heat for 5 minutes or until heated through (do not boil).

Yield: 6 servings.

CHERRY BRIE TOSSED SALAD

toni borden, wellington, florida

Draped in a light vinaigrette and sprinkled with almonds, this pretty salad is a variation of a recipe that's been passed around for years at school and church functions and even birthday parties. Everyone wants the recipe. Try different cheeses if you like.

DRESSING:
- 1 cup cider vinegar
- 1/2 cup sugar
- 1/4 cup olive oil
- 1 teaspoon ground mustard
- 1-1/2 teaspoons poppy seeds

SALAD:
- 2 tablespoons butter
- 3/4 cup sliced almonds
- 3 tablespoons sugar
- 8 cups torn romaine
- 8 ounces Brie *or* Camembert, rind removed, cubed
- 1 package (6 ounces) dried cherries

1 In a jar with a tight-fitting lid, combine the dressing ingredients; shake until sugar is dissolved.

2 For salad, in a heavy skillet, melt butter over medium heat. Add almonds and cook and stir until nuts are toasted, about 4 minutes. Sprinkle with sugar; cook and stir until sugar is melted, about 3 minutes. Spread on foil to cool; break apart.

3 In a salad bowl, combine the romaine, cheese and cherries. Shake dressing; drizzle over salad. Sprinkle with sugared almonds and toss to coat.

Yield: 10 servings.

CHUNKY CRANBERRY SALAD

joyce butterfield, nancy, kentucky

I found this recipe while taking a cooking class. Full of mixed fruit, celery and nuts, it's a lively alternative to jellied cranberry sauce. When cranberries are in season, I buy extra and freeze them so I can make this salad year-round.

      4 cups fresh *or* frozen cranberries
3-1/2 cups unsweetened pineapple juice
      2 envelopes unflavored gelatin
   1/2 cup cold water
      2 cups sugar
      1 can (20 ounces) unsweetened pineapple tidbits, drained
      1 cup chopped pecans
      1 cup green grapes, chopped
   1/2 cup finely chopped celery
      2 teaspoons grated orange peel

1   In a large saucepan, combine the cranberries and pineapple juice. Cook over medium heat until berries pop, about 15 minutes.

2   Meanwhile, in a small bowl, sprinkle gelatin over cold water; let stand for 5 minutes. In a large bowl, combine the berry mixture, sugar and softened gelatin. Chill until partially set.

3   Fold in the pineapple, pecans, grapes, celery and orange peel. Pour into individual serving dishes. Chill until firm.

Yield: 12 servings.

CLAM CHOWDER

melba horne, macon, georgia

Here's a quick chowder that's been in my family for more than 30 years. I make a big pot to take to an annual party at work. It's always a hit. Served with crusty bread and a green salad, it's the perfect meal for a chilly evening.

      6 bacon strips, diced
   1/2 cup finely chopped onion
      2 cans (10-3/4 ounces *each*) condensed cream of potato soup, undiluted
1-1/2 cups milk
      3 cans (6-1/2 ounces *each*) minced clams, undrained
      1 tablespoon lemon juice
   1/4 teaspoon dried thyme
   1/4 teaspoon pepper
Minced fresh parsley

1   In a large skillet, cook bacon over medium heat until crisp. Using a slotted spoon, remove to paper towels; drain, reserving 1 tablespoon drippings.

2   In the same skillet, saute onion in reserved drippings until tender. Stir in soup and milk. Add the clams, lemon juice, thyme, pepper and bacon; cook until heated through. Garnish with parsley.

Yield: 5 servings.

GORGONZOLA PEAR SALAD

melinda singer, tarzana, california

Tired of tossed salads? Here's an irresistible variation featuring pears that makes an attractive and tasty first course. The cheese and pecans are nice additions. You'll appreciate how easy it is.

- 3 medium pears, cored and halved
- 3 tablespoons olive oil
- 1/2 teaspoon salt
- 6 cups spring mix salad greens
- 2 plum tomatoes, seeded and chopped
- 1 cup crumbled Gorgonzola cheese
- 1/2 cup pecan halves, toasted
- 3/4 cup balsamic vinaigrette

1 Place pears in an ungreased 13-in. x 9-in. x 2-in. baking dish. Drizzle with oil and sprinkle with salt. Bake, uncovered, at 400° for 25-30 minutes, basting occasionally with cooking juices.

2 In a large salad bowl, combine the greens, tomatoes, cheese and pecans. Drizzle with dressing and toss to coat. Divide among six serving plates; top each with a pear half.

Yield: 6 servings.

CRANBERRY RICE SALAD

taste of home test kitchen

Our home economists devised this make-ahead recipe with the hectic holidays in mind. Cranberries and green onions add a bit of color.

- 1 cup uncooked long grain rice
- 3/4 cup dried cranberries
- 2 green onions, sliced
- 2 tablespoons sugar
- 1/2 teaspoon dried minced onion
- 1/2 teaspoon poppy seeds
- 1/8 teaspoon paprika
- 1 tablespoon white wine vinegar
- 1 tablespoon cider vinegar
- 2 tablespoons canola oil
- 3/4 cup sliced almonds, toasted

1 Cook rice according to package directions; drain and rinse with cold water. In a large bowl, combine the rice, cranberries and green onions.

2 In a small bowl, combine the sugar, minced onion, poppy seeds and paprika; whisk in the vinegars and oil. Drizzle over rice mixture and toss to coat. Cover and refrigerate for up to 2 hours. Just before serving, stir in the almonds.

Yield: 5 servings.

BUTTERNUT BISQUE

kristin arnett, elkhorn, wisconsin

I've served this wonderful soup to family as well as company. It's especially good to prepare in the cool fall months.

- 3-1/2 pounds butternut squash, peeled, seeded and cubed
- 1 cup sliced carrots
- 1 medium tart apple, peeled and chopped
- 1/2 cup chopped shallots
- 2 tablespoons olive oil
- 3 large tomatoes, seeded and chopped
- 4 cups chicken broth
- 1-1/4 cups half-and-half cream
- 1-1/2 teaspoons salt
- 1/4 teaspoon cayenne pepper
- 3/4 cup frozen corn, thawed
- 2 tablespoons minced chives

Sour cream and additional chives, optional

1. In a large bowl, toss the squash, carrots, apple, shallots and oil. Transfer to a large roasting pan.

2. Bake, uncovered, at 400° for 1 hour or until browned and tender, stirring twice. Cool slightly. Place in a food processor; cover and process until almost smooth.

3. In a Dutch oven or soup kettle, cook tomatoes over medium heat for 5 minutes. Add the pureed vegetables, broth, cream, salt and cayenne; heat through (do not boil). Stir in the corn and chives. Garnish servings with sour cream and chives if desired.

Yield: 10 servings.

PINEAPPLE LIME GELATIN

wanda weathermon, comanche, texas

This recipe was passed down by my mother. We make it often, but especially at Christmas and Thanksgiving. With the marshmallows, pecans and whipped cream, the sweet salad can even be served as a light dessert.

- 1 package (3 ounces) lime gelatin
- 2 cups boiling water, *divided*
- 16 large marshmallows
- 1 package (3 ounces) cream cheese, softened
- 1 can (8 ounces) unsweetened crushed pineapple, undrained
- 1 cup heavy whipping cream, whipped
- 1 cup chopped pecans
- 2 to 3 drops green food coloring, optional

1. In a large bowl, dissolve gelatin in 1 cup boiling water; set aside.

2. In a small saucepan, combine marshmallows and remaining water. Cook over low heat until the marshmallows are melted, stirring occasionally. Stir into gelatin. Refrigerate until partially set.

3. In a large bowl, beat cream cheese until smooth. Beat in pineapple. Fold in the gelatin mixture, whipped cream, pecans and the food coloring if desired. Pour into a 6-cup mold coated with cooking spray. Refrigerate until set. Unmold onto a serving plate.

Yield: 12 servings.

BREAKFAST & BRUNCH

PEACH
COBBLER
COFFEE
CAKE
P. 143

RHUBARB-RIBBON BRUNCH CAKE

mary blenk, cumberland, maine

My dad has always had a flourishing rhubarb patch. So when I saw this contest, I knew I should try to create a recipe with his endless supply. This cake can be served as a coffee cake at breakfast or an elegant finish to a special meal.

- 3/4 cup sugar
- 3 tablespoons cornstarch
- 1/4 teaspoon ground cinnamon
- 1/8 teaspoon ground nutmeg
- 1/3 cup cold water
- 2-1/2 cups sliced fresh *or* frozen rhubarb
- 3 to 4 drops food coloring, optional

BATTER:
- 2-1/4 cups all-purpose flour
- 3/4 cup sugar
- 3/4 cup cold butter, cubed
- 1/2 teaspoon *each* baking powder and baking soda
- 1/2 teaspoon salt
- 1 egg, lightly beaten
- 1 carton (6 ounces) vanilla yogurt
- 1 teaspoon vanilla extract

TOPPING:
- 1 egg, beaten
- 8 ounces Mascarpone cheese
- 1/4 cup sugar
- 1/2 cup *each* chopped pecans and flaked coconut

1 In a large saucepan, combine the sugar, cornstarch, cinnamon, nutmeg and water until smooth. Add rhubarb. Bring to a boil; cook and stir for 2 minutes or until thickened. Add food coloring if desired. Set aside.

2 In a large bowl, combine flour and sugar; cut in butter until mixture resembles coarse crumbs. Set aside 1 cup for topping. Add the baking powder, baking soda and salt to remaining crumb mixture. In a small bowl, combine the egg, yogurt and vanilla; stir into batter until smooth. Spread into a greased 9-in. springform pan.

3 Combine the egg, Mascarpone cheese and sugar; spoon over batter. Top with rhubarb mixture. Add pecans and coconut to reserved crumb mixture; sprinkle over top.

4 Bake at 350° for 60-65 minutes or until a toothpick inserted near the center comes out clean. Cool on a wire rack for 20 minutes; remove sides of pan. Cool completely.

Yield: 12 servings.

Editor's Note: If using frozen rhubarb, measure rhubarb while still frozen, then thaw completely. Drain in a colander, but do not press liquid out.

OVEN-BAKED WESTERN OMELET

d'shon mccarty, morenci, arizona

The very first time I served this luscious omelet to my husband and young daughters, it became a Yuletide tradition! Now I always double the savory recipe and sometimes substitute cheddar for Swiss cheese.

- 3 green onions, sliced
- 1/2 cup chopped sweet red pepper
- 1 tablespoon canola oil
- 6 eggs, lightly beaten
- 1 cup (4 ounces) shredded Swiss cheese
- 6 ounces cubed fully cooked ham
- 1/3 cup water

1 In a 10-in. ovenproof skillet, saute the onions and red pepper in oil for 5 minutes. In a large bowl, combine the eggs, cheese, ham and water. Pour over vegetable mixture. Bake, uncovered, at 375° for 15-20 minutes or until set.

Yield: 6 servings.

ALMOND RING COFFEE CAKE

vie spence, woburn, massachusetts
The coffee cake gets a delicate almond flavor from the extract in the filling and the glaze.

- 3-1/2 to 3-3/4 cups all-purpose flour, *divided*
- 1 package (1/4 ounce) active dry yeast
- 1 cup milk
- 1/3 cup butter
- 1/3 cup sugar
- 1/2 teaspoon salt
- 1 egg

FILLING:

- 1/4 cup butter, softened
- 1/2 cup sugar
- 1/2 teaspoon almond extract

GLAZE:

- 2 to 3 tablespoons milk
- 1 teaspoon almond extract
- 1-3/4 cups confectioners' sugar

Sliced almonds, toasted, optional

1 In a large bowl, combine 2 cups flour and yeast. In a saucepan, heat the milk, butter, sugar and salt to 120°-130°. Add to dry ingredients; beat until moistened. Add egg; beat for 3 minutes. Stir in enough remaining flour to form a soft dough.

2 Turn onto floured surface; knead until smooth and elastic, about 4-6 minutes. Place in a greased bowl, turning once to grease top. Cover and let rise in a warm place until doubled, about 1 hour.

3 Punch dough down. Turn on a lightly floured surface; roll into an 18-in. x 12-in. rectangle. In a small bowl, beat filling ingredients until smooth. Spread over dough to within 1 in. of edges.

4 Roll up jelly-roll style, starting with a long side; pinch seam to seal. Place on a greased baking sheet, sealing ends to form a ring. Cover and let rise until doubled, about 30 minutes.

5 Bake at 375° for 20-25 minutes or until golden. Remove from pan to a wire rack to cool.

6 In a small bowl, combine milk and almond extract; whisk in confectioners' sugar until smooth. Drizzle over coffee cake. Sprinkle with almonds if desired.

Yield: 8-10 servings.

CREAM CHEESE SCRAMBLED EGGS

jacque hunt, heyburn, idaho
My mother-in-law introduced me to this recipe, and now it's my kids' favorite breakfast. The rich taste makes it special enough for Christmas morning, but it won't take up a lot of time.

- 1 package (3 ounces) cream cheese, softened
- 2 tablespoons half-and-half cream
- 8 eggs
- 1/3 cup grated Parmesan cheese
- 1/2 teaspoon lemon-pepper seasoning
- 1/8 teaspoon salt
- 1/2 cup real bacon bits
- 2 tablespoons butter

1 In a small bowl, beat cream cheese and cream until smooth. Beat in the eggs, Parmesan cheese, lemon-pepper and salt. Stir in bacon.

2 In a large skillet, melt butter; add egg mixture. Cook and stir over medium heat until eggs are completely set.

Yield: 4 servings.

APPLE RAISIN CREPES

darlene brenden, salem, oregon

I've been making and eating these delectable breakfast treats for as long as I can remember. They look impressive but are quick and easy to prepare. Heating the filled crepes a second time turns them golden brown and adds a wonderful crispness.

- 1-1/2 cups all-purpose flour
- 1/4 cup sugar
- 1 cup milk
- 6 tablespoons water
- 1/4 cup canola oil
- 1 egg

FILLING:
- 5 cups thinly sliced peeled tart apples
- 1 cup sugar
- 1/2 cup raisins
- 2 teaspoons ground cinnamon
- 1 tablespoon confectioners' sugar

1 For batter, in a small bowl, combine flour and sugar. Add the milk, water, oil and egg. Cover and refrigerate for 1 hour.

2 In a large saucepan, combine the apples, sugar, raisins and cinnamon. Cook and stir over medium heat for 8-10 minutes or until apples are tender; set aside.

3 Heat a lightly greased 8-in. nonstick skillet; pour 3 tablespoons of batter into the center of skillet. Lift and tilt pan to evenly coat bottom. Cook until top appears dry; turn and cook 15-20 seconds longer. Remove to a wire rack. Repeat with remaining batter, greasing skillet as needed. When cool, stack crepes with waxed paper or paper towels in between.

4 With a slotted spoon, fill each crepe with 1/4 cup of apples; roll up. On a lightly greased griddle or in a large skillet, cook crepes over medium heat for 3-4 minutes on each side or until golden brown. Sprinkle with confectioners' sugar. Serve immediately with remaining sauce from apples.

Yield: 1 dozen.

GRANDMA'S HONEY MUFFINS

darlis wilfer, west bend, wisconsin

I can remember my grandma making these delicious muffins—we'd eat them nice and warm, fresh from the oven! She was a "pinch of this" and "handful of that" kind of cook, so getting the ingredient amounts correct for the recipe was a challenge. Now it's a family treasure!

- 2 cups all-purpose flour
- 1/2 cup sugar
- 3 teaspoons baking powder
- 1/2 teaspoon salt
- 1 egg
- 1 cup milk
- 1/4 cup butter, melted
- 1/4 cup honey

1 In a large bowl, combine the flour, sugar, baking powder and salt. In another bowl, whisk the egg, milk, butter and honey; stir into dry ingredients just until moistened.

2 Fill greased or paper-lined muffin cups three-fourths full. Bake at 400° for 15-18 minutes or until a toothpick inserted near the center comes out clean. Remove from pan to a wire rack. Serve warm.

Yield: 1 dozen.

WALNUT PEAR COFFEE CAKE

darlene spalding, lynden, washington

This moist coffee cake goes great with a cup of coffee at breakfast. It also makes a delicious snack or dessert. It will disappear in minutes.

- 1 cup chopped walnuts
- 1/3 cup packed brown sugar
- 1 teaspoon ground cinnamon
- 1/3 cup all-purpose flour
- 1/4 cup cold butter

FILLING:

- 2 medium ripe pears, peeled and sliced (about 2 cups)
- 2 teaspoons lemon juice
- 1/2 cup butter, softened
- 1 cup sugar
- 2 eggs
- 1 teaspoon vanilla extract
- 1-3/4 cups all-purpose flour
- 3/4 teaspoon baking powder
- 1/2 teaspoon baking soda
- 1/4 teaspoon salt
- 1 cup (8 ounces) sour cream
- 1/2 cup chopped walnuts

1 In a small bowl, combine walnuts, brown sugar and cinnamon; set aside. Place flour in a small bowl; cut in butter until mixture resembles coarse crumbs. Stir in 3/4 cup of nut mixture; set aside for topping. Set aside remaining nut mixture for filling.

2 In a small bowl, toss the pears with lemon juice; set aside. In a another bowl, cream the butter and sugar until light and fluffy. Add eggs, one at a time, beating well after each addition. Beat in vanilla. Combine the flour, baking powder, baking

soda and salt; gradually add to creamed mixture alternately with sour cream, beating well after each addition.

3 Spread two-thirds of the batter into a greased 9-in. springform pan. Top with the reserved nut mixture, pears and remaining batter. Sprinkle with walnuts and reserved topping mixture.

4 Bake at 350° for 50-55 minutes or until a toothpick inserted near the center comes out clean. Cool on a wire rack for 10 minutes. Carefully run a knife around edge of pan to loosen; remove sides of pan. Cool for 1 hour before cutting.

Yield: 12 servings.

TURKEY SAUSAGE PATTIES

janice wuertzer, dubuque, iowa

Eat smart—starting with this homemade turkey sausage. If you like garlic, try substituting it for the sage.

- 1 small onion, finely chopped
- 1/4 cup dry bread crumbs
- 1 teaspoon rubbed sage
- 1/2 teaspoon salt
- 1/2 teaspoon paprika
- 1/4 teaspoon pepper
- 1 pound lean ground turkey
- 2 teaspoons canola oil

1 In a large bowl, combine the onion, bread crumbs, sage, salt, paprika and pepper. Crumble turkey over mixture and mix well. Shape into six patties. Cover and refrigerate for 2 hours.

2 In a large nonstick skillet over medium heat, cook patties in oil for 7 minutes on each side or until meat is no longer pink.

Yield: 6 patties.

SAGE ONION QUICHE

shelley johnson, indianapolis, indiana

I reach for this recipe often because it's so versatile. You can serve it for brunch, as a side dish or as a meatless entree. The fresh sage adds great flavor to the onions.

2 large onions, thinly sliced
2 tablespoons butter
2 tablespoons minced fresh sage
1 teaspoon minced fresh thyme *or* 1/4 teaspoon dried thyme
1 unbaked pastry shell (9 inches)
1 cup (4 ounces) shredded cheddar cheese
4 eggs
1 can (12 ounces) evaporated milk
1/2 teaspoon salt
1/8 teaspoon pepper
1/8 teaspoon ground nutmeg

1 In a large skillet, saute onions in butter until tender; drain. Stir in sage and thyme. Spoon into pastry shell. Sprinkle with cheese. In a bowl, whisk the eggs, milk, salt, pepper and nutmeg. Pour over cheese.

2 Bake at 425° for 15 minutes. Reduce heat to 375°; bake 20-25 minutes longer or until a knife inserted near the center comes out clean. Let stand for 10 minutes before cutting.

Yield: 6-8 servings.

APPLE PECAN MUFFINS

carol stine, dayton, ohio

Apple, pecans and coconut give these cinnamon-spiced muffins a hearty yet tender texture. The apple-flavored glaze is delicious and adds a touch of sweetness.

1/4 cup butter, softened
1/3 cup sugar
2 tablespoons brown sugar
1 egg
1/2 cup milk
1-1/2 cups all-purpose flour
2 teaspoons baking powder
1/2 teaspoon salt
1/2 teaspoon ground cinnamon
1 medium tart apple, peeled and finely chopped
1/2 cup chopped pecans, toasted
1/4 cup flaked coconut

GLAZE:
1 cup confectioners' sugar
2 tablespoons unsweetened apple juice

1 In a large bowl, cream butter and sugars until light and fluffy. Beat in egg. Stir in milk. Combine the flour, baking powder, salt and cinnamon; add to creamed mixture just until moistened. Fold in the apple, pecans and coconut.

2 Fill greased or paper-lined muffin cups three-fourths full. Bake at 400° for 15-20 minutes or until a toothpick inserted near the center comes out clean. Cool for 5 minutes before removing from pan to a wire rack. Combine glaze ingredients until smooth; drizzle over muffins. Serve warm.

Yield: 11 muffins.

BROCCOLI QUICHE CREPE CUPS

kristin arnett, elkhorn, wisconsin

When I was very young and just learning to cook, this was one of the first recipes I made. I still prepare these and my children do, too!

- 1-1/2 cups milk
- 3 eggs
- 1 cup all-purpose flour
- 1/4 teaspoon salt

FILLING:

- 1 package (10 ounces) frozen broccoli with cheese sauce
- 3 bacon strips, diced
- 1/2 cup chopped onion
- 2 eggs
- 1/4 cup milk

1 In a blender, combine the milk, eggs, flour and salt; cover and process until smooth. Cover and refrigerate for 1 hour. Heat a lightly greased 8-in. nonstick skillet over medium heat; pour 2 tablespoons batter into the center of skillet. Lift and tilt pan to coat bottom evenly. Cook until top appears dry; turn and cook 15-20 seconds longer. Remove to a wire rack. Repeat with remaining batter, greasing skillet as needed. When cool, stack crepes with waxed paper or paper towels in between.

2 Line each of four 6-oz. custard cups with a crepe; set aside. Freeze remaining crepes in a freezer bag, leaving waxed paper between each crepe, for up to 3 months.

3 For filling, cook broccoli according to package directions. Cut up any larger pieces of broccoli. In a microwave-safe bowl, microwave bacon on high for 2 minutes; drain. Add the onion; microwave on

high for 3 minutes or until tender. Beat eggs and milk; stir in broccoli mixture and bacon mixture. Spoon into prepared crepe cups.

4 Bake, uncovered, at 350° for 30-35 minutes or until a knife inserted near the center comes out clean. Remove from the custard cups and serve immediately.

Yield: 4 servings.

APPLE SPICE MUFFINS

beckie lapointe, abbotsford, british columbia

I came up with this recipe when I was out of my usual muffin-making ingredients. I improvised, and the results were terrific!

- 2 cups all-purpose flour
- 1 cup granola without raisins
- 2/3 cup sugar
- 3 teaspoons baking powder
- 1 teaspoon salt
- 1/2 teaspoon ground cinnamon
- 1/4 teaspoon ground nutmeg
- 2 eggs
- 2/3 cup unsweetened apple juice
- 1/4 cup canola oil
- 1-1/2 cups grated peeled apples

1 In a large bowl, combine the first seven ingredients. In another bowl, whisk the eggs, apple juice and oil. Stir into dry ingredients just until moistened. Fold in apples.

2 Fill greased or paper-lined muffin cups three-fourths full. Bake at 400° for 18-20 minutes or until a toothpick inserted near the center comes out clean. Cool for 5 minutes before removing from pan to a wire rack. Serve warm.

Yield: 1 dozen.

CRANBERRY COFFEE CAKE

doris brearley, vestal, new york

This recipe was given to me by a former neighbor. The yummy cake relies on baking mix, canned cranberry sauce and an easy nut topping, so it's truly a quick bread.

    2   cups biscuit/baking mix
    2   tablespoons sugar
  2/3   cup milk
    1   egg, lightly beaten
  2/3   cup jellied cranberry sauce

TOPPING:
  1/2   cup chopped walnuts
  1/2   cup packed brown sugar
  1/2   teaspoon ground cinnamon

GLAZE:
    1   cup confectioners' sugar
    2   tablespoons milk
  1/4   teaspoon vanilla extract

1   In a large bowl, combine the biscuit mix, sugar, milk and egg. Pour into a greased 8-in. square baking dish. Drop cranberry sauce by teaspoonfuls over batter. Combine topping ingredients; sprinkle over cranberry sauce.

2   Bake at 400° for 18-23 minutes or until golden brown. Cool on a wire rack.

3   In a small bowl, combine the glaze ingredients; drizzle over coffee cake.

Yield: 9 servings.

SPINACH CHEESE STRATA

mary laffey, indianapolis, indiana

Here's a delicious brunch dish for the holidays. I usually garnish with red and green pepper rings overlapped in the center for a festive touch.

  1/2   cup chopped onion
  1/4   cup chopped sweet red pepper
  1/4   cup chopped green pepper
    2   tablespoons butter
    1   package (10 ounces) frozen chopped spinach, thawed and well drained
    2   cups Wheat Chex
  1/2   cup shredded cheddar cheese
  1/2   cup shredded Swiss cheese
    6   eggs
    2   cups milk
  1/3   cup crumbled cooked bacon
    1   teaspoon Dijon mustard
    1   teaspoon salt
  1/4   teaspoon white pepper

1   In a large skillet, saute the onion and peppers in butter until crisp-tender. Remove from the heat. Stir in spinach and cereal. Spoon into a greased 11-in. x 7-in. baking dish. Sprinkle with cheese.

2   In a large bowl, combine the eggs, milk, bacon, mustard, salt and pepper. Pour over cheese. Bake at 325° for 45-50 minutes or until knife inserted near the center comes out clean. Let stand for 10 minutes before cutting.

Yield: 6-8 servings.

Freezing Peppers

Diced green, red and sweet yellow peppers can be frozen for up to 6 months without blanching them first. When you need some diced peppers, you can just get them out of the freezer.—Taste of Home Test Kitchen

COCONUT CHOCOLATE MUFFINS

sonia daily, midland, michigan
With a rich, dark chocolate flavor and luscious cream cheese-coconut topping, these irresistible muffins taste more like a decadent dessert than a morning treat.

    1/2 cup cream cheese, softened
      3 tablespoons sugar
      2 tablespoons all-purpose flour
      1 egg
      1 cup (6 ounces) semisweet chocolate chips, *divided*
    1/2 cup flaked coconut
    1/3 cup chopped pecans, toasted
BATTER:
  1-1/2 cups all-purpose flour
      1 cup packed brown sugar
    1/4 cup baking cocoa
      1 teaspoon baking soda
    1/4 teaspoon ground cinnamon
      1 cup brewed coffee, room temperature
    1/3 cup canola oil
      2 tablespoons cider vinegar

1 In a small bowl, beat the cream cheese, sugar and flour until smooth. Beat in egg. Stir in 2/3 cup chocolate chips; set aside. In another bowl, combine the coconut, pecans and remaining chips; set aside.

2 In a large bowl, combine the flour, brown sugar, cocoa, baking soda and cinnamon. Whisk the coffee, oil and vinegar; stir into dry ingredients just until moistened.

3 Fill paper-lined muffin cups half full. Drop a rounded tablespoonful of cream cheese mixture into the center of each; sprinkle with 1 tablespoon coconut mixture.

4 Bake at 350° for 20-25 minutes or until a toothpick inserted near the comes out clean. Cool for 5 minutes before removing from pans to wire racks. Serve warm.

Yield: 14 muffins.

SPICED SAUSAGE PATTIES

heather madgwick, garden city, kansas
You've never tasted sausage quite like this before! The secret to this special recipe from South Africa lies in the spices, which include coriander, cloves, allspice and nutmeg. I've been cooking for a while, and this is one of my favorite recipes.

  2-1/2 pounds ground beef
    1/2 pound ground pork
  2-1/4 teaspoons salt
  1-1/2 teaspoons ground coriander
      1 to 1-1/2 teaspoons ground allspice
    3/4 teaspoon ground cloves
    3/4 teaspoon pepper
    1/2 teaspoon ground nutmeg
    1/4 cup cider vinegar

1 Crumble beef and pork into a large bowl. Combine the seasonings; sprinkle over meat. Add vinegar and mix well. Cover and refrigerate for 1 hour.

2 Shape the meat mixture into 2-1/2-in. patties. In a large skillet, cook the patties over medium heat for 4-5 minutes on each side or until a meat thermometer reads 160° and juices run clear.

Yield: 2-1/2 dozen.

CREPES FLORENTINE

sue a. jurack, mequon, wisconsin

Bring this spectacular dish to the table and you'll receive many compliments on the presentation! The rich Mornay-sauced spinach and creamy mushroom mixtures are beautifully layered between crepes.

- 2-1/2 cups milk
- 4 eggs
- 1/4 cup butter, melted
- 2 cups all-purpose flour
- 1/4 teaspoon salt

FILLING:

- 8 tablespoons butter, *divided*
- 5 tablespoons all-purpose flour
- 1/4 teaspoon *each* salt and pepper

Dash ground nutmeg

- 2-1/4 cups milk
- 1/3 cup heavy whipping cream
- 1 cup (4 ounces) shredded Gruyere cheese *or* Swiss cheese, *divided*
- 1-1/2 cups finely chopped fresh mushrooms
- 1 shallot, finely chopped
- 1 package (8 ounces) cream cheese, softened
- 1 egg
- 2 packages (10 ounces *each*) frozen chopped spinach, thawed and squeezed dry
- 2 tablespoons shredded Parmesan cheese

1 For crepes, in a large bowl, combine the milk, eggs and butter. Combine flour and salt; add to milk mixture and mix well. Cover and refrigerate for 1 hour.

2 Heat a lightly greased 8-in. nonstick skillet; pour 2 tablespoons batter into the center of skillet. Lift and tilt pan to evenly coat bottom. Cook until top appears dry; turn and cook 15-20 seconds longer. Remove to a wire rack. Repeat with remaining batter, adding butter to skillet as needed. When cool, stack crepes with waxed paper or paper towels in between.

3 For filling, in a large saucepan, melt 5 tablespoons butter. Stir in the flour, salt, pepper and nutmeg until smooth; gradually add the milk. Bring to a boil; cook and stir for 2 minutes or until thickened. Reduce heat to low; stir in the cream and 3/4 cup Gruyere cheese. Cook and stir until cheese is melted. Remove from heat.

4 In a skillet, saute the mushrooms and shallot in 2 tablespoons butter until tender. In a small bowl, beat cream cheese and egg until smooth. Beat in mushroom mixture. Add enough cheese sauce to achieve a spreadable consistency. In a large bowl, combine the spinach and 1/2 cup cheese

sauce until blended. Add the additional sauce if needed to achieve a spreadable consistency.

5 To assemble, on two greased 9-in. ovenproof pie or tart pans, layer a crepe, spinach mixture, another crepe, then mushroom mixture. Repeat five more times. Pour remaining sauce over the stacks. Sprinkle with remaining Gruyere and Parmesan cheeses. Dot with remaining butter. Cover and refrigerate for 1 hour.

6 Remove from refrigerator 15 minutes before baking. Bake at 350° for 55-60 minutes or until bubbly and golden and a thermometer reads 160°. Let stand for 5 minutes before cutting. Cut into wedges.

Yield: 8-12 servings.

Editor's Note: This dish can be served at a brunch, luncheon or as a very special side dish. Be sure to use an attractive ovenproof plate so it can be brought from the oven right to the table. The crepes can be made in advance and frozen, and the dish can be assembled the morning of your party.

How Much is a Dash?

Traditionally, a dash is a very small amount of seasoning added with a quick downward stroke of the hand. It's generally between 1/16 and a scant 1/8 teaspoon.
—Taste of Home Test Kitchen

CREPE QUICHE CUPS

sheryl riley, unionville, missouri
I enjoy trying new recipes, especially when entertaining family and friends. These unique crepe cups hold a delicious sausage-and-egg filling.

    2 eggs
    1 cup plus 2 tablespoons milk
    2 tablespoons butter, melted
    1 cup all-purpose flour
  1/8 teaspoon salt
FILLING :
  1/2 pound bulk pork sausage
  1/4 cup chopped onion
    3 eggs
  1/2 cup milk
  1/2 cup mayonnaise
    2 cups (8 ounces) shredded cheddar cheese

1 For crepe batter, in a small bowl, beat the eggs, milk and butter. Combine flour and salt; add to egg mixture and mix well. Cover and refrigerate for 1 hour.

2 In a small skillet, cook sausage and onion over medium heat until meat is no longer pink; drain. In a large bowl, whisk eggs, milk and mayonnaise. Stir in sausage mixture and cheese; set aside.

3 Heat a lightly greased 8-in. nonstick skillet. Stir crepe batter; pour 2 tablespoons into center of skillet. Lift and tilt pan to coat bottom evenly. Cook until top appears dry; turn and cook 15-20 seconds longer.

4 Remove to a wire rack. Repeat with remaining batter, greasing skillet as needed. When cool, stack crepes with waxed paper or paper towels in between.

5 Line greased muffin cups with crepes; fill two-thirds full with sausage mixture. Bake at 350° for 15 minutes. Cover loosely with foil; bake 10-15 minutes longer or until a knife inserted near the center comes out clean.

Yield: 16 servings.

BERRY-FILLED DOUGHNUTS

ginny watson, broken arrow, oklahoma
Just four readily available ingredients are all you'll need for this sure-to-be-popular treat. Folks will never guess that a tube of buttermilk biscuits are the base for these golden, jelly-filled doughnuts.

    4 cups canola oil
    1 tube (7-1/2 ounces) refrigerated buttermilk biscuits, separated into 10 biscuits
  3/4 cup seedless strawberry jam
    1 cup confectioners' sugar

1 In an electric skillet or deep-fat fryer, heat oil to 375°. Fry biscuits, a few at a time, for 1-2 minutes on each side or until golden brown. Drain on paper towels.

2 Cut a small hole in the corner of a pastry or plastic bag; insert a very small plastic tip. Fill bag with jam. Push the tip through the side of each doughnut to fill with jam. Dust with confectioners' sugar while warm. Serve immediately.

Yield: 10 servings.

SCRAMBLED EGG BRUNCH BREAD

julie deal, china grove, north carolina

This attractive bread is brimming with eggs, ham and cheese, making it a real meal in one. By using refrigerated crescent rolls, it's a snap to prepare.

>   2 tubes (8 ounces *each*) refrigerated crescent rolls
>   4 ounces thinly sliced deli ham, julienned
>   4 ounces cream cheese, softened
>   1/2 cup milk
>   8 eggs
>   1/4 teaspoon salt
> Dash pepper
>   1/4 cup chopped sweet red pepper
>   2 tablespoons chopped green onion
>   1 teaspoon butter
>   1/2 cup shredded cheddar cheese

1 Unroll each tube of crescent dough (do not separate rectangles). Place side by side on a greased baking sheet with long sides touching; seal seams and perforations. Arrange ham lengthwise down center third of rectangle.

2 In a large bowl, beat cream cheese and milk until smooth. Separate one egg; set egg white aside. Add the egg yolk, salt, pepper and remaining eggs to cream cheese mixture; mix well. Stir in red pepper and onions.

3 In a large skillet, melt butter; add egg mixture. Cook and stir over medium heat just until set. Remove from the heat. Spoon scrambled eggs over ham. Sprinkle with cheese.

4 On each long side of dough, cut 1-in.-wide strips to the center to within 1/2 in. of filling. Starting at one end, fold alternating strips at an angle across the filling. Pinch ends to seal and tuck under.

5 Beat reserved egg white; brush over dough. Bake at 375° for 25-28 minutes or until golden brown.

Yield: 6 servings.

BREAKFAST RICE PUDDING

sue draheim, waterford, wisconsin

My husband makes this rice pudding quite often for our breakfast. It's hearty and nutritious.

> 1-1/3 cups uncooked long grain *or* basmati rice
>   1 can (15-1/4 ounces) peach halves, drained
>   1 cup canned *or* frozen pitted tart cherries, drained
>   1 cup heavy whipping cream
>   1/2 cup packed brown sugar, *divided*
>   1/4 cup old-fashioned oats
>   1/4 cup flaked coconut
>   1/4 cup chopped pecans
>   1/4 cup butter, melted

1 Cook rice according to package directions. In a large bowl, combine the rice, peaches, cherries, cream and 1/4 cup brown sugar. Transfer to a greased 1-1/2 quart baking dish.

2 Combine the oats, coconut, pecans, butter and remaining brown sugar; sprinkle over rice. Bake, uncovered, at 375° for 25-30 minutes or until golden brown.

Yield: 8 servings.

SPICED MIXED FRUIT

barb biedenstein, centennial, colorado
Delicious fresh fruit is hard to come by around Christmas, so this recipe calling for dried and canned fruits is a welcome treat.

- 2 packages (8 ounces *each*) mixed dried fruit
- 1 can (15 ounces) fruit cocktail, undrained
- 1 cup raisins
- 1 cup apple cider *or* juice
- 1/2 cup brandy *or* additional apple cider *or* juice
- 4-1/2 teaspoons chopped candied ginger
- 1-1/2 teaspoons ground cardamom
- 1-1/2 teaspoons ground allspice
- 2 medium apples, chopped
- 1 cup fresh *or* frozen cranberries

1 In a 3-qt. baking dish, combine the first eight ingredients. Cover and bake at 350° for 35-40 minutes or until fruit is softened.

2 Stir in apples and cranberries. Bake, uncovered, for 15-20 minutes or until apples are tender. Serve warm or at room temperature.

Yield: 6-1/2 cups.

BREAKFAST BURRITOS

linda wells, st. mary's, georgia
Burritos for breakfast? Why not! These zesty little handfuls will wake up your taste buds and start your day with a smile. And you can make and freeze them ahead, then just pop them into the microwave for a quick meal.

- 1 pound bulk pork sausage
- 1-1/2 cups frozen Southern-style hash brown potatoes
- 1/4 cup diced onion
- 1/4 cup diced green *or* red pepper
- 4 eggs, beaten
- 12 flour tortillas (8 inches), warmed
- 1/2 cup shredded cheddar cheese

Picante sauce and sour cream, optional

1 In a large skillet, cook sausage over medium heat until no longer pink; drain. Add the potatoes, onion and pepper; cook and stir for 6-8 minutes or until tender. Add eggs; cook and stir until set. Spoon filling off center on each tortilla. Sprinkle with cheese. Fold sides and ends over filling and roll up. Serve with picante sauce and sour cream if desired.

2 **To freeze and reheat burritos:** Wrap each burrito in waxed paper and foil. Freeze for up to 1 month. To use, remove foil and waxed paper. Place one burrito on a microwave-safe plate. Microwave on high for 2 to 2-1/4 minutes or until a meat thermometer reads 165°, turning burrito over once. Let stand for 20 seconds.

Yield: 12 servings.

Editor's Note: This recipe was tested in a 1,100-watt microwave.

SWEDISH PANCAKES

susan johnson, lyons, kansas

When we spend the night at my mother-in-law's house, our kids beg her to make these crepe-like pancakes for breakfast. They're a little lighter than traditional pancakes, so my family can eat a lot!

- 2 cups milk
- 4 eggs
- 1 tablespoon canola oil
- 1-1/2 cups all-purpose flour
- 3 tablespoons sugar
- 1/4 teaspoon salt

Lingonberries *or* raspberries

Seedless raspberry jam *or* fruit spread, warmed

Whipped topping

1 In a blender, combine the first six ingredients. Cover and process until blended. Heat a lightly greased 8-in. nonstick skillet; pour 1/4 cup batter into center of each. Lift and tilt pan to evenly coat bottom. Cook until top appears dry; turn and cook 15-20 seconds longer.

2 Repeat with the remaining batter, adding oil to skillet as needed. Stack pancakes with waxed paper or paper towels in between. Reheat in the microwave if desired.

3 Fold pancakes into quarters; serve with berries, raspberry jam and whipped topping.

Yield: 5 servings (20 pancakes).

BLUEBERRY-STUFFED FRENCH TOAST

myrna koldenhoven, sanborn, iowa

I came across this recipe in a newspaper several years ago. The special berry-filled French toast is truly company fare.

- 1-1/2 cups fresh *or* frozen blueberries
- 3 tablespoons sugar, *divided*
- 8 slices Italian bread (1-1/4 inches thick)
- 4 eggs
- 1/2 cup orange juice
- 1 teaspoon grated orange peel

Dash salt

BLUEBERRY ORANGE SAUCE:

- 3 tablespoons sugar
- 1 tablespoon cornstarch
- 1/8 teaspoon salt
- 1/4 cup *each* orange juice and water
- 1-1/2 cups orange segments
- 1 cup fresh *or* frozen blueberries
- 1/3 cup sliced almonds

1 In a small bowl, combine blueberries and 2 tablespoons sugar. Cut a pocket in the side of each slice of bread. Fill each pocket with about 3 tablespoons berry mixture.

2 In a shallow bowl, whisk the eggs, orange juice, orange peel, salt and remaining sugar. Carefully dip both sides of bread in egg mixture (do not squeeze out filling). Place in a greased 15-in. x 10-in. x 1-in. baking pan. Bake at 400° for 7-1/2 minutes on each side; turning gently.

3 Meanwhile, in a small saucepan, combine the sugar, cornstarch and salt. Gently whisk in orange juice and water until smooth. Bring to a boil; cook and stir for 1-2 minutes or until thickened. Reduce heat; stir in oranges and blueberries. Cook for 5 minutes or until heated through. Serve over French toast; sprinkle with almonds.

Yield: 8 servings.

crepes for another use. Crepes may be frozen for up to 3 months.

5 Pipe filling onto the center of each remaining crepe. Top with 2 tablespoons pie filling. Fold side edges of crepe to the center. Drizzle with fudge topping and garnish with whipped topping. Serve immediately.

Yield: 8 servings.

MINI SPINACH FRITTATAS

nancy statkevicus, tucson, arizona

These mini frittatas are a cinch to make and just delicious. The recipe doubles easily for a crowd and even freezes well for added convenience.

      1 cup ricotta cheese
    3/4 cup grated Parmesan cheese
    2/3 cup chopped fresh mushrooms
      1 package (10 ounces) frozen chopped spinach, thawed and squeezed dry
      1 egg
    1/2 teaspoon dried oregano
    1/4 teaspoon salt
    1/4 teaspoon pepper
     24 slices pepperoni

1 In a small bowl, combine the first eight ingredients. Place a slice of pepperoni in each of 24 greased miniature muffin cups. Fill muffin cups three-fourths full with cheese mixture.

2 Bake at 375° for 20-25 minutes or until a toothpick comes out clean. Carefully run a knife around edges of muffin cups to loosen. Serve warm.

Yield: 2 dozen.

CHOCOLATE-CHERRY CREAM CREPES

kimberly witt, minot, north dakota

My son calls me a gourmet cook whenever I make his favorite crepes. Sometimes, for a change, I substitute apple pie filling for the cherries and top the golden crepes with warm caramel sauce.

  1-1/4 cups milk
      3 eggs
      2 tablespoons butter, melted
    3/4 cup all-purpose flour
      1 tablespoon sugar
    1/4 teaspoon salt
      1 package (8 ounces) cream cheese, softened
    1/2 cup confectioners' sugar
      1 teaspoon vanilla extract
      1 can (21 ounces) cherry pie filling

Chocolate fudge ice cream topping and whipped topping

1 In a large bowl, combine milk, eggs and butter. Combine the flour, sugar and salt; add to egg mixture and mix well. Cover; refrigerate for 1 hour.

2 For filling, in a small bowl, beat cream cheese until fluffy. Beat in confectioners' sugar and vanilla until smooth; set aside.

3 Heat a lightly greased 8-in. nonstick skillet; pour 2 tablespoons batter into the center of skillet. Lift and tilt pan to evenly coat bottom. Cook until top appears dry; turn and cook 15-20 seconds longer.

4 Remove to a wire rack. Repeat with remaining batter, greasing skillet as needed. Stack crepes with waxed paper between. Cover and freeze 10

JACK CHEESE OVEN OMELET

aurel roberts, vancouver, washington

Although it's simple, the omelet looks like you fussed. Sometimes I toss in mushrooms and cheddar cheese for a different flavor.

- 8 bacon strips, diced
- 4 green onions, sliced
- 8 eggs
- 1 cup milk
- 1/2 teaspoon seasoned salt
- 2-1/2 cups (10 ounces) shredded Monterey Jack cheese, *divided*

1 In a large skillet, cook bacon until crisp. Drain, reserving 1 tablespoon drippings. Set bacon aside. Saute onion in drippings until tender; set aside.

2 In a large bowl, beat eggs. Add milk, seasoned salt, 2 cups cheese, bacon and sauteed onions. Transfer to a greased shallow 2-qt. baking dish. Bake, uncovered, at 350° for 35-40 minutes. Sprinkle with remaining cheese.

Yield: 6 servings.

GLAZED POPPY SEED DOUGHNUTS

at hawryliw, saskatoon, saskatchewan

Light as a feather, these pretty glazed doughnuts are ny husband's all-time favorites. They're something to celebrate any time of year!

- 1 tablespoon active dry yeast
- 1 teaspoon plus 1/2 cup sugar, *divided*
- 1 cup warm water (110° to 115°)
- 2/3 cup warm milk (110° to 115°)
- 1/3 cup poppy seeds
- 1 cup warm mashed potatoes (prepared without added milk and butter)
- 3 eggs
- 1/2 cup shortening
- 1 teaspoon salt
- 1 teaspoon ground cinnamon
- 7 to 8 cups all-purpose flour

Oil for deep-fat frying

GLAZE:
- 1/2 cup sugar
- 1/4 cup milk
- 1/4 cup butter, cubed
- 1/2 cup confectioners' sugar
- 1/4 teaspoon salt
- 1/4 teaspoon vanilla extract

1 In a large bowl, dissolve yeast and 1 teaspoon sugar in warm water. In another bowl, combine milk and poppy seeds. Let each bowl stand for 5 minutes. Add the potatoes, eggs, shortening, salt, cinnamon, poppy seed mixture and 3 cups flour to the yeast mixture. Beat until smooth. Stir in enough remaining flour to form a soft dough.

2 Turn onto a floured surface; knead until smooth and elastic, about 6-8 minutes. Place in a greased bowl, turning once to grease top. Cover and let rise in a warm place until doubled, about 1 hour.

3 Punch dough down. Turn onto a lightly floured surface; divide into fourths. Roll out each portion to 1/2-in. thickness. Cut with a lightly floured 2-1/2-in. doughnut cutter. Place on greased baking sheets. Cover and let rise for 30 minutes.

4 In an electric skillet or deep-fat fryer, heat oil to 375°. Fry doughnuts, a few at a time, for 1-1/2 minutes on each side or until golden brown. Drain on paper towels.

5 In a saucepan, bring sugar, milk and butter to a boil. Cook and stir for 1 minute. Remove from heat; cool completely. Stir in confectioners' sugar, salt and vanilla until smooth. Drizzle over doughnuts.

Yield: 3-1/2 dozen.

FESTIVE FRENCH PANCAKES

diane aune, sacramento, california

Not quite as thin as true crepes, these light-as-a-feather pancakes are topped with preserves and a dusting of confectioners' sugar. They're elegant, so easy to make and say "Joyeux Noel" with delicious French flair!

- 2/3 cup milk
- 2 eggs
- 1/3 cup water
- 1/2 teaspoon vanilla extract
- 3/4 cup all-purpose flour
- 2 tablespoons confectioners' sugar
- 1 teaspoon baking powder
- 1/2 teaspoon salt

Preserves of your choice, optional

Additional confectioners' sugar, optional

1 In a blender, combine the milk, eggs, water and vanilla; cover and process until well blended. Combine the flour, confectioners' sugar, baking powder and salt; add to egg mixture. Cover and process until smooth.

2 Heat a lightly greased 8-in. nonstick skillet over medium heat; pour 2 tablespoons batter into the center of skillet. Lift and tilt pan to coat bottom evenly. Cook until top appears dry; turn and cook 15-20 seconds longer. Remove to a wire rack. Repeat with remaining batter, greasing skillet as needed. Spread preserves over pancakes if desired; roll up. Sprinkle with confectioners' sugar if desired.

Yield: 8 pancakes.

VEGETABLE FRITTATA

alice parker, moultrie, georgia

This fresh-tasting dish is an easy all-in-one meal. The bacon, eggs and hash browns make it filling. The green broccoli and red paprika give it a look that fits the season.

- 4 bacon strips, cut into 1/2-inch pieces
- 2 cups frozen shredded hash browns, thawed
- 1 cup chopped broccoli
- 1/2 cup chopped green pepper
- 1/2 cup chopped red onion
- 1/2 to 1 teaspoon dried rosemary, crushed
- 6 eggs
- 3 tablespoons water
- 1/2 teaspoon salt
- 1/4 teaspoon pepper
- 1/4 teaspoon paprika

1 In a 8-in. ovenproof skillet, cook the bacon until crisp. Drain, reserving 2 tablespoons drippings in the skillet. Remove bacon to paper towel. To the skillet, add hash browns, broccoli, green pepper, onion and rosemary; cover and cook over low heat until hash browns are golden brown and vegetables are tender, about 10 minutes. Remove from the heat and set aside.

2 Beat eggs, water, salt and pepper; pour over hash browns. Top with bacon and paprika. Bake uncovered, at 350° for 12-15 minutes or until eggs are completely set.

Yield: 4-6 servings.

PETITE SAUSAGE QUICHES

dawn stitt, hesperia, michigan

You won't be able to eat just one of these cute mini quiches. Filled with savory sausage, Swiss cheese and a dash of cayenne, the mouth-watering morsels will disappear fast from the breakfast or buffet table.

- 1 cup butter, softened
- 2 packages (3 ounces *each*) cream cheese, softened
- 2 cups all-purpose flour

FILLING:

- 6 ounces bulk Italian sausage
- 1 cup (4 ounces) shredded Swiss cheese
- 1 tablespoon minced chives
- 2 eggs
- 1 cup half-and-half cream
- 1/4 teaspoon salt

Dash cayenne pepper

1 In a large bowl, beat the butter, cream cheese and flour until smooth. Shape tablespoonfuls of dough into balls; press onto the bottom and up the sides of greased miniature muffin cups.

2 In a large skillet, cook sausage over medium heat until no longer pink; drain. Sprinkle sausage, Swiss cheese and chives into muffin cups. In a small bowl, beat eggs, cream, salt and pepper until blended. Pour into shells.

3 Bake at 375° for 28-30 minutes or until browned. Serve warm.

Yield: 3 dozen.

HOT CURRIED FRUIT

maryellen hays, wolcottville, indiana

Attractive and full of flavor, this comforting fruit dish makes a great accompaniment to any hearty breakfast casserole. The spices give it special character.

- 1 can (20 ounces) unsweetened pineapple chunks
- 1 can (16 ounces) pitted dark sweet cherries, drained
- 1 can (15-1/4 ounces) pear halves, drained
- 1 can (15-1/4 ounces) peach halves, drained
- 3/4 cup packed brown sugar
- 1/4 cup butter, melted
- 1 teaspoon curry powder
- 1 teaspoon ground cinnamon
- 1/2 teaspoon ground nutmeg

1 Drain pineapple, reserving juice. In a greased 2-qt. baking dish, combine the pineapple, cherries, pears and peaches. In a small bowl, combine the brown sugar, butter, curry, cinnamon, nutmeg and reserved juice; pour over fruit.

2 Cover and bake at 350° for 35-45 minutes or until heated through.

Yield: 8 servings.

mixture. Pour into ungreased 1-cup souffle dishes or custard cups. Place in a shallow baking pan. Add 1 in. of hot water to pan.

4 Bake, uncovered, at 325° for 20 minutes. Remove custard cups to wire racks to cool. Cover and refrigerate for up to 4 hours.

5 Remove from the refrigerator 30 minutes before baking. Uncover; sprinkle with remaining cheese. Bake at 425° for 15-20 minutes or until puffed and golden brown.

Yield: 4 servings.

MEAT-LOVER'S OMELET ROLL

roberta gibbs, kamiah, idaho
This is our favorite breakfast to prepare for company. When I make it for just my husband and myself, we get to enjoy the luscious leftovers!

- 1 cup mayonnaise, *divided*
- 1 tablespoon prepared mustard
- 1-1/2 teaspoons prepared horseradish
- 1-1/2 teaspoons plus 1/4 cup finely chopped onion, *divided*
- 2 tablespoons all-purpose flour
- 12 eggs, *separated*
- 1 cup milk
- 1/2 teaspoon salt
- 1/8 teaspoon pepper
- 1/2 cup finely chopped celery
- 2 teaspoons canola oil
- 1 cup cubed fully cooked ham
- 3/4 cup cooked pork sausage, drained and crumbled
- 8 bacon strips, cooked and crumbled
- 1 cup (4 ounces) shredded Swiss cheese

1 For mustard sauce, in a small bowl, combine 1/2 cup mayonnaise, mustard, horseradish and 1-1/2 teaspoons onion until blended. Refrigerate until serving. Line a 15-in. x 10-in. x 1-in. baking pan with waxed paper; grease the paper and set aside.

2 In a large saucepan, combine flour and remaining mayonnaise until smooth. In a large bowl, whisk egg yolks until thickened. Add the milk, salt and pepper; whisk into flour mixture. Cook over medium-low heat for 6-7 minutes or until slightly thickened. Remove from the heat. Cool for 15 minutes.

3 In a large bowl, beat egg whites until stiff peaks form. Gradually fold into egg yolk mixture. Spread into prepared pan. Bake at 425° for 12-15 minutes or until golden brown.

TWICE-BAKED CHEESE SOUFFLES

taste of home test kitchen
You'll easily impress guests with these individual cheese souffles from our home economists. Partially bake and refrigerate them early in the morning. Then simply sprinkle with cheese and finish baking when you're ready.

- 3 tablespoons butter
- 1/4 cup all-purpose flour
- 2 cups plus 2 tablespoons milk
- 1/4 teaspoon onion powder
- 1/4 teaspoon salt
- 1/8 teaspoon ground nutmeg
- 1/8 teaspoon pepper
- 2 cups (8 ounces) shredded cheddar cheese, *divided*
- 3 eggs, *separated*

1 In a saucepan, melt butter. Stir in the flour until smooth. Gradually add milk, onion powder, salt, nutmeg and pepper. Bring to a boil; cook and stir for 2 minutes or until thickened. Reduce heat; add 1 cup cheese and stir until melted. Remove from the heat; set aside.

2 In a small bowl, beat egg yolks until thick and lemon-colored, about 3 minutes. Stir in 1/3 cup hot cheese sauce. Return all to the pan; cook and stir for 1-2 minutes. Cool completely.

3 In large bowl, beat egg whites on high speed until stiff peaks form. Gently fold into cooled cheese

1-1/2 teaspoons sugar
1-1/2 teaspoons white wine vinegar
   1 garlic clove, minced
1/2 teaspoon salt
1/4 teaspoon dried oregano

1 Place one sheet of phyllo dough on a work surface; brush with butter. Top with another sheet of phyllo; brush with butter. Cut into six 4-1/2-in. squares. (Keep remaining phyllo dough covered with plastic wrap to avoid drying out.) Repeat with remaining phyllo and butter.

2 Stack three squares of layered phyllo in each of four greased muffin cups, rotating squares so corners do not overlap. Sprinkle 1 teaspoon of cheese into each cup. Top with one egg. Sprinkle with green onion, salt and pepper. Place on a baking sheet. Bake at 350° for 25-30 minutes or until the eggs are completely set and the pastry is golden brown.

3 Meanwhile, in a saucepan, combine the salsa ingredients. Bring to a boil over medium heat. Reduce heat; simmer, uncovered, for 10 minutes or until onion is tender. Serve with egg cups.

Yield: 4 servings.

4 Meanwhile, in a large skillet, saute celery and remaining onion in oil until crisp-tender. Add the ham, sausage and bacon; heat through and keep warm.

5 Remove omelet from oven. Run a knife around edges to loosen; invert onto a kitchen towel. Gently peel off waxed paper. Sprinkle cheese over omelet to within 1 in. of edges. Top with meat mixture. Roll up from a short side. Transfer to a serving platter, seam side down. Cut with a serrated knife. Serve with mustard sauce.

Yield: 8 servings.

EGG BLOSSOMS

barbara nowakowski, north tonawanda, new york
These cute phyllo dough shells are filled with a savory combination of Parmesan cheese, egg and green onion. The flaky cups are served atop a warm homemade salsa.

   4 sheets phyllo dough (14 inches x 9 inches)
   2 tablespoons butter, melted
   4 teaspoons grated Parmesan cheese
   4 eggs
   4 teaspoons finely chopped green onion
1/4 teaspoon salt
1/8 teaspoon pepper

SALSA:
   1 can (14-1/2 ounces) diced tomatoes, undrained
   1 small onion, chopped

CORNMEAL HAM CAKES

priscilla gilbert, indian harbour beach, florida
These cakes are great for breakfast, but my husband and I also enjoy them for supper.

- 1/2 cup all-purpose flour
- 1/2 cup cornmeal
- 2 tablespoons sugar
- 1/2 teaspoon baking powder
- 1/4 teaspoon baking soda
- 1/8 teaspoon salt
- 2 eggs, lightly beaten
- 1 cup buttermilk
- 3 tablespoons butter, melted
- 1 teaspoon vanilla extract
- 1-1/2 cups diced fully cooked ham

PINEAPPLE MAPLE SYRUP:
- 1 cup diced fresh pineapple
- 1/4 teaspoon ground cinnamon
- 1 tablespoon butter
- 1 cup maple syrup

1   In a large bowl, combine the first six ingredients. Combine the eggs, buttermilk, butter and vanilla; stir into dry ingredients until well blended. Fold in ham. Pour batter by 1/4 cupfuls onto a greased hot griddle. Turn when bubbles form on top; cook until second side is golden brown.

2   For syrup, in a small saucepan, saute pineapple and cinnamon in butter for 4-6 minutes or until pineapple is browned. Stir in maple syrup. Serve with pancakes.

Yield: 4 servings.

GRAPEFRUIT ALASKA

peg atzen, hackensack, minnesota
You'll easily impress guests with this recipe. It takes some time to prepare, but the rave reviews I receive make it all worth it.

- 4 large grapefruit
- 2 teaspoons rum extract
- 1/2 cup heavy whipping cream, whipped
- 3 egg whites
- 1 teaspoon cornstarch
- 1/4 teaspoon cream of tartar
- 1/4 cup sugar
- 8 maraschino cherries

1   Halve grapefruit and section; remove membranes. Return grapefruit sections to grapefruit halves. Drizzle 1/4 teaspoon rum extract over each. Top with 1 rounded tablespoon of whipped cream; place on an ungreased foil-lined baking sheet.

2   In a large bowl, beat the egg whites, cornstarch and cream of tartar on medium speed until soft peaks form. Gradually beat in sugar, 1 tablespoon at a time, on high until stiff glossy peaks form and sugar is dissolved. Mound 1/2 cup on each grapefruit half; spread meringue to edges to seal. Bake at 350° for 15 minutes or until meringue is browned. Top each with a cherry. Serve immediately.

Yield: 8 servings.

GREEN 'N' GOLD EGG BAKE

muriel paceleo, montgomery, new york

I need just five ingredients to assemble this pretty casserole. The firm squares have a delicious spinach flavor that's welcome at breakfast or dinner.

- 1 cup seasoned bread crumbs, *divided*
- 2 packages (10 ounces *each*) frozen chopped spinach, thawed and squeezed dry
- 3 cups (24 ounces) 4% cottage cheese
- 1/2 cup grated Romano *or* Parmesan cheese
- 5 eggs

1. Sprinkle 1/4 cup bread crumbs into a greased 8-in. square baking dish. Bake at 350° for 3-5 minutes or until golden brown.

2. Meanwhile, in a large bowl, combine the spinach, cottage cheese, Romano cheese, three eggs and remaining crumbs. Spread over the baked crumbs. Beat remaining eggs; pour over spinach mixture.

3. Bake, uncovered, at 350° for 45 minutes or until a knife inserted near the center comes out clean. Let stand for 5-10 minutes before serving.

Yield: 9 servings.

GINGERBREAD PANCAKES

michelle smith, sykesville, maryland

I wake 'em up Christmas morning with the delightful aroma of these fluffy pancakes. They've got a great gingerbread flavor and pretty fruit topping! You can substitute boysenberry, blueberry or strawberry syrup for maple, if you'd like a tasty change.

- 1 cup all-purpose flour
- 2 tablespoons sugar
- 1 teaspoon baking powder
- 1/2 teaspoon ground cinnamon
- 1/4 teaspoon ground ginger
- 1/4 teaspoon ground allspice
- 1 egg
- 3/4 cup milk
- 2 tablespoons molasses
- 1 tablespoon canola oil
- 6 tablespoons maple pancake syrup
- 3/4 cup apple pie filling, warmed
- 3 tablespoons dried cranberries

1. In a large bowl, combine the first six ingredients. Combine the egg, milk, molasses and oil; stir into dry ingredients just until moistened.

2. Pour batter by 1/4 cupfuls onto a greased hot griddle; turn when bubbles form on top. Cook until the second side is golden brown.

3. To serve, place two pancakes on each plate; drizzle with 2 tablespoons syrup. Top with 1/4 cup apple pie filling; sprinkle with cranberries.

Yield: 3 servings.

SPINACH BRUNCH PIE

gertie kwant, stanwood, washington

You won't believe how easy it is to assemble this egg dish. With tomatoes, eggs and spinach, every bite is colorful and flavorful.

- 1 package (10 ounces) frozen chopped spinach, thawed and squeezed dry
- 1 teaspoon white vinegar
- 1/2 teaspoon ground nutmeg
- 3 eggs
- 1 cup (8 ounces) 4% cottage cheese
- 1 cup (8 ounces) sour cream
- 1/2 cup biscuit/baking mix
- 1/4 cup butter, melted
- 3 small tomatoes, thinly sliced
- 2 tablespoons shredded Parmesan cheese

1 In a small bowl, combine the spinach, vinegar and nutmeg. Spread into a greased 9-in. pie plate. In a blender, combine the eggs, cottage cheese, sour cream, biscuit mix and butter; cover and process until smooth. Pour over spinach mixture.

2 Bake, uncovered, at 350° for 25-30 minutes or until almost set. Arrange tomato slices over the top; sprinkle with Parmesan cheese. Bake 5-10 minutes longer or untila thermometer reads 160°. Let stand for 10 minutes before serving.

Yield: 6 servings.

CRANBERRY SURPRISE MUFFINS

helen howley, mount laurel, new jersey

This recipe has been in my family since 1943, so these muffins have been enjoyed during the holidays for many years. The "surprise" is a dollop of cranberry sauce in the center. We like to eat them fresh from the oven.

- 2 cups all-purpose flour
- 2 tablespoons sugar
- 3 teaspoons baking powder
- 1/2 teaspoon salt
- 2 eggs
- 1 cup milk
- 1/4 cup butter, melted
- 1 cup jellied cranberry sauce

1 In a large bowl, combine the flour, sugar, baking powder and salt. In another bowl, whisk the eggs, milk and butter. Stir into the dry ingredients just until moistened.

2 Fill 12 greased muffin cups one-fourth full. Drop a rounded tablespoonful of cranberry sauce into each cup. Top with the remaining batter.

3 Bake at 400° for 12-15 minutes or until muffin tops spring back when lightly touched. Cool for 5 minutes before removing from pan to a wire rack. Serve warm.

Yield: 1 dozen.

Editor's Note: These muffins are best served the day they're made.

TOFFEE APPLE FRENCH TOAST

renee endress, galva, illinois

I love quick breakfast recipes that can be put together the night before, saving time on busy mornings. I created this dish by incorporating my family's favorite apple dip with French toast. The winning combination is perfect for overnight guests.

- 8 cups cubed French bread (1-inch cubes)
- 2 medium tart apples, peeled and chopped
- 1 package (8 ounces) cream cheese, softened
- 3/4 cup packed brown sugar
- 1/4 cup sugar
- 1-3/4 cups milk, *divided*
- 2 teaspoons vanilla extract, *divided*
- 1/2 cup English toffee bits *or* almond brickle chips
- 5 eggs

1 Place half of the bread cubes in a greased 13-in. x 9-in. baking dish; top with apples. In a large bowl, beat the cream cheese, sugars, 1/4 cup milk and 1 teaspoon vanilla until smooth; stir in toffee the bits. Spread over apples. Top with remaining bread cubes.

2 In another bowl, beat the eggs and remaining milk and vanilla until blended; pour over the bread. Cover and refrigerate overnight.

3 Remove from the refrigerator 30 minutes before baking. Bake, uncovered, at 350° for 35-45 minutes or until a knife inserted near the center comes out clean.

Yield: 8 servings.

FRUITED DUTCH BABY

shirley robertson, versailles, missouri

This traditional oven-baked pancake is a sensational way to showcase fruit, and it makes an ideal holiday breakfast or brunch. If you prefer, sprinkle with powdered sugar or serve it with other fresh fruit or canned pie filling.

- 1 tablespoon butter
- 3/4 cup all-purpose flour
- 1 tablespoon sugar
- 1/4 teaspoon salt
- 3 eggs, lightly beaten
- 3/4 cup milk
- 1-1/2 cups sliced fresh strawberries
- 2 medium firm bananas, sliced

Whipped cream, optional

- 1/4 cup flaked coconut, toasted

1 Place butter in a 9-in. pie plate. Place in a 400° oven for 5 minutes or until melted. Meanwhile, in a large bowl, combine the flour, sugar and salt. Stir in eggs and milk until smooth. Pour into prepared pie plate. Bake for 15-20 minutes or until golden brown.

2 In a large bowl, combine the strawberries and bananas. Using a slotted spoon, place fruit in center of pancake. Top with whipped cream if desired. Sprinkle with toasted coconut. Serve immediately.

Yield: 6 servings.

APRICOT-COCONUT FRENCH TOAST

jean groen, apache junction, arizona

I look for easy food to prepare for various functions. This breakfast dish has always brought raves and recipe requests! Leftovers, if there are any, are wonderful. Just microwave them for 15 seconds per slice.

- 1/2 cup chopped dried apricots
- 1/2 cup water
- 1/4 cup butter, melted
- 2/3 cup flaked coconut, toasted
- 1/4 cup sugar
- 1-1/4 teaspoons ground cinnamon
- 7 eggs
- 1-3/4 cups milk
- 1 teaspoon vanilla extract
- Pinch salt
- 16 slices French bread (1 inch thick)
- Maple syrup

1 In a small microwave-safe bowl, heat apricots and water on high for 2 minutes or until mixture comes to a boil. Let stand for 5 minutes; drain.

2 Pour butter into a 15-in. x 10-in. x 1-in. baking pan and tilt to coat bottom. Sprinkle with coconut and apricots. Combine sugar and cinnamon; sprinkle over fruit.

3 In a large shallow bowl, whisk the eggs, milk, vanilla and salt. Dip bread into egg mixture; soak for 1 minute. Place slices close together over coconut mixture. Cover and refrigerate overnight.

4 Remove from the refrigerator 30 minutes before baking. Bake, uncovered, at 375° for 20-25 minutes or until golden brown. Serve with syrup.

Yield: 8 servings.

Editor's Note: A dark baking pan is not recommended for this recipe.

COUNTRY BRUNCH PIE

karen corn, greenfield, indiana

This egg pie makes a great brunch dish with fruit and muffins, or serve it for lunch with tossed greens and French bread.

- Pastry for single-crust pie (9 inches)
- 1/2 pound bulk pork sausage
- 3/4 cup shredded part-skim mozzarella cheese
- 4 eggs
- 1 cup half-and-half cream
- 1 can (4 ounces) mushroom stems and pieces, drained
- 1/4 cup chopped green pepper
- 1/4 cup chopped sweet red pepper
- 2 tablespoons chopped onion

1 Line a 9-in. deep-dish pie plate with pastry. Trim to 1/2 in. beyond edge of plate; flute edges. Line pastry shell with a double thickness of heavy-duty foil. Bake at 400° for 5 minutes. Remove foil; bake 5 minutes longer.

2 In a small skillet, cook sausage over medium heat until no longer pink; drain. Spoon sausage into crust; sprinkle with cheese. In a small bowl, combine the eggs, cream, mushrooms, peppers and onion; pour over cheese.

3 Bake at 375° for 40-45 minutes or until a knife inserted near the center comes out clean. Let pie stand for 10 minutes before cutting.

Yield: 6-8 servings.

CHERRY CRESCENT COFFEE CAKE

valerie belley, st. louis, missouri

A can of pie filling and a couple tubes of crescent rolls help me assemble this sweet treat. It's the perfect addition to hot cups of coffee and good conversation.

- 1 package (8 ounces) cream cheese, softened
- 3/4 cup confectioners' sugar, *divided*
- 1 egg
- 1/2 teaspoon vanilla extract
- 2 tubes (8 ounces *each*) refrigerated crescent rolls
- 1 can (21 ounces) cherry pie filling
- 2 to 3 teaspoons milk

1 In a small bowl, beat cream cheese and 1/4 cup confectioners' sugar until smooth. Add egg; beat just until combined. Stir in vanilla; set aside.

2 Unroll crescent dough and separate into triangles. Set four triangles aside. Place remaining triangles on a greased 14-in. pizza pan, forming a ring with wide ends facing outer edge of pan and pointed ends toward the center; leave a 3-in. hole in the center. Lightly press seams together.

3 Spread cream cheese mixture over dough to within 1/2 in. of edges. Top with pie filling to within 1/2 in. of cream cheese edges. Cut reserved triangles into thirds, starting at the wide end and ending at the point. Arrange over pie filling with points facing outer edge of pan, forming spokes. Press ends at center and outer edge to seal.

4 Bake at 375° for 15-20 minutes or until golden brown. Cool on a wire rack. Combine remaining confectioners' sugar and enough milk to achieve drizzling consistency; drizzle over coffee cake.

Yield: 12 servings.

SWEET POTATO MUFFINS

susan bracken, state college, pennsylvania

Minced gingerroot and dried orange peel enhance the taste of these spiced muffins. I especially love the whipped ginger butter served with these warm holiday treats.

- 1-1/2 cups all-purpose flour
- 1 cup plus 1 tablespoon sugar, *divided*
- 3 teaspoons baking powder
- 3 teaspoons grated orange peel
- 1-1/2 teaspoons ground ginger
- 1 teaspoon baking soda
- 1/4 teaspoon salt
- 2 eggs, lightly beaten
- 1 cup cold mashed sweet potatoes (prepared without milk *or* butter)
- 1/4 teaspoon ground cinnamon

GINGER BUTTER:
- 1/2 cup butter, softened
- 2 tablespoons finely chopped crystallized ginger

1 In a large bowl, combine the flour, 1 cup sugar, baking powder, orange peel, ginger, baking soda and salt. Whisk eggs and sweet potatoes; stir into dry ingredients just until moistened.

2 Fill greased or paper-lined muffin cups two-thirds full. Combine cinnamon and remaining sugar; sprinkle over batter.

3 Bake at 400° for 18-22 minutes or until a toothpick inserted near the center comes out clean. Cool for 5 minutes before removing from pans to wire racks.

4 In a small bowl, combine the ginger butter ingredients. Serve with warm muffins.

Yield: 1 dozen.

JOLLY JELLY DOUGHNUTS

lee bremson, kansas city, missouri
Just looking at these fat, festive, jelly-filled doughnuts will make your mouth water. Serve them warm, and you'll find folks licking sugar from their fingers and asking you for seconds.

- 2 packages (1/4 ounce *each*) active dry yeast
- 2 cups warm milk (110° to 115°)
- 7 cups all-purpose flour, *divided*
- 4 egg yolks
- 1 egg
- 1/2 cup sugar
- 1 teaspoon salt
- 2 teaspoons grated lemon peel
- 1/2 teaspoon vanilla extract
- 1/2 cup butter, melted

Oil for deep-fat frying

Red jelly of your choice

Additional sugar

1 In a large bowl, dissolve yeast in warm milk. Add 2 cups flour; mix well. Let stand in a warm place for 30 minutes. Add the egg yolks, egg, sugar, salt, lemon peel and vanilla; mix well. Beat in butter and remaining flour. Do not knead. Cover and let dough rise in a warm place until doubled, about 45 minutes.

2 Punch dough down. On a lightly floured surface, roll out to 1/2 in. thickness. Cut with a 2-1/2-in. biscuit cutter. Place on lightly greased baking sheets. Cover and let rise until nearly double, about 35 minutes.

3 In a deep-fat fryer or electric skillet, heat oil to 375°. Fry doughnuts, a few at a time, for 1-1/2 to

2 minutes on each side or until lightly browned. Drain on paper towels.

4 Cool for 2-3 minutes; cut a small slit with a sharp knife on one side of each doughnut. Cut a small hole in the corner of a pastry or plastic bag; insert a very small round tip. Fill with jelly. Fill each doughnut with about 1 teaspoon jelly. Carefully roll doughnuts in sugar. Serve warm.

Yield: About 2-1/2 dozen.

CREAMY HAM 'N' EGG CASSEROLE

dixie terry, goreville, illinois
Have leftover cooked potatoes or eggs on hand? Here's a terrific way to use them up! This breakfast main dish is a great way to fill up family members before they leave for work, school or wherever they need to be.

- 2 medium cooked potatoes, peeled and sliced
- 4 hard-cooked eggs, chopped
- 1 cup diced fully cooked ham
- 1/2 teaspoon salt
- 1/4 teaspoon pepper
- 1 egg
- 1-1/2 cups (12 ounces) sour cream
- 1/4 cup dry bread crumbs
- 1 tablespoon butter, melted

1 In a large bowl, combine the potatoes, cooked eggs, ham, salt and pepper. Combine the raw egg and sour cream; add to the potato mixture and gently toss to coat. Transfer to a greased 11-in. x 7-in. baking dish.

2 Toss bread crumbs and butter; sprinkle over casserole. Bake, uncovered, at 350° for 20 minutes or until a thermometer reaches 160°.

Yield: 6 servings.

GREATEST GRANOLA

jonie daigle, greensburg, pennsylvania

After clipping granola recipes for years, I chose my favorite ingredients from each one, added a few of my own and came up with this tasty version. Try different combinations of dried fruit, nuts and flavored yogurt for a variety of interesting blends.

- 2 cups old-fashioned oats
- 1 cup Grape-Nuts
- 1/2 cup sliced almonds
- 1/2 cup honey
- 1/3 cup canola oil
- 1/4 cup packed brown sugar
- 1-1/2 teaspoons vanilla extract
- 1/4 teaspoon ground cinnamon
- 1 cup crisp rice cereal
- 1/2 cup toasted wheat germ
- 1/2 cup chopped dried apricots
- 1/2 cup dried cranberries, chopped

Yogurt flavor of your choice, optional

1 In a large bowl, combine the oats, Grape-Nuts and almonds. Spread onto a greased, foil-lined 15-in. x 10-in. x 1-in. baking pan. Coat mixture with cooking spray. Bake, uncovered, at 300° for 20 minutes, stirring once.

2 Meanwhile, in a small saucepan, combine the honey, oil and brown sugar. Cook and stir over low heat until heated through. Remove from the heat; stir in vanilla and cinnamon.

3 Stir cereal and wheat germ into oat mixture. Drizzle with honey mixture; stir to coat. Bake 5-10 minutes longer or until golden brown. Cool on a wire rack.

4 Break granola into pieces. Sprinkle with apricots and cranberries and mix well. Store in an airtight container. Serve with yogurt if desired.

Yield: about 8 cups.

BRUNCH RISOTTO

jennifer dines, brighton, massachusetts

This light, flavorful and inexpensive risotto makes a surprising addition to a traditional brunch menu. It's gotten lots of compliments from my friends.

- 5-1/4 to 5-3/4 cups reduced-sodium chicken broth
- 3/4 pound Italian turkey sausage links, casings removed
- 2 cups uncooked arborio rice
- 1 garlic clove, minced
- 1/4 teaspoon pepper
- 1 tablespoon olive oil
- 1 medium tomato, chopped

1 In a large saucepan, heat broth and keep warm. In a large nonstick skillet, cook sausage until no longer pink; drain and set aside.

2 In the same skillet, saute the rice, garlic and pepper in oil for 2-3 minutes. Return sausage to skillet. Carefully stir in 1 cup heated broth. Cook and stir until all of the liquid is absorbed.

3 Add remaining broth, 1/2 cup at a time, stirring constantly. Allow liquid to absorb between additions. Cook just until risotto is creamy and rice is almost tender. Total cooking time is about 20 minutes. Add tomato; cook and stir until heated through. Serve immediately.

Yield: 8 servings.

ASPARAGUS CHEESE QUICHE

sheryl long, lincolnton, north carolina

The fluffy texture of this quiche practically melts in your mouth! The green asparagus and red tomatoes on top make this a natural for the holidays.

- 1/2 **pound fresh asparagus, trimmed and halved lengthwise**
- 1 **cup (8 ounces) sour cream**
- 1 **cup (8 ounces) 4% cottage cheese**
- 2 **egg whites**
- 1 **egg**
- 2 **tablespoons butter, melted**
- 5 **tablespoons grated Parmesan cheese,** *divided*
- 1/4 **cup all-purpose flour**
- 1/2 **teaspoon baking powder**
- 1/4 **teaspoon salt**
- 1 **plum tomato, sliced**

1 In a large saucepan, bring 4 cups water to a boil. Add asparagus; cover and boil for 3 minutes. Drain and immediately place asparagus in ice water. Drain and pat dry. Arrange half of the spears in a spoke pattern in a greased 9-in. pie plate.

2 In a blender, combine the sour cream, cottage cheese, egg whites, egg and butter; cover and process until smooth. Add 3 tablespoons Parmesan cheese, flour, baking powder and salt; cover and process until blended. Carefully pour over asparagus. Arrange remaining asparagus in a spoke pattern over the top. Sprinkle with remaining Parmesan cheese.

3 Bake at 350° for 25-30 minutes or until a knife inserted near the center comes out clean. Garnish with the sliced tomato. Let stand for 10 minutes before slicing.

Yield: 6 servings.

LEMON PULL-APART COFFEE CAKE

mary tallman, arbor vitae, wisconsin

I found this recipe in a newspaper and make it often. I like to bake this coffee cake when unexpected company stops in, and I need something speedy to go with a cup of coffee.

- 1/4 **cup sugar**
- 1/4 **cup chopped walnuts**
- 1/4 **cup golden raisins**
- 2 **tablespoons butter, melted**
- 2 **teaspoons grated lemon peel**
- 1 **tube (12 ounces) refrigerated buttermilk biscuits**

GLAZE:
- 1/2 **cup confectioners' sugar**
- 1 **tablespoon lemon juice**

1 In a large bowl, combine the first five ingredients. Separate biscuits and cut each into quarters; toss with sugar mixture. Place in a greased 9-in. round baking pan.

2 Bake at 400° for 20-25 minutes or until golden brown. Immediately invert onto a wire rack. Combine glaze ingredients until smooth; drizzle over warm coffee cake.

Yield: 10 servings.

CHICKEN 'N' HAM FRITTATA

ruth allen, hebron, kentucky

Because my family is busy, we often gather for Sunday brunch to discuss plans for the upcoming week over servings of this hearty egg dish. It's colorful and special enough to prepare for holiday get-togethers, too.

- 1/2 cup chopped green onions
- 2 garlic cloves, minced
- 2 tablespoons canola oil
- 1-1/4 cups chopped yellow summer squash
- 1 cup chopped zucchini
- 1/2 cup *each* chopped sweet yellow pepper and chopped sweet red pepper
- 1 teaspoon minced fresh gingerroot
- 2 cups cubed cooked chicken breast
- 1 cup chopped deli ham
- 6 eggs
- 3/4 cup mayonnaise
- 1/4 teaspoon prepared horseradish
- 1/4 teaspoon pepper
- 1 cup (4 ounces) shredded Monterey Jack cheese

1 In a large ovenproof skillet, saute the onions and garlic in oil for 1 minute. Add the yellow squash, zucchini, peppers and ginger; cook and stir for 8 minutes or until vegetables are crisp-tender. Add the chicken and ham; cook 1 minute longer or until heated through. Remove from the heat.

2 In a large bowl, whisk the eggs, mayonnaise, horseradish and pepper until blended. Pour into skillet.

3 Bake, uncovered, at 350° for 25-30 minutes or until eggs are completely set. Sprinkle with cheese; cover and let stand for 5 minutes or until cheese is melted.

Yield: 6 servings.

PEACH COBBLER COFFEE CAKE

virginia krites, cridersville, ohio

"Absolutely delicious" is how our taste-testers described this comforting coffee cake.

- 1 cup butter, softened
- 1 cup sugar
- 2 eggs
- 3 teaspoons vanilla extract
- 3 cups all-purpose flour
- 1 teaspoon *each* baking powder and baking soda
- 1/2 teaspoon salt
- 1-1/4 cups sour cream
- 1 can (21 ounces) peach pie filling
- 1 can (15-1/4 ounces) sliced peaches, drained

TOPPING:
- 1 cup packed brown sugar
- 1 cup all-purpose flour
- 1/2 cup quick-cooking oats
- 1/4 teaspoon ground cinnamon
- 1/2 cup cold butter, cubed

GLAZE:
- 1 cup confectioners' sugar
- 1 to 2 tablespoons milk

1 In a large bowl, cream butter and sugar until light and fluffy. Add eggs, one at a time, beating well after each addition. Beat in vanilla. Combine flour, baking powder, baking soda and salt; add to creamed mixture alternately with sour cream. Beat just until combined.

2 Pour half of the batter into a greased 13-in. x 9-in. baking dish. Combine pie filling and peaches; spread over batter. Drop remaining batter by tablespoonfuls over filling.

3 For topping, combine the brown sugar, flour, oats and cinnamon in a bowl. Cut in butter until mixture is crumbly. Sprinkle over batter.

4 Bake at 350° for 70-75 minutes or until a toothpick inserted near the center comes out clean. Cool on a wire rack. Combine glaze ingredients; drizzle over coffee cake.

Yield: 12 servings.

OVERNIGHT ASPARAGUS STRATA

lynn licata, sylvania, ohio

I've made this tasty egg dish for breakfast, brunch and even as a Christmas dinner side dish. With its English muffin crust, this is not your run-of-the-mill strata. Friends always ask for the recipe.

- 1 pound fresh asparagus, trimmed and cut into 1-inch pieces
- 4 English muffins, split and toasted
- 2 cups (8 ounces) shredded Colby-Monterey Jack cheese, *divided*
- 1 cup diced fully cooked ham
- 1/2 cup chopped sweet red pepper
- 8 eggs
- 2 cups milk
- 1 teaspoon salt
- 1 teaspoon ground mustard
- 1/4 teaspoon pepper

1 In a large saucepan, bring 8 cups water to a boil. Add asparagus; cover and cook for 3 minutes. Drain and immediately place asparagus in ice water. Drain and pat dry.

2 Arrange six English muffin halves, cut side up, in a greased 13-in. x 9-in. x 2-in. baking dish. Fill in spaces with remaining muffin halves. Sprinkle with 1 cup cheese, asparagus, ham and red pepper. In a bowl, whisk the eggs, milk, salt, mustard and pepper; pour over muffins. Cover and refrigerate overnight.

3 Remove from the refrigerator 30 minutes before baking. Sprinkle with remaining cheese. Bake, uncovered, at 375° for 40-45 minutes or until a knife inserted near the edge comes out clean. Let stand for 5 minutes before cutting.

Yield: 6-8 servings.

GIGANTIC CINNAMON ROLLS

kathy wells, brodhead, wisconsin

These large, luscious cinnamon rolls are always a hit at my parent's Christmas brunch. The recipe yields two, so you can keep one and give the other as a gift.

- 1/2 cup sugar
- 1/2 cup packed brown sugar
- 2 teaspoons ground cinnamon
- 2 loaves (1 pound *each*) frozen bread dough, thawed
- 1/2 cup butter, melted
- 1/2 cup chopped pecans
- 1-1/4 cups confectioners' sugar
- 6 teaspoons milk
- 1/2 teaspoon vanilla extract

1 In a shallow bowl, combine sugars and cinnamon; set aside. On a lightly floured surface, roll each loaf of dough into a 12-in. x 4-in. rectangle. Cut each rectangle lengthwise into four 1-in. strips. Roll each into an 18-in.-long rope. Dip in butter, then roll in sugar mixture.

2 Coil one rope in the center of a greased 12-in. pizza pan. Add three more ropes, pinching ends together to fill one pan. Repeat with remaining ropes on a second pizza pan. Sprinkle with pecans and remaining cinnamon-sugar. Cover and let rise in a warm place until doubled, about 45 minutes.

3 Bake at 350° for 20-30 minutes or until golden brown. In a small bowl, combine confectioners' sugar, milk and vanilla until smooth. Drizzle over warm rolls.

Yield: 2 rolls (6-8 servings each).

SUNSHINE CREPES

mary hobbs, campbell, missouri

My family wanted just a light brunch and coffee this year for Christmas morning, so I whipped up these sweet and fruity crepes that were a big hit with everyone!

> 2/3 cup milk
> 2 eggs
> 1 tablespoon canola oil
> 1/2 cup all-purpose flour
> 1 teaspoon sugar
> 1/4 teaspoon salt

FILLING:

> 1 can (20 ounces) crushed pineapple, drained
> 1 can (11 ounces) mandarin oranges, drained
> 1 teaspoon vanilla extract
> 1 carton (8 ounces) frozen whipped topping, thawed

Confectioners' sugar

1 In a large bowl, beat the milk, eggs and oil. Combine the flour, sugar and salt; add to the milk mixture and mix well. Cover and refrigerate for 1 hour.

2 Coat an 8-in. nonstick skillet with cooking spray; heat over medium heat. Stir crepe batter; pour 2 tablespoons into center of skillet. Lift and tilt pan to coat bottom evenly. Cook until top appears dry; turn and cook 15-20 seconds longer. Remove to a wire rack. Repeat with remaining batter, coating skillet as needed. When cool, stack crepes with waxed paper or paper towels in between.

3 For filling, in a large bowl, combine the pineapple, oranges and vanilla; fold in whipped topping. Spoon 1/3 cup down the center of each crepe; roll up. Dust with confectioners' sugar.

Yield: 6 servings.

HOT FRUIT COMPOTE

joyce moynihan, lakeville, minnesota

This sweet and colorful fruit compote is perfect with an egg casserole at a holiday brunch. It can bake right alongside the eggs, so everything is conveniently done at the same time.

> 2 cans (15-1/4 ounces *each*) sliced pears, drained
> 1 can (29 ounces) sliced peaches, drained
> 1 can (20 ounces) unsweetened pineapple chunks, drained
> 1 package (20 ounces) pitted dried plums
> 1 jar (16 ounces) unsweetened applesauce
> 1 can (21 ounces) cherry pie filling
> 1/4 cup packed brown sugar

1 In a large bowl, combine the first five ingredients. Pour into a 13-in. x 9-in. x 2-in. baking dish coated with cooking spray. Spread pie filling over fruit mixture; sprinkle with brown sugar.

2 Cover and bake at 350° for 40-45 minutes or until bubbly. Serve warm.

Yield: 20 servings.

BIG PINE FRENCH TOAST

jan mccormick, rosemount, minnesota

In this flavorful spin on French toast, slices of bread are coated with eggnog, fried to golden-brown perfection and arranged in a tree shape.

- 2 cups eggnog
- 8 slices day-old bread
- 8 pork sausage links

Green colored sugar

Confectioners' sugar

- 4 orange slices and fresh herbs, optional

1 Pour eggnog into a shallow bowl; dip both sides of bread in eggnog. In a nonstick skillet, toast bread over medium heat for 2 minutes on each side or until golden brown. Meanwhile, in another skillet, brown the sausage.

2 Cut French toast diagonally; place four slices, overlapping slightly, on each serving plate for the tree. Place two sausages at the bottom for the trunk. Sprinkle with sugars. Add an orange slice for the sun and herbs for grass if desired.

Yield: 4 servings.

Editor's Note: This recipe was tested with commercially prepared eggnog.

SAUSAGE-MUSHROOM BREAKFAST BAKE

diane babbitt, ludlow, massachusetts

My mom shared this delicious recipe when I needed to bring a dish to a breakfast potluck. Everyone there loved it.

- 1 pound bulk pork sausage
- 2 cups sliced fresh mushrooms
- 6 cups cubed bread
- 2 cups (8 ounces) shredded sharp cheddar cheese
- 1 cup chopped fresh tomatoes
- 10 eggs, lightly beaten
- 3 cups milk
- 2 teaspoons ground mustard
- 1/2 teaspoon salt
- 1/4 teaspoon pepper

1 In a large skillet, cook sausage and mushrooms over medium heat until meat is no longer pink; drain. Place half of the bread cubes in a greased 13-in. x 9-in. x 2-in. baking dish; top with 2 cups sausage mixture and half of the cheese and tomatoes. Repeat layers. In a large bowl, combine the eggs, milk, mustard, salt and pepper; pour over bread mixture.

2 Bake, uncovered, at 350° for 50-55 minutes or until a knife inserted near the center comes out clean. Let stand for 10 minutes before serving.

Yield: 12 servings.

CHILE RELLENOS QUICHE

linda miritello, mesa, arizona

To me, nothing sparks up a meal more than the smoky flavor of roasted green chilies. This is a quick and easy recipe, and I usually have the ingredients on hand, so when I don't know what to fix for brunch or even dinner, I make this quiche.

Pastry for single-crust pie (9 inches)
- 2 tablespoons cornmeal
- 1-1/2 cups (6 ounces) shredded Monterey Jack cheese
- 1 cup (4 ounces) shredded cheddar cheese
- 1 can (4 ounces) chopped green chilies
- 3 eggs
- 3/4 cup sour cream
- 1 tablespoon minced fresh cilantro
- 2 to 4 drops hot pepper sauce, optional

1. Line the unpricked pastry shell with a double thickness of heavy-duty foil. Bake at 450° for 8 minutes. Remove foil; bake 5 minutes longer. Cool on a wire rack. Reduce heat to 350°.

2. Sprinkle cornmeal over bottom of pastry shell. In a bowl, combine the cheeses; set aside 1/2 cup for topping. Add chilies to the remaining cheese mixture; sprinkle into crust.

3. In a small bowl, whisk the eggs, sour cream, cilantro and hot pepper sauce if desired. Pour into crust; sprinkle with reserved cheese mixture.

4. Bake for 35-40 minutes or until a knife inserted near the center comes out clean. Let stand for 5 minutes before cutting.

Yield: 6 servings.

GINGERBREAD WAFFLES

taste of home test kitchen

So folks could enjoy the flavor of gingerbread at breakfast, our Test Kitchen home economists share this recipe. The waffles are so pretty with a light sprinkling of confectioners' sugar.

- 1 cup all-purpose flour
- 1-1/2 teaspoons baking powder
- 1 teaspoon ground ginger
- 3/4 teaspoon ground cinnamon
- 1/2 teaspoon baking soda
- 1/4 teaspoon salt
- 1/8 teaspoon ground cloves
- 1/3 cup packed brown sugar
- 1 egg, *separated*
- 3/4 cup buttermilk
- 1/4 cup molasses
- 3 tablespoons butter, melted
- 1/8 teaspoon cream of tartar

Confectioners' sugar, optional

1. In a large bowl, combine the first seven ingredients. In a small bowl, beat the brown sugar and egg yolk until fluffy; add the buttermilk, molasses and butter. Stir into dry ingredients just until combined.

2. In another small bowl, beat the egg white and cream of tartar until stiff peaks form. Gently fold into batter. Quickly spoon onto a preheated waffle iron. Bake according to manufacturer's directions until golden brown. Sprinkle with confectioners' sugar if desired.

Yield: 8 waffles.

ASPARAGUS PIE

mary lou wayman, salt lake city, utah

This hearty quiche is as attractive as it is flavorful! It looks complicated to make but is actually a simple recipe. The secret is the crust—it's refrigerated pizza dough that I season with basil and Parmesan cheese. It almost seems too nice to cut, but we're always glad we did when we taste a slice.

- 1/4 pound fresh asparagus, trimmed
- 2 teaspoons canola oil
- 1/2 cup grated Parmesan cheese
- 2 teaspoons dried basil
- 1 package (13.8 ounces) refrigerated pizza crust
- 3 bacon strips, diced
- 1 medium onion, chopped
- 5 eggs
- 1/2 cup milk
- 1/8 teaspoon salt
- **Dash ground nutmeg**
- 1-1/2 cups (6 ounces) shredded Swiss cheese
- 1 tablespoon all-purpose flour

1 In a large saucepan, bring 1/2 in. of water to a boil. Add asparagus; cover and boil for 3 minutes. Drain and immediately place asparagus in ice water. Drain and pat dry. Toss with oil; set aside.

2 In a small bowl, combine Parmesan cheese and basil; sprinkle half over work surface. Place pizza dough on surface; roll into a 12-in. circle. Sprinkle with remaining Parmesan mixture; gently press into dough with a rolling pin. Transfer to a greased 9-in. springform pan. Press dough onto the bottom and 1-1/2 in. up the sides of pan.

3 Line unpricked dough with a double thickness of heavy-duty foil. Bake at 425° for 8 minutes. Remove foil; bake 5 minutes longer. Place on a wire rack. Reduce heat to 350°.

4 In a small skillet, cook bacon over medium heat until crisp; using a slotted spoon, remove bacon to paper towels. Drain, reserving 1 tablespoon drippings. In the drippings, saute onion until tender; drain.

5 In a large bowl, whisk the eggs, milk, salt and nutmeg. Stir in bacon and onion. Toss the Swiss cheese and flour; stir into egg mixture. Pour into the crust. Arrange asparagus in a spoke-like pattern on top.

6 Place pan on a baking sheet. Bake for 35-40 minutes or until a knife inserted near the center comes out clean. Let stand for 10 minutes before removing sides of pan. Cut into wedges.

Yield: 6 servings.

FROSTED FRUIT SALAD

ann fox, austin, texas

This breakfast recipe is easy, light, delicious and uses up the bananas and apples I always have on hand.

- 2 large apples, cut into 3/4-inch cubes
- 2 medium firm bananas, sliced
- 2 teaspoons lemon juice
- 1 carton (6 ounces) fat-free reduced-sugar raspberry yogurt
- 1/4 cup raisins
- 1 tablespoon sunflower kernels

1 In a large bowl, combine apples and bananas. Sprinkle with lemon juice; toss to coat. Stir in the yogurt, raisins and sunflower kernels. Serve immediately.

Yield: 6 servings.

HOMEMADE BREADS

MOCHA-
CINNAMON
COFFEE
CAKE
P. 181

CHOCOLATE CHIP CINNAMON ROLLS

patty wynn, pardeeville, wisconsin

I started adding chocolate chips to my cinnamon rolls because several children didn't like the raisins in them. My family loves them now.

- 4 packages (1/4 ounce *each*) active dry yeast
- 2-1/2 cups warm water (110° to 115°)
- 3 cups warm milk (110° to 115°)
- 1/2 cup butter, softened
- 2 eggs
- 3/4 cup honey
- 4 teaspoons salt
- 14 cups all-purpose flour

FILLING:
- 6 tablespoons butter, softened
- 2-1/4 cups packed brown sugar
- 1 package (12 ounces) miniature semisweet chocolate chips
- 3 teaspoons ground cinnamon

GLAZE:
- 3 cups confectioners' sugar
- 6 tablespoons butter, softened
- 1 teaspoon vanilla extract
- 6 to 8 tablespoons milk

1 In a large bowl, dissolve yeast in warm water; let stand 5 minutes. Add milk, butter, eggs, honey, salt and 3 cups flour; beat on low for 3 minutes. Stir in enough remaining flour to form a soft dough.

2 Turn onto a floured surface; knead until smooth and elastic, 6-8 minutes. Place in a large greased bowl; turning once. Cover and let rise in a warm place until doubled, about 1 hour.

3 Punch dough down. Turn onto a floured surface; divide into four pieces. Roll each into a 14-in. x 8-in. rectangle; spread with butter. Combine the brown sugar, chips and cinnamon; sprinkle over dough to within 1/2 in. of edges and press into dough.

4 Roll up jelly-roll style, starting with a long side; pinch seam to seal. Cut each into 12 slices. Place cut side down in four greased 13-in. x 9-in.

baking dishes. Cover and let rise until doubled, about 30 minutes.

5 Bake at 350° for 25-30 minutes or until golden brown. Cool for 5 minutes; remove from pans to wire racks.

6 For glaze, in a large bowl, combine confectioners' sugar, butter, vanilla and enough milk to achieve desired consistency; drizzle over rolls.

Yield: 4 dozen.

Editor's Note: This recipe can be halved to fit into a mixing bowl.

BLENDER YEAST ROLLS

regena newton, oktaha, oklahoma

If you're looking for a quick and easy homemade yeast roll, you'll want to try this recipe. Use your blender to combine the wet ingredients before stirring in the flour. No kneading required, either.

- 1 cup warm milk (110° to 115°)
- 1 package (1/4 ounce) active dry yeast
- 1/4 cup sugar
- 2 eggs
- 1/4 cup canola oil
- 3-1/4 cups all-purpose flour
- 1 teaspoon salt

1 In a blender, combine the warm milk, yeast, sugar, eggs and oil; cover and process on low speed for 30 seconds or until blended.

2 In a large bowl, combine the flour and salt. Add yeast mixture; stir with a spoon until combined (do not knead). Cover and let rise in a warm place until doubled, about 30 minutes.

3 Stir down dough. Fill greased muffin cups half full. Cover and let rise until doubled, about 30 minutes.

4 Bake at 350° for 18-20 minutes or until golden. Remove from pans to wire racks. Serve warm.

Yield: about 1 dozen.

POPPY SEED SWEET ROLLS

ruth stahl, shepherd, montana

When I don't plan on serving these sweet rolls the same day I prepare them, I tuck them into the freezer. Then I can surprise my family with a batch when they least expect it!

- 2 tablespoons active dry yeast
- 1/4 cup warm water (110° to 115°)
- 3 tablespoons sugar, *divided*
- 1-1/2 cups warm buttermilk (110° to 115°)
- 1/2 cup canola oil
- 1 teaspoon salt
- 1/2 teaspoon baking soda
- 4 to 4-1/2 cups all-purpose flour

FILLING:

- 1 package (8 ounces) cream cheese, softened
- 1/4 cup butter, softened
- 1 cup packed brown sugar
- 2 tablespoons all-purpose flour
- 1 teaspoon vanilla extract
- 1 cup chopped pecans
- 2 tablespoons poppy seeds

ICING:

- 2 cups confectioners' sugar
- 4 teaspoons milk
- 1 teaspoon vanilla extract

1 In a large bowl, dissolve yeast in warm water. Add 1 tablespoon sugar; let stand for 5 minutes. Add the buttermilk, oil, salt, baking soda, 3 cups flour and remaining sugar; beat until smooth. Stir in enough remaining flour to form a soft dough.

2 Turn onto a lightly floured surface; knead until smooth and elastic, about 6-8 minutes. Place in a greased bowl, turning once to grease top. Cover and let rise in a warm place for 30 minutes.

3 Punch dough down. Turn onto a floured surface; divide in half. Roll each portion into a 15-in. x 9-in. rectangle.

4 For filling, in a small bowl, beat cream cheese and butter until fluffy. Beat in the brown sugar, flour and vanilla until smooth. Stir in nuts and poppy seeds. Spread over rectangles. Roll up jelly-roll style, starting with a long side; pinch seams to seal.

5 Cut into 1-in. pieces. Place 2 in. apart on greased baking sheets. Cover and let rise for 30 minutes.

6 Bake at 375° for 12-15 minutes until golden brown. Remove from pans to wire racks to cool. Combine icing ingredients; drizzle over rolls.

Yield: about 2-1/2 dozen.

BAKED HERB PUFFS

dorothy smith, el dorado, arkansas

Ground mustard, parsley and green onions make these puffs a nice addition to any meal. I often freeze them, then reheat for a few minutes in the oven.

- 1 cup water
- 1/2 cup butter
- 1 teaspoon ground mustard
- 1/4 teaspoon salt
- 1/8 teaspoon pepper
- 1 cup all-purpose flour
- 4 eggs
- 1/3 cup minced fresh parsley
- 1/4 cup chopped green onions

1 In a large saucepan, bring the water, butter, mustard, salt and pepper to a boil. Add flour all at once and stir until a smooth ball forms. Remove from the heat; let stand for 5 minutes. Add eggs, one at a time, beating well after each addition. Continue beating until mixture is smooth and shiny. Add parsley and green onions; mix well.

2 Drop by 2 tablespoonfuls 2 in. apart onto greased baking sheets. Bake at 400° for 18-20 minutes or until golden brown. Cut a slit in each to allow steam to escape; bake 5 minutes longer. Remove to a wire rack to cool.

Yield: 1-1/2 dozen.

CHOCOLATE-FILLED CRESCENTS

carol formholtz, deltona, florida

I always get compliments and recipe requests for these rich, flaky rolls drizzled with chocolate. They're great for brunch, dessert or a midday coffee treat!

- 3 tablespoons butter, softened
- 1 cup confectioners' sugar
- 1 tablespoon milk
- 1 teaspoon vanilla extract
- 1/4 cup baking cocoa
- 3 tablespoons finely chopped pecans
- 2 tubes (8 ounces *each*) refrigerated crescent rolls

CHOCOLATE GLAZE:
- 1 cup confectioners' sugar
- 2 tablespoons baking cocoa
- 2 tablespoons plus 1 teaspoon water
- 2 tablespoons butter, melted
- 1/2 teaspoon vanilla extract

1   In a small bowl, cream butter and confectioners' sugar until light and fluffy. Beat in milk and vanilla. Gradually add cocoa and mix well. Stir in pecans.

2   Unroll crescent dough and separate into triangles. Spread about 2 rounded teaspoons of filling over each triangle to within 1/4 in. of edges. Roll up each from the wide end. Place point side down 2 in. apart on ungreased baking sheets. Curve ends to form crescent shapes.

3   Bake at 375° for 12-15 minutes or until golden brown. Remove to wire racks; cool slightly. In a small bowl, whisk glaze ingredients until smooth; drizzle over crescents.

Yield: 16 servings.

CRANBERRY-NUT POPPY SEED BREAD

sandra fish, newberg, oregon

As a former home economics teacher, I love to experiment with recipes. One day I decided to add poppy seeds to my family's favorite cranberry bread. Everyone loved it!

- 4 cups all-purpose flour
- 2 cups sugar
- 2 teaspoons salt
- 1 teaspoon baking soda
- 1/2 teaspoon baking powder
- 2 eggs
- 1-1/2 cups orange juice
- 1/2 cup canola oil
- 3 tablespoons poppy seeds
- 2 tablespoons grated orange peel
- 2 cups chopped fresh *or* frozen cranberries
- 1-1/2 cups chopped nuts

1   In a large bowl, combine the flour, sugar, salt, baking soda and baking powder. In another bowl, whisk the eggs, orange juice, oil, poppy seeds and orange peel. Stir into dry ingredients just until moistened. Fold in cranberries and nuts.

2   Spoon into two greased 8-in. x 4-in. loaf pans. Bake at 350° for 60-65 minutes or until a toothpick inserted near the center comes out clean (cover loosely with foil if tops brown too quickly). Cool for 10 minutes before removing from pans to wire racks to cool completely.

Yield: 2 loaves (12 slices each).

Measuring Chopped Nuts

In our recipes, if the word "chopped" comes before the ingredient, then chop the ingredient before measuring. If the word "chopped" comes after the ingredient, then chop after measuring.—Taste of Home Test Kitchen

CREAM-FILLED CINNAMON COFFEE CAKE

arlene wengerd, millersburg, ohio

Repeat guests phone ahead to request my cinnamony coffee cake for breakfast. You can prepare it in advance and refrigerate, or welcome company with its fresh-baked aroma.

- 1/2 **cup butter, softened**
- 1 **cup sugar**
- 2 **eggs**
- 1 **teaspoon vanilla extract**
- 1-1/2 **cups all-purpose flour**
- 1/2 **teaspoon** *each* **baking soda and salt**
- 1 **cup (8 ounces) sour cream**

TOPPING:
- 1/2 **cup sugar**
- 1/2 **cup chopped pecans**
- 2 **teaspoons ground cinnamon**

FILLING:
- 1 **tablespoon cornstarch**
- 3/4 **cup milk**
- 1/4 **cup butter, softened**
- 1/4 **cup shortening**
- 1/2 **cup sugar**
- 1/2 **teaspoon vanilla extract**

1 In a large bowl, cream butter and sugar until light and fluffy. Add eggs, one at a time, beating well after each addition. Beat in vanilla. Combine the flour, baking soda and salt; add to creamed mixture alternately with sour cream, beating just until combined.

2 Pour into two greased and waxed paper-lined 9-in. round baking pans. Combine the topping ingredients; sprinkle over batter. Lightly cut through with a knife to swirl.

3 Bake at 350° for 20-25 minutes or until a toothpick comes out clean. Cool for 10 minutes; remove from pans to wire racks to cool completely.

4 In a small saucepan, combine cornstarch and milk until smooth. Bring to a boil; cook and stir for 1-2 minutes or until thickened. Cover and refrigerate until chilled. In a small bowl, cream butter, shortening and sugar until light and fluffy. Add vanilla and chilled milk mixture; beat on medium speed until smooth and creamy, about 10 minutes.

5 Place one cake on a serving plate; spread with filling. Top with remaining cake. Store in refrigerator.

Yield: 8-10 servings.

WALNUT ZUCCHINI MUFFINS

harriet stichter, milford, indiana

Shredded zucchini adds moistness to these tender muffins dotted with raisins and chopped walnuts. If you have a surplus of zucchini in summer, as most of us do, this is a good way to use some of it.

- 1 **cup all-purpose flour**
- 3/4 **cup whole wheat flour**
- 2/3 **cup packed brown sugar**
- 2 **teaspoons baking powder**
- 3/4 **teaspoon ground cinnamon**
- 1/2 **teaspoon salt**
- 2 **eggs**
- 3/4 **cup milk**
- 1/2 **cup butter, melted**
- 1 **cup** *each* **shredded zucchini and chopped walnuts**
- 1/2 **cup raisins**

1 In a large bowl, combine the first six ingredients. In another bowl, whisk the eggs, milk and butter; stir into dry ingredients just until moistened. Fold in the zucchini, walnuts and raisins.

2 Fill greased muffin cups three-fourths full. Bake at 375° for 18-20 minutes or until a toothpick inserted near the center comes out clean. Cool for 5 minutes before removing from pan to a wire rack. Serve warm.

Yield: 1 dozen.

HOLIDAY BRAIDS

sally hook, montgomery, texas

Once you slice into one of these braids, it will disappear quickly. The cream cheese, brown sugar and fruit tucked inside the flaky crust create an unforgettable combination.

- 2 tablespoons active dry yeast
- 1 cup warm milk (110° to 115°)
- 4 eggs
- 1/2 cup butter, softened
- 1/3 cup sugar
- 2 tablespoons grated orange peel
- 1-1/2 teaspoons vanilla extract
- 1 teaspoon salt
- 4 to 5 cups all-purpose flour

FILLING:
- 1 package (8 ounces) cream cheese, softened
- 1 cup packed brown sugar
- 1 egg
- 2 tablespoons grated orange peel
- 1 teaspoon ground cinnamon
- 1 cup *each* chopped pecans and dried cranberries

GLAZE:
- 1 cup confectioners' sugar
- 1 to 2 tablespoons milk

1 In a large bowl, dissolve yeast in warm milk. Add the eggs, butter, sugar, orange peel, vanilla, salt and 2 cups flour. Beat on medium speed for 3 minutes. Stir in enough remaining flour to form a soft dough (dough will be sticky).

2 Turn onto a floured surface; knead until smooth and elastic, about 6-8 minutes. Place in a greased bowl, turning once to grease top. Cover and let rise in a warm place until doubled, about 1 hour.

3 In a small bowl, beat cream cheese and brown sugar until smooth. Beat in the egg, orange peel and cinnamon; set aside.

4 Turn dough onto a lightly floured surface; divide in half. On greased baking sheets, roll each portion into a 15-in. x 9-in. rectangle. Spread filling down the center of each; sprinkle with pecans and cranberries.

5 On each long side, cut 3/4-in.-wide strips about 2 in. into center. Starting at one end, fold alternating strips at an angle across filling. Pinch ends to seal. Cover and let rise until doubled, about 45 minutes.

6 Bake at 375° for 15-20 minutes or until golden brown. Remove from pans to wire racks. Combine glaze ingredients; drizzle over braids. Serve warm.

Yield: 2 loaves (12 slices each).

CHOCOLATE-PECAN STICKY BUNS

tammy logan, clinton, tennessee

You won't believe how delicious this super-easy, four-ingredient recipe is! These rolls have chocolate kisses tucked inside that guests will love.

- 1 can (15 ounces) coconut-pecan frosting
- 1 cup pecan halves
- 2 tubes (12 ounces *each*) refrigerated buttermilk biscuits
- 20 milk chocolate kisses

1 Spread frosting over the bottom of a greased 9-in. square baking pan. Arrange pecans over frosting; set aside.

2 Flatten each biscuit to 1/4-in. thickness. Place a chocolate kiss on one side of each biscuit. Fold edges of dough over kiss; pinch edges to seal. Arrange biscuits, flat side down, over pecans.

3 Bake at 400° for 25-30 minutes or until golden brown. Cool on a wire rack for 5 minutes. Invert onto a serving plate; serve immediately.

Yield: 20 servings.

SUN-DRIED TOMATO 'N' BASIL WREATH

teresa morancie, brewer, maine

I added to a family recipe to create this bright and pretty wreath. Served with herb butter, it makes a special accompaniment to holiday meals.

- 1/2 cup boiling water
- 1/4 cup sun-dried tomatoes (not packed in oil)
- 1/2 cup fat-free milk
- 1/4 cup grated Parmesan cheese
- 3 tablespoons butter
- 2 tablespoons sugar
- 4-1/2 teaspoons minced fresh basil
- 1/2 teaspoon salt
- 1 package (1/4 ounce) active dry yeast
- 2 tablespoons warm water (110° to 115°)
- 1 egg, beaten
- 2-1/4 to 2-1/2 cups all-purpose flour

HERB BUTTER:
- 1 tablespoon butter
- 2-1/4 teaspoons minced fresh basil
- 1-1/2 teaspoons grated Parmesan cheese
- 1-1/2 teaspoons olive oil

1 Pour boiling water over tomatoes; let stand 15 minutes. In a saucepan, combine the next six ingredients. Drain and chop tomatoes; add to pan. Cook and stir mixture over low heat until sugar is dissolved. Remove from heat; cool slightly.

2 In a large bowl, dissolve yeast in warm water. Add tomato mixture, egg and 2 cups flour; beat until smooth. Stir in enough remaining flour to form a soft dough. Knead on a floured surface until smooth, about 6-8 minutes. Place in a bowl coated with cooking spray; turn once to coat top. Cover and let rise until doubled, about 1 hour.

3 In a small saucepan, melt butter; add the basil, Parmesan and oil. Keep warm. Punch dough down; divide into three portions. Shape each into an 18-in. rope.

4 Brush with half of herb butter. Place ropes on a baking sheet coated with cooking spray; braid and shape into a wreath. Pinch ends to seal. Cover and let rise until doubled, about 40 minutes.

5 Brush with remaining herb butter. Bake at 350° for 20-25 minutes or until golden brown. Remove to a wire rack.

Yield: 1 loaf (12 slices).

MARASCHINO CHERRY MINI LOAVES

linda murch, litchfield, minnesota

I've been making these breads as Christmas gifts for my neighbors for years. Each moist slice is dotted with cherries, chocolate and nuts.

- 1 jar (10 ounces) maraschino cherries
- 2 cups all-purpose flour
- 1 cup sugar
- 2 teaspoons baking powder
- 1/2 teaspoon salt
- 3 eggs
- 1 cup chopped walnuts
- 1/2 cup miniature semisweet chocolate chips
- 1/2 cup chopped dates

1 Drain cherries, reserving 1/4 cup juice; set aside. In a large bowl, combine the flour, sugar, baking powder and salt. In another bowl, whisk eggs and reserved juice; stir into dry ingredients just until moistened. Fold in the walnuts, chocolate chips, dates and cherries.

2 Spoon into three greased 5-3/4-in. x 3-in. x 2-in. loaf pans. Bake at 325° for 40-45 minutes or until a toothpick inserted near the center comes out clean. Cool for 10 minutes before removing from pans to a wire rack to cool completely. Wrap and store for 24 hours before serving.

Yield: 3 mini loaves (6 slices each).

SWEDISH PASTRY RINGS

myra pratt, fairview, pennsylvania

Although my family is of Polish and German descent, we sure enjoy this sweet bit of Sweden! Mom was always sure to make this for Easter breakfast.

2-1/4 cups all-purpose flour
   2 tablespoons plus 1 teaspoon sugar, *divided*
   1 teaspoon salt
1/2 cup cold butter
   1 package (1/4 ounce) active dry yeast
1/4 cup warm water (110° to 115°)
1/4 cup warm evaporated milk (110° to 115°)
   1 egg
1/4 cup dried currants *or* raisins

FILLING:
1/4 cup butter, softened
1/2 cup packed brown sugar
1/2 cup chopped pecans

BROWNED BUTTER GLAZE:
   2 tablespoons butter
   1 cup confectioners' sugar
1/2 teaspoon vanilla extract
   3 to 4 teaspoons evaporated milk

1 In a large bowl, combine flour, 2 tablespoons sugar and salt. Cut in butter until mixture resembles fine crumbs. In a large another large bowl, dissolve yeast and remaining sugar in warm water. Add milk, egg and crumb mixture; beat until well blended. Stir in currants. Cover and refrigerate overnight.

2 Line two baking sheets with foil and grease the foil; set aside. For filling, in a small bowl, cream butter and brown sugar until light and fluffy; stir in pecans.

3 Punch down dough. Turn onto a lightly floured surface; divide in half. Roll each portion into a 14-in. x 7-in. rectangle; spread filling to within 1/2 in. of edges. Roll up jelly-roll style, starting with a long side; pinch seams to seal.

4 Place loaves seam side down on prepared pans; pinch ends together to form a ring. With scissors, cut from outside edge two-thirds of the way toward center of ring at 1-in. intervals. Separate strips slightly; twist to allow filling to show. Cover and let rise in a warm place until doubled, about 45 minutes.

5 Bake at 350° for 18-22 minutes or until golden brown. Remove from pans to wire racks to cool.

6 For glaze, in a small saucepan, cook butter over medium heat until lightly browned, stirring constantly. Remove from the heat. Stir in confectioners' sugar, vanilla and enough milk to achieve desired consistency. Drizzle over pastry rings.

Yield: 2 pastry rings (12-16 servings each).

CHERRY-ALMOND DROP SCONES

helen phillips, eaton, colorado

This easy treat is studded with dried cherries and crunchy almonds. Pair with a cup of steaming cocoa, coffee or tea for a quick winter warm-up!

2-1/4 cups all-purpose flour
   2 tablespoons sugar
2-1/4 teaspoons baking powder
1/2 teaspoon *each* baking soda and salt
   1 cup reduced-fat vanilla yogurt
1/4 cup butter, melted
   1 egg, lightly beaten
1/4 teaspoon almond extract
1/2 cup *each* dried cherries, chopped and slivered almonds

1 In a large bowl, combine the flour, sugar, baking powder, baking soda and salt. In another bowl, combine the yogurt, butter, egg and extract. Stir into dry ingredients just until moistened. Fold in cherries and almonds.

2 Drop by heaping tablespoonfuls 2 in. apart onto a baking sheet coated with cooking spray. Bake at 400° for 15-18 minutes or until lightly browned. Remove to wire racks. Serve warm.

Yield: 14 scones.

CINNAMON APPLE MUFFINS

louise gilbert, quesnel, british columbia

Even the finicky eaters in my family enjoy these lovely muffins. The cinnamon-honey butter is a tasty accompaniment.

- 1-1/2 cups all-purpose flour
- 1/2 cup sugar
- 1-3/4 teaspoons baking powder
- 1/2 teaspoon salt
- 1/2 teaspoon ground cinnamon
- 1/8 teaspoon ground nutmeg
- 1 egg
- 1/2 cup milk
- 3 tablespoons canola oil
- 3 tablespoons unsweetened applesauce
- 1 medium McIntosh apple, peeled and grated

TOPPING:

- 1/4 cup packed brown sugar
- 1 tablespoon all-purpose flour
- 2 tablespoons cold butter
- 1/2 cup quick-cooking oats

CINNAMON-HONEY BUTTER:

- 1/2 cup butter, softened
- 1/4 cup honey
- 1/2 teaspoon ground cinnamon

1 In a large bowl, combine the flour, sugar, baking powder, salt, cinnamon and nutmeg. In another bowl, whisk the egg, milk, oil and applesauce. Stir into dry ingredients just until moistened. Fold in apple. Fill greased or paper-lined muffin cups half full.

2 For topping, in a small bowl, combine brown sugar and flour; cut in butter until crumbly. Add oats. Sprinkle over muffins.

3 Bake at 350° for 18-22 minutes or until a toothpick inserted near the center comes out clean. Cool for 5 minutes before removing from pan to a wire rack.

4 In a small bowl, beat the butter, honey and cinnamon until blended. Serve with warm muffins. Refrigerate leftover butter.

Yield: 1 dozen.

MAPLE-OAT DINNER ROLLS

helen davis, waterbury, vermont

I'm in my 80s, but I still like to bake for my children, grandchildren and great-grandchildren. These hearty rolls are one of our favorites.

- 1 package (1/4 ounce) active dry yeast
- 1/2 cup warm water (110° to 115°), *divided*
- 1/2 cup warm strong brewed coffee (110° to 115°)
- 1/2 cup old-fashioned oats
- 1/4 cup sugar
- 1/4 cup maple syrup
- 1 egg
- 3 tablespoons shortening
- 1 teaspoon salt
- 3 to 3-1/2 cups bread flour
- 1 tablespoon butter, melted

1 In a large bowl, dissolve yeast in 1/4 cup warm water. Add the coffee, oats, sugar, syrup, egg, shortening, salt, remaining water and 2 cups flour. Beat until smooth. Stir in enough remaining flour to form a soft dough.

2 Turn onto a floured surface; knead until smooth and elastic, about 6-8 minutes. Place in a greased bowl, turning once to grease top. Cover and let rise in a warm place until doubled, about 1 hour.

3 Punch down dough. Turn onto a floured surface; divide into four portions. Divide each portion into six pieces; shape each into a ball. Place in a greased 13-in. x 9-in. baking pan. Cover and let rise until doubled, about 30 minutes.

4 Bake at 350° for 25-30 minutes or until golden brown. Brush rolls with butter. Remove from pan to a wire rack. Serve warm.

Yield: 2 dozen.

PISTACHIO PUMPKIN BREAD

kathy kittell, lenexa, kansas
A few years ago during the holiday season, a friend shared this delightful recipe with me. Since then, I've made it every holiday and shared it with family and friends. The cute little loaves blend pumpkin, pistachio, rum and raisins with festive results.

> 1 package (14 ounces) pumpkin quick bread/muffin mix
> 2 eggs
> 1 cup water
> 3 tablespoons canola oil
> 1/4 to 1/2 teaspoon rum extract
> 1/2 cup raisins
> 1/2 cup chopped pistachios

GLAZE:
> 1/4 cup sugar
> 2 tablespoons water
> 1 tablespoon butter
> 1/4 teaspoon rum extract

1 In a large bowl, combine the bread mix, eggs, water, oil and extract just until blended. Stir in the raisins and pistachios. Transfer to three greased 5-3/4-in. x 3-in. x 2-in. loaf pans.

2 Bake at 375° for 30-35 minutes or until a toothpick inserted near the center comes out clean. Cool for 5 minutes.

3 Meanwhile, in a small saucepan, combine the sugar, water and butter. Bring to a boil; cook and stir for 3 minutes or until sugar is dissolved. Remove from the heat; stir in extract.

4 Remove loaves from pans to wire racks. With a toothpick, poke holes in the top of each loaf; brush with glaze. Cool completely.

Yield: 3 mini loaves (4 slices each).

Editor's Note: Wrap the bread in colored cellophane, tie with festive ribbon and give as a gift.

CHERRY COFFEE CAKE

gail buss, westminster, maryland
With its pretty layer of cherries and crunchy streusel topping, this coffee cake is great for breakfast. Or you can even serve it for dessert.

> 1 package (18-1/4 ounces) yellow cake mix, *divided*
> 1 cup all-purpose flour
> 1 package (1/4 ounce) active dry yeast
> 2/3 cup warm water (120° to 130°)
> 2 eggs, lightly beaten
> 1 can (21 ounces) cherry pie filling
> 1/3 cup cold butter

GLAZE:
> 1 cup confectioners' sugar
> 1 tablespoon corn syrup
> 1 to 2 tablespoons water

1 In a large bowl, combine 1-1/2 cups cake mix, flour, yeast and water until smooth. Stir in eggs until blended. Transfer to a greased 13-in. x 9-in. baking dish. Gently spoon pie filling over top.

2 In a small bowl, place remaining cake mix; cut in butter until crumbly. Sprinkle over filling.

3 Bake at 350° for 35-40 minutes or until lightly browned. Cool on a wire rack. Combine the confectioners' sugar, corn syrup and enough water to achieve desired consistency. Drizzle over cake.

Yield: 12-16 servings.

Lightly Beaten Eggs

When a recipe calls for eggs that are lightly beaten, just beat the egg with a fork until the yolk and white are combined. If you beat them more, you may impact the result of the recipe.—Taste of Home Test Kitchen

ALMOND PASTRY PUFFS

betty claycomb, alverton, pennsylvania

This tender, nutty coffee cake is one of my favorite brunch treats. It looks and tastes so special, people won't believe you made it yourself. It's good that the recipe makes two!

- 2 **cups all-purpose flour,** *divided*
- 1/4 **teaspoon salt**
- 1 **cup cold butter,** *divided*
- 2 **tablespoons plus 1 cup cold water,** *divided*
- 1/4 **teaspoon almond extract**
- 3 **eggs**

FROSTING:

- 1-1/2 **cups confectioners' sugar**
- 2 **tablespoons butter, softened**
- 4 **teaspoons water**
- 1/4 **teaspoon almond extract**
- 2/3 **cup chopped almonds, toasted**

1 In a large bowl, combine 1 cup flour and salt; cut in 1/2 cup butter until mixture resembles coarse crumbs. Add 2 tablespoons cold water; stir with a fork until blended. Shape dough into a ball; divide in half. Place dough 3 in. apart on an ungreased baking sheet; pat each into a 12-in. x 3-in. rectangle.

2 In a large saucepan, bring remaining butter and water to a boil. Remove from the heat; stir in extract and remaining flour until a smooth ball forms. Remove from the heat; let stand for 5 minutes. Add eggs, one at a time, beating well after each addition. Continue beating until mixture is smooth and shiny.

3 Spread over rectangles. Bake at 400° for 18-20 minutes or until the topping is lightly browned. Cool for 5 minutes before removing from pan to wire racks.

4 For frosting, in a small mixing bowl, combine the confectioners' sugar, butter, water and extract; beat until smooth. Spread over pastries; sprinkle with almonds.

Yield: 2 pastries (11 servings each).

WALNUT-FILLED STOLLEN

mary faulk, cambridge, wisconsin

My grandmother made date stollen every Christmas. Over the years, I replaced Grandmother's date filling with nuts. You can also top off this sweet yeast bread with either a vanilla glaze, drizzle or frosting to suit your family's taste.

- 1 **package (1/4 ounce) active dry yeast**
- 1 **cup warm milk (110° to 115°)**
- 1/2 **cup butter, softened**
- 1/2 **cup sugar**
- 2 **eggs**
- 1 **teaspoon salt**
- 4 **to 4-1/2 cups all-purpose flour**

FILLING:

- 3 **cups chopped walnuts**
- 1 **cup packed brown sugar**
- 2 **tablespoons half-and-half cream**
- 1 **tablespoon vanilla extract**
- 2 **teaspoons ground cinnamon**

Vanilla frosting

1 In a large mixing bowl, dissolve yeast in warm milk. Add the butter, sugar, eggs, salt and 2 cups flour; beat until smooth. Stir in enough remaining flour to form a soft dough. Turn onto a floured surface; knead until smooth and elastic, about 6-8 minutes. Place in a greased bowl, turning once to grease top. Cover and let rise in a warm place until doubled, about 1-1/4 hours.

2 Punch the dough down; divide into thirds. Shape each portion into a 12-in. x 7-in. oval. In a bowl,

combine the walnuts, brown sugar, cream, vanilla and cinnamon. Spread down the middle third of each stollen. Fold a long side over to within 1 in. of opposite side; press edge lightly to seal. Place on greased baking sheets; curve ends slightly. Cover and let rise until nearly doubled, about 45 minutes.

3 Bake at 350° for 15-20 minutes or until golden brown. Remove to wire racks to cool. Top with vanilla frosting.

Yield: 3 loaves.

WALNUT-CRUSTED WHEAT LOAVES

taste of home test kitchen

This moist, flavorful round bread has a wonderful balance of both white and wheat flours. Pass a basket of wedges with creamy butter.

    3   cups whole wheat flour
2-3/4   to 3 cups all-purpose flour
    3/4 cup toasted wheat germ
    2   packages (1/4 ounce *each*) active dry yeast
    2   teaspoons salt
    2   cups water
    1/2 cup honey
    1/3 cup shortening
    2   eggs
    1   cup chopped walnuts

GLAZE:
    1/4 cup sugar
    1/4 cup water
    1/4 cup chopped walnuts

1 In a large bowl, combine the whole wheat flour, 2-1/2 cups all-purpose flour, wheat germ, yeast and salt. In a small saucepan, heat the water, honey and shortening to 120°-130°. Add to dry ingredients; beat just until moistened. Add eggs; beat until smooth. Stir in walnuts and enough remaining all-purpose flour to form a soft dough.

2 Turn onto a floured surface; knead until smooth and elastic, about 5-6 minutes. Place in a greased bowl, turning once to grease top. Cover and let rise in a warm place until doubled, about 1 hour.

3 Punch dough down. Turn onto a lightly floured surface; divide in half. Shape each portion into a ball; flatten slightly. Place on two greased baking sheets. Cover and let rise in a warm place until doubled, about 35 minutes.

4 For glaze, in a saucepan, bring sugar and water to a boil. Cook for 2 minutes or until thickened. Brush over top of loaves. With a sharp knife, make several shallow slashes across the top of loaves. Sprinkle with walnuts.

5 Bake at 375° for 30-35 minutes or until golden brown. Remove from pans to wire racks to cool.

Yield: 2 loaves (12 slices each).

CHERRY NUT BREAD

melissa gentner, tecumseh, michigan

Chopped pecans and maraschino cherries perk up this pound cake-like bread. The pretty slices are delicious with a crisp golden crust. This is my husband's favorite bread, and I love to make it.

- 2 cups butter, softened
- 3 cups sugar
- 5 eggs, *separated*
- 1 teaspoon vanilla extract
- 5 cups all-purpose flour
- 1 teaspoon baking soda
- 1/2 teaspoon baking powder
- 1/2 teaspoon salt
- 1 cup buttermilk
- 2 jars (10 ounces *each*) maraschino cherries, drained and chopped
- 1 cup chopped pecans

1 In a large mixing bowl, cream butter and sugar. Add egg yolks and vanilla; mix well. Combine the flour, baking soda, baking powder and salt; add to the creamed mixture alternately with buttermilk just until blended (batter will be thick). In a small mixing bowl, beat egg whites until stiff peaks form. Fold into batter. Fold in cherries and pecans.

2 Transfer to four greased and floured 8-in. x 4-in. x 2-in. loaf pans. Bake at 350° for 50-55 minutes or until a toothpick inserted near the center comes out clean and loaves are golden brown. Cool for 10 minutes before removing from pans to wire racks.

Yield: 4 loaves.

STRAWBERRY CHEESECAKE MUFFINS

iris linkletter, summerside, prince edward island

My mother-in-law has been a great inspiration to me in the kitchen. These fruity muffins are often part of our Sunday dinner menu.

- 1 package (3 ounces) cream cheese, softened
- 1/4 cup confectioners' sugar
- 2-1/2 cups all-purpose flour
- 3 teaspoons baking powder
- 1/2 teaspoon salt
- 1 egg
- 1-1/4 cups milk
- 1/2 cup packed brown sugar
- 1/3 cup butter, melted
- 1 teaspoon grated lemon peel
- 1/4 teaspoon almond extract
- 1/4 cup strawberry jam

1 In a small bowl, beat the cream cheese and confectioners' sugar until smooth; set aside. In a large bowl, combine the flour, baking powder and salt. In another small bowl, whisk the egg, milk, brown sugar, butter, lemon peel and almond extract. Stir into dry ingredients just until moistened.

2 Spoon half of the batter into greased muffin cups. Top each with 1 tablespoon cream cheese mixture and 1 teaspoon jam. Top with remaining batter.

3   Bake at 375° for 18-20 minutes or until a tooth-
    pick comes out clean. Cool for 5 minutes before
    removing from pan to a wire rack.

Yield: 1 dozen.

PRETZEL WREATHS

roberta spieker, fort collins, colorado
Youngsters love to lend a hand with this recipe.
Our two girls help me measure, pour, stir, shape...and,
of course, eat the chewy pretzel rounds when
they're done!

    1   package (1/4 ounces) active dry yeast
    1-1/2 cups warm water (110° to 115°)
    4   cups all-purpose flour
    1   tablespoon sugar
    1   teaspoon salt
    1   egg white, lightly beaten
    Coarse salt *or* colored sugar

1   In a large bowl, dissolve yeast in water. Add 2 cups
    flour, sugar and salt. Beat until smooth. Stir in
    enough remaining flour to form a soft dough.

2   Turn onto a floured surface; knead until smooth
    and elastic, about 6 minutes. Cover and let rest
    for 15 minutes. Divide dough into 16 portions. Roll
    each portion into a 15-in. rope. Fold each rope in
    half and twist two or three times; shape into a
    circle and pinch ends together.

3   Place on greased baking sheets. Brush with egg
    white; sprinkle with salt or sugar. Bake at 425° for
    12-15 minutes.

Yield: 16 pretzels.

WHITE CHOCOLATE BERRY MUFFINS

mary lou wayman, salt lake city, utah
Santa himself might stop by just to get a taste of
these rich, moist muffins studded with white
chocolate chips and juicy raspberries. They're sure
to brighten any table.

    1   package (8 ounces) cream cheese, softened
    1   cup sugar
    2   eggs
    1   teaspoon vanilla extract
    1-1/2 cups all-purpose flour
    2   teaspoons baking powder
    1/2 teaspoon salt
    1   cup fresh raspberries
    1/2 cup vanilla *or* white chips

1   In a large bowl, beat cream cheese and sugar
    until smooth. Add eggs, beat in well after each ad-
    dition. Stir in vanilla. Combine the flour, baking
    powder and salt; add to cream cheese mixture
    just until blended. Fold in raspberries and chips.

2   Fill greased or paper-lined muffin cups two-thirds
    full. Bake at 375° for 20-25 minutes or until a
    toothpick comes out clean. Cool for 5 minutes be-
    fore removing from pan to a wire rack.

Yield: 1 dozen.

MOIST APPLESAUCE FRUITCAKE

pauline woodyard, humble, texas
The recipe for this flavorful cake has been handed down in my husband's family for four generations.

- 1 cup chopped mixed candied fruit
- 1 cup finely chopped pecans
- 1 cup finely chopped walnuts
- 1 cup raisins
- 1/2 cup chopped dried apricots
- 1/2 cup chopped dried apples
- 2-1/2 cups all-purpose flour, *divided*
- 1 cup butter, softened
- 2 cups sugar
- 2 eggs
- 2 cups applesauce
- 2 teaspoons vanilla *or* rum extract
- 2 teaspoons baking soda
- 2 teaspoons ground cinnamon
- 1 teaspoon salt
- 1 teaspoon ground nutmeg
- 1 teaspoon ground cloves
- 1 teaspoon ground allspice

1 In a bowl, combine the first six ingredients; add 1 cup flour. Stir to coat. In a mixing bowl, cream butter and sugar; add eggs and mix well. Add the applesauce and vanilla extract. Combine the baking soda, cinnamon, salt, nutmeg, cloves, allspice and remaining flour; stir into applesauce mixture. Stir in fruit mixture. Pour into a greased and floured 10-in. tube pan.

2 Bake at 325° for 60-65 minutes or until a toothpick inserted near the center comes out clean. Cool for 10 minutes before removing from pan to a wire rack to cool completely.

Yield: 12-16 servings.

ORANGE CRANBERRY BREAD

ron gardner, grand haven, michigan
With this recipe, you can enjoy two moist loaves of bread that are packed with the zesty taste of cranberries and orange peel. I suggest serving slices toasted with butter or cream cheese.

- 2-3/4 cups all-purpose flour
- 2/3 cup sugar
- 2/3 cup packed brown sugar
- 3-1/2 teaspoons baking powder
- 1 teaspoon salt
- 1/2 teaspoon ground cinnamon
- 1/4 teaspoon ground nutmeg
- 1 egg
- 1 cup milk
- 1/2 cup orange juice
- 3 tablespoons canola oil
- 2 to 3 teaspoons grated orange peel
- 2 cups coarsely chopped fresh *or* frozen cranberries
- 1 large apple, peeled and chopped

1 In a large bowl, combine the flour, sugars, baking powder, salt, cinnamon and nutmeg. Whisk the egg, milk, orange juice, oil and orange peel; stir into dry ingredients just until blended. Fold in the cranberries and apple.

2 Pour into two greased 8-in. x 4-in. x 2-in. loaf pans. Bake at 350° for 50-55 minutes or until a toothpick inserted near the center comes out clean. Cool for 10 minutes before removing from pans to wire racks.

Yield: 2 loaves (16 slices each).

CHOCOLATE CHIP CARAMEL ROLLS

julia holm, northfield, minnesota

As a teenager, I keep active with sports and friends. But baking is my favorite hobby. My five older brothers eat these delicious breakfast rolls right out of the oven!

    1 package (1/4 ounce) active dry yeast
 3/4 cup warm water (110° to 115°)
 3/4 cup warm milk (110° to 115°)
    3 tablespoons canola oil
 1/4 cup sugar
1-1/2 teaspoons salt
3-3/4 to 4-1/2 cups all-purpose flour
 3/4 cup miniature semisweet chocolate chips

FILLING:
 1/4 cup butter, softened
 1/3 cup sugar
    2 tablespoons ground cinnamon
    1 cup miniature semisweet chocolate chips

SYRUP:
    1 cup packed brown sugar
 3/4 cup heavy whipping cream

1 In a large bowl, dissolve yeast in warm water. Add the milk, oil, sugar, salt and 3 cups flour; beat on medium speed for 3 minutes. Stir in enough remaining flour to form a firm dough.

2 Turn onto a floured surface; knead in chocolate chips until dough is smooth and elastic, about 6-8 minutes. Place in a greased bowl, turning once to grease top. Cover and let rise in a warm place until doubled, about 1 hour.

3 Punch dough down. Turn onto a lightly floured surface. Roll into an 18-in. x 12-in. rectangle. Spread butter over dough to within 1/2 in. of edges. Combine sugar and cinnamon; sprinkle over butter. Sprinkle with chocolate chips; gently press into dough. Roll up jelly-roll style, starting with a long side; pinch the seam to seal. Cut into 12 slices.

4 Combine brown sugar and cream; pour into a greased 13-in. x 9-in. x 2-in. baking dish. Arrange rolls cut side up over syrup. Cover and let rise until doubled, about 50 minutes.

5 Bake at 375° for 30-35 minutes or until golden brown. Cool for 10 minutes before removing to a serving platter. Serve warm.

Yield: 1 dozen.

CRANBERRY CORN BREAD

sylvia gidwani, milford, new jersey

During the holidays, I make several pans of this sweet cake-like corn bread for family and friends. Whole blueberries—coated in flour—can be used in place of the cranberries.

 1/2 cup butter, softened
    1 cup sugar
    2 eggs
1-1/2 cups all-purpose flour
    1 cup cornmeal
    2 teaspoons baking powder
 1/2 teaspoon salt
1-1/2 cups buttermilk
    1 cup cranberries, halved

1 In a bowl, cream butter and sugar until light and fluffy. Add eggs; mix well. Combine the flour, cornmeal, baking powder and salt. Add to creamed mixture alternately with buttermilk. Fold in cranberries.

2 Transfer to a greased 9-in. square baking pan. Bake at 375° for 40-45 minutes or until a toothpick inserted near the center comes out clean. Serve warm.

Yield: 9-12 servings.

CRANBERRY SWEET POTATO MUFFINS

diane musil, lyons, illinois

Bold autumn flavors of sweet potatoes, cranberries and cinnamon give seasonal appeal to these muffins. I recommended them for a change-of-pace treat with a meal, packed into a lunch box or as a snack.

- 1-1/2 cups all-purpose flour
-   1/2 cup sugar
-     2 teaspoons baking powder
-   3/4 teaspoon salt
-   1/2 teaspoon ground cinnamon
-   1/2 teaspoon ground nutmeg
-     1 egg
-   1/2 cup milk
-   1/2 cup cold mashed sweet potatoes (without added butter *or* milk)
-   1/4 cup butter, melted
-     1 cup chopped fresh *or* frozen cranberries

Cinnamon-sugar

1   In a large bowl, combine the flour, sugar, baking powder, salt, cinnamon and nutmeg. In a small bowl, combine the egg, milk, sweet potatoes and butter; stir into dry ingredients just until moistened. Fold in cranberries.

2   Fill greased or paper-line muffin cups half full. Sprinkle with cinnamon-sugar. Bake at 375° for 18-22 minutes or until a toothpick inserted in muffins comes out clean. Cool in pan 10 minutes before removing to a wire rack. Serve warm.

Yield: 1 dozen.

HERB POTATO ROLLS

lonna smith, woodruff, wisconsin

My grandma always made these rolls. She enjoyed them as a child in Germany. I practiced for years before I finally perfected the recipe!

-     5 to 5-1/2 cups all-purpose flour
-     1 cup mashed potato flakes
-     2 packages (1/4 ounce *each*) active dry yeast
-     1 tablespoon sugar
-     1 tablespoon minced chives
-     2 teaspoons salt
-     2 teaspoons minced fresh parsley
-     2 cups milk
-   1/2 cup sour cream
-     2 eggs

1   In a large small bowl, combine 3 cups flour, potato flakes, yeast, sugar, chives, salt and parsley. In a small saucepan, heat milk and sour cream to 120°-130° add to dry ingredients. Beat on medium speed for 2 minutes. Add eggs and 1/2 cup flour; beat 2 minutes longer. Stir in enough remaining flour to form a soft dough. Turn onto a floured surface; knead until smooth and elastic, about 6-8 minutes. Place in a greased bowl, turning once to grease top. Cover and let rise in a warm place until doubled, about 45 minutes.

2   Punch dough down. Turn onto a lightly floured surface; divide into 24 pieces. Shape each into a roll. Place in a greased 13-in. x 9-in. x 2-in. baking pan. Cover and let rise until doubled, about 35 minutes.

3   Bake at 375° for 30-35 minutes or until golden brown. Remove to wire racks.

Yield: 2 dozen.

FEATHER WHOLE WHEAT ROLLS

leann sain, orem, utah

My grandmother and mother have made this recipe famous in our family as well as our community. We never sit down to Thanksgiving or Christmas dinner without these melt-in-your-mouth rolls.

- 4 tablespoons active dry yeast
- 2 tablespoons plus 2/3 cup sugar, *divided*
- 2 cups warm water (110° to 115°)
- 2 cups warm milk (110° to 115°)
- 4 eggs, lightly beaten
- 2/3 cup canola oil
- 2 teaspoons salt
- 4 cups whole wheat flour
- 4-1/2 to 5 cups all-purpose flour
- 1/4 cup butter, melted

1 In a large bowl, dissolve yeast and 2 tablespoons sugar in warm water. Add the milk, eggs, oil, salt, remaining sugar and whole wheat flour. Beat until smooth. Stir in enough all-purpose flour to form a soft dough (dough will be sticky). Do not knead. Cover and refrigerate for 8 hours.

2 Punch dough down. Divide into thirds. Cover and refrigerate two portions. Turn the remaining portion onto a lightly floured surface; roll or pat to 1/2-in. thickness. Cut with a lightly floured 2-1/2-in. biscuit cutter. Repeat with remaining dough. Place rolls 2-1/2-in. apart on greased baking sheets. Cover and let rise in a warm place until doubled, about 2 hours.

3 Bake at 425° for 8-12 minutes or until golden brown. Brush with butter. Remove to wire racks.

Yield: about 5 dozen.

WHITE CHOCOLATE CRANBERRY BREAD

ruth burrus, zionsville, indiana

Tangy cranberries complement the appealing vanilla-citrus flavor of this quick bread. The fine texture of the holiday loaf is similar to a pound cake.

- 1/2 cup butter-flavored shortening
- 1 cup sugar
- 3 eggs
- 1/2 cup buttermilk
- 3 tablespoons orange juice
- 1 teaspoon grated lemon peel
- 1 teaspoon vanilla extract
- 1/2 cup vanilla *or* white chips, melted and cooled
- 2-1/4 cups all-purpose flour
- 1/2 teaspoon salt
- 1/4 teaspoon baking soda
- 1 cup dried cranberries

1 In a large mixing bowl, cream shortening and sugar. Add eggs, one at a time, beating well after each addition. Beat in the buttermilk, orange juice, lemon peel and vanilla. Stir in melted chips. Combine the flour, salt and baking soda; gradually add to creamed mixture. Stir in cranberries.

2 Pour into a greased and floured 9-in. x 5-in. x 3-in. loaf pan. Bake at 350° for 55-60 minutes or until a toothpick inserted near the center comes out clean. Cool for 10 minutes before removing from pan to a wire rack to cool completely.

Yield: 1 loaf.

CHERRY-GO-ROUND

kathy mccreary, wichita, kansas
This fancy coffee cake is surprisingly easy. It makes a great homemade gift.

 1 package (1/4 ounce) active dry yeast
 1/4 cup warm water (110° to 115°)
 1 cup warm milk (110° to 115°)
 1/2 cup sugar
 1/2 cup butter, softened
 1 egg
 1 teaspoon salt
 4-1/2 to 5 cups all-purpose flour
FILLING:
 2 cans (16 ounces *each*) pitted tart cherries, well drained
 1/2 cup all-purpose flour
 1/2 cup packed brown sugar
 1/2 cup chopped pecans
ICING:
 1 cup confectioners' sugar
 1/4 teaspoon vanilla extract
 1 to 2 tablespoons milk

1 In a large bowl, dissolve yeast in warm water. Add the milk, sugar, butter, egg, salt and 2 cups flour. Beat until smooth. Stir in enough remaining flour to form a soft dough.

2 Turn onto a lightly floured surface; knead until smooth and elastic, about 6-8 minutes. Place in a greased bowl, turning once to grease top. Cover and refrigerate for at least 2 hours or overnight.

3 Line two baking sheets with foil and grease well; set aside. Punch dough down. Turn onto a lightly floured surface; divide in half. Roll each portion into a 14-in. x 7-in. rectangle. Spread cherries over dough to within 1/2 in. of edges. Combine flour, brown sugar and pecans; sprinkle over cherries.

4 Roll up jelly-roll style, starting with a long side; pinch seams and tuck ends under. Place seam side down on prepared baking sheets; pinch ends together to form a ring. With kitchen scissors, cut from outside edge two-thirds of the way toward center of ring at 1-in. intervals. Separate strips slightly and twist to allow filling to show. Cover and let rise until doubled, about 1 hour.

5 Bake at 350° for 20-25 minutes or until golden brown. Remove from pans to wire racks.

6 In a small bowl, combine the confectioners' sugar, vanilla and enough milk to achieve desired consistency; drizzle over warm coffee cakes.

Yield: 2 coffee cakes.

GINGERBREAD MUFFINS

kelly trupkiewicz, fort collins, colorado
Growing up, I adored my mom's gingerbread cake with lemon sauce, so I re-created the combination for my family. The spice- and molasses-flavored muffins spread with homemade lemon curd are a new-generation favorite.

LEMON CURD:
 2/3 cup sugar
 3/4 teaspoon cornstarch

1/3 cup lemon juice

5 egg yolks, lightly beaten

1/4 cup butter, cubed

2 teaspoons grated lemon peel

MUFFINS:

2 cups all-purpose flour

1/4 cup sugar

2-1/2 teaspoons baking powder

2 teaspoons ground ginger

1 teaspoon ground cinnamon

1/4 teaspoon salt

1/4 teaspoon ground cloves

1 egg

3/4 cup milk

1/4 cup canola oil

1/4 cup molasses

1 In a large heavy saucepan, combine the sugar, cornstarch and lemon juice until smooth. Cook and stir over medium-high heat until thickened and bubbly. Reduce heat to low; cook and stir for 2 minutes longer. Remove from the heat. Stir a small amount of hot filling into egg yolks; return all to the pan, stirring constantly. Bring to a gentle boil; cook and stir for 2 minutes. Remove from the heat; gently stir in butter and lemon peel until blended. Pour into a large bowl; cover surface with plastic wrap. Cover and refrigerate until serving.

2 In a large bowl, combine the flour, sugar, baking powder, ginger, cinnamon, salt and cloves. In another bowl, whisk the egg, milk, oil and molasses until smooth; stir into dry ingredients just until moistened. Fill paper-lined muffin cups half full. Bake at 375° for 15-20 minutes or until a toothpick comes out clean. Cool for 5 minutes before removing from pan to a wire rack. Serve warm with lemon curd.

Yield: 1 dozen (1 cup lemon curd).

HOLIDAY CRANBERRY YEAST BREAD

joan hallford, north richland hills, texas

Wonderful aromas permeate the house while this bread is baking. My family loves it hot from the oven. The cranberries give each slice a yummy hint of sweet-tart flavor...and the whole wheat flour adds a healthy touch to our holiday menus.

1-1/2 cups fresh or frozen cranberries, halved

1/3 cup packed brown sugar

1/3 cup molasses

1-1/4 cups warm water (110° to 115°), *divided*

1 tablespoon active dry yeast

1 tablespoon honey

2 tablespoons butter, melted

1 teaspoon salt

1/4 teaspoon ground allspice

2-1/2 cups whole wheat flour

1-1/2 to 2 cups all-purpose flour

1 In a small bowl, combine the cranberries, brown sugar and molasses; let stand for 1 hour. Stir in 1 cup warm water.

2 In a large bowl, dissolve the yeast in remaining warm water. Add honey; let stand for 5 minutes. Beat in the butter, salt, allspice, whole wheat flour, 1 cup all-purpose flour and cranberry mixture until smooth. Stir in enough remaining flour to form a soft dough.

3 Turn onto a lightly floured surface; knead until smooth and elastic, about 6-8 minutes. Place in a large bowl coated with cooking spray, turning once to coat top. Cover and let rise until doubled, about 1 hour.

4 Punch dough down and turn onto a floured surface; shape into a loaf. Place in a 9-in. x 5-in. x 3-in. loaf pan coated with cooking spray. Cover and let rise until doubled, about 30 minutes.

5 Bake at 350° for 50-60 minutes or until golden brown. Remove from pan to wire rack to cool.

Yield: 1 loaf.

ORANGE-HAZELNUT SPIRAL ROLLS

loraine meyer, bend, oregon

By adapting a popular coffee cake recipe, I came up with these scrumptious rolls. I make them for my family throughout the year.

        5 to 5-1/2 cups all-purpose flour, *divided*
        1 cup mashed potato flakes
    1/4 cup sugar
        2 packages (1/4 ounce *each*) quick-rise yeast
        1 teaspoon salt
        2 teaspoons grated orange peel
        1 cup milk
    1/2 cup butter, cubed
    1/2 cup sour cream
    1/4 cup water
        2 eggs

FILLING:

    1/3 cup butter, softened
        1 cup confectioners' sugar
        1 cup ground hazelnuts

GLAZE:

    1/2 cup sugar
    1/4 cup orange juice concentrate
    1/4 cup sour cream
        2 tablespoons butter

1   In a large bowl, combine 4 cups flour, potato flakes, sugar, yeast, salt and orange peel. In saucepan, heat the milk, butter, sour cream and water to 120°-130°. Add to dry ingredients; beat just until moistened. Add eggs; beat until smooth. Stir in enough remaining flour to form stiff dough.

2   Turn onto floured surface; knead until smooth and elastic, about 6-8 minutes. Place in greased bowl, turning once to grease top. Cover; let dough rest in a warm place for 20 minutes.

3   Punch dough down. Turn onto a floured surface; roll into a 22-in. x 14-in. rectangle. For the filling, combine butter, confectioners' sugar and nuts.

Spread lengthwise over half of the dough. Fold the dough over the filling, forming a 22-in. x 7-in. rectangle. Cut into 7-in. x 3/4-in. strips.

4   Twist each strip 4 or 5 times and shape into a ring. Pinch ends together. Place on two greased 15-in. x 10-in. x 1-in. baking pans. Cover and let rise for 30 minutes or until doubled.

5   Bake at 375° for 17-20 minutes or until golden brown. Remove to wire racks. Meanwhile, in a saucepan, combine glaze ingredients over medium heat. Bring to boil; boil and stir for 3 minutes or until thickened. Remove from the heat. Drizzle over warm rolls.

Yield: about 2 dozen.

YUMMY YEAST ROLLS

emma rea, columbia, missouri

These golden brown rolls are light, tender and a cinch to make. To cut out the biscuits, we just use the top of a drinking glass.

        2 to 2-1/2 cups all-purpose flour
        3 tablespoons sugar
        1 package (1/4 ounce) quick-rise yeast
    1/2 teaspoon salt
    3/4 cup warm water (120° to 130°)
        2 tablespoons butter, melted

1   In a large bowl, combine 1-1/2 cups flour, sugar, yeast and salt. Add water and butter; beat on medium speed for 3 minutes or until smooth. Stir in enough remaining flour to form a soft dough.

2   Turn onto a well-floured surface; knead until smooth and elastic, about 4-6 minutes. Cover and let rest for 10 minutes. Roll dough to 3/8-in. thickness; cut with a lightly floured 2-1/2-in. biscuit cutter. Place 2 in. apart on a greased baking sheet. Cover and let rise in a warm place until doubled, about 30 minutes.

3   Bake at 375° for 11-14 minutes or until lightly browned. Remove to a wire rack.

Yield: about 1 dozen.

CHRISTMAS BANANA BREAD

phyllis schmalz, kansas city, kansas

This bread is a pretty addition to the table during the holidays. Cherries, walnuts and chocolate chips give festive flair to the loaf of moist banana bread.

- 1/2 cup butter, softened
- 1 cup sugar
- 2 eggs
- 2 cups all-purpose flour
- 1 teaspoon baking soda
- 1/4 teaspoon salt
- 1-1/4 cups mashed ripe bananas (about 3 medium)
- 1/2 cup chopped walnuts
- 1/2 cup semisweet chocolate chips
- 1/4 cup chopped maraschino cherries

1 In a large bowl, cream butter and sugar until light and fluffy. Add eggs, one at a time, beating well after each addition. Combine the flour, baking soda and salt; gradually add to creamed mixture. Beat in the bananas just until combined. Stir in the walnuts, chocolate chips and cherries.

2 Pour into a greased 9-in. x 5-in. x 3-in. loaf pan. Bake at 350° for 70-80 minutes or until a toothpick inserted near the center comes out clean. Cool for 10 minutes before removing from pan to a wire rack.

Yield: 1 loaf (16 slices).

CREAMY CHOCOLATE CRESCENTS

bill hughes, dolores, colorado

"Homemade" chocolate-filled treats are easy when you start with convenient refrigerated crescent rolls. They're impressive yet easy to serve for breakfast with a cup of coffee or tea or as a midday snack.

- 2 packages (3 ounces *each*) cream cheese, softened
- 1/4 cup butter, softened
- 1/2 cup confectioners' sugar
- 2 tablespoons cornstarch
- 2 cups (12 ounces) semisweet chocolate chips, melted
- 1/2 teaspoon vanilla extract
- 4 tubes (8 ounces *each*) refrigerated crescent rolls

GLAZE:

- 2 eggs
- 1 tablespoon butter, melted
- 1/2 teaspoon almond extract

Confectioners' sugar, optional

1 In a large bowl, beat the cream cheese, butter and sugar until fluffy. Add the cornstarch, melted chocolate and vanilla; beat until smooth. Unroll crescent roll dough; separate into triangles.

2 In a small bowl, whisk together eggs, butter and extract. Brush some over dough. Drop rounded teaspoonfuls of chocolate mixture at the wide end of each triangle; roll up from the wide end. Place point side down on greased baking sheets; curve ends slightly. Brush with remaining glaze.

3 Bake at 350° for 10-15 minutes or until golden. Remove from pans to cool on wire racks. Dust with confectioners' sugar if desired.

Yield: about 2-1/2 dozen.

MAPLE PECAN COFFEE TWIST

carolyn strube, garden city, texas
Making sweet breads has been a hobby of mine since I was a teenager. The addition of maple flavoring gives this coffee cake a tasty twist.

   1   **package (1/4 ounce) active dry yeast**
1/4   **cup warm water (110° to 115°)**
3/4   **cup warm milk (110° to 115°)**
1/2   **cup mashed potatoes**
1/2   **cup shortening**
1/4   **cup sugar**
   2   **eggs**
   1   **teaspoon maple flavoring**
1/2   **teaspoon salt**
   4   **to 5 cups all-purpose flour**

FILLING:
1/2   **cup sugar**
1/2   **cup finely chopped pecans**
   1   **teaspoon ground cinnamon**
   1   **teaspoon maple flavoring**
   6   **tablespoons butter, softened**

GLAZE:
1-1/2   **cups confectioners' sugar**
1/4   **teaspoon maple flavoring**
   2   **to 3 tablespoons milk**

1 In a large bowl, dissolve yeast in warm water. Add the milk, potatoes, shortening, sugar, eggs, maple flavoring, salt and 2 cups flour. Beat until smooth. Stir in enough remaining flour to form a soft dough.

2 Turn onto a floured surface; knead until smooth and elastic, about 6-8 minutes. Place in a greased bowl, turning once to grease top. Cover and let rise in a warm place until doubled, about 1 hour.

3 For filling, combine the sugar, pecans, cinnamon and maple flavoring; set aside. Punch dough down. Turn onto a lightly floured surface; divide into thirds. Roll each portion into a 14-in. circle; place one circle on a greased baking sheet or 14-in. pizza pan.

4 Spread with a third of the butter; sprinkle with a third of the filling. Top with a second circle of dough; spread with butter and top with filling. Repeat with remaining dough, butter and filling; pinch to seal.

5 Carefully place a glass in the center of the circle. With scissors, cut from outside edge just to the glass, forming 16 wedges. Remove glass; twist each wedge five to six times. Pinch ends to seal and tuck under.

6 Cover and let rise until doubled, about 30 minutes. Bake at 375° for 25-30 minutes or until golden brown.

7 In a small bowl, combine the confectioners' sugar and flavoring and enough milk to achieve desired consistency; set aside. Carefully remove bread from pan by running a metal spatula under it to loosen; transfer to a wire rack. Drizzle with glaze. Serve slightly warm or cool completely.

Yield: 16 servings.

CRANBERRY SWIRL LOAF

darlene brenden, salem, oregon
My mother made this bread with dates, but I use cranberries instead. Either way, it's delicious.

   3   **to 3-1/2 cups all-purpose flour**
1/3   **cup sugar**
   1   **package (1/4 ounce) quick-rise yeast**
1/2   **teaspoon salt**

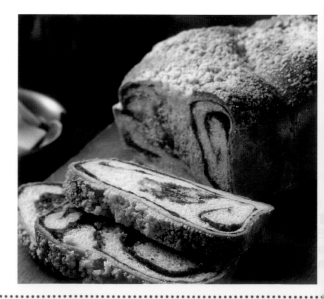

1/2 cup water

1/2 cup milk

1/3 cup butter, cubed

FILLING:

1 cup chopped fresh *or* frozen cranberries

1/4 cup packed brown sugar

1/4 cup water

1 tablespoon butter

1/2 cup chopped walnuts

1 tablespoon lemon juice

TOPPING:

2 tablespoons all-purpose flour

2 tablespoons sugar

2 tablespoons cold butter, *divided*

1 In a large bowl, combine 1 cup flour, sugar, yeast and salt. In a saucepan, heat the water, milk and butter to 120°-130°. Add to dry ingredients; beat just until moistened. Stir in enough remaining flour to form a soft dough.

2 Turn onto a floured surface; knead until smooth and elastic, about 5-7 minutes. Place in a greased bowl, turning once to grease top. Cover and let rise in a warm place until doubled, about 1 hour.

3 For filling, in a small saucepan, combine the cranberries, brown sugar and water. Cook over medium heat until berries pop, about 15 minutes. Remove from the heat; stir in the butter, walnuts and lemon juice. Cool.

4 Punch dough down. Turn onto a lightly floured surface; roll into a 20-in. x 10-in. rectangle. Spread filling to within 1/2 in. of edges. Roll up jelly-roll style, starting with a long side; pinch seam to seal. Place in a zigzag pattern in a greased 9-in. x 5-in. x 3-in. loaf pan.

5 For topping, in a small bowl, combine flour and sugar; cut in 1 tablespoon butter until crumbly. Melt remaining butter; brush over dough. Sprinkle with topping. Cover and let rise until doubled, about 40 minutes.

6 Bake at 350° for 40-45 minutes or until bread sounds hollow when tapped. Carefully remove from pan to a wire rack to cool.

Yield: 1 loaf (16 slices).

BRAIDED ONION LOAF

linda knoll, jackson, michigan

This recipe won the blue ribbon for "Best Loaf of Bread" at our county fair a few years ago. One bite and you'll see why the tender, savory slices appealed to the judges.

1 package (1/4 ounce) active dry yeast

3/4 cup warm water (110° to 115°)

1/2 cup warm milk (110° to 115°)

1/4 cup butter, softened

1 egg

1/4 cup sugar

1-1/2 teaspoons salt

4 to 4-1/2 cups all-purpose flour

FILLING:

1/4 cup butter, softened

3/4 cup dried minced onion

1 tablespoon grated Parmesan cheese

1 teaspoon paprika

1 teaspoon garlic salt, optional

Melted butter

1 In a large bowl, dissolve yeast in warm water. Add the milk, butter, egg, sugar, salt and 2 cups flour; beat until smooth. Add enough of the remaining flour to form a soft dough.

2 Turn onto a floured surface; knead until smooth and elastic, about 6-8 minutes. Place in a greased bowl, turning once to grease top. Cover and let rise in a warm place until doubled, about 1 hour.

3 For filling, in a bowl, combine the butter, onion, Parmesan cheese, paprika and garlic salt if desired; set aside. Punch dough down; turn onto a lightly floured surface. Divide into thirds. Roll each portion into a 20-in. x 4-in. rectangle. Spread filling over rectangles. Roll up jelly-roll style, starting from a long side.

4 Place ropes on an ungreased baking sheet; braid. Pinch ends to seal and tuck under. Cover and let rise until doubled, about 45 minutes.

5 Bake at 350° for 30-35 minutes or until golden brown. Brush with melted butter. Remove from pan to a wire rack.

Yield: 1 loaf.

CHRISTMAS TREE SWEET ROLLS

lori daniels, beverly, west virginia

Every Christmas Eve, I make a special bread to enjoy the next morning while opening gifts. I often share one of the "trees" with a neighbor.

2	packages (1/4 ounce *each*) active dry yeast
2-1/2	cups warm water (110° to 115°), *divided*
1/2	cup nonfat dry milk powder
1/2	cup canola oil
2	tablespoons sugar
2	teaspoons salt
7	to 8 cups all-purpose flour

FILLING:

1	package (8 ounces) cream cheese, softened
1/3	cup sugar
1	teaspoon vanilla extract
1/4	teaspoon ground cinnamon
1	can (8 ounces) crushed pineapple, well drained
1/2	cup chopped red and green candied cherries
1/4	cup chopped pecans

GLAZE:

2	cups confectioners' sugar
2	tablespoons milk
1	tablespoon butter, softened
1	teaspoon vanilla extract

Red candied cherries and green colored sugar

1 In a large bowl, dissolve yeast in 1/2 cup warm water. Add the milk powder; oil, sugar, salt, remaining water and 2 cups flour. Beat on medium speed for 2 minutes. Stir in enough remaining flour to form a soft dough. Turn onto a floured surface; knead until smooth and elastic, about 1 hour.

2 Meanwhile, in a medium bowl, beat the cream cheese, sugar, vanilla and cinnamon until blended. Stir in the pineapple, cherries and pecans; set aside.

3 Punch dough down. Turn onto a lightly floured surface; divide in half. Roll each portion into an 11-in. x 9-in. rectangle. Spread filling to within 1/2 in. of edges. Roll up each rectangle jelly-roll style, starting with a long side; pinch seam to seal.

4 To form a tree, cut each log into 11 slices, 1 in. each. Cover two baking sheets with foil and grease well. Center one slice near the top of each prepared baking sheet for treetop. Arrange slices with sides touching in three more rows, adding one slice for each row, forming a tree. Center the remaining slice below the tree trunk. Cover and let the dough rise until doubled, about 30 minutes.

5 Bake at 350° for 20-25 minutes or until golden brown. Transfer foil with trees to wire racks; cool for 20 minutes.

6 For glaze, in a bowl, beat the confectioners' sugar, milk, butter and vanilla until smooth. Transfer to a small pastry or plastic bag; cut a small hole in a corner of the bag. Pipe garland on trees. Decorate with cherries and colored sugar.

Yield: 2 trees (11 rolls each).

CHRISTMAS CRANBERRY ROLLS

margery rice, bedford, new hampshire

Cranberries are one of our favorite foods, and this is a much-requested recipe. I've been making these pretty sweet rolls for years.

3-3/4	cups all-purpose flour
1/4	cup sugar
1	package (1/4 ounce) active dry yeast
1	teaspoon salt
1-1/4	cups milk
1/4	cup canola oil
1	egg
3	tablespoons butter
3/4	cup packed brown sugar
3	tablespoons corn syrup
1	cup fresh cranberries, halved
1/2	cup chopped citron *or* mixed candied fruit
1/2	cup chopped pecans
2	teaspoons grated lemon peel

TOPPING:

2/3	cup sugar
1	teaspoon ground cinnamon
6	tablespoons butter, melted

1. In a large mixing bowl, combine 1-3/4 cups flour, sugar, yeast and salt. In a saucepan, heat milk and oil to 120°-130°. Add to the dry ingredients; mix well. Add egg; beat well. Add enough remaining flour to form a soft dough. Turn onto a floured surface; knead until smooth and elastic, about 6-8 minutes. Place in a greased bowl, turning once to grease top. Cover and let rise until doubled, about 1 hour.

2. Meanwhile, melt butter in a small saucepan; stir in brown sugar and corn syrup. Spread into two greased 9-in. round baking pans; set aside. Combine cranberries, citron, pecans and lemon peel; sprinkle over brown sugar mixture.

3. Punch dough down; turn onto a lightly floured surface. Divide into 30 pieces; roll each piece into a 1-1/2-in. ball. In a small bowl, combine sugar and cinnamon. Place melted butter in another bowl. Roll each ball in butter, then in cinnamon-sugar. Place 15 balls in each pan. Cover and let rise until doubled, about 1 hour. Bake at 375° for 22-27 minutes or until golden brown. Cool for 5 minutes before inverting onto serving plates.

Yield: 2-1/2 dozen.

EASY-DOES-IT FRUITCAKE

omaine wetzel, ronks, pennsylvania

These miniature loaves are chock-full of tempting fruit and nuts. The glaze makes them extra moist and tasty. They are wonderful to give as gifts and fun to serve to holiday guests and family.

- 3 **cups all-purpose flour,** *divided*
- 1 **pound chopped candied fruit**
- 2 **packages (8 ounces** *each***) pitted dates, chopped**
- 1 **package (15 ounces) raisins**
- 1 **cup chopped walnuts**
- 1 **cup chopped pecans** *or* **almonds**
- 1 **cup butter, softened**
- 1-1/4 **cups packed brown sugar**
- 4 **eggs**
- 1 **teaspoon baking soda**
- 1 **teaspoon salt**
- 1 **teaspoon ground cinnamon**
- 1 **teaspoon ground cloves**
- 1/4 **cup orange juice**

GLAZE:
- 1 **cup confectioners' sugar**
- 2 **tablespoons milk**

1. In large bowl, combine 1/4 cup flour, candied fruit, dates, raisins and nuts; toss until well coated; set aside.

2. In another large bowl, cream butter and brown sugar until light and fluffy. Add eggs, one at a time, beating well after each addition. Combine the baking soda, salt, cinnamon, cloves and remaining flour; gradually add to creamed mixture alternately with orange juice, beating well after each addition. Stir in fruit and nut mixture; mix well.

3. Spoon into five greased 5-3/4-in. x 3-in. x 2-in. baking pans (pans will be full). Bake at 325° for 1 hour. Cover with foil; bake 10-15 minutes longer or until a toothpick inserted near the center comes out clean. Let stand for 10 minutes before removing from pans to wire racks.

4. In a small bowl, combine glaze ingredients until smooth. With a pastry brush, brush glaze over warm loaves. Cool completely.

Yield: 5 loaves.

BRAIDED WREATH BREAD

janet uram, willowick, ohio

I make this attractive bread to celebrate Santa Lucia Day on December 13. This Swedish custom is the symbolic start of Christmas in Scandinavia. It's a festival of lights that brightens the short, dark days of winter.

- 1 package (1/4 ounce) active dry yeast
- 1/4 cup warm water (110° to 115°)
- 1/3 cup warm milk (110° to 115°)
- 1/4 cup sugar
- 1/4 cup butter, cubed
- 1 egg
- 1 teaspoon grated orange peel
- 1/2 teaspoon salt
- 1/2 teaspoon orange extract
- 2-1/2 to 3 cups all-purpose flour

GLAZE:
- 1 egg

1 In a large bowl, dissolve yeast in warm water. Add the milk, sugar, butter, 1 egg, orange peel, salt, extract and 1 cup flour; beat until smooth. Stir in enough remaining flour to form a soft dough.

2 Turn onto a floured surface; knead until smooth and elastic, about 6-8 minutes. Place in a greased bowl, turning once to grease top. Cover and let rise in a warm place until doubled, about 1 hour.

3 Punch dough down; divide into thirds. Roll each portion into a 20-in. rope. Braid the ropes; shape into a wreath and pinch ends to seal. Place on a greased baking sheet. Cover and let rise in a warm place until doubled, about 45 minutes.

4 For glaze, beat egg; lightly brush over dough. Bake at 350° for 30-35 minutes or until golden brown. Cool for 10 minutes before removing from pan to a wire rack to cool.

Yield: 12 servings.

CINNAMON CHIP SCONES

barbara humiston, tampa, florida

These scones will melt in your mouth. They're delicious hot, warm or even cold!

- 3-1/4 cups all-purpose flour
- 1/3 cup plus 2 tablespoons sugar, *divided*
- 2-1/2 teaspoons baking powder
- 1/2 teaspoon baking soda
- 1/2 teaspoon salt
- 3/4 cup cold butter, cubed
- 1 cup buttermilk
- 1 package (10 ounces) cinnamon-flavored baking chips
- 2 tablespoons butter, melted

1 In a large bowl, combine the flour, 1/3 cup sugar, baking powder, baking soda and salt. Cut in butter until mixture resembles coarse crumbs. Stir in buttermilk just until moistened. Fold in chips.

2 Turn onto a lightly floured surface; knead gently 10-12 times or until dough is no longer sticky. Divide in half; gently pat or roll each portion into a 7-in. circle. Brush with butter and sprinkle with remaining sugar.

3 Cut each circle into six wedges. Separate wedges and place on an ungreased baking sheet. Bake at 425° for 10-13 minutes or until lightly browned. Serve warm.

Yield: 1 dozen.

FREEZER CRESCENT ROLLS

kristine buck, payson, utah

Bake up sweet convenience with this freezer-friendly dough. This recipe was handed down to me from my aunt, an awesome cook! I love having homemade rolls available any time I want, especially during the holidays.

    3 teaspoons active dry yeast
    2 cups warm water (110° to 115°)
  1/2 cup butter, softened
  2/3 cup nonfat dry milk powder
  1/2 cup sugar
  1/2 cup mashed potato flakes
    2 eggs
1-1/2 teaspoons salt
    6 to 6-1/2 cups all-purpose flour

1   In a large bowl, dissolve yeast in warm water. Add the butter, milk powder, sugar, potato flakes, eggs, salt and 3 cups flour. Beat until smooth. Stir in enough remaining flour to form a firm dough.

2   Turn onto a heavily floured surface; knead 8-10 times. Divide dough in half. Roll each portion into a 12-in. circle; cut each circle into 16 wedges. Roll up wedges from the wide ends and place point side down 2 in. apart on waxed paper-lined baking sheets. Curve the ends to form crescents.

3   Cover and freeze. When firm, transfer to a large resealable plastic freezer bag. Freeze for up to 4 weeks.

4   **To use frozen rolls:** Arrange frozen rolls 2 in. apart on baking sheets coated with cooking spray. Cover and thaw in the refrigerator overnight. Let rise in a warm place for 1 hour or until doubled. Bake at 350° for 15-17 minutes or until golden brown. Serve warm.

Yield: 32 rolls.

SIMPLE STOLLEN

shirley glaab, hattiesburg, mississippi

When it comes to seasonal sweets, this easy Christmas stollen is a recipe I know I can count on. It's made with baking powder instead of yeast, so it requires no rising.

2-1/4 cups all-purpose flour
  1/2 cup sugar
1-1/2 teaspoons baking powder
  1/4 teaspoon salt
    7 tablespoons cold butter, *divided*
    1 cup ricotta cheese
  1/2 cup chopped mixed candied fruit
  1/2 cup raisins
  1/3 cup slivered almonds, toasted
    1 teaspoon vanilla extract
  1/2 teaspoon almond extract
  1/2 teaspoon grated lemon peel
    1 egg
    1 egg yolk

Confectioners' sugar

1   In a large bowl, combine the flour, sugar, baking powder and salt. Cut in 6 tablespoons butter until mixture resembles fine crumbs. In a small bowl, combine the ricotta, candied fruit, raisins, almonds, extracts, lemon peel, egg and yolk. Stir into dry ingredients just until moistened.

2   Turn onto a floured surface; knead five times. Roll dough into a 10-in. x 8-in. oval. Fold a long side over to within 1 in. of opposite side; press edge lightly to seal. Place on a greased baking sheet; curve ends slightly.

3   Bake at 350° for 40-45 minutes or until golden brown. Melt remaining butter; brush over loaf. Remove to a wire rack to cool completely. Dust with confectioners' sugar.

Yield: 1 loaf.

Editor's Note: This recipe does not contain yeast.

WALNUT-FILLED COFFEE CAKES

debbie johnson, centertown, missouri

At our house, holiday mornings just would not be the same without these wonderful sugary-cinnamon loaves. They also make lovely gifts.

- 1 package (1/4 ounce) active dry yeast
- 4 tablespoons sugar, *divided*
- 1 cup warm water (110° to 115°)
- 2 eggs
- 1 cup butter, softened
- 1 cup milk
- 1 teaspoon salt
- 5 to 6 cups all-purpose flour

FILLING:
- 1 cup packed brown sugar
- 1/2 cup all-purpose flour
- 1 teaspoon ground cinnamon
- 6 tablespoons cold butter, cubed
- 1/2 cup chopped walnuts

GLAZE:
- 1-1/2 cups confectioners' sugar
- 4 teaspoons orange juice

1 In a large bowl, dissolve yeast and 1 tablespoon sugar in warm water; let stand 5 minutes. Add the eggs, butter, milk, salt, 5 cups flour and remaining sugar; beat until smooth. Stir in enough remaining flour to form a soft dough (dough will be sticky). Cover; refrigerate overnight.

2 For filling, in a small bowl, combine the brown sugar, flour and cinnamon; cut in butter until mixture resembles coarse crumbs. Stir in walnuts.

3 Punch dough down. On a floured surface, roll into a 21-in. circle; cut into four wedges. Spread filling over dough to within 1/2 in. of edges. Roll up each wedge from the wide end.

4 Place point side down on baking sheets coated with cooking spray. Curve ends to form crescents. Cut slits in pastry. Cover and let rise in a warm place until doubled, about 1 hour.

5 Bake at 350° for 15-20 minutes or until golden brown. Remove from pans to wire racks to cool. Combine glaze ingredients; drizzle over coffee cakes. Cut each into 12 slices.

Yield: 4 coffee cakes (12 slices each).

BANANA WHEAT BREAD

louise myers, pomeroy, ohio

A subtle banana flavor comes through in this moist whole wheat loaf. Flecked with poppy seeds, the sweet slices are wonderful warm or toasted and spread with butter.

- 3/4 cup water (70° to 80°)
- 1/4 cup honey
- 1 egg, lightly beaten
- 4-1/2 teaspoons canola oil
- 1 medium ripe banana, sliced
- 2 teaspoons poppy seeds
- 1 teaspoon salt
- 1/2 teaspoon vanilla extract
- 1-3/4 cups bread flour
- 1-1/2 cups whole wheat flour
- 2-1/4 teaspoons active dry yeast

1 In bread machine pan, place all ingredients in order suggested by manufacturer. Select basic bread setting. Choose crust color and loaf size if available. Bake according to bread machine directions (check dough after 5 minutes of mixing; add 1 to 2 tablespoons of water or flour if needed).

Yield: 1 loaf (1-1/2 pounds, 16 slices).

Editor's Note: We recommend you do not use a bread machine's time-delay feature for this recipe.

SANTA'S SURPRISE GINGERBREAD MUFFINS

edie despain, logan, utah

Cranberry-raspberry sauce is the luscious surprise tucked inside these mouthwatering muffins.

    1/2 cup butter, softened
    1/2 cup sugar
    1/2 cup packed brown sugar
      2 eggs
    1/2 cup molasses
      3 cups all-purpose flour
  1-1/2 teaspoons ground cinnamon
      1 teaspoon baking soda
    1/4 teaspoon *each* ground ginger, cloves and
         allspice
      1 cup buttermilk
    1/2 cup cranberry-raspberry sauce

1 In a large bowl, cream butter and sugars until light and fluffy. Add eggs, one at a time, beating well after each addition. Beat in the molasses. Combine the flour, cinnamon, baking soda, ginger, cloves and allspice; add to the creamed mixture alternately with buttermilk.

2 Fill 16 greased or paper-lined muffin cups half full; spoon about 1-1/2 teaspoons cranberry-raspberry sauce over each. Top with remaining batter. Bake at 350° for 25-30 minutes or until a toothpick inserted near the center comes out clean. Cool for 10 minutes before removing from pans to wire racks to cool completely.

Yield: 16 muffins.

DILLY ONION DINNER ROLLS

carol faulkner, sunman, indiana

These light, golden rolls are packed with savory onion and dill. The dough can also be rolled out and cut with a biscuit cutter.

      1 package (1/4 ounce) active dry yeast
    1/4 cup warm water (110° to 115°)
      1 cup (8 ounces) 4% cottage cheese
      1 egg
      2 tablespoons sugar
      2 tablespoons dried minced onion
      3 tablespoons butter, softened, *divided*
      3 teaspoons dill seed, *divided*
      1 teaspoon salt
  2-1/4 to 2-1/2 cups all-purpose flour

1 In a bowl, dissolve yeast in warm water. In a small saucepan, heat cottage cheese to 110°-115°. Add cottage cheese, egg, sugar, onion, 1 tablespoon butter, 2 teaspoons dill seed, salt and 1 cup flour to yeast mixture; beat until well combined. Stir in enough remaining flour to form a stiff dough.

2 Turn onto a floured surface; knead until smooth and elastic, about 6-8 minutes. Place in a greased bowl, turning once to grease top. Cover and let rise in a warm place until doubled, about 1 hour.

3 Punch the dough down. Turn onto a lightly floured surface; divide dough in half. Roll each portion into a 14-in. x 6-in. rectangle. Spread with 1 tablespoon butter.

4 With the dull edge of a table knife, score dough widthwise at 2-in. intervals. Using those marks as a guideline, make score marks widthwise across dough. Fold dough accordion-style, back and forth along creased lines. Cut folded dough into 1-in. pieces. Place each piece cut side down in a greased muffin cup.

5 Melt remaining butter; brush over dough. Sprinkle with remaining dill seed. Cover and let rise until doubled, about 30 minutes.

6 Bake at 375° for 15-17 minutes or until golden brown. Remove from pan to a wire rack.

Yield: 1 dozen.

ALMOND COFFEE CAKE

mary shivers, ada, oklahoma

This cake is doubly delicious due to the cream cheese and vanilla chip filling. One piece always leads to another!

- 1 loaf (1 pound) frozen bread dough, thawed
- 1 package (8 ounces) cream cheese, softened
- 1/4 cup sugar
- 1 egg
- 1/2 teaspoon almond extract
- 3/4 cup vanilla *or* white chips
- 1 tablespoon milk

GLAZE:
- 1 cup confectioners' sugar
- 1/4 teaspoon almond extract
- 1 to 2 tablespoons milk
- 1/2 cup slivered almonds, toasted

1 On a lightly floured surface, roll dough into a 15-in. x 9-in. rectangle. Transfer to a lightly greased baking sheet.

2 In a small bowl, beat cream cheese and sugar until smooth. Add egg and extract; mix well (filling will be soft). Spread down center of rectangle; sprinkle with chips. On each long side, cut 1-in.-wide strips, about 1/2 in. from filling.

3 Starting at one end, fold alternating strips at an angle across filling. Seal ends. Cover and let rise in a warm place until doubled, about 1 hour.

4 Brush with milk. Bake at 350° for 20-30 minutes or until golden brown. Cool on a wire rack.

5 For glaze, in a small bowl, combine confectioners' sugar and extract. Stir in enough milk to achieve desired consistency. Drizzle over coffee cake. Sprinkle with almonds.

Yield: 8-10 servings.

CHOCOLATE PUMPKIN BREAD

taste of home test kitchen

Save time during the busy holiday season with a moist chocolaty bread. The two pumpkin-flavored loaves can be made ahead of time and then frozen for special events.

- 3-1/3 cups all-purpose flour
- 3 cups sugar
- 4 teaspoons pumpkin pie spice
- 2 teaspoons baking soda
- 1 teaspoon salt
- 1/2 teaspoon baking powder
- 4 eggs
- 1 can (15 ounces) solid-pack pumpkin
- 2/3 cup water
- 2/3 cup canola oil
- 2 cups (12 ounces) semisweet chocolate chips
- 1 cup sliced almonds, toasted

1 In a large bowl, combine the first six ingredients. In another bowl, combine the eggs, pumpkin, water and oil; stir into dry ingredients just until moistened. Stir in chocolate chips and almonds.

2 Pour into two greased 9-in. x 5-in. loaf pans. Bake at 350° for 70-75 minutes or until a toothpick inserted near the center comes out clean. Cool for 10 minutes before removing from pans to wire racks to cool completely. Wrap in foil and freeze for up to 3 months.

3 **To use frozen bread:** Thaw at room temperature.

Yield: 2 loaves (16 slices each).

FEATHERLIGHT ROLLS

terri duhon, bryan, texas
Aptly named for their light texture, these tender rolls from my mom were a favorite of family and friends alike. They're just as tasty the next day.

2 packages (1/4 ounce *each*) active dry yeast
1/2 cup warm water (110° to 115°)
1 tablespoon plus 1/3 cup sugar, *divided*
1 cup warm milk (110° to 115°)
1/3 cup shortening
2 eggs
1-1/2 teaspoons salt
4 to 5 cups all-purpose flour

1 In a large bowl, dissolve yeast in warm water. Stir in 1 tablespoon sugar; let stand for 5 minutes. Add milk, shortening, eggs, salt, 3 cups flour and remaining sugar. Beat on medium speed for 2 minutes. Stir in enough remaining flour to form a soft dough (mixture will be sticky). Do not knead. Cover and refrigerate overnight.

2 Punch dough down. Turn onto a lightly floured surface; divide into 24 portions. Divide each portion into three pieces; shape each into a ball. Place three balls in each greased muffin cup. Cover and let rise in a warm place until doubled, about 1-3/4 hours.

3 Bake at 350° for 13-15 minutes or until golden. Remove from pans to wire racks. Serve warm.

Yield: 2 dozen.

CHRISTMAS MORNING CROISSANTS

tish stevenson, grand rapids, michigan
Growing up in France, I often enjoyed buttery croissants for breakfast with steaming cups of hot chocolate. I've tried to re-create the experience for my family with this recipe, and now, it's a Christmas tradition.

2 packages (1/4 ounce *each*) active dry yeast
1 cup warm water (110° to 115°)
1-1/4 cups cold butter, *divided*
5 cups all-purpose flour
1/3 cup sugar
1-1/2 teaspoons salt
3/4 cup evaporated milk
2 eggs
1 tablespoon water

1 In a large bowl, dissolve yeast in warm water; let stand for 5 minutes. Melt 1/4 cup butter; set aside. Combine 1 cup flour, sugar and salt; add to yeast mixture. Add the milk, 1 egg and melted butter; beat until smooth.

2 Place remaining flour in a large bowl; cut in remaining butter until crumbly. Add yeast mixture; mix well. Do not knead. Cover; refrigerate overnight.

3 Punch dough down. Turn onto a lightly floured surface; knead about six times. Divide dough into four pieces. Roll each piece into a 16-in. circle; cut each circle into eight wedges.

4 Roll up wedges from the wide ends and place point side down 3 in. apart on ungreased baking sheets. Curve ends to form crescents. Cover and let rise in a warm place for 1 hour.

5 Beat water and remaining egg; brush over rolls. Bake at 325° for 20-25 minutes or until lightly browned. Serve warm.

Yield: 32 rolls.

CAPPUCCINO MUFFINS

susan wagers, minot, north dakota

These airy muffins capture the wonderful flavor of coffee. Folks are pleasantly surprised to find a creamy chocolate center.

- 2-1/2 cups all-purpose flour
- 2/3 cup sugar
- 2-1/2 teaspoons baking powder
- 1-1/2 teaspoons ground cinnamon
- 3/4 teaspoon salt
- 1/2 teaspoon baking soda
- 1 egg
- 1-1/3 cups buttermilk
- 3 tablespoons canola oil
- 4-1/2 teaspoons instant coffee granules
- 2 teaspoons vanilla extract
- 12 chocolate kisses

TOPPING:

- 2 tablespoons sugar
- 1/2 teaspoon ground cinnamon

1 In a large bowl, combine the flour, sugar, baking powder, cinnamon, salt and baking soda. In another bowl, beat the egg, buttermilk, oil, coffee granules and vanilla until coffee granules are dissolved. Stir into dry ingredients just until moistened.

2 Spoon 2 tablespoons batter into greased muffin cups. Place a chocolate kiss in the center of each; top with remaining batter. Combine sugar and cinnamon; sprinkle over batter.

3 Bake at 425° for 16-20 minutes or until a toothpick inserted near the center comes out clean. Cool for 5 minutes before removing from pan to a wire rack. Serve warm.

Yield: 1 dozen.

PEACHY ROLLS

renae jacobson, elm creek, nebraska

I adapted a peach sauce recipe, using it on top of frozen cinnamon rolls, for this quick breakfast. Fix them the night before and you can pop them into the oven as soon as you get up.

- 2 cups frozen unsweetened sliced peaches, thawed and chopped
- 1/2 cup packed brown sugar
- 1/2 cup orange juice
- 1 teaspoon ground cinnamon
- 1 teaspoon vanilla extract
- 2 packages (19 ounces *each*) freezer-to-oven cinnamon rolls

1 In a small saucepan, combine the first five ingredients. Bring to a boil; cook and stir for 2 minutes. Pour into a greased 13-in. x 9-in. baking dish; top with cinnamon rolls.

2 Bake at 350° for 35-40 minutes or until golden brown. Cool for 10 minutes before inverting onto a serving plate. Drizzle with contents of frosting packets from the cinnamon rolls if desired. Serve warm.

Yield: 1 dozen.

Editor's Note: This recipe was tested with Rhodes Any Time Cinnamon Rolls, which are available in foil pans in the freezer section.

MOCHA-CINNAMON COFFEE CAKE

bette mintz, glendale, california
This tender coffee cake is so yummy and sweet, it doesn't need frosting.

- 3/4 cup chopped walnuts
- 1/3 cup sugar
- 1 tablespoon baking cocoa
- 1 teaspoon instant coffee granules
- 1 teaspoon ground cinnamon

BATTER:
- 3/4 cup butter, softened
- 1-1/2 cups sugar
- 4 eggs
- 1 teaspoon vanilla extract
- 2-1/4 cups all-purpose flour
- 2 teaspoons baking powder
- 1 teaspoon baking soda
- 1-1/2 cups (12 ounces) sour cream
- 1/2 cup semisweet chocolate chips

1. In a small bowl, combine the first five ingredients; set aside. In a large bowl, cream butter and sugar until light and fluffy. Add eggs, one at a time, beating well after each addition. Beat in vanilla. Combine the flour, baking powder and baking soda; add to creamed mixture alternately with sour cream just until combined. Stir in chocolate chips.

2. Pour a third of the batter into a greased 10-in. fluted tube pan. Sprinkle with half of the walnut mixture; repeat layers. Top with remaining batter.

3. Bake at 350° for 40-45 minutes or until a toothpick inserted near center comes out clean. Cool for 10 minutes before removing to a wire rack.

Yield: 12-16 servings.

CELEBRATION BRAID

marcia vermaire, fruitport, michigan
During the holidays, I sometimes make a couple of these golden loaves a day to give as gifts. Everyone in our family loves them any time of year. The recipe originated from one for Jewish challah, which I began making over a decade ago.

- 2 packages (1/4 ounce *each*) active dry yeast
- 1 cup warm water (110° to 115°)
- 1/3 cup butter, softened
- 1/4 cup sugar
- 1 teaspoon salt
- 2 eggs
- 4-1/2 to 5 cups all-purpose flour
- 1 egg yolk
- 1 tablespoon cold water

1. In a large bowl, dissolve the yeast in warm water. Add the butter, sugar, salt, eggs and 3 cups flour. Beat on medium speed for 3 minutes. Stir in enough remaining flour to form a soft dough.

2. Turn onto a floured surface; knead until smooth and elastic, about 6-8 minutes. Place in a greased bowl, turning once to grease top. Cover and let rise in a warm place until doubled, about 1 hour.

3. Punch dough down. Turn onto a lightly floured surface; divide into four pieces. Shape each piece into an 18-in. rope. Place ropes parallel to each other on a greased baking sheet.

4. Beginning from the right side, braid dough by placing the first rope over the second rope, under the third and over the fourth. Repeat three or four times, beginning each time from the right side. Pinch ends to seal and tuck under.

5. Cover; let rise until doubled, about 45 minutes. Beat egg yolk and water; brush over braid. Bake at 350° for 20-25 minutes or until golden brown. Remove from pan to a wire rack to cool.

Yield: 1 loaf.

GINGERBREAD LOAF

barbara severson, tularosa, new mexico

As a diabetic, I tend to stick with tried-and-true recipes. I added spices to a well-liked oatmeal bread for this loaf, and it's the best my bread machine has ever turned out. It tastes great warm with tea or coffee.

    1   cup plus 1 tablespoon water (70° to 80°)
  1/2 cup molasses
    1   tablespoon canola oil
    3   cups bread flour
    1   cup old-fashioned oats
1-1/2 teaspoons ground cinnamon
    1   to 1-1/2 teaspoons ground ginger
    1   teaspoon salt
  1/2 teaspoon grated orange peel
  1/4 teaspoon *each* ground nutmeg and ground cloves
    1   package (1/4 ounce) active dry yeast

1   In bread machine pan, place all ingredients in order suggested by manufacturer. Select basic bread setting. Choose crust color and loaf size if available.

2   Bake according to bread machine directions (check dough after 5 minutes of mixing; add 1 to 2 tablespoons of water or flour if needed).

Yield: 1 loaf (16 slices).

CRANBERRY UPSIDE-DOWN MUFFINS

michele briasco-brin, fall river, massachusetts

Fresh cranberries are readily available here, so I cook with them often. The sweet-tart taste of these pretty muffins adds a festive touch to special-occasion suppers.

1-3/4 cups fresh *or* frozen cranberries
  3/4 cup sugar
  1/8 teaspoon ground nutmeg
BATTER:
1-3/4 cups all-purpose flour
  1/3 cup sugar
    2 teaspoons baking powder
  1/4 teaspoon salt
    1 egg
  3/4 cup milk
  1/4 cup canola oil
  1/2 teaspoon lemon extract
  1/3 cup chopped walnuts

1   In a small saucepan, combine cranberries and sugar. Cover and cook over low heat until juice forms. Uncover; cook and stir over medium heat for 10 minutes or until berries pop. Stir in nutmeg; cool slightly. Spoon into 12 paper-lined muffin cups; set aside.

2   In a large bowl, combine the flour, sugar, baking powder and salt. In another bowl, whisk the egg, milk, oil and lemon extract; stir into dry ingredients just until moistened. Stir in walnuts. Spoon over cranberry mixture.

3   Bake at 400° for 18-22 minutes or until a toothpick comes out clean. Cool for 10 minutes before removing from pan to a wire rack. Carefully remove paper liners and serve muffins warm, cranberry side up.

Yield: 1 dozen.

Freezing Bread

It's best to store bread at room temperature in a cool, dry place for up to 2-3 days. Heat and humidity cause homemade bread to mold. Storing it in the refrigerator turns it stale quickly. To keep bread soft, store in an airtight plastic bag.—Taste of Home Test Kitchen

DAZZLING DESSERTS

CREAMY
RASPBERRY
DESSERT
P. 191

RASPBERRY-CREAM CHOCOLATE TORTE

mary beth jung, hendersonville, north carolina

This spectacular torte looks and tastes like it came from a European bakery. Although it takes some time to make, each step is actually very easy.

2/3 cup butter, softened
1 cup sugar
3 eggs
2 teaspoons vanilla extract
2 cups all-purpose flour
3/4 cup baking cocoa
1-1/2 teaspoons baking powder
1/2 teaspoon baking soda
1-1/3 cups milk

FILLING:

1 package (10 ounces) frozen unsweetened raspberries, thawed
1 envelope unflavored gelatin
1 cup heavy whipping cream
1/4 cup confectioners' sugar
1/2 teaspoon vanilla extract

GANACHE:

1/2 cup semisweet chocolate chips
3 tablespoons heavy whipping cream

1 In a large bowl, cream butter and sugar until light and fluffy. Beat in eggs and vanilla. Combine the flour, cocoa, baking powder and soda; gradually add to creamed mixture alternately with milk, beating well after each addition.

2 Line a greased 15-in. x 10-in. x 1-in. baking pan with waxed paper; grease the paper. Spread batter evenly into pan. Bake at 350° for 15-20 minutes or until cake springs back when lightly touched in center. Cool for 10 minutes before removing from pan to a wire rack; carefully remove paper. Cool completely.

3 For filling, puree raspberries in a food processor. Strain, reserving juice and discarding seeds. Place juice in a small saucepan. Sprinkle with gelatin; let stand for 1 minute. Cook and stir over low heat until gelatin is completely dissolved. Cool to room temperature.

4 In a small bowl, beat the cream until it begins to thicken. Add confectioners' sugar and vanilla; beat until stiff peaks form. Gently fold into raspberry mixture.

5 Trim the edges from cake. Cut into four 7-1/2-in. x 4-1/2-in. rectangles. Place one rectangle on a serving platter; spread with a third of the filling. Repeat layers twice. Top with remaining rectangle.

6 For ganache, place chocolate chips and cream in a small saucepan. Cook and stir over low heat until chocolate is melted. Cool until thickened, about 10 minutes. Spread over torte. Refrigerate for 2 hours before serving.

Yield: 8-10 servings.

Troubleshooting Cakes

There are several factors that may cause a cake to sink in the center after baking. The most important one is oven temperature. An oven that is not hot enough can cause the cake to rise and then sink. Check the accuracy of your oven temperature with an oven thermometer. Too short of a baking time can cause similar results. Use a toothpick to check the cake's doneness. The toothpick should come out clean and the sides of the cake may start pulling from the cake pan. An incorrect proportion of ingredients may cause a cake to sink. Too much sugar, liquid or leavening as well as too little flour could be the culprit. Other reasons a cake may sink include undermixing the batter, moving the cake during baking or baking in a pan that's too small for the amount of batter.
—Taste of Home Test Kitchen

DECADENT BROWNIE SWIRL CHEESECAKE

taste of home test kitchen

It may look fancy, but this cheesecake is so simple. The secret is the speedy crust—it's from a packaged brownie mix! You don't need to be an experienced cook to make the elegant chocolate swirls on top—anyone can do it!

- 1 package fudge brownie mix
  (13-inch x 9-inch pan size)

FILLING:

- 4 packages (8 ounces *each*) cream cheese, softened
- 1 cup sugar
- 4 eggs, lightly beaten
- 3 teaspoons vanilla extract *or* 1 teaspoon almond extract and 2 teaspoons vanilla extract

Fresh raspberries, optional

Chocolate curls, optional

1. Prepare brownie mix according to package directions for chewy fudge brownies. Set aside 2/3 cup batter; spread remaining batter into a greased 9-in. springform pan.

2. Place pan on a double thickness of heavy-duty foil (about 18 in. square). Securely wrap foil around pan. Bake at 350° for 25-28 minutes (brownies will barely test done). Cool for 10 minutes on a wire rack.

3. In a large bowl, beat cream cheese and sugar until smooth. Beat in eggs and vanilla on low speed just until combined. Stir 1/3 cup into reserved brownie batter; set aside. Spoon half the cheesecake batter into crust; dollop with half of reserved chocolate cheesecake batter. Repeat layers. Cut through batter with a knife to swirl the chocolate cheesecake batter.

4. Place in a larger baking pan; add 1 in. of hot water to larger pan. Bake at 325° for 1-1/2 hours or until surface is no longer shiny and center is almost set.

5. Remove pan from water bath and foil. Cool on a wire rack for 10 minutes. Carefully run a knife around the edge of pan to loosen; cool 1 hour longer. Refrigerate overnight. Remove sides of pan. Garnish with raspberries and chocolate curls if desired.

Yield: 16 servings.

BREAD PUDDING

evette rios, westfield, massachusetts

Back in 13th-century England, bread pudding was called "poor man's pudding." Leftover bread was simply soaked in water, then seasoned with sugar and spices. Today's version features eggs, milk, butter and raisins.

- 3 eggs
- 3 cans (12 ounces *each*) evaporated milk
- 1-1/4 cups sugar
- 1/4 cup butter, melted
- 1/2 to 1 cup raisins
- 1 teaspoon ground cinnamon
- 2 teaspoons vanilla extract
- 1/2 teaspoon salt
- 1 loaf (1 pound) bread, cut into cubes

1. In a large bowl, beat the eggs. Add milk, sugar, butter, raisins, cinnamon, vanilla and salt; mix well. Add bread cubes; stir gently.

2. Pour into a greased 13-in. x 9-in. baking dish. Bake at 325° for 50-60 minutes or until a knife inserted near the center comes out clean. Serve warm or cold. Store in the refrigerator.

Yield: 12-16 servings.

CHOCOLATE MOCHA TORTE

abby slavings, buchanan, michigan

A mocha filling is spread between the layers of this fabulous chocolate cake that's piled high with flavor.

CAKE:
- 1/2 cup baking cocoa
- 1/2 cup boiling water
- 2-1/2 cups all-purpose flour
- 1-1/2 teaspoons baking soda
- 1/2 teaspoon salt
- 2/3 cup butter, softened
- 1-3/4 cups sugar
- 2 eggs
- 1 teaspoon vanilla extract
- 1 cup buttermilk

FILLING:
- 5 tablespoons all-purpose flour
- 1 cup milk
- 1 cup butter, softened
- 1 cup sugar
- 1/2 teaspoon instant coffee granules
- 2 teaspoons water
- 2 teaspoons baking cocoa
- 1 teaspoon vanilla extract
- 1 cup chopped pecans

FROSTING:
- 1/2 cup shortening
- 1/4 cup butter
- 2 tablespoons plus 1-1/2 teaspoons evaporated milk
- 1 tablespoon boiling water
- 1-1/2 teaspoons vanilla extract

Dash salt
- 3-3/4 cups confectioners' sugar, *divided*

Pecan halves, optional

1 For cake, make a paste of cocoa and water; cool and set aside. Sift together the flour, baking soda and salt; set aside. In a large bowl, cream butter and sugar until light and fluffy. Add eggs, one at a time, beating well after each addition. Beat in vanilla. Blend in cocoa mixture. Add flour mixture alternately with the buttermilk, beating well after each addition.

2 Pour into two greased and floured 9-in. round baking pans. Bake at 350° for 35 minutes or until a toothpick inserted near the center comes out clean. Cool for 10 minutes before removing from pans to wire racks to cool completely.

3 For filling, in a saucepan, combine flour and milk until smooth. Bring to a boil over low heat; cook and stir for 1-2 minutes or until thickened. Remove from the heat; cool.

4 Meanwhile, cream butter and sugar until light and fluffy. Dissolve coffee in water; add to creamed mixture along with cocoa, vanilla and cooled milk mixture. Beat until fluffy, about 5 minutes. Fold in nuts.

5 Split each cake into two horizontal layers. Place bottom layer on a serving plate; top with a third of the filling. Repeat layers twice. Top with remaining cake layer.

6 For frosting, in a large bowl, cream shortening and butter until light and fluffy. Add the milk, water, vanilla, salt and half of confectioners' sugar. Beat well. Add remaining confectioners' sugar and beat until smooth and fluffy. Spread over top and sides of cake. Garnish with pecan halves if desired.

Yield: 16 servings.

No Buttermilk on Hand?

There are a number of substitutes for buttermilk in baking. For each cup of buttermilk, you can use 1 tablespoon of white vinegar or lemon juice plus enough milk to measure 1 cup. Stir, then let stand for 5 minutes. You can also use 1 cup of plain yogurt or 1-3/4 teaspoons cream of tartar plus 1 cup milk. Another option is to keep powdered buttermilk blend on hand. You can reconstitute the amount needed for your recipe in just seconds. SACO Cultured Buttermilk Blend is found near dry and canned milk in most grocery stores.—Taste of Home Test Kitchen

CRANBERRY-TOPPED LEMON TARTS

ruth lee, troy, ontario

The delicious combination of colors and tangy-sweet flavors makes this a very special finale. You'll receive a ton of compliments on your culinary expertise.

- 2 cups all-purpose flour
- 3 tablespoons sugar
- 3/4 teaspoon salt
- 1 cup cold butter, cubed

TOPPING:
- 3 cups fresh *or* frozen cranberries
- 1-1/4 cups sugar
- 1/4 cup water

FILLING:
- 5 eggs
- 1-1/2 cups sugar
- 3/4 cup lemon juice
- 4 teaspoons grated lemon peel
- 1/3 cup butter, softened

GARNISH:
- 1 medium lemon, cut into 1/4-inch slices
- 1/2 cup sugar
- 1/4 cup water

1 In a large bowl, combine the flour, sugar and salt; cut in butter until mixture resembles coarse crumbs. Stir until dough forms a ball. Divide into eight portions; press each onto the bottom and up the sides of eight 4-in. tart pans.

2 Cover and refrigerate for 20 minutes. Bake at 350° for 20-25 minutes or until golden brown. Cool on wire racks.

3 In a large saucepan, combine the cranberries, sugar and water. Cook over medium heat until berries have popped, about 20 minutes.

4 Meanwhile, in a small heavy saucepan over medium heat, whisk the eggs, sugar, lemon juice and lemon peel until blended. Add butter; cook, whisking constantly, until mixture is thickened and coats the back of a metal spoon.

5 Transfer to a small bowl; cover and refrigerate for 1 hour. Transfer berry topping to another bowl; refrigerate until serving.

6 Spoon filling into tart shells. Chill, uncovered, until set. For garnish, in a small saucepan, bring lemon slices, sugar and water to a boil. Reduce heat; simmer, uncovered, for 20-25 minutes or until lemon is tender. Cut slices in half; chill.

7 Just before serving, spoon cranberry topping over tarts. Garnish with lemon slices.

Yield: 8 servings.

MINT DIP WITH BROWNIES

carol klein, franklin square, new york

My sister shared this simple recipe with me many years ago. The cool, refreshing dip also tastes terrific with fresh strawberries.

- 1 package fudge brownie mix (8-inch square pan size)
- 3/4 cup sour cream
- 2 tablespoons brown sugar
- 2 tablespoons green creme de menthe

1 Prepare and bake brownies according to package directions. Cool on a wire rack. Meanwhile, in a small bowl, combine the sour cream, brown sugar and creme de menthe; cover and refrigerate until serving.

2 Cut the brownies into 1-in. diamonds. Serve with mint dip.

Yield: 1 dozen (3/4 cup dip).

PEPPERMINT FREEZER PIE

kelli bucy, massena, iowa

Pretty peppermint ice cream plus fudgy chocolate plus fluffy meringue equals this perfect pie! The lovely dessert has become a holiday tradition. You can make and freeze it well in advance.

 2 squares (1 ounce *each*) unsweetened chocolate
 3 tablespoons butter
2/3 cup evaporated milk
1/2 cup sugar
 1 teaspoon vanilla extract
 1 quart peppermint ice cream, softened
 1 pastry shell (9 inches), baked

MERINGUE:
 3 egg whites
 6 tablespoons sugar
 1 tablespoon water
1/4 teaspoon cream of tartar
1/2 teaspoon vanilla extract
 3 tablespoons crushed peppermint-stick candy

1 In a heavy saucepan, melt chocolate and butter over low heat. Stir in milk and sugar. Cook and stir for 8 minutes or until sugar is dissolved. Remove from the heat; stir in vanilla. Cool completely.

2 Spread half of the ice cream into pastry shell; freeze until firm. Spread half of the chocolate mixture over ice cream; freeze until set. Repeat layers. Freeze for several hours or overnight.

3 In a heavy saucepan, combine the egg whites, sugar, water and cream of tartar. With a hand mixer, beat on low speed for 1 minute. Continue beating over low heat until mixture reaches 160°, about 12 minutes.

4 Pour into bowl of a heavy-duty stand mixer; add vanilla. Beat on high until frosting forms stiff peaks, about 7 minutes. Fold in the peppermint candy. Spread over top of pie. Cover and freeze until serving. Pie may be frozen for up to 2 months.

Yield: 6-8 servings.

STRAWBERRY ANGEL DESSERT

theresa mathis, tucker, georgia

This is a wonderful meal finale for any occasion and is a great way to serve dessert to a crowd. Every time I make this attractive treat, someone asks for the recipe.

1-1/2 cups sugar
 5 tablespoons cornstarch
 1 package (3 ounces) strawberry gelatin
 2 cups water
 2 pounds fresh strawberries, hulled, *divided*
 1 package (8 ounces) cream cheese, softened
 1 can (14 ounces) sweetened condensed milk
 1 carton (12 ounces) frozen whipped topping, thawed
 1 prepared angel food cake (16 ounces), cut into 1-inch cubes

1 For glaze, in a large saucepan, combine sugar, cornstarch and gelatin. Add water and stir until smooth. Cook and stir over medium-high heat until mixture begins to boil. Cook and stir 1-2 minutes longer or until thickened. Remove from the heat; cool completely. Cut half of the strawberries into quarters; fold into glaze.

2 In a small bowl, beat cream cheese until smooth. Beat in milk until blended. Fold in whipped topping.

3 In a 4-qt. clear glass bowl, layer half of the cake cubes, glaze and cream mixture. Repeat layers. Cut remaining strawberries in half and arrange over the top. Cover and refrigerate for at least 2 hours or overnight.

Yield: 12-16 servings.

WHITE CHOCOLATE BREAD PUDDING

kathy rundle, fond du lac, wisconsin

A delectable white chocolate sauce is the crowning touch on servings of this comforting cinnamon bread pudding.

- 16 slices cinnamon bread, crusts removed, cubed
- 1 cup dried cranberries
- 3/4 cup vanilla *or* white chips
- 3/4 cup chopped pecans
- 1/4 cup butter, melted
- 6 eggs
- 4 cups milk
- 3/4 cup plus 1 tablespoon sugar, *divided*
- 1 teaspoon vanilla extract
- 1/4 teaspoon *each* ground cinnamon and ground allspice

SAUCE:
- 2/3 cup heavy whipping cream
- 2 tablespoons butter
- 8 squares (1 ounce *each*) white baking chocolate, chopped

1 In a greased 13-in. x 9-in. baking dish, layer half of the bread cubes, cranberries, vanilla chips and pecans. Repeat layers. Drizzle with butter.

2 In a large bowl, beat the eggs, milk, 3/4 cup sugar, vanilla, cinnamon and allspice until blended; pour over bread mixture. Let stand for 15-30 minutes.

3 Sprinkle with remaining sugar. Bake, uncovered, at 375° for 55-65 minutes or until a knife inserted near the center comes out clean. Cover loosely with foil during the last 15 minutes if top browns too quickly.

4 In a small saucepan, bring cream and butter to a boil. Add chocolate and remove from the heat (do not stir). Let stand for 5 minutes; whisk until smooth. Serve with warm bread pudding.

Yield: 12 servings (1-1/2 cups sauce).

MAPLE PUMPKIN PIE

lisa varner, greenville, south carolina

Tired of traditional pumpkin pie? The maple syrup in this special pie provides a subtle but terrific enhancer.

- 2 eggs
- 1 can (15 ounces) solid-pack pumpkin
- 1 cup evaporated milk
- 3/4 cup sugar
- 1/2 cup maple syrup
- 1 teaspoon pumpkin pie spice
- 1/4 teaspoon salt

Pastry for single-crust pie (9 inches)

MAPLE WHIPPED CREAM:
- 1 cup heavy whipping cream
- 2 tablespoons confectioners' sugar
- 1 tablespoon maple syrup
- 1/4 teaspoon pumpkin pie spice

Chopped pecans, optional

1 In a large bowl, combine the first seven ingredients; beat until smooth. Pour into crust.

2 Bake at 425° for 15 minutes. Reduce heat to 350°. Bake 45-50 minutes longer or until crust is golden brown and top of pie is set (cover edges with foil during the last 15 minutes to prevent over-browning if necessary). Cool on a wire rack for 1 hour. Refrigerate overnight or until set.

3 In a small bowl, beat the cream, confectioners' sugar, syrup and pumpkin pie spice until stiff peaks form. Pipe or dollop onto pie. Sprinkle with pecans if desired. Refrigerate leftovers.

Yield: 8 servings.

APPLE DUMPLINGS

robin lendon, cincinnati, ohio

These warm, comforting dumplings are great alone or served with a scoop of vanilla ice cream. They are covered in a luscious caramel sauce.

   3 cups all-purpose flour
   1 teaspoon salt
   1 cup shortening
 1/3 cup cold water
   8 medium tart apples, peeled and cored
   8 teaspoons butter
   9 teaspoons cinnamon-sugar, *divided*

SAUCE:

1-1/2 cups packed brown sugar
   1 cup water
 1/2 cup butter, cubed

1   In a large bowl, combine flour and salt; cut in shortening until crumbly. Gradually add water, tossing with a fork until dough forms a ball. Divide into eight portions. Cover and refrigerate for at least 30 minutes or until easy to handle.

2   Roll each portion of dough between two lightly floured sheets of waxed paper into a 7-in. square. Place an apple on each square. Place 1 teaspoon butter and 1 teaspoon cinnamon-sugar in the center of each apple.

3   Gently bring up corners of pastry to each center; pinch edges to seal. If desired, cut out apple leaves and stems from dough scraps; attach to dumplings with water. Place in a greased 13-in. x 9-in. baking dish. Sprinkle with remaining cinnamon-sugar.

4   In a large saucepan, combine sauce ingredients. Bring just to a boil, stirring until blended. Pour over apples.

5   Bake at 350° for 50-55 minutes or until apples are tender and pastry is golden brown, basting occasionally with sauce. Serve warm.

Yield: 8 servings.

CHOCOLATE CHIP RASPBERRY BARS

bev cudrak, coaldale, alberta

These buttery bars combine the magical duo of chocolate and raspberry. My husband found this recipe in a farm paper, so I made it. The results were out of this world.

1-3/4 cups all-purpose flour
   1 cup sugar
   1 cup cold butter
   1 egg
 1/2 teaspoon almond extract
   1 cup seedless raspberry jam
 1/2 cup miniature semisweet chocolate chips

1   In a large bowl, combine flour and sugar. Cut in butter until mixture resembles coarse crumbs. Stir in egg and extract just until moistened. Set aside 1 cup crumb mixture for topping.

2   Press the remaining mixture into a greased 11-in. x 7-in. baking pan. Bake at 350° for 5 minutes. Spread with jam and sprinkle with reserved crumb mixture. Bake 35-40 minutes longer or until golden brown.

3   Sprinkle with chocolate chips. Return to the oven for 30 seconds or until chips are glossy. Cool completely on a wire rack. Cut into bars.

Yield: about 3 dozen.

CARAMEL CHOCOLATE CAKE

gloria guadron, fishers, indiana

I love to make this impressive cake for guests or to take to potlucks. Spread with an easy butterscotch frosting and draped with a caramel-nut topping, it looks like it took all day, yet it's quite simple to make.

  1 package (18-1/4 ounces) German chocolate cake mix
3/4 cup packed brown sugar
  6 tablespoons butter, cubed
  2 tablespoons heavy whipping cream
1/2 cup finely chopped pecans
  1 package (3.4 ounces) instant butterscotch pudding mix
  1 cup cold milk
2-1/2 cups whipped topping

1   Prepare and bake cake according to package directions for two 9-in. round baking pans. Cool for 10 minutes before removing from pans to wire racks to cool completely.

2   Meanwhile, in a small saucepan, combine the brown sugar, butter and cream. Cook and stir over low heat until sugar is dissolved. Increase heat to medium. Do not stir. Cook for 3-6 minutes or until bubbles form in center of mixture and color is amber brown. Remove from the heat; stir in pecans. Cool at room temperature for 30 minutes, stirring occasionally.

3   In a small bowl, whisk pudding mix and milk for 2 minutes. Let stand for 2 minutes or until soft-set. Fold in whipped topping. Cover and refrigerate until thickened, about 20 minutes.

4   Place one cake layer on a serving platter; spread with 3/4 cup pudding mixture. Top with remaining cake layer; spread remaining pudding mixture over top and sides of cake.

5   If necessary, reheat pecan mixture in a microwave for up to 30 seconds to achieve a spreading consistency. Spoon pecan mixture around edge of cake. Store in the refrigerator.

Yield: 10-12 servings.

YULETIDE POUND CAKE

lorraine caland, thunder bay, ontario

I always serve this beautiful cake when we decorate our Christmas tree. It's not too sweet for the little ones, who can snack on it without getting too full for the appetizer part of the evening.

  1 cup butter, softened
1/2 cup shortening
  3 cups sugar
  5 eggs
  1 teaspoon *each* vanilla and rum extract
  3 cups all-purpose flour
  1 teaspoon baking powder
  1 cup (8 ounces) sour cream
GLAZE:
  1 cup confectioners' sugar
  2 to 3 teaspoons milk

1   In a large bowl, cream the butter, shortening and sugar until light and fluffy. Add eggs, one at a time, beating well after each addition. Beat in extracts. Combine flour and baking powder; gradually add to creamed mixture alternately with sour cream just until combined.

2   Pour into a greased and floured 10-in. fluted tube pan. Bake at 350° for 60-70 minutes or until a toothpick inserted near the center comes out clean.

3   Cool for 10 minutes before removing from pan to a wire rack to cool completely. Combine glaze ingredients; drizzle over cake.

Yield: 12-16 servings.

CREAMY RASPBERRY DESSERT

julianne johnson, grove city, minnesota

Do-ahead and delicious, this dessert is a favorite because of its pretty color, creamy texture and terrific flavor. A light, no-bake filling makes it quick. Try garnishing with fresh berries and sprigs of mint.

- 1 cup graham cracker crumbs
- 3 tablespoons sugar
- 1/4 cup butter, melted

FILLING

- 1 package (10 ounces) frozen raspberries, thawed
- 1/4 cup cold water
- 1 envelope unflavored gelatin
- 1 package (8 ounces) cream cheese, softened
- 1/2 cup sugar
- 1 cup heavy whipping cream, whipped

Fresh raspberries and whipped cream for garnish

1 In a bowl, combine crumbs, 3 tablespoons sugar and butter. Press onto bottom of an 8-in. or 9-in. springform pan. Bake at 350° for 10 minutes. Cool.

2 Meanwhile, for filling, drain the raspberries and reserve juice. Set berries aside. In a small saucepan, combine the juice, cold water and gelatin. Let stand for 5 minutes.

3 Cook and stir over low heat until gelatin dissolves. Remove from the heat; cool for 10 minutes.

4 In a small bowl, beat cream cheese and sugar until blended. Add berries and gelatin mixture; beat on low until thoroughly blended. Chill until partially set. Watch carefully, as mixture will set

up quickly. Gently fold in whipped cream. Spoon into the crust. Chill for 6 hours or overnight.

5 Just before serving, run knife around edge of pan to loosen. Remove sides of pan. Top with fresh raspberries and whipped cream.

Yield: 10 servings.

CANDY APPLE WALNUT PIE

serita bratcher, morrison, tennessee

The South is known for apple pies, but this one is not your typical apple pie! The filling includes red-hot candies, and instead of a regular double crust, you crumble a frozen pastry shell and sprinkle it over the top. You can peel the apples if you wish or leave them unpeeled.

- 6 cups sliced tart apples
- 2/3 cup chopped walnuts
- 1/2 cup red-hot candies
- 1/3 cup plus 2 tablespoons sugar, *divided*
- 1/3 cup all-purpose flour
- 2 frozen deep-dish pastry shells (9 inches)

1 In a large bowl, combine the apples, walnuts, Red-Hots, 1/3 cup sugar and flour; toss to coat. Spoon into one pastry shell. Crumble the remaining pastry shell into 1/2-in. pieces; toss with remaining sugar. Sprinkle over filling.

2 Place on a baking sheet. Bake at 375° for 50-60 minutes or until filling is bubbly and crust is golden brown. Cool completely on a wire rack before cutting.

Yield: 6-8 servings.

PEPPERMINT CAKE LOG

robyn anderson, sugar grove, illinois

Each Christmas, my husband asks for only one thing
...this chocolate mint cake roll! This fluffy filling pairs
well with the tender cake.

- 1/2 cup all-purpose flour
- 1/3 cup baking cocoa
- 1/4 teaspoon baking powder
- 1/4 teaspoon baking soda
- 4 eggs, *separated*
- 1/3 cup plus 1/2 cup sugar, *divided*
- 1 teaspoon vanilla extract
- 1/3 cup water
- 1 tablespoon confectioners' sugar

FILLING:
- 1 cup heavy whipping cream
- 1/4 cup confectioners' sugar
- 1/3 cup crushed peppermint candies

GLAZE:
- 2 tablespoons butter
- 2 tablespoons baking cocoa
- 2 tablespoons water
- 1 cup confectioners' sugar
- 1/2 teaspoon vanilla extract

1 Line a greased 15-in. x 10-in. x 1-in. baking pan
   with waxed paper; grease the paper and set aside.
   Combine the flour, cocoa, baking powder and
   baking soda; set aside.

2 In large bowl, beat egg yolks, 1/3 cup sugar and
   vanilla until thick and lemon-colored. Add dry
   ingredients alternately with water just until blended. In a small bowl, beat egg whites on medium
   speed until soft peaks form. Gradually beat in
   remaining sugar, 1 tablespoon at a time, until
   stiff glossy peaks form. Fold into yolk mixture.

3 Spread batter evenly in prepared pan. Bake at
   375° for 12-15 minutes or until cake springs back
   when lightly touched. Cool for 5 minutes. Invert
   cake onto a kitchen towel dusted with 1 table-

spoon confectioners' sugar. Gently peel off waxed
paper. Roll up cake in the towel jelly-roll style,
starting with a short side. Cool completely on a
wire rack.

4 For filling, in a small bowl, beat cream until soft
   peaks form. Gradually beat in confectioners'
   sugar until stiff peaks form. Fold in crushed
   candies. Unroll cake; spread filling to within 1/2
   in. of edges. Roll up again. Cover and refrigerate
   for at least 1 hour.

5 For glaze, combine the butter, cocoa and water
   in a small saucepan. Cook and stir over low heat
   until smooth. Remove from the heat. Whisk in
   confectioners' sugar and vanilla until smooth.
   Drizzle over cake. Refrigerate leftovers.

Yield: 10 servings.

BANANA ICE CREAM PUFFS

pam olson, holland, michigan

These tender golden puffs are filled with rich banana
ice cream and drizzled with hot fudge—making
them pretty and tasty enough to draw a sleighful of
compliments!

- 1 cup sugar
- 1 package (3.4 ounces) cook-and-serve banana
  cream pudding mix
- 3 tablespoons all-purpose flour
- 1/2 teaspoon salt
- 5 cups milk
- 4 eggs, lightly beaten
- 4 cups heavy whipping cream
- 1-3/4 cups mashed ripe banana (about 4 medium)
- 2 tablespoons vanilla extract

CREAM PUFFS:
- 2 cups water
- 1 cup butter
- 2 teaspoons sugar

1/4 teaspoon salt

2 cups all-purpose flour

8 eggs

Hot fudge *or* chocolate ice cream topping

Chopped nuts

1   In a saucepan, combine the sugar, pudding mix, flour and salt; gradually stir in milk until smooth. Cook and stir over medium heat until thickened and bubbly. Reduce heat; cook and stir 2 minutes longer. Remove from the heat.

2   Stir a small amount of hot filling into eggs. Return all to the pan, stirring constantly. Bring to a gentle boil; cook and stir for 2 minutes. Press plastic wrap onto the surface of pudding mixture. Refrigerate until chilled, about 4 hours.

3   Stir in the cream, bananas and vanilla. Fill cylinder of ice cream freezer two-thirds full; freeze according to manufacturer's directions. Refrigerate remaining mixture until ready to freeze. Allow ice cream to ripen in the refrigerator freezer for 2-4 hours.

4   In a large saucepan, bring the water, butter, sugar and salt to a boil. Add flour all at once and stir until a smooth ball forms. Remove from the heat; let stand for 5 minutes. Add eggs, two at a time, beating well after each addition. Continue beating until mixture is smooth and shiny.

5   Drop by 2 rounded tablespoonfuls 3 in. apart onto greased baking sheets. Bake at 400° for 20-25 minutes or until golden brown. Remove to wire racks. Immediately split puffs open; remove tops and set aside. Discard soft dough from inside. Cool puffs.

6   To serve, spoon banana ice cream into cream puffs; replace tops. Drizzle with hot fudge topping and sprinkle with nuts.

Yield: About 2 dozen puffs and 3 quarts ice cream.

CHOCOLATE CREPES

taste of home test kitchen

If you think crepes are merely breakfast fare, we insist you try these cream-filled crepes for dessert!

1-1/2 cups milk

3 eggs

3 tablespoons water

2 tablespoons canola oil

1-1/2 teaspoons vanilla extract

1-1/2 cups all-purpose flour

1/4 cup sugar

1/4 cup baking cocoa

1/8 teaspoon salt

FILLING:

1 package (8 ounces) cream cheese, softened

1/4 cup sugar

1/2 cup sour cream

1/2 teaspoon vanilla extract

1/3 cup creme de cacao

1 carton (8 ounces) frozen whipped topping, thawed

FUDGE SAUCE:

3/4 cup semisweet chocolate chips

1/4 cup butter

1/2 cup sugar

2/3 cup half-and-half cream

10 mint Andes candies, chopped, optional

1   For batter, place the first nine ingredients in a blender or food processor. Cover and process until smooth. Refrigerate for 1 hour.

2   Meanwhile, in a large mixing bowl, beat cream cheese and sugar until light and fluffy. Beat in sour cream and vanilla. Fold in creme de cacao and whipped topping. Cover and refrigerate for at least 1 hour.

3   For the fudge sauce, in a large saucepan, melt chocolate chips and butter over low heat. Stir in sugar and cream. Bring to a boil. Reduce heat; simmer, uncovered, for 10 minutes. Set aside and keep warm.

4   Heat a lightly greased 8-in. nonstick skillet; pour 2 tablespoons batter into center of skillet. Lift and tilt pan to evenly coat bottom. Cook until top appears dry; turn and cook 15-20 seconds longer. Remove to a wire rack. Repeat with remaining batter, greasing skillet as needed. When cool, stack crepes with waxed paper or paper towels in between.

5   Spoon 1/4 cup filling down the center of each crepe; roll up. Top with fudge sauce. Sprinkle with mint candies if desired.

Yield: 10 servings.

FROZEN PEPPERMINT DELIGHT

pam lancaster, willis, virginia

If you're looking for a dessert that's festive, delicious and easy to make, this is the one for you. Drizzled in hot fudge sauce and loaded with pretty peppermint pieces, this tempting treat will have guests asking for seconds.

- 1 package (14 ounces) cream-filled chocolate sandwich cookies, crushed
- 1/2 cup butter, melted
- 1 gallon peppermint ice cream, slightly softened
- 1 carton (12 ounces) frozen whipped topping, thawed
- 1 jar (11-3/4 ounces) hot fudge ice cream topping, warmed

Crushed peppermint candy

1 In a bowl, combine cookie crumbs and butter. Press into an ungreased 13-in. x 9-in. x 2-in. dish. Spread ice cream over crust; top with whipped topping. Cover and freeze until solid. May be frozen for up to 2 months.

2 Just before serving, drizzle with hot fudge topping and sprinkle with peppermint candy.

Yield: 12-15 servings.

STEAMED CHOCOLATE PUDDING

mary kelley, minneapolis, minnesota

Warm and comforting, this special pudding is timeless. You'll love its chocolaty goodness and tender texture.

- 2 tablespoons butter, softened
- 1 cup sugar
- 1 egg
- 2 squares (1 ounce *each*) unsweetened chocolate, melted and cooled
- 1-3/4 cups all-purpose flour

- 1 teaspoon salt
- 1/4 teaspoon cream of tartar
- 1/4 teaspoon baking soda
- 1 cup milk

VANILLA SAUCE:

- 1/2 cup sugar
- 1 tablespoon cornstarch

Dash salt

- 1 cup cold water
- 2 tablespoons butter
- 1 teaspoon vanilla extract

Dash ground nutmeg

1 In a large bowl, beat the butter and sugar until crumbly. Beat in egg. Stir in chocolate. Combine the flour, salt, cream of tartar and baking soda; gradually add to creamed mixture alternately with milk, beating well just until combined.

2 Pour into a well-greased 7-cup pudding mold; cover. Place mold on a rack in a deep kettle; add 1 in. of hot water to pan. Bring to a gentle boil; cover and steam for 2 to 2-1/4 hours or until top springs back when lightly touched, adding water as needed.

3 Remove mold to a wire rack; cool for 15 minutes. Meanwhile, in a small saucepan, combine the sugar, cornstarch and salt. Stir in water until smooth. Bring to a boil; cook and stir for 2 minutes or until thickened. Remove from the heat; stir in the butter, vanilla and nutmeg.

4 Unmold pudding onto a serving plate; cut into wedges. Serve warm with sauce.

Yield: 6-8 servings (1-1/2 cups sauce).

GINGER PLUM TART

taste of home test kitchen

Looking for a quick dessert that's pretty as a picture? Try this mouth-watering tart. For an extra-special effect, crown it with a scoop of ice cream, yogurt or a dollop of whipped topping.

Pastry for single-crust pie (9 inches)
- 3-1/2 cups sliced unpeeled fresh plums
- 3 tablespoons plus 1 teaspoon coarse sugar, *divided*
- 1 tablespoon cornstarch
- 2 teaspoons finely chopped crystallized ginger
- 1 egg white
- 1 tablespoon water

1 Roll pastry into a 12-in. circle. Transfer to a large baking sheet lined with parchment paper. In a large bowl, combine plums, 3 tablespoons sugar and cornstarch. Arrange plums in a pinwheel pattern over pastry to within 2 in. of edges; sprinkle with ginger. Fold edges of pastry over plums.

2 Beat egg white and water; brush over pastry. Sprinkle with remaining sugar. Bake at 400° for 20-25 minutes or until crust is lightly browned. Cool for 15 minutes before removing from pan to a serving platter.

Yield: 8 servings.

WHITE CHOCOLATE TORTE

norma van devander, calais, maine

Looking for a change from heavy, chocolate desserts? Try this white chocolate cake! It's wonderfully moist and slices into beautiful wedges.

- 1 cup butter, softened
- 2 cups sugar
- 4 squares (1 ounce *each*) white baking chocolate, melted and cooled
- 4 eggs
- 1-1/2 teaspoons clear vanilla extract
- 3 cups all-purpose flour

- 1 teaspoon baking soda
- 1 cup buttermilk
- 1/2 cup water
- 1/2 cup chopped pecans, toasted

FROSTING:
- 2 packages (one 8 ounces, one 3 ounces) cream cheese, softened
- 1/3 cup butter, softened
- 4 squares (1 ounce *each*) white baking chocolate, melted and cooled
- 1-1/2 teaspoons clear vanilla extract
- 6-1/2 cups confectioners' sugar

White chocolate curls

1 Line three greased 9-in. round baking pans with waxed paper and grease the paper; set aside. In a large bowl, cream butter and sugar until light and fluffy. Beat in chocolate. Add eggs, one at a time, beating well after each. Beat in vanilla. Combine flour and baking soda; gradually add to creamed mixture alternately with buttermilk and water, beating well after each addition. Fold in pecans. Pour batter into prepared pans.

2 Bake at 350° for 23-27 minutes or until a toothpick inserted near the center comes out clean. Cool for 10 minutes before removing from pans to wire racks; discard waxed paper.

3 For frosting, in a large bowl, beat cream cheese and butter until fluffy. Beat in chocolate and vanilla. Gradually add confectioners' sugar until smooth. Spread frosting between layers and over top and sides of cake. Garnish with chocolate curls. Store in the refrigerator.

Yield: 14-16 servings.

MOCHA MERINGUE CUPS

helen davis, waterbury, vermont

No one can resist a rich mocha filling sitting on top of a crisp, chewy meringue cup. My family expects me to make these treats for many special occasions throughout the year.

> 3 egg whites
> 1/4 teaspoon cream of tartar
>
> Dash salt
>
> 1 cup sugar
>
> CHOCOLATE FILLING:
> 2 cups milk chocolate chips
> 1 cup heavy whipping cream
> 1 teaspoon instant coffee granules
> 1 teaspoon vanilla extract

1 Place egg whites in a small bowl; let stand at room temperature for 30 minutes. Add the cream of tartar and salt; beat on medium speed until soft peaks form.

2 Gradually beat in sugar, 1 tablespoon at a time, on high until stiff glossy peaks form and sugar is dissolved.

3 Spoon meringue into eight mounds on parchment-lined baking sheets. Shape into 3-in. cups with the back of a spoon. Bake at 275° for 45-50 minutes. Turn oven off; leave meringues in oven for 1 hour.

4 Remove from the oven and cool on baking sheets. When completely cooled, remove meringues from the paper and store in an airtight container at room temperature. For filling, in a microwave, melt the chocolate chips, cream and coffee granules; stir until smooth. Stir in vanilla. Transfer to a small bowl; refrigerate until chilled.

5 Beat until stiff peaks form. Immediately spoon into a pastry bag or plastic bag with a #20 star tip. Pipe filling into meringue cups. Refrigerate until serving.

Yield: 8 servings.

POMEGRANATE POACHED PEARS

bev jones, brunswick, missouri

Pears can benefit from an overnight soak in poaching liquid in the fridge. They'll pick up more flavor and the pomegranate's ruby color. Guests will enjoy identifying the subtle tastes in the reduction sauce from wine, rosemary and fruit juices.

> 3 cups dry red wine *or* red grape juice
> 1 bottle (16 ounces) pomegranate juice
> 1 cup water
> 1/2 cup sugar
> 1/4 cup orange juice
> 2 tablespoons grated orange peel
> 3 fresh rosemary sprigs (4 inches)
> 1 cinnamon stick (3 inches)
> 6 medium pears
> 6 orange slices
> 6 tablespoons Mascarpone cheese

1 In a Dutch oven, combine the first eight ingredients. Core pears from the bottom, leaving stems intact. Peel pears; place on their sides in the pan. Bring to a boil. Reduce heat; cover and simmer for 25-30 minutes or until pears are almost tender. Remove with a slotted spoon; cool

2 Strain poaching liquid and return to Dutch oven. Bring to a boil; cook until reduced to 1 cup, about 45 minutes. Discard rosemary and cinnamon. Place an orange slice on each serving plate; top with 1 tablespoon cheese and a pear. Drizzle with poaching liquid.

Yield: 6 servings.

- 1 cup finely chopped walnuts, toasted
- 1/2 cup flaked coconut
- 1/2 teaspoon cream of tartar

FILLING FROSTING:
- 1 cup raspberry preserves, warmed
- 2 packages (one 8 ounces, one 3 ounces) cream cheese, softened
- 3/4 cup butter, softened
- 6-1/2 cups confectioners' sugar
- 2 teaspoons vanilla extract
- 1/2 cup chopped walnuts

1 Let the eggs stand at room temperature for 30 minutes. In a large bowl, cream the shortening, butter and sugar until light and fluffy. Add egg yolks, one at a time, beating well after each addition. Beat in vanilla. Combine the flour and baking soda; add to creamed mixture alternately with buttermilk, beating well after each addition. Stir in walnuts and coconut.

2 In another large bowl and with clean beaters, beat egg whites and cream of tartar on high speed until stiff peaks form. Fold a fourth of egg whites into the batter, then fold in remaining whites.

3 Pour into three greased and floured 9-in. round baking pans. Bake at 350° for 24-28 minutes or top springs back lightly when touched. Cool for 10 minutes before removing from pans to wire racks to cool completely.

4 Spread raspberry preserves over the top of two cake layers. Refrigerate for 30 minutes. Meanwhile, in a large bowl, beat the cream cheese, butter and confectioners' sugar until fluffy. Beat in vanilla.

5 Place one raspberry topped cake layer on a serving plate. Spread with some of the frosting. Repeat with second raspberry topped cake layer. Top with plain cake layer. Spread remaining frosting over the top and sides of cake. Sprinkle with nuts. Store in the refrigerator.

Yield: 16 servings.

BLACK FOREST TART

taste of home test kitchen
Cherry pie filling and a melted chocolate drizzle tastefully top a rich, fudgy dessert from our home economists.

- 1-1/4 cups chocolate wafer crumbs
- 1/4 cup sugar
- 1/4 cup butter, melted

FILLING:
- 1/2 cup butter

- 6 squares (1 ounce *each*) semisweet chocolate, chopped
- 3 eggs
- 2/3 cup sugar
- 1 teaspoon vanilla extract
- 1/4 teaspoon salt
- 2/3 cup all-purpose flour

TOPPING:
- 1 can (21 ounces) cherry pie filling
- 2 squares (1 ounce *each*) semisweet chocolate, chopped
- 1 tablespoon heavy whipping cream

1 In a small bowl, combine wafer crumbs and sugar; stir in butter. Press onto the bottom and up the sides of a lightly greased 11-in. fluted tart pan with removable bottom. Place pan on a baking sheet. Bake at 350° for 8-10 minutes or until lightly browned. Cool on a wire rack.

2 In a microwave-safe bowl, melt butter and chocolate; stir until smooth. Cool for 10 minutes. In a large bowl, beat the eggs, sugar, vanilla and salt until thickened, about 4 minutes. Blend in chocolate mixture. Add flour; mix well.

3 Pour into crust; spread evenly. Bake at 350° for 25-30 minutes or until a toothpick inserted near the center comes out clean. Cool completely on a wire rack.

4 Spread pie filling over the top. In a small microwave-safe bowl, combine chocolate and cream. Microwave on high for 20-30 seconds or until chocolate is melted; stir until smooth. Cool for 5 minutes, stirring occasionally. Drizzle over tart. Chill until set.

Yield: 12 servings.

Editor's Note: This tart is best served the day it is prepared. This recipe was tested in a 1,100-watt microwave.

CHERRY BERRY CHEESECAKE

susan knittle-hunter, evanston, wyoming
I found this merry prize-winning recipe in a magazine years ago. It's been a Yuletide tradition at our house ever since.

- 2-1/4 cups sliced almonds, toasted
- 1/4 cup confectioners' sugar
- 1 teaspoon grated orange peel
- 3/4 teaspoon ground cinnamon
- 1/4 teaspoon ground nutmeg
- 1/4 cup butter, melted

FRUIT FILLING:
- 1 can (21 ounces) cherry pie filling
- 1 cup whole-berry cranberry sauce
- 3 tablespoons sugar
- 1 teaspoon lemon juice
- 1 envelope unflavored gelatin

CREAM CHEESE FILLING:
- 2 packages (3 ounces *each*) cream cheese, softened
- 3 tablespoons confectioners' sugar
- 2 tablespoons plain yogurt

Additional sliced almonds

1 Place the almonds in a food processor; cover and process until finely ground. Transfer to a bowl; add the confectioners' sugar, orange peel, cinnamon and nutmeg. Stir in butter. Press onto the bottom and 1 in. up the sides of a greased 9-in. springform pan. Bake at 350° for 9-11 minutes or until lightly browned; cool.

2 In a large saucepan, combine the pie filling, cranberry sauce, sugar and lemon juice. Sprinkle gelatin over cranberry mixture. Stir until combined; let stand for 1 minute. Cook over low heat until gelatin is completely dissolved, stirring gently. Remove from the heat. Chill until slightly thickened.

3 Meanwhile, in a large bowl, beat the cream cheese, confectioners' sugar and yogurt until smooth. Spread evenly over cooled crust. Spoon fruit filling over the cream cheese layer. Refrigerate for at least 6 hours or overnight. Sprinkle with sliced almonds. Refrigerate overnight.

4 Remove sides of pan. Refrigerate leftovers.

Yield: 12 servings.

DATE PUDDING

opal hamer, st. petersburg, florida
This pudding has been our family's favorite holiday dessert for years. At Christmas, I top each with green-tinted whipped cream and a red maraschino cherry.

- 3/4 cup chopped dates
- 1/2 cup chopped walnuts
- 6 tablespoons sugar
- 1 egg
- 2 tablespoons milk
- 1/2 teaspoon vanilla extract
- 2 tablespoons all-purpose flour
- 1/2 teaspoon baking powder

Dash salt
- 1 tablespoon butter

Whipped cream

1 In a bowl, combine the dates, walnuts and sugar. In another bowl, beat egg, milk and vanilla. Add to date mixture; mix well. Combine flour, baking powder and salt; add to the date mixture.

2 Spread into a greased 1-qt. baking dish; dot with butter. Bake at 325° for 30 minutes or until a knife inserted near the center comes out clean. Serve with whipped cream.

Yield: 2 servings.

CRANBERRY MOUSSE

pauline tucker, baldwinville, massachusetts

We live about 100 miles from Cape Cod, which is known for its cranberries. I found this recipe at the Cranberry World Visitors Center. When I made it for our fellowship group at church, everyone wanted the recipe. You'll be surprised it's so easy to make with just four ingredients.

- 1 can (16 ounces) jellied cranberry sauce
- 1 cup cranberry juice
- 1 package (3 ounces) cranberry *or* raspberry gelatin
- 1 cup heavy whipping cream, whipped

1 In a large saucepan, bring the cranberry sauce and juice to a boil; cook and stir until smooth. Stir in the gelatin until dissolved. Cool slightly; transfer to a bowl. Refrigerate for 1 hour or until mixture begins to thicken.

2 Fold in the whipped cream. Spoon into dessert dishes. Chill for 3-4 hours or until firm.

Yield: 6 servings.

RICOTTA NUT TORTE

karen albert, prineville, oregon

This pretty layered Italian cake is called cassata. It takes some time to prepare this eye-catching dessert but it conveniently chills overnight.

- 2 cartons (15 ounces *each*) ricotta cheese
- 1-1/2 cups sugar
- 1 teaspoon vanilla extract
- 1 cup chopped pecans
- 1 milk chocolate candy bar (7 ounces), grated

BATTER:
- 2/3 cup shortening
- 1-2/3 cups sugar
- 3 eggs
- 1-1/2 teaspoons vanilla extract
- 2-1/2 cups all-purpose flour
- 2-1/2 teaspoons baking powder
- 1 teaspoon salt
- 1-1/4 cups milk

FROSTING:
- 2 cups heavy whipping cream
- 1/4 cup confectioners' sugar
- 1/2 teaspoon vanilla extract

Whole hazelnuts and chocolate curls, optional

1 For filling, in a small bowl, beat ricotta cheese and sugar until smooth; beat in vanilla. Fold in pecans and chocolate. Cover and refrigerate.

2 In a large bowl, cream the shortening and sugar until light and fluffy. Add eggs, one at a time, beating well after each addition. Beat in the vanilla. Combine the flour, baking powder and salt; add to the creamed mixture alternately with milk, beating well after each addition.

3 Pour into three waxed paper-lined 9-in. round baking pans. Bake at 350° for 25-30 minutes or until a toothpick inserted near the center comes out clean. Cool for 10 minutes before removing from pans to wire racks to cool completely.

4 Cut each cake in half. Place one bottom layer on a serving plate; spread with 1 cup filling. Repeat layers four times. Top with the remaining cake. Cover and refrigerate overnight.

5 In a bowl, beat the cream until thickened. Add confectioners' sugar and vanilla; beat until stiff peaks form. Spread over top and sides of cake. Garnish with hazelnuts and chocolate curls if desired. Refrigerate leftovers.

Yield: 12 servings.

CROWN JEWEL GELATIN PIE

elaine augustine, manchester, connecticut
This colorful pie—an old family favorite—couldn't be easier for busy holiday cooks to make. The stained-glass look of gelatin cubes adds a festive note.

- 1 package (3 ounces) raspberry gelatin
- 3 cups boiling water, *divided*
- 2 cups cold water, *divided*
- 1 package (3 ounces) lime gelatin
- 1 package (3 ounces) black cherry gelatin
- 1 cup pineapple juice
- 1/4 cup sugar
- 1 package (3 ounces) strawberry gelatin
- 1-1/2 cups heavy whipping cream
- 2 graham cracker crust (9 inches)

1 In a small bowl, dissolve raspberry gelatin in 1 cup boiling water; stir in 1/2 cup cold water. Pour into a 9-in. x 5-in. x 3-in. loaf pan coated with cooking spray. Repeat with lime and black cherry gelatin, using two more loaf pans. Refrigerate until firm, about 2 hours. Cut each into 1/2-in. cubes.

2 In a saucepan, combine the pineapple juice and sugar. Bring to a boil. Add strawberry gelatin and stir until dissolved. Add remaining cold water. Transfer to large bowl. Refrigerate until thickened but not firm, about 1-1/4 hours.

3 In a large chilled bowl, beat cream until soft peaks form. Fold whipped cream into strawberry gelatin mixture. Gently stir in the cubed gelatin. Spoon mixture into crust. Refrigerate until firm, about 2 hours.

Yield: 2 pies (6-8 servings each).

CHOCOLATE HAZELNUT GATEAU

michelle krzmarzick, redondo beach, california
Gateau is the French word for any rich and fancy cake. I think you'll agree this dense chocolate dessert has just the right amount of sweetness.

- 2/3 cup butter, softened
- 3/4 cup sugar
- 3 eggs, *separated*
- 1 cup (6 ounces) semisweet chocolate chips, melted and cooled
- 1 teaspoon vanilla extract
- 3/4 cup all-purpose flour
- 1/2 teaspoon salt
- 1/4 cup milk
- 2/3 cup ground hazelnuts, toasted

GLAZE:
- 3 tablespoons butter
- 2 tablespoons light corn syrup
- 1 tablespoon water
- 1 cup (6 ounces) semisweet chocolate chips

Toasted slivered almonds and fresh mint leaves

1 In a large bowl, cream butter and sugar until light and fluffy. Beat in egg yolks, melted chocolate and vanilla. Combine the flour and salt; gradually add to creamed mixture alternately with milk, beating well after each addition. Stir in the hazelnuts.

2 In a small bowl, beat egg whites until stiff peaks form; carefully fold into batter. Spread into a greased 9-in. springform pan. Place pan on a baking sheet.

3 Bake at 350° for 30-35 minutes or until a toothpick inserted near the center comes out clean. Cool on wire rack for 10 minutes. Carefully run a knife around edge of pan to loosen; remove sides of pan. Cool completely. In a small saucepan, bring the butter, corn syrup and water to a boil; stirring constantly. Remove from the heat. Add the chocolate chips; stir until smooth. Cool to room temperature. Spread over top and sides of gateau. Garnish with almonds and mint.

Yield: 12 servings.

TRADITIONAL CHEESECAKE

taste of home test kitchen
Here's a basic cheesecake that tastes great alone or with any number of garnishes.

- 1 cup graham cracker crumbs
- 1 tablespoon sugar
- 3 tablespoons cold butter

FILLING:
- 4 packages (8 ounces *each*) cream cheese, softened
- 1-1/4 cups sugar
- 1 tablespoon lemon juice
- 2 teaspoons vanilla extract
- 3 eggs, lightly beaten

Raspberry sauce and sour cream, optional

1 In a small bowl, combine cracker crumbs and sugar; cut in butter until crumbly. Grease the sides only of a 9-in. springform pan; press crumb mixture onto bottom of pan. Place on a baking sheet. Bake at 350° for 10 minutes. Cool on a wire rack.

2 In a large bowl, beat the cream cheese, sugar, lemon juice and vanilla until smooth. Add eggs; beat on low speed just until combined. Pour over crust. Return pan to baking sheet.

3 Bake at 350° for 45-55 minutes or until center is almost set. Cool on a wire rack for 10 minutes. Carefully run a knife around edge of pan to loosen; cool 1 hour longer.

4 Refrigerate overnight. Just before serving, remove sides of pan. Serve with raspberry sauce and sour cream if desired. Refrigerate leftovers.

Yield: 12 servings.

CHEESE-FILLED SHORTBREAD TARTLETS

cathy walerius, mound, minnesota
Bite-size treats are a nice addition to a dessert buffet. You can store cooled, baked tart shells in an airtight container at room temperature overnight or in the freezer for a few weeks.

- 1 package (8 ounces) cream cheese, softened
- 1 cup sweetened condensed milk
- 1/3 cup lemon juice
- 1 teaspoon vanilla extract
- 1 cup butter, softened
- 1-1/2 cups all-purpose flour
- 1/2 cup confectioners' sugar
- 1 tablespoon cornstarch

Fresh raspberries and mint leaves

1 In a small bowl, beat cream cheese until smooth. Gradually beat in milk, lemon juice and vanilla. Cover and refrigerate for 8 hours or overnight.

2 In another small bowl, beat the butter, flour, confectioners' sugar and cornstarch until smooth. Roll into 1-in. balls. Place in greased miniature muffin cups; press onto the bottom and up the sides. Prick with a fork.

3 Bake at 325° for 20-25 minutes or until golden brown. Immediately run a knife around each tart to loosen completely. Cool in pans on wire racks.

4 Pipe or spoon 1 tablespoon cheese filling into each tart shell. Cover and refrigerate until set. Just before serving, garnish with raspberries and mint.

Yield: 3 dozen.

FROSTY GINGER PUMPKIN SQUARES

kathryn reeger, shelocta, pennsylvania

My family loves getting together to sample good food. While pumpkin makes it perfect for the holidays, this ice cream dessert is requested year-round. Everyone enjoys it.

- 1/4 cup butter, melted
- 1 cup crushed graham cracker (about 16 squares)
- 1 cup crushed gingersnaps (about 18 cookies)
- 2 cups canned pumpkin
- 1 cup sugar
- 1/2 to 1 teaspoon ground cinnamon
- 1/2 teaspoon salt
- 1/2 teaspoon ground ginger
- 1/4 teaspoon ground nutmeg
- 1 cup chopped walnuts
- 1/2 gallon vanilla ice cream, softened slightly

1 In a large bowl, combine the butter and crushed graham crackers and gingersnaps. Press half of the crumb mixture into an ungreased 13-in. x 9-in. x 2-in. dish.

2 In a large bowl, combine the pumpkin, sugar, cinnamon, salt, ginger and nutmeg. Stir in the walnuts. Fold in softened ice cream. Spoon into crust. Sprinkle remaining crumb mixture over top. Freeze until firm, about 3 hours.

Yield: 12-15 servings.

GIFT-WRAPPED CHOCOLATE CAKE

(PICTURED ON NEXT PAGE)

taste of home test kitchen

Family and friends will be impressed when you present this rich, glazed cake at a get-together.

- 2 teaspoons plus 3/4 cup butter, softened
- 1-1/2 cups sugar
- 3 eggs, *separated*
- 3 tablespoons *each* water and canola oil
- 1-1/2 teaspoons vanilla extract
- 1/2 cup all-purpose flour
- 1/2 cup plus 1 tablespoon baking cocoa
- 3/4 cup chopped pecans
- 1/8 teaspoon cream of tartar
- 1/8 teaspoon salt

GLAZE:

- 8 squares (1 ounce *each*) semisweet chocolate, chopped
- 1/2 cup heavy whipping cream

Chocolate Bow (recipe below)

1 Line the bottom of a 9-in. springform pan with foil; grease foil and sides of pan with 2 teaspoons butter; set aside. Melt remaining butter. In a mixing bowl, beat butter and sugar. Add egg yolks, one at a time, beating well after each. Beat in the water, oil and vanilla; mix well. Combine flour and cocoa; gradually add to egg mixture. Stir in pecans.

2 In another mixing bowl, beat egg whites on medium speed until foamy. Add cream of tartar and salt; beat on high until stiff peaks form. Fold into chocolate mixture. Pour into prepared pan. Bake at 350° for 45-50 minutes or until top begins to crack slightly and a toothpick comes out with moist crumbs. Cool on wire rack for 10 minutes. Carefully run a knife around the edge of pan to loosen; cool 1 hour longer. Refrigerate overnight.

3 To assemble, invert cake onto a waxed paper-lined baking sheet. Remove foil; set aside. In a heavy saucepan, heat chocolate and cream over very low heat until chocolate in melted (do not boil); stir until smooth. Remove from the heat. Cool if necessary until mixture reaches spreading consistency.

4 Slowly pour over cake, smoothing sides with a metal spatula to evenly coat. Chill until set. Carefully transfer cake to a flat serving plate. Top with Chocolate Bow. (See recipe below.) Refrigerate leftovers.

Yield: 10-12 servings.

CHOCOLATE BOW

(PICTURED ON NEXT PAGE)

debbie gauthier, timmins, ontario

What a beautiful sight this is on top of your favorite cake! It takes some time to prepare but can be made a month in advance and stored in an airtight container.

- 1 cup plus 2 tablespoons vanilla *or* white chips, *divided*
- 4 teaspoons shortening
- 1/2 large marshmallow

1. Cut three 6-in. squares from freezer paper. Cut each square into six 1-in. strips. Set aside four strips. Place remaining strips shiny side up on a waxed paper-lined work surface.

2. In a microwave, melt 1 cup vanilla chips and shortening; stir until smooth. Working quickly with a few strips at a time, spread chocolate beyond three sides of the strips onto the waxed paper, leaving 1/2 in. at one short end.

3. Immediately peel each strip from work surface; place on clean waxed paper. Let strips dry just until barely set but still pliable, about 1 minute. (If chocolate strips become to stiff, warm in the microwave for a few seconds.)

4. With paper side out, press ends of chocolate strips together. Stand strips on edges on a waxed paper-lined baking sheet. Chill until set, about 10 minutes. Carefully remove freezer paper.

5. For ribbons, coat four reserved strips with chocolate; peel strips from work surface. On an inverted 9-in. x 1-1/2-in. round baking pan, place strips, chocolate side down at 90-degree angles to each other and drape 1-1/4 in. over side of pan. (If necessary, use a drop of chocolate under the bottom edge to hold in place. With a toothpick, press the strip onto the dab of chocolate.) Chill until set; remove freezer paper.

6. Melt remaining chips in the microwave. Fill a plastic bag with melted chocolate; cut a small hole in the corner. Place marshmallow half, cut side down, in the center of a piece of waxed paper. Secure six chocolate loops around edge of marshmallow with melted chocolate; press ends down. Layer five more loops on top with the ends touching. Secure with chocolate. Coat the top of marshmallow with remaining chocolate; place

remaining loops in center, pressing down. Let dry for 1 hour or overnight. Carefully peel waxed paper from bow. Place ribbons and bow on top of the cake.

Yield: 1 white chocolate bow for a 9-in. round or springform cake.

RED RASPBERRY MOUSSE DESSERT

edna hoffman, hebron, indiana

When I need a light and refreshing finish to a special meal, I make this fluffy, fruity mousse. Ladyfingers add an elegant look to this pretty dessert.

> 2 packages (3 ounces *each*) raspberry gelatin
> 1-3/4 cups boiling water
> 2 packages (10 ounces *each*) frozen sweetened raspberries, thawed
> 2 cups heavy whipping cream, whipped
> 23 ladyfingers

Fresh mint, raspberries and additional whipped cream, optional

1. In a large bowl, dissolve gelatin in boiling water. Stir in raspberries. Refrigerate until partially thickened. Fold in whipped cream.

2. Arrange the ladyfingers with rounded side out around the sides of an ungreased 9-in. springform pan. Carefully spoon the raspberry mixture into pan. Cover and refrigerate until firm. Garnish with mint, raspberries and whipped cream if desired.

Yield: 12 servings.

CHOCOLATE CHIP COOKIE CHEESECAKE

kathleen gualano, cary, illinois

Our daughter first astounded us with her cooking talents when she made this cheesecake at 13 years of age. With a unique cookie crumb crust and extra-creamy filling, people think this dessert was made by a gourmet baker!

- 2 cups chocolate chip cookie crumbs (about 28 cookies)
- 3 tablespoons sugar
- 5 tablespoons butter, melted

FILLING:

- 5 packages (8 ounces *each*) cream cheese, softened
- 1-1/4 cups sugar
- 3 tablespoons all-purpose flour
- 5 eggs
- 2 egg yolks
- 1/4 cup sour cream
- 1 teaspoon grated orange peel
- 1/2 teaspoon vanilla extract
- 1 cup miniature semisweet chocolate chips

TOPPING:

- 1 cup (8 ounces) sour cream
- 2 tablespoons sugar
- 1 teaspoon vanilla extract
- 1 tablespoon chocolate chip cookie crumbs

1 In a large bowl, combine cookie crumbs and sugar; stir in butter. Press onto the bottom and 2 in. up the sides of a greased 9-in. springform pan; set aside.

2 In another large bowl, beat the cream cheese and sugar until smooth. Add flour; mix well. Add eggs and egg yolks; beat on low speed just until combined. Beat in sour cream, orange peel and vanilla just until combined. Stir in chocolate chips. Pour over crust. Place pan on a baking sheet.

3 Bake at 325° for 65-75 minutes or until center is almost set. Remove from the oven; let stand for 5 minutes. Combine the sour cream, sugar and vanilla; spread over filling. Return to the oven for 8 minutes. Cool on a wire rack for 10 minutes.

4 Carefully run a knife around edge of pan to loosen. Cool 1 hour longer. Refrigerate overnight. Remove sides of pan. Garnish with cookie crumbs.

Yield: 12-14 servings.

STRAWBERRY SCHAUM TORTE

diane krisman, hales corners, wisconsin

This recipe was handed down from my German grandma. She took great pride in serving this delicate dessert. Whenever I make it, I'm filled with warm memories of childhood.

- 8 egg whites
- 1 tablespoon white vinegar
- 1 teaspoon vanilla extract
- 1/4 teaspoon salt
- 2 cups sugar
- 3 cups sliced fresh strawberries
- 1-1/2 cups whipped cream

1 Place egg whites in a large mixing bowl and let stand at room temperature for 30 minutes. Beat the egg whites, vinegar, vanilla and salt on medium speed until soft peaks form. Gradually beat in sugar, about 2 tablespoons at a time, on high until stiff glossy peaks form and sugar is dissolved.

2 Spread into a greased 10-in. springform pan. Bake at 300° for 50-60 minutes or until lightly browned. Remove to a wire rack to cool (meringue will fall). Serve with strawberries and whipped cream. Store leftovers in the refrigerator.

Yield: 12 servings.

CRANBROSIA GELATIN MOLD

gladys mccollum abee, mckee, kentucky

Guests ooh and aah when I bring out this fancy fruit-filled ring. Garnished with mint, sugared cranberries and mandarin oranges, it's a showstopper.

- 2 cups fresh *or* frozen cranberries, coarsely ground
- 1 cup sugar
- 1 can (11 ounces) mandarin oranges
- 1 can (8 ounces) sliced pineapple
- 2 envelopes unflavored gelatin
- 1 cup (8 ounces) sour cream
- 1 cup heavy whipping cream
- 2 tablespoons confectioners' sugar

1 In a bowl, combine cranberries and sugar. Let stand for 30 minutes or until sugar is dissolved, stirring occasionally. Drain juice from oranges and pineapple, reserving 3/4 cup juice. Cut pineapple into small pieces. Set fruit aside.

2 In a small saucepan, sprinkle the gelatin over reserved juice; let stand for 1 minute. Cook and stir over low heat until gelatin is dissolved, about 2 minutes. Add to cranberry mixture; stir in the oranges and pineapple. Fold in sour cream.

3 In a small bowl, beat cream until it begins to thicken. Add confectioners' sugar; beat until soft peaks form. Fold into fruit mixture. Pour into a 6-cup ring mold or 12 individual molds lightly coated with cooking spray. Refrigerate until set. Unmold before serving.

Yield: 10-12 servings.

DELICIOUS STUFFED BAKED APPLES

glenda ardoin, hessmer, louisiana

Baked apples are always a welcome sight at the dinner table on frigid fall evenings. This dressed-up version also features raisins, cranberries and apricots in individual servings.

- 1/2 cup golden raisins
- 1/2 cup dried cranberries
- 1/4 cup chopped dried apricots
- 2-1/4 cups cranberry-apple juice
- 1/3 cup cranberry juice concentrate
- 4 large Golden Delicious apples
- 1/3 cup packed brown sugar
- 3/4 teaspoon ground allspice, *divided*
- 1/4 cup butter, melted

1 In a small bowl, combine the raisins, cranberries and apricots. In a small saucepan, bring juice and concentrate to a boil. Pour over dried fruit; let stand for 15 minutes.

2 Meanwhile, core apples, leaving bottoms intact. Peel the top third of each apple; place in a greased 8-in. square baking dish.

3 Drain fruit mixture, reserving juice. Stir brown sugar and 1/2 teaspoon allspice into fruit; spoon into apples. Drizzle with butter. Pour 3/4 cup reserved juice around apples.

4 Cover and bake at 350° for 50 minutes. Uncover; bake 10-15 minutes longer or until tender. Meanwhile, in a small saucepan, bring remaining reserved juice and allspice to a boil; cook until liquid is reduced to 1/4 cup. Serve with baked apples.

Yield: 4 servings.

CREAM PUFF DESSERT

denise wahl, lockport, illinois

Inspired by classic cream puffs, this recipe is a wonderful treat. I've served it at Cub Scout banquets, birthday parties and holidays. I'm a regular baker, and this dessert is one of my all-time favorites.

- 1 cup water
- 1/2 cup butter
- 1/4 teaspoon salt
- 1 cup all-purpose flour
- 4 eggs

FILLING:
- 1 package (8 ounces) cream cheese, softened
- 2-1/2 cups cold milk
- 2 packages (3.4 ounces *each*) instant vanilla pudding mix

TOPPING:
- 1 carton (8 ounces) frozen whipped topping, thawed

Chocolate syrup

1 In a saucepan over medium heat, bring the water, butter and salt to a boil. Add flour all at once and stir until a smooth ball forms. Continue beating until smooth and shiny. Remove from the heat; let stand for 5 minutes. Add the eggs, one at a time, beating well after each addition.

2 Pour into a greased 15-in. x 10-in. x 1-in. baking pan. Bake at 400° for 28-30 minutes or until puffed and golden brown. Cool on a wire rack.

3 For filling, in a large bowl, beat the cream cheese, milk and pudding mixes until smooth. Spread over the crust; refrigerate for 20 minutes. Spread with whipped topping. Store in the refrigerator. Just before serving, drizzle with chocolate syrup.

Yield: 15 servings.

CRANBERRY SHORTBREAD BARS

taste of home test kitchen

Colorful and tasty, these bars and a glass of milk make the perfect treat after a dusty afternoon of raking leaves. Wrapped in colored cellophane and ribbons, this recipe is pretty enough to double as a quick holiday gift.

- 1 cup butter, softened
- 1/2 cup confectioners' sugar
- 1 egg
- 1-1/2 cups all-purpose flour
- 1/2 cup flaked coconut
- 1/8 teaspoon salt
- 1/2 cup sugar
- 1/2 cup packed brown sugar
- 3 tablespoons cornstarch
- 1 package (12 ounces) fresh *or* frozen cranberries
- 1 cup unsweetened apple juice
- 1 cup chopped walnuts
- 2 squares (1 ounce *each*) white baking chocolate, melted

1 In a large bowl, cream butter and confectioners' sugar until light and fluffy. Beat in egg. Combine the flour, coconut and salt; gradually add to creamed mixture and mix well. Set aside 1 cup for topping. Spread remaining mixture into a greased 13-in. x 9-in. baking dish. Bake at 425° for 10 minutes.

2 Meanwhile, in a small saucepan, combine the sugars and cornstarch. Stir in cranberries and apple juice. Bring to a boil. Reduce heat; cook and stir for 5 minutes or until thickened. Remove from the heat; stir in walnuts.

3 Spread over crust. Sprinkle with reserved crumb mixture. Bake for 20-25 minutes or until golden brown and bubbly. Cool on a wire rack. Drizzle with white chocolate. Cut into bars.

Yield: 2 dozen.

WHITE CHOCOLATE PUMPKIN CHEESECAKE

phyllis schmalz, kansas city, kansas

Just pour the spiced pumpkin filling over the delectable gingersnap crust, bake and refrigerate overnight. The final touch is an almond topping.

- 1-1/2 cups crushed gingersnap cookies (about 32 cookies)
- 1/4 cup butter, melted
- 3 packages (8 ounces *each*) cream cheese, softened
- 1 cup sugar
- 3 eggs, lightly beaten
- 1 teaspoon vanilla extract
- 5 squares (1 ounce *each*) white baking chocolate, melted and cooled
- 3/4 cup canned pumpkin
- 1 teaspoon ground cinnamon
- 1/4 teaspoon ground nutmeg

ALMOND TOPPING:
- 1/2 cup chopped almonds
- 2 tablespoons butter, melted
- 1 teaspoon sugar

1 In a small bowl, combine gingersnap crumbs and butter. Press onto the bottom of a greased 9-in. springform pan; set aside.

2 In a bowl, beat cream cheese and sugar until smooth. Add eggs and vanilla; beat on low speed just until combined. Stir in melted white chocolate.

3 Combine pumpkin and spices; gently fold into cream cheese mixture. Pour over crust. Place pan on a baking sheet.

4 Bake at 350° for 55-60 minutes or until center is just set. Cool on a wire rack for 10 minutes. Meanwhile, combine the topping ingredients; spread in

a shallow baking pan. Bake for 10 minutes or until golden brown, stirring twice. Cool.

5 Carefully run a knife around edge of springform pan to loosen; cool 1 hour longer. Refrigerate overnight. Transfer topping to an airtight container; store in the refrigerator.

6 Just before serving, remove sides of pan; sprinkle topping over cheesecake. Refrigerate leftovers.

Yield: 12 servings.

NEVER-FAIL PECAN PIE

beverly materne, reeves, louisiana

This was my mother-in-law's recipe. Her famous pecan pies were always a hit—I have never seen anyone not enjoy every mouthful! She was kind enough to pass this recipe on to me, and it's one that I really enjoy making.

- 2 eggs, well beaten
- 1/2 cup sugar
- 1 cup dark corn syrup
- 1 tablespoon all-purpose flour
- 1/4 teaspoon salt
- 1 teaspoon vanilla extract
- 1 cup pecan halves
- 1 unbaked pie shell (9 inches)

1 Combine eggs, sugar, corn syrup, flour, salt and vanilla. Stir in pecans. Pour into pie shell. Cover pastry edges with foil to prevent excess browning. Bake at 350° for 30 minutes. Remove foil and bake another 15 minutes or until golden brown.

Yield: 6-8 servings.

CHOCOLATE GANACHE CAKE

kathy kittell, lenexa, kansas

Here's to that chocolate fix we all need. I use cream in both the filling and glaze of this ultra-rich dessert.

- 3/4 cup butter, softened
- 1-1/2 cups sugar
- 1 egg
- 1 teaspoon vanilla extract
- 1 cup buttermilk
- 3/4 cup sour cream
- 2 cups all-purpose flour
- 2/3 cup baking cocoa
- 1 teaspoon baking soda
- 1/4 teaspoon salt

FILLING:
- 4 squares (1 ounce *each*) semisweet chocolate
- 1 cup heavy whipping cream
- 1/2 teaspoon vanilla extract

GLAZE:
- 8 squares (1 ounce *each*) semisweet chocolate
- 1/4 cup butter, cubed
- 3/4 cup heavy whipping cream

1 In a large bowl, cream the butter and sugar until light and fluffy. Add egg and vanilla; beat for 2 minutes. Combine buttermilk and sour cream. Combine flour, cocoa, baking soda and the salt; add to creamed mixture alternately with the buttermilk mixture, beating well after each addition.

2 Pour into two greased and waxed paper-lined 9-in. round baking pans. Bake at 350° for 20-25 minutes or until a toothpick comes out clean. Cool for 10 minutes; remove from pans to wire racks to cool completely.

3 In a heavy saucepan, melt chocolate with cream over low heat. Remove from the heat; stir in vanilla. Transfer to a small bowl; chill until slightly thickened, stirring occasionally. Beat on medium speed until light and fluffy. Chill until mixture achieves spreading consistency.

4 For glaze, in a heavy saucepan, melt chocolate and butter. Gradually add cream; heat until just warmed. Chill until slightly thickened.

5 Place one cake layer on a serving plate; spread with filling. Top with remaining cake layer. Slowly pour glaze over top of cake. Chill until serving.

Yield: 12-14 servings.

RICOTTA CHEESECAKE

georgiann franklin, canfield, ohio

When I was a nurse, my coworkers and I regularly swapped recipes during lunch breaks. This creamy cheesecake was one of the best I received.

- 1-1/4 cups graham cracker crumbs
- 3 tablespoons sugar
- 1/3 cup butter, melted

FILLING:
- 2 cartons (15 ounces *each*) ricotta cheese
- 1 cup sugar
- 3 eggs, lightly beaten
- 2 tablespoons all-purpose flour
- 1 teaspoon vanilla extract
- 1 can (14-1/2 ounces) pitted tart cherries, optional

1 In a bowl, combine the graham cracker crumbs and sugar; stir in butter. Press onto the bottom and 1 in. up the sides of a greased 9-in. springform pan.

2 Place on a baking sheet. Bake at 400° for 6-8 minutes or until crust is lightly browned around the edges. Cool on a wire rack.

3 In a large bowl, beat ricotta cheese on medium speed for 1 minute. Add sugar; beat for 1 minute. Add eggs; beat just until combined. Beat in flour and vanilla. Pour into crust.

4 Place pan on a baking sheet. Bake at 350° for 50-60 minutes or until center is almost set. Cool on a wire rack for 10 minutes. Carefully run a knife around edge of pan to loosen; cool 1 hour longer. Refrigerate overnight. Remove sides of pan. Serve with cherries if desired. Refrigerate leftovers.

Yield: 12 servings.

LACY FRUIT CUPS WITH SABAYON SAUCE

taste of home test kitchen

This fruity dessert from our home economists is a refreshing change of pace from heavy desserts.

- 3 tablespoons butter
- 3 tablespoons brown sugar
- 3 tablespoons light corn syrup
- 2 tablespoons plus 2 teaspoons all-purpose flour
- 1/3 cup ground pecans
- 1/4 teaspoon vanilla extract
- 5 egg yolks
- 1/2 cup rose *or* marsala wine
- 1/3 cup sugar
- 2 medium pink grapefruit, peeled and sectioned
- 2 medium blood oranges *or* tangerines, peeled and sectioned
- 3/4 cup fresh raspberries

1 In a small saucepan, melt butter over low heat. Stir in brown sugar and corn syrup; cook and stir until mixture comes to a boil. Remove from the heat. Stir in flour. Fold in pecans and vanilla.

2 Drop by tablespoonfuls 3 in. apart onto parchment paper-lined baking sheets. Bake at 325° for 8-10 minutes or until golden brown. Cool for 30-60 seconds. Working quickly, peel cookies off paper and immediately drape over inverted 6-oz. custard cups; cool completely.

3 In a small saucepan, combine the egg yolks, wine and sugar. Cook and stir over medium heat until mixture reaches 160° or is thick enough to coat the back of a metal spoon.

4 Divide the grapefruit, oranges and berries among cookie cups; top with sauce. Serve immediately.

Yield: 8 servings.

Editor's Note: If the cookies become firm before they are draped over custard cups, warm them on the baking sheet for 1 minute to soften.

CARAMEL-PECAN APPLE PIE

gloria castro, santa rosa, california

You'll love the smell in your kitchen—and the smiles on everybody's faces—when you make this scrumptious pie that's drizzled with caramel sauce. It's takes me back home to Virginia and being at my granny's table.

- 7 cups sliced peeled tart apples
- 1 teaspoon lemon juice
- 1 teaspoon vanilla extract
- 3/4 cup chopped pecans
- 1/3 cup packed brown sugar
- 3 tablespoons sugar
- 4-1/2 teaspoons ground cinnamon
- 1 tablespoon cornstarch
- 1/4 cup caramel ice cream topping, room temperature
- 1 unbaked pastry shell (9 inches)
- 3 tablespoons butter, melted

STREUSEL TOPPING:
- 3/4 cup all-purpose flour
- 2/3 cup chopped pecans
- 1/4 cup sugar
- 6 tablespoons cold butter
- 1/4 cup caramel ice cream topping, room temperature

1 In a large bowl, toss the apples with lemon juice and vanilla. Combine pecans, sugars, cinnamon and the cornstarch; add to apple mixture and toss to coat. Pour the caramel topping over bottom of pastry shell; top with the apple mixture (shell will be full). Drizzle with butter.

2 In a small bowl, combine the flour, pecans and sugar. Cut in butter until the mixture resembles coarse crumbs. Sprinkle over filling.

3 Bake at 350° for 55-65 minutes or until filling is bubbly and topping is browned. Immediately drizzle with caramel topping. Cool on a wire rack.

Yield: 8 servings.

CHERRY-CHOCOLATE CREAM PUFFS

christopher fuson, marysville, ohio

I developed this fancy and fun chocolate-filled cream puff that is perfect for cherry lovers. I enjoy cooking and playing with ideas for new recipes.

- 1 cup water
- 1/3 cup butter, cubed
- 1 tablespoon sugar
- 1/8 teaspoon salt
- 1 cup all-purpose flour
- 4 eggs

CHERRY-CHOCOLATE FILLING:

- 1 carton (8 ounces) frozen whipped topping, thawed
- 1/2 cup sugar
- 1/4 cup milk
- 6 squares (1 ounce *each*) semisweet chocolate, chopped
- 3/4 pound fresh *or* frozen sweet cherries, pitted and chopped

Confectioners' sugar

1 In a small saucepan over medium heat, bring water, butter, sugar and salt to a boil. Add flour all at once; stir until a smooth ball forms. Remove from the heat; let stand for 5 minutes. Add eggs, one at a time, beating well after each addition. Continue beating until smooth and shiny.

2 Drop by 2 rounded tablespoonfuls 3 in. apart onto greased baking sheets. Bake at 400° for 30-35 minutes or until golden brown. Remove to wire racks. Immediately split puffs open; remove tops and set aside. Discard soft dough from inside. Cool puffs.

3 Let whipped topping stand at room temperature for 30 minutes. Meanwhile, in a small saucepan over medium heat, bring sugar and milk to a boil; cook and stir until sugar is dissolved. Reduce heat to low; stir in chocolate until melted. Transfer to a large bowl. Cool to room temperature, about 25 minutes, stirring occasionally. Fold in whipped topping.

4 Fill each cream puff with a heaping tablespoonful of cherries; top with chocolate filling. Replace tops. Dust with confectioners' sugar; serve immediately. Refrigerate leftovers.

Yield: 10 servings.

GINGER PEACH UPSIDE-DOWN CAKE

june tubb, viroqua, wisconsin

I made this cake often when our children were young. It takes only five ingredients but looks so festive and tastes so good!

- 1/4 cup butter, melted
- 1/2 cup packed brown sugar
- 1 can (15-1/4 ounces) sliced peaches, drained and patted dry
- 1/4 cup red candied cherries, halved
- 1 package (14-1/2 ounces) gingerbread cake/cookie mix

1 In a small bowl, combine butter and brown sugar. Spoon into an ungreased 10-in. fluted tube pan. Alternately arrange peaches and cherries in pan.

2 Prepare gingerbread batter according to package directions for cake; carefully pour over fruit.

3 Bake at 350° for 35-40 minutes or until a toothpick inserted near the center comes out clean. Cool for 5 minutes before inverting onto a serving plate. Cool completely before cutting.

Yield: 12 servings.

MINT ICE CREAM TORTE

taste of home test kitchen

It's great to have an impressive dessert like this one on hand for unexpected company. This from-the-freezer favorite is perfect to wow guests during the Christmas season.

- 20 cream-filled chocolate sandwich cookies, crushed
- 1/4 cup butter, melted
- 10 mint Andes candies, melted
- 1/2 gallon mint chocolate chip ice cream, *divided*
- 1 jar (11-3/4 ounces) hot fudge ice cream topping

1 In a small bowl, combine cookie crumbs and butter. Press half of the mixture into a greased 9-in. springform pan. Spread melted candies over crust. Top with half of the ice cream.

2 Place 1/4 cup hot fudge topping in a small bowl; cover and refrigerate until serving. In another bowl, combine remaining topping and crumb mixture; spread over ice cream. Cover and freeze for 2 hours or until firm.

3 Top with remaining ice cream. Cover and freeze for 8 hours or overnight until firm. Remove from the freezer 5 minutes before serving. Warm reserved fudge topping and use to garnish torte.

Yield: 12 servings.

CRAN-RASPBERRY PIE

eddie stott, mt. juliet, tennessee

Sweet raspberry gelatin tames the tartness of cranberries and pineapple in this holiday pie. The fluffy marshmallow-flavored topping is simply amazing! Plan on having seconds.

- 1 package (3 ounces) raspberry gelatin
- 1 cup boiling water
- 1 cup whole-berry cranberry sauce
- 1 can (8 ounces) unsweetened crushed pineapple, drained
- 1 graham cracker crust (9 inches)
- 2 cups miniature marshmallows
- 1/4 cup sweetened condensed milk
- 1/2 teaspoon vanilla extract
- 1 cup heavy whipping cream, whipped

1 In a large bowl, dissolve gelatin in boiling water. Stir in cranberry sauce and pineapple. Chill until partially set. Pour into crust. Refrigerate until set.

2 Meanwhile, in a heavy saucepan, combine marshmallows and milk. Cook and stir over medium-low heat until marshmallows are melted. Remove from heat. Stir in vanilla. Transfer to a large bowl. Cover and let stand until cooled to room temperature.

3 Whisk in one-third of the whipped cream until smooth (mixture will be stringy at first). Fold in the remaining whipped cream. Spread over gelatin layer. Refrigerate until set.

Yield: 6-8 servings.

CHOCOLATE-MARBLED CHEESECAKE DESSERT

marjorie runyan, middleburg, pennsylvania

This recipe features three kinds of chocolate—baking cocoa, hot fudge topping and chocolate chips! A small piece is all you need to round out a holiday dinner.

- 1/2 cup butter, softened
- 1 cup sugar, *divided*
- 1 cup all-purpose flour
- 1/4 cup baking cocoa
- 1/4 teaspoon salt
- 2 packages (8 ounces *each*) cream cheese, softened
- 2 eggs, lightly beaten
- 1 teaspoon vanilla extract
- 1/2 cup hot fudge ice cream topping
- 1/4 cup semisweet chocolate chips, melted

Milk chocolate *or* striped chocolate kisses, optional

1 In a small bowl, cream butter and 1/2 cup sugar until light and fluffy. Combine the flour, cocoa and salt; gradually add to creamed mixture and mix well. Press into a greased 8-in. square baking dish; set aside.

2 In a large bowl, beat cream cheese and remaining sugar until smooth. Add eggs and vanilla; beat on low speed just until combined. Remove 1 cup to a small bowl; beat in fudge topping. Spread 1 cup over crust; spread with remaining cream cheese mixture.

3 Stir melted chips into remaining fudge mixture; drop by teaspoonfuls over cream cheese layer. Cut through batter with a knife to swirl.

4 Bake at 350° for 40-45 minutes or until a toothpick inserted near the center comes out clean. Cool on a wire rack. Garnish with kisses if desired. Store in the refrigerator.

Yield: 12-16 servings.

CINNAMON APPLE CRUMB PIE

carolyn ruch, new london, wisconsin

Here's a dessert any busy hostess could love! It goes together in minutes, but it looks and tastes like you fussed. It is easily doubled to feed any size gathering.

- 1 can (21 ounces) apple pie filling
- 1 unbaked pastry shell (9 inches)
- 1/2 teaspoon ground cinnamon
- 4 tablespoons butter, *divided*
- 1-1/2 to 2 cups crushed pecan shortbread cookies

1 Pour pie filling into pastry shell. Sprinkle with cinnamon and dot with 1 tablespoon butter. Melt remaining butter. Place cookie crumbs in a small bowl; stir in butter until coarse crumbs form. Sprinkle over filling. Cover edges of pastry loosely with foil.

2 Bake at 450° for 10 minutes. Reduce heat to 350°; remove foil and bake for 40-45 minutes or until crust is golden brown and filling is bubbly. Cool on a wire rack for at least 2 hours.

Yield: 6-8 servings.

NANTUCKET CRANBERRY TART

jackie zack, riverside, connecticut

While guests are enjoying a bountiful meal, this eye-catching tart can be baking to perfection in the oven. Because it calls for very few ingredients, it's quick to assemble.

- 1 package (12 ounces) fresh *or* frozen cranberries, thawed
- 1 cup sugar, *divided*
- 1/2 cup sliced almonds
- 2 eggs
- 3/4 cup butter, melted
- 1 teaspoon almond extract
- 1 cup all-purpose flour
- 1 tablespoon confectioners' sugar

1 In a small bowl, combine the cranberries, 1/2 cup sugar and almonds. Transfer to a greased 11-in. fluted tart pan with a removable bottom. Place on a baking sheet.

2 In a small bowl, beat the eggs, butter, extract and remaining sugar. Beat in flour just until moistened (batter will be thick). Spread evenly over berries.

3 Bake at 325° for 40-45 minutes or until a toothpick inserted near the center comes out clean. Cool on a wire rack. Dust with confectioners' sugar. Refrigerate leftovers.

Yield: 12 servings.

RASPBERRY BROWNIE DESSERT

ann vick, rosemount, minnesota

This is such an easy dessert that everyone goes crazy over. I have brought it to church and work potlucks, and everyone always begs for more. It goes together in a snap.

- 1 package fudge brownie mix (13-inch x 9-inch pan size)
- 2 cups heavy whipping cream, *divided*
- 1 package (3.3 ounces) instant white chocolate pudding mix
- 1 can (21 ounces) raspberry pie filling

1 Prepare and bake brownies according to package directions, using a greased 13-in. x 9-in. baking pan. Cool completely on a wire rack.

2 In a small bowl, combine 1 cup cream and pudding mix; stir for 2 minutes or until very thick. In a small bowl, beat remaining cream until stiff peaks form; fold into pudding. Carefully spread over brownies; top with the pie filling. Cover and refrigerate for at least 2 hours before cutting.

Yield: 15-18 servings.

APPLE-RAISIN BUNDT CAKE

maryellen hays, wolcottville, indiana

This moist, old-fashioned dessert has a pleasant blend of spices and is loaded with nuts and raisins.

- 3/4 cup butter, softened
- 1-1/2 cups sugar
- 1 cup plus 2 tablespoons strawberry jam
- 3-1/3 cups all-purpose flour
- 1-1/2 teaspoons baking soda
- 1-1/2 teaspoons ground nutmeg
- 3/4 teaspoon *each* ground allspice, cloves and cinnamon
- 1-1/2 cups buttermilk
- 1-3/4 cups raisins
- 3/4 cup chopped walnuts
- 3/4 cup chopped peeled apple

GLAZE:
- 1 cup confectioners' sugar
- 4 teaspoons milk

1 In a large bowl, cream butter and sugar until light and fluffy. Stir in jam. Combine the flour, baking soda and spices; add into creamed mixture alternately with buttermilk, beating well after each addition. Stir in the raisins, walnuts and apple. Pour into a greased and floured 10-in. fluted tube pan.

2 Bake at 350° for 1 hour or until a toothpick inserted near the center comes out clean. Cool for 10 minutes before removing from pan to a wire rack. Combine glaze ingredients; drizzle over cake.

Yield: 12-16 servings.

CRANBERRY CHEESECAKE TART

diane halferty, corpus christi, texas

I created this recipe to reduce the sugar and fat in the original high-calorie version. Although it uses sugar substitute and reduced-fat ingredients, you can't tell the difference between this dessert and the original.

Pastry for single-crust pie (9 inches)
- 1/3 cup sugar
- 2 tablespoons cornstarch
- 2/3 cup water
- 3 cups fresh *or* frozen cranberries

Sugar substitute equivalent to 1 tablespoon sugar
- 1 package (8 ounces) reduced-fat cream cheese
- 1-1/2 cups reduced-fat whipped topping, *divided*
- 1 teaspoon grated lemon peel

1 Press pastry onto the bottom and up the sides of a 10-in. tart pan with removable bottom. Bake at 400° for 9-11 minutes or until lightly browned. Cool on a wire rack.

2 In a large saucepan, combine the sugar, cornstarch and water until smooth. Add cranberries. Bring to a boil over medium heat. Reduce heat to low; cook and stir for 3-5 minutes or until thickened and berries have popped. Remove from the heat; cool to room temperature. Stir in the sugar substitute.

3 In a small bowl, beat cream cheese and 1 cup whipped topping until smooth; add lemon peel. Spread over pastry; top with cranberry mixture. Refrigerate for 2-4 hours or until set. Garnish with remaining whipped topping.

Yield: 10 servings.

Editor's Note: This recipe was tested with Splenda no-calorie sweetener.

GRASSHOPPER PIE

sally vandermus, rochester, minnesota

After a hearty meal, this light, refreshing pie hits the spot. Chocolate and mint are definitely meant for each other. I make this festive treat at Christmas and whenever my son comes to visit. He loves it with sweet cherries on top.

- 2/3 cup semisweet chocolate chips
- 2 tablespoons heavy whipping cream
- 2 teaspoons shortening
- 1 cup finely chopped walnuts

FILLING:
- 35 large marshmallows
- 1/4 cup milk
- 1/4 teaspoon salt
- 3 tablespoons green creme de menthe
- 3 tablespoons clear creme de cacao
- 1-1/2 cups heavy whipping cream, whipped

Chocolate curls, optional

1 Line a 9-in. pie plate with foil; set aside. In a large heavy saucepan, combine the chocolate chips, cream and shortening; cook over low heat until chips are melted. Stir in walnuts. Pour into prepared pie plate; spread evenly over bottom and sides of plate. Refrigerate for 1 hour or until set.

2 In a large heavy saucepan, combine the marshmallows, milk and salt; cook over low heat until marshmallows are melted, stirring occasionally. Remove from the heat; stir in creme de menthe and creme de cacao. Refrigerate for 1 hour or until slightly thickened.

3 Carefully remove foil from chocolate crust and return crust to pie plate. Fold whipped cream into filling; pour into crust. Refrigerate overnight. Garnish with chocolate curls if desired.

Yield: 6-8 servings.

CHOCOLATE DESSERT DELIGHT

lee ann stidman, spirit lake, idaho

My friends refer to this unbelievably rich ice cream dessert as "death by chocolate" before they ask for seconds! It's a yummy, festive, do-ahead treat.

- 2 cups chocolate graham cracker crumbs (about 32 squares)
- 1/2 cup butter, melted
- 1/2 cup chopped walnuts
- 1 tablespoon sugar

FILLING:
- 1/2 gallon chocolate ice cream, softened
- 1 jar (12-1/4 ounces) *each* caramel ice cream and hot fudge toppings
- 1/2 cup miniature semisweet chocolate chips
- 1/2 cup chopped walnuts

TOPPING:
- 2 cups heavy whipping cream
- 3 tablespoons sugar
- 1 tablespoon baking cocoa
- 1 teaspoon vanilla extract
- 1/2 teaspoon instant coffee granules

Additional miniature chocolate chips and chopped walnuts

1 For crust, combine the crumbs, butter, walnuts and sugar; press into an ungreased 13-in. x 9-in. x 2-in. baking pan. Bake at 350° for 10 minutes; cool completely.

2 Spread half of the ice cream over crust; spoon caramel and hot fudge toppings over ice cream. Sprinkle with chocolate chips and walnuts; freeze until firm. Spread with remaining ice cream over the top. Cover with plastic wrap. Freeze at least 2 hours.

3 In a large bowl, beat cream until stiff peaks form. Fold in sugar, cocoa, vanilla and coffee granules. Pipe or spoon onto dessert. Sprinkle with additional chocolate chips and walnuts. Return to freezer until 10 minutes before serving.

Yield: 16-20 servings.

WHITE CHOCOLATE-STRAWBERRY TIRAMISU

anna ginsberg, austin, texas

This decadent dessert is a twist on traditional Italian tiramisu. My family loves the unusual addition of white chocolate and fresh strawberries.

- 2 cups heavy whipping cream
- 1 package (8 ounces) cream cheese, softened
- 4 ounces Mascarpone cheese
- 9 squares (1 ounce *each*) white baking chocolate, melted and cooled
- 1 cup confectioners' sugar, *divided*
- 1 teaspoon vanilla extract
- 2 packages (3 ounces *each*) ladyfingers, split
- 2/3 cup orange juice
- 4 cups sliced fresh strawberries

Chocolate syrup, optional

1   In a large bowl, beat the cream until soft peaks form; set aside. In another large bowl, beat cheeses until light and fluffy. Beat in the chocolate, 1/2 cup confectioners' sugar and vanilla. Fold in 2 cups whipped cream.

2   Brush half of the ladyfingers with half of the orange juice; arrange in a 13-in. x 9-in. x 2-in. dish. Spread with 2 cups cream cheese mixture; top with 2 cups of berries. Brush remaining ladyfingers with remaining orange juice; arrange over berries.

3   In a large bowl, combine remaining cream cheese mixture and confectioners' sugar; fold in remaining whipped cream. Spread over ladyfingers. Top with remaining berries. Refrigerate until serving. Just before serving, drizzle with chocolate syrup if desired. Refrigerate leftovers.

Yield: 15 servings.

DOUBLE NUT BAKLAVA

kari caven, post falls, idaho

It may take some time to make this rich, buttery treat, but it's well worth the effort! The blend of coconut, pecans and macadamia nuts is irresistible.

- 1-1/4 cups flaked coconut, toasted
- 1/2 cup finely chopped macadamia nuts
- 1/2 cup finely chopped pecans
- 1/2 cup packed brown sugar
- 1 teaspoon ground allspice
- 1-1/4 cups butter, melted
- 1 package phyllo dough (16 ounces, 14-inch x 9-inch sheet size), thawed
- 1 cup sugar
- 1/2 cup water
- 1/4 cup honey

1   In a large bowl, combine the first five ingredients; set aside. Brush a 13-in. x 9-in. x 2-in. baking pan with some of the butter. Unroll the sheets of phyllo dough; trim to fit into pan.

2   Layer 10 sheets of phyllo in prepared pan, brushing each with butter. (Keep remaining dough covered with plastic wrap and a damp towel to prevent it from drying out.) Sprinkle with a third of the nut mixture. Repeat layers twice. Top with five phyllo sheets, brushing each with butter. Brush top sheet of phyllo with butter.

3   Using a sharp knife, cut into 36 diamond shapes. Bake at 350° for 30-35 minutes or until golden brown. Cool completely on a wire rack.

4   In a small saucepan, bring the sugar, water and honey to a boil. Reduce heat; simmer for 5 minutes. Pour hot syrup over baklava. Cover and let stand overnight.

Yield: 3 dozen.

CRUMB-TOPPED CHERRY PIE

sandy jenkins, elkhorn, wisconsin

This pie was my dad's favorite and one my mom made often for Sunday dinner. We had a farm, so Mom made her own butter and ice cream, and she used our fresh dairy products for this pie's great topping.

- 1-1/4 cups all-purpose flour
- 1/2 teaspoon salt
- 1/2 cup canola oil
- 2 tablespoons milk

FILLING:

- 1-1/3 cups sugar
- 1/3 cup all-purpose flour
- 2 cans (14-1/2 ounces each) pitted tart cherries, drained
- 1/4 teaspoon almond extract

TOPPING:

- 1/2 cup all-purpose flour
- 1/2 cup sugar
- 1/4 cup cold butter
- 1 cup heavy whipping cream
- 1 tablespoon confectioners' sugar
- 1/8 teaspoon vanilla extract

1 In a bowl, combine flour and salt. Combine oil and milk; stir into flour mixture with a fork just until blended. Pat evenly onto the bottom and up the sides of a 9-in. pie plate; set aside.

2 In a bowl, combine filling ingredients; pour into crust. For topping, combine flour and sugar in a small bowl; cut in butter until crumbly. Sprinkle over filling.

3 Bake at 425° for 35-45 minutes or until crust is golden brown and filling is bubbly. Cool on a wire rack.

4 Just before serving, in a small mixing bowl, beat cream until it begins to thicken. Add confectioners' sugar and vanilla; beat until soft peaks form. Serve with pie.

Yield: 6-8 servings.

CRANBERRY CHEESECAKE

joy monn, stockbridge, georgia

Refreshing cranberries, lemon juice and orange peel complement the cheesecake's sweet filling. This is my favorite Christmas dessert to make as a gift. It really appeals to people who don't care for chocolate.

- 1-1/2 cups cinnamon graham cracker crumbs (about 8 whole crackers)
- 1/4 cup sugar
- 1/3 cup butter, melted

FILLING:

- 4 packages (8 ounces each) cream cheese, softened
- 1 can (14 ounces) sweetened condensed milk
- 1/4 cup lemon juice
- 4 eggs
- 1-1/2 cups chopped fresh or frozen cranberries
- 1 teaspoon grated orange peel

Sugared cranberries and orange peel strips, optional

1 In a bowl, combine cracker crumbs and sugar; stir in butter. Press onto the bottom of a greased 9-in. springform pan; set aside.

2 In a mixing bowl, beat cream cheese and milk until smooth. Beat in lemon juice until smooth. Add eggs; beat on low speed just until combined. Fold in cranberries and orange peel. Pour over the crust. Place on pan on a baking sheet. Bake at 325° for 60-70 minutes or until center is almost set. Cool on a wire rack for 10 minutes.

3 Carefully run a knife around edge of pan to loosen. Cool 1 hour longer. Refrigerate for at least 6 hours or overnight. Remove sides of pan. Garnish with sugared cranberries and orange peel if desired.

Yield: 12 servings.

POACHED PEARS IN RASPBERRY SAUCE

clara coulston, washington court house, ohio

This fruity recipe is just right for anyone who loves elegant desserts, but not the extra pounds associated with so many of them.

- 8 medium Bosc pears
- 2 cups pear juice
- 1 cinnamon stick (3 inches)
- 1-1/2 teaspoons minced fresh gingerroot
- 1 teaspoon whole cloves
- 1/4 teaspoon ground nutmeg
- 1 tablespoon cornstarch
- 1/2 cup cranberry juice
- 2 cups fresh raspberries *or* 1 package (12 ounces) frozen unsweetened raspberries, thawed
- 2 tablespoons maple syrup

1 Core pears from the bottom, leaving stems intact. Peel pears. If necessary, cut 1/4 in. from bottom so pears will sit flat. Place in a Dutch oven. Add the pear juice, cinnamon stick, ginger, cloves and nutmeg. Cover; bring to a boil. Reduce heat; simmer for 25-30 minutes or until pears are tender.

2 Remove the pears and place in serving dishes. Discard cinnamon stick and cloves from poaching liquid. In a small bowl, combine cornstarch and cranberry juice until smooth; stir into liquid. Bring to a boil; cook and stir for 2 minutes or until thickened. Add raspberries and syrup. Remove from the heat; cool slightly.

3 In a blender or food processor, puree raspberry sauce in batches until smooth. Strain and discard seeds. Pour sauce over pears. Serve warm, at room temperature or chilled.

Yield: 8 servings.

GINGERBREAD WITH CHANTILLY CREAM

pam holloway, marion, louisiana

An old-fashioned family favorite, this treat has never lost its popularity during the holidays. A blend of ginger, cinnamon and nutmeg makes the bread extra flavorful, and my guests always comment on the "cute" dollop of whipped cream on top!

- 1/2 cup shortening
- 2 tablespoons sugar
- 1 tablespoon brown sugar
- 1 egg
- 1 cup hot water
- 1 cup molasses
- 2-1/4 cups all-purpose flour
- 1 teaspoon baking soda
- 1 teaspoon ground ginger
- 1 teaspoon ground cinnamon
- 3/4 teaspoon salt
- 1/8 teaspoon ground nutmeg

CHANTILLY CREAM:
- 1 cup heavy whipping cream
- 1 teaspoon confectioners' sugar
- 1/4 teaspoon vanilla extract

1 In a large bowl, cream the shortening and sugars until light and fluffy. Beat in egg; mix well. Beat in water and molasses. Combine the flour, baking soda, ginger, cinnamon, salt and nutmeg; gradually add to creamed mixture.

2 Pour into a greased 9-in. square baking pan. Bake at 350° for 33-37 minutes or until a toothpick inserted near the center comes out clean.

3 In a small bowl, beat cream until it begins to thicken. Add confectioners' sugar and vanilla; beat until stiff peaks form. Serve with warm gingerbread.

Yield: 9 servings.

CRAN-APPLE COBBLER

jo ann sheehan, ruther glen, virginia

My cranberry-packed cobbler is the crowning glory of many of our late fall and winter meals. My family isn't big on pies, so this favorite is preferred at our Thanksgiving and Christmas celebrations. The aroma of cinnamon and fruit is irresistible.

- 2-1/2 cups sliced peeled apples
- 2-1/2 cups sliced peeled firm pears
- 1 to 1-1/4 cups sugar
- 1 cup fresh *or* frozen cranberries, thawed
- 1 cup water
- 3 tablespoons quick-cooking tapioca
- 3 tablespoons red-hot candies
- 1/2 teaspoon ground cinnamon
- 2 tablespoons butter

TOPPING:
- 3/4 cup all-purpose flour
- 2 tablespoons sugar
- 1 teaspoon baking powder
- 1/4 teaspoon salt
- 1/4 cup cold butter, cubed
- 3 tablespoons milk

Vanilla ice cream

1 In a large saucepan, combine the first eight ingredients; let stand for 5 minutes. Cook and stir over medium heat until mixture comes to a full rolling boil, about 18 minutes. Transfer cran-apple mixture to a greased 2-qt. baking dish; dot with butter.

2 In a small bowl, combine the flour, sugar, baking powder and salt in a bowl. Cut in butter until mixture resembles coarse crumbs. Stir in milk until a soft dough forms.

3 Drop topping by heaping tablespoonfuls onto the hot fruit. Bake at 375° for 30-35 minutes or until golden brown. Serve warm with ice cream.

Yield: 6-8 servings.

PUMPKIN PIES FOR A GANG

edna hoffman, hebron, indiana

When I think of cooking for a crowd this time of year, pumpkin pie always comes to mind. Guests love this traditional treat, and the recipe is perfect for a large gathering. It fills eight pie shells!

- 4 packages (15 ounces *each*) refrigerated pie pastry
- 16 eggs, lightly beaten
- 4 cans (29 ounces *each*) solid-pack pumpkin
- 1/2 cup dark corn syrup
- 9 cups sugar
- 1-1/4 cups all-purpose flour
- 1 cup nonfat dry milk powder
- 4 teaspoons salt
- 4 teaspoons *each* ground ginger, cinnamon and nutmeg
- 1 teaspoon ground cloves
- 8 cups milk

1 Unroll pastry; line eight 9-in. pie plates with one sheet of pastry. Flute edges; set aside. In a large bowl, combine the eggs, pumpkin and corn syrup. In another bowl, combine the dry ingredients; place half in each of two large bowls. Stir half of the pumpkin mixture into each bowl. Gradually stir in milk until smooth.

2 Pour into pie shells. Bake at 350° for 60-70 minutes or until a knife inserted near the center comes out clean. Cool on wire racks. Store in the refrigerator.

Yield: 8 pies (6-8 servings each).

RASPBERRY VANILLA TRIFLE

joyce toth, wichita falls, texas

When I was growing up, my English mother made this as the centerpiece at our traditional Christmas Day tea. Presented in a cut glass bowl, it's absolutely stunning.

- 2 cups milk
- 1 package (3 ounces) cook-and-serve vanilla pudding mix
- 1 loaf (10-3/4 ounces) frozen pound cake, thawed
- 1/4 cup seedless raspberry jam
- 1/4 cup orange juice
- 10 soft macaroon cookies
- 2 cups fresh *or* frozen unsweetened raspberries, thawed and drained
- 1 cup heavy whipping cream
- 2 tablespoons confectioners' sugar
- 1/4 cup sliced almonds, toasted

1 In a small saucepan, combine milk and pudding mix. Cook and stir over medium heat until mixture comes to a full boil. Cool. Cut cake into 1-in. slices; spread with jam. Cut into 1-in. cubes. Place cubes jam side up in a 3-qt. trifle or glass bowl. Drizzle with orange juice.

2 Place macaroons in a food processor, cover and pulse until coarse crumbs form. Set aside 1/4 cup crumbs for garnish; sprinkle remaining crumbs over cake cubes. Top with berries and pudding. Cover and refrigerate overnight.

3 Just before serving, in a small bowl, beat cream until thickened. Beat in confectioners' sugar until stiff peaks form. Spread over trifle. Sprinkle with almonds and reserved macaroon crumbs.

Yield: 10-12 servings.

CARAMEL PECAN PIE

diana bartelings, rock creek, british columbia

Of all my pecan pie recipes, this is the most decadent. It oozes goodness. Even my two young sons, both hockey players, eat it slowly to enjoy every delicious bite.

- 1-2/3 cups all-purpose flour
- 1/4 teaspoon salt
- 1/2 cup cold butter
- 1/3 cup sweetened condensed milk
- 2 egg yolks

FILLING:
- 1-1/2 cups sugar
- 1/2 cup plus 2 tablespoons butter
- 1/3 cup maple syrup
- 3 eggs
- 3 egg whites
- 1/2 teaspoon vanilla extract
- 2 cups ground pecans

1 In a bowl, combine flour and salt; cut in butter until mixture resembles coarse crumbs. Combine milk and egg yolks; stir into crumb mixture until dough forms a ball. Press onto the bottom and up the sides of an ungreased 9-in. deep-dish pie plate; flute edges. Cover and refrigerate.

2 In a large saucepan, combine the sugar, butter and syrup; bring to a boil over medium heat, stirring constantly. Remove from the heat.

3 In a large bowl, beat the eggs, egg whites and vanilla. Gradually add hot syrup mixture. Stir in pecans. Pour into pastry shell.

4 Cover edges loosely with foil. Bake at 350° for 35-40 minutes or until set. Cool on a wire rack. Refrigerate leftovers.

Yield: 6-8 servings.

LINZER TART

karen ehatt, chester, maryland

This lovely versatile tart shows up regularly at family gatherings. I can customize it for any holiday occasion by using different-shaped cookie cutouts or different fruit fillings. And even my picky children gobble it up!

- 1/2 cup butter, softened
- 3/4 cup sugar
- 1 egg
- 1/2 teaspoon grated lemon peel
- 1/2 cup slivered almonds, toasted
- 1-1/2 cups all-purpose flour
- 1 teaspoon ground cinnamon
- 1/4 teaspoon salt
- 1 jar (18 ounces) raspberry preserves

1 In a large bowl, cream the butter and sugar until light and fluffy. Add egg and lemon peel; mix well. Place almonds in a blender, cover and process until ground. Combine the almonds, flour, cinnamon and salt; gradually add to creamed mixture until well blended. Remove 1/3 cup of dough. Roll between two sheets of waxed paper to 1/8-in. thickness. Freeze for 8-10 minutes or until firm.

2 Press remaining dough evenly onto the bottom and up the sides of an ungreased 11-in. fluted tart pan with removable bottom. Spread raspberry preserves over crust. Remove remaining dough from freezer; using small cookie cutters, cut out desired shapes. Place over preserves.

3 Bake at 375° for 20-25 minutes or until crust is golden brown and filling is bubbly. Cool for 10 minutes. Loosen sides of pan. Cool completely on a wire rack. Remove sides of pan.

Yield: 10-12 servings.

MOCHA LATTE PARFAITS

taste of home test kitchen

When hosting a small dinner party, try serving these pretty parfaits. Assemble them earlier in the day for a no-fuss dessert!

- 1 cup (6 ounces) semisweet chocolate chips, *divided*
- 1/2 teaspoon shortening
- Chocolate jimmies
- 3 tablespoons half-and-half cream
- 2 egg yolks, lightly beaten
- 2 teaspoons vanilla extract
- 1 teaspoon instant coffee granules

LATTE CREAM:
- 2 teaspoons instant coffee granules
- 1-1/2 cups heavy whipping cream, *divided*
- 1/3 cup confectioners' sugar

1 In a microwave-safe bowl, melt 1/2 cup chocolate chips with shortening; stir until smooth. Dip rims of four parfait glasses in chocolate; sprinkle with jimmies. Let stand until set.

2 In a small saucepan, combine the cream, egg yolks, vanilla, coffee granules and remaining chocolate chips. Cook and stir over medium heat until mixture reaches 160° or is thick enough to coat the back of a metal spoon. Cool, stirring several times.

3 In a small bowl, dissolve coffee granules in 1 tablespoon whipping cream. Add remaining cream; beat cream mixture until it begins to thicken. Add confectioners' sugar; beat until soft peaks form. Fold 1-1/2 cups of cream mixture into cooled chocolate mixture.

4 Spoon about 1/4 cup chocolate mousse into each parfait glass; spoon or pipe about 1/4 cup cream mixture over mousse. Repeat layers. Refrigerate for at least 2 hours.

Yield: 4 servings.

OLD-FASHIONED JAM CAKE

janet robinson, lawrenceburg, kentucky

I remember my aunt telling me she made this cake often when she was a young girl. Through the years, she made improvements to it, and her cake become a real family favorite. It has been a popular staple at our reunions.

- 1 cup raisins
- 1 can (8 ounces) crushed pineapple, undrained
- 2-1/2 cups all-purpose flour
- 1/3 cup baking cocoa
- 1 teaspoon baking soda
- 1 teaspoon *each* ground cinnamon and ground nutmeg
- 1/2 teaspoon ground cloves
- 1 cup butter, softened
- 1 cup sugar
- 4 eggs
- 1 jar (12 ounces) *or* 1 cup blackberry jam
- 2/3 cup buttermilk
- 1 cup chopped pecans

CARAMEL ICING:

- 1 cup butter, cubed
- 2 cups packed brown sugar
- 1/2 cup milk
- 3-1/2 to 4 cups confectioners' sugar

1 In a bowl, combine raisins and pineapple; soak for several hours or overnight.

2 Combine dry ingredients; set aside. In a large bowl, cream butter and sugar until light and fluffy. Add eggs, one at a time, beating well after each

addition. Add the jam and buttermilk to creamed mixture alternately with dry ingredients; mix well. Stir in raisin mixture and nuts.

3 Spread into two greased and floured 9-in. round baking pans. Bake at 350° for 50 minutes or until a toothpick inserted near the center comes out clean. Cool for 10 minutes before removing to wire racks to cool completely.

4 For the icing, melt butter over medium heat. Stir in sugar and milk. Bring to a boil. Remove from the heat; cool until just warm. Beat in enough confectioners' sugar to achieve a spreading consistency. Frost cake.

Yield: 12-16 servings.

CINNAMON POACHED APPLES

libby orendorff, uniontown, arkansas

For a lighter holiday dessert, try these spicy and sweet apples. They're refreshing served chilled, but my family also likes them warm.

- 2 cups sugar
- 2 cups water
- 1/4 cup red-hot candies
- 6 small tart apples, cored and peeled

1 In a large saucepan, bring the sugar, water and red-hots to a boil. Cook and stir until red-hots are dissolved, about 5 minutes. Reduce heat; carefully add apples. Cover and simmer for 15 minutes or just until apples are tender, turning once.

2 With a slotted spoon, remove apples to a large bowl. Bring syrup to a boil; cook, uncovered, until reduced to about 1-1/2 cups. Cool. Pour syrup over apples; cover and refrigerate until serving.

Yield: 6 servings.

SWEET
TREATS

SUGARED
CHERRY
JEWELS
P. 236

CHOCOLATE CARAMEL CANDY

jane meek, pahrump, nevada

This dazzling treat tastes like a Snickers bar but has homemade flavor beyond compare. When I entered it in a recipe contest at our harvest festival, it won five ribbons, including grand prize and the judges' special award.

- 2 teaspoons butter
- 1 cup milk chocolate chips
- 1/4 cup butterscotch chips
- 1/4 cup creamy peanut butter

FILLING:
- 1/4 cup butter
- 1 cup sugar
- 1/4 cup evaporated milk
- 1-1/2 cups marshmallow creme
- 1/4 cup creamy peanut butter
- 1 teaspoon vanilla extract
- 1-1/2 cups chopped salted peanuts

CARAMEL LAYER:
- 1 package (14 ounces) caramels
- 1/4 cup heavy whipping cream

ICING:
- 1 cup (6 ounces) milk chocolate chips
- 1/4 cup butterscotch chips
- 1/4 cup creamy peanut butter

1 Line a 13-in. x 9-in. pan with foil; butter the foil with 2 teaspoons butter and set aside. In a small saucepan, combine the milk chocolate chips, butterscotch chips and peanut butter; stir over low heat until melted and smooth. Spread into prepared pan. Refrigerate until set.

2 For filling, in a small heavy saucepan, melt butter over medium heat. Add sugar and milk; bring to a gentle boil. Reduce heat to medium-low; boil and stir for 5 minutes. Remove from

the heat; stir in the marshmallow creme, peanut butter and vanilla. Add peanuts. Spread over first layer. Refrigerate until set.

3 For caramel layer, in a small heavy saucepan, combine caramels and cream; stir over low heat until melted and smooth. Cook and stir 4 minutes longer. Spread over the filling. Refrigerate until set.

4 For icing, in another saucepan, combine chips and peanut butter; stir over low heat until melted and smooth. Pour over the caramel layer. Refrigerate for at least 4 hours or overnight.

5 Remove from the refrigerator 20 minutes before cutting. Remove from pan and cut into 1-in. squares. Store in an airtight container.

Yield: about 8 dozen.

PEPPERMINT COOKIES

donna lock, fort collins, colorado

These drop cookies have a touch of peppermint candy in every bite. They're so easy to make and taste so good, that you should plan on making more than one batch for the holidays.

- 2/3 cup butter-flavored shortening
- 1/4 cup sugar
- 1 egg
- 1-1/2 cups all-purpose flour
- 1/2 teaspoon baking powder
- 1/2 teaspoon salt
- 1/2 cup crushed peppermint candies

1 In a large bowl, cream shortening and sugar until light and fluffy. Beat in egg. Combine the flour, baking powder and salt; gradually stir into creamed mixture and mix well. Fold in candy.

2 Drop by teaspoonfuls onto greased baking sheets. Bake at 350° for 10-12 minutes or until edges of cookies just begin to brown. Remove to wire racks to cool.

Yield: 3-1/2 dozen.

PEPPERMINT LOLLIPOPS

taste of home test kitchen

These splendid suckers are a fun and festive treat to share at Christmas. There are endless color and design options...so let your creative juices flow!

- 1-1/2 cups sugar
- 3/4 cup water
- 2/3 cup light corn syrup
- 1/2 teaspoon cream of tartar
- 1/2 teaspoon peppermint oil
- Green and red paste food coloring
- 10 lollipop sticks

1 Butter 10 assorted metal cookie cutters and place on a parchment paper-lined baking sheet; set aside. In a large heavy saucepan, combine sugar, water, corn syrup and cream of tartar. Cook and stir over medium heat until sugar is dissolved. Bring to a boil. Cook, without stirring, until a candy thermometer reads 300° (hard-crack stage).

2 Remove from the heat. Stir in oil, keeping face away from mixture as odor is very strong. Spoon 1/4 cup sugar mixture into two ramekins or custard cups; tint one green and one red.

3 Immediately pour remaining sugar mixture into prepared cookie cutters. Drizzle with green and red mixtures; cut through with a toothpick to swirl. Remove cutters just before lollipops are set; firmly press a lollipop stick into each.

Yield: 10 lollipops.

Editor's Note: Peppermint Lollipops were tested with LorAnn peppermint oil. It can be found at candy and cake decorating supply shops or at www.lorannoils.com. We recommend that you test your candy thermometer before each use by bringing water to a boil; the thermometer should read 212°. Adjust your recipe temperature up or down based on your test.

BAVARIAN MINT FUDGE

sue tucker, edgemoor, south carolina

My sister-in-law sent this chocolate candy to us one Christmas, and it's been a traditional holiday treat in our home ever since. With just six ingredients, it couldn't be any simpler to make.

- 1-1/2 teaspoons plus 1 tablespoon butter, *divided*
- 2 cups (12 ounces) semisweet chocolate chips
- 1 package (11-1/2 ounces) milk chocolate chips
- 1 can (14 ounces) sweetened condensed milk
- 1 teaspoon peppermint extract
- 1 teaspoon vanilla extract

1 Line an 11-in. x 7-in. pan with foil and grease the foil with 1-1/2 teaspoons butter; set aside.

2 In a heavy saucepan, melt the chocolate chips and remaining butter over low heat; stir until smooth. Remove from the heat; stir in the milk and extracts until well blended. Spread into prepared pan. Refrigerate until set.

3 Using the foil, lift fudge out of the pan. Discard the foil; cut fudge into 1-in. squares. Store in the refrigerator.

Yield: about 2-1/2 pounds.

CHOCOLATE CARAMEL THUMBPRINTS

elizabeth marino, san juan capistrano, california

Covered in chopped nuts and drizzled with chocolate, these cookies are delicious and pretty. Everybody looks forward to munching on them during the holidays.

- 1/2 cup butter, softened
- 2/3 cup sugar
- 1 egg, *separated*
- 2 tablespoons milk
- 1 teaspoon vanilla extract
- 1 cup all-purpose flour
- 1/3 cup baking cocoa
- 1/4 teaspoon salt
- 1 cup finely chopped pecans

FILLING:

- 12 to 14 caramels
- 3 tablespoons heavy whipping cream
- 1/2 cup semisweet chocolate chips
- 1 teaspoon shortening

1 In a large bowl, cream butter and sugar until light and fluffy. Beat in egg yolk, milk and vanilla. Combine the flour, cocoa and salt; gradually add to creamed mixture and mix well. Cover and refrigerate for 1 hour or until easy to handle.

2 Roll into 1-in. balls. Beat egg white. Place egg whites in a shallow bowl. Place nuts in another shallow bowl. Dip balls into egg white and coat with nuts.

3 Place 2 in. apart on greased baking sheets. Using the end of a wooden spoon handle, make a 3/8-to 1/2-in. indentation in the center of each ball. Bake at 350° for 10-12 minutes or until set. Remove to wire racks to cool.

4 Meanwhile, in a large heavy saucepan, melt caramels with cream over low heat; stir until

smooth. Using about 1/2 teaspoon caramel mixture, fill each cookie. In a microwave, melt chocolate chips and shortening; stir until smooth. Drizzle over cookies.

Yield: about 2-1/2 dozen.

CRANBERRY ALMOND BARK

elizabeth hodges, regina beach, saskatchewan

The addition of dried cranberries makes this almond bark extra special. It looks impressive but is really quick and easy to make.

- 8 squares (1 ounce *each*) white baking chocolate
- 3 squares (1 ounce *each*) semisweet chocolate
- 3/4 cup whole blanched almonds, toasted
- 3/4 cup dried cranberries

1 In a microwave, melt white chocolate at 70% power for 1 minute; stir. Microwave at additional 10- to 20-second intervals, stirring until smooth. Repeat with semisweet chocolate. Stir almonds and cranberries into white chocolate. Thinly spread onto a waxed paper-lined baking sheet.

2 With a spoon, drizzle semisweet chocolate over the white chocolate. Cut through with a knife to swirl. Chill until firm. Break into pieces. Refrigerate in an airtight container.

Yield: 1 pound.

Toasting Nuts

To toast nuts, spread in a 15-in. x 10-in. x 1-in. baking pan. Bake at 350° for 5-10 minutes or until lightly browned, stirring occasionally. Or, spread in a dry nonstick skillet and heat over low heat until lightly browned, stirring occasionally.—Taste of Home Test Kitchen

BUTTERSCOTCH EGGNOG STARS

cheryl hemmer, swansea, illinois

These yellow star-shaped cookies with a "stained-glass" center are almost too pretty to eat! But they have a rich eggnog flavor that is irresistible. They take a little time and patience to prepare, but they're worth every minute!

- 2/3 **cup butter, softened**
- 1 **cup sugar**
- 1 **egg**
- 1/4 **cup eggnog**
- 2 **cups all-purpose flour**
- 3/4 **teaspoon baking powder**
- 1/4 **teaspoon salt**
- 1/4 **teaspoon ground nutmeg**
- 1/2 **cup crushed hard butterscotch candies**

OPTIONAL ICING:
- 1-1/2 **cups confectioners' sugar**
- 1/4 **teaspoon rum extract**
- 2 **to 3 tablespoons eggnog**

Yellow colored sugar

1. In a large bowl, cream butter and sugar until light and fluffy. Beat in egg and eggnog. Combine the flour, baking powder, salt and nutmeg; gradually add to creamed mixture and mix well. Divide dough in half.

2. On a lightly floured surface, roll out one portion at a time to 1/4-in. thickness. Cut with floured 3-1/2-in. star cutter. Cut out centers with a 1-1/2-in. star cutter. Line baking sheets with foil; grease foil.

3. Place large star cutouts on prepared baking sheets. Sprinkle 1 teaspoon candy in center of each. Repeat with remaining dough; reroll small cutouts if desired.

4. Bake at 375° for 6-8 minutes or until edges are golden brown. Cool on baking sheets for 5 minutes. Carefully slide foil and cookies from baking sheets onto wire racks to cool.

5. For icing if desired, beat confectioners' sugar, rum extract and enough eggnog to achieve drizzling consistency. Drizzle over cooled cookies if desired. Sprinkle with colored sugar if desired. Let stand until hardened.

Yield: about 3 dozen.

Editor's Note: This recipe was tested with commercially prepared eggnog.

CRUNCHY CHOCOLATE CUPS

elizabeth prestie, preeceville, saskatchewan

These sweet, crunchy morsels are super-easy to make but are always popular on my cookie and candy tray for the holidays.

- 1 **package (12 ounces) semisweet chocolate chips**
- 1 **package (11 ounces) butterscotch chips**
- 1 **package (10 ounces) peanut butter chips**
- 1 **cup coarsely crushed cornflakes**
- 1/2 **cup chopped peanuts, optional**

1. In a microwave-safe bowl, melt the chocolate chips, butterscotch chips and peanut butter chips over low heat; stir until smooth. Stir in cornflakes. Add peanuts if desired. Let stand for 10-15 minutes or until slightly cooled.

2. Drop by teaspoonfuls into miniature foil cups placed on a 15-in. x 10-in. x 1-in. baking sheet. Refrigerate until set.

Yield: about 5 dozen.

SECRET KISS COOKIES

karen owen, rising sun, indiana

Here's a recipe that's literally sealed with a kiss. This cookie is bound to satisfy any sweet tooth.

- 1 cup butter, softened
- 1/2 cup sugar
- 1 teaspoon vanilla extract
- 2 cups all-purpose flour
- 1 cup finely chopped walnuts
- 30 milk chocolate kisses
- 1-1/3 cups confectioners' sugar, *divided*
- 2 tablespoons baking cocoa

1 In a large bowl, cream butter, sugar and vanilla until light and fluffy. Gradually add the flour and mix well. Fold in the walnuts. Refrigerate dough for 2-3 hours or until firm.

2 Shape into 1-in. balls. Flatten the balls and place a chocolate kiss in the center of each; pinch dough together around kiss. Place 2 in. apart on ungreased baking sheets.

3 Bake at 375° for 12 minutes or until set but not browned. Cool for 1 minute; remove from pans to wire racks.

4 Sift together 2/3 cup confectioners' sugar and the cocoa. While the cookies are still warm, roll half in the cocoa mixture and half in the remaining confectioners' sugar. Cool completely. Store in an airtight container.

Yield: 2-1/2 dozen.

HOLIDAY SPRITZ COOKIES

taste of home test kitchen

These crisp, buttery cookies make a perfect welcome gift or sweet party treat. Color the dough in Christmas colors and use a cookie press to make all kinds of fun shapes.

- 1/2 cup butter, softened
- 1 cup sugar
- 1 egg
- 2 tablespoons milk
- 1/2 teaspoon vanilla extract
- 2-1/4 cups cake flour
- 1/2 teaspoon salt

Food coloring, optional

Holiday sprinkles and colored sugars

1 In a small bowl, cream butter and sugar until light and fluffy. Beat in the egg, milk and vanilla. Combine flour and salt; gradually add to creamed mixture just until combined. Stir in food coloring if desired. Cover and chill for at least 2 hours.

2 Fill cookie press and form into desired shapes on ungreased baking sheets. Decorate with sprinkles and colored sugars.

3 Bake at 400° for 8 minutes or until edges just begin to brown. Cool on wire racks.

Yield: about 5 dozen.

Chill Cookie Sheets

Some recipes for spritz cookies say to chill the dough, but this makes pressing difficult. Instead, I chill my cookie sheets. The room-temperature dough presses out quickly, and the chilled sheets keep the dough from spreading too fast.—Arlene M., Brecksville, Ohio

WHITE CHOCOLATE PEPPERMINT FUDGE

sue schindler, barnesville, minnesota

I make many batches of this minty fudge to give as Christmas gifts. It's a nice change from milk chocolate candy.

- 1-1/2 teaspoons plus 1/4 cup butter, softened, *divided*
- 2 cups sugar
- 1/2 cup sour cream
- 12 squares (1 ounce *each*) white baking chocolate, chopped
- 1 jar (7 ounces) marshmallow creme
- 1/2 cup crushed peppermint candy
- 1/2 teaspoon peppermint extract

1 Line a 9-in. square pan with foil. Grease the foil with 1-1/2 teaspoons butter; set aside.

2 In a large heavy saucepan, combine the sugar, sour cream and remaining butter. Cook and stir over medium heat until sugar is dissolved. Bring to a rapid boil; cook and stir until a candy thermometer reads 234° (soft-ball stage), about 5 minutes.

3 Remove from the heat; stir in white chocolate and marshmallow creme until melted. Fold in peppermint candy and extract. Pour into prepared pan. Chill until firm.

4 Using foil, lift fudge out of pan. Gently peel off foil; cut fudge into 1-in. squares. Store in refrigerator.

Yield: 2 pounds.

Editor's Note: We recommend that you test your candy thermometer before each use by bringing water to a boil; the thermometer should read 212°. Adjust your recipe temperature up or down based on your test.

CAPPUCCINO TRUFFLES

ellen swenson, newport center, vermont

Dark chocolate, mocha and cinnamon is a delectable combination. These candies are so smooth and rich, I could eat them all in one sitting. Make a lot, because they also make great presents.

- 1 tablespoon boiling water
- 2 teaspoons instant coffee granules
- 2-1/2 teaspoons ground cinnamon, *divided*
- 1/3 cup heavy whipping cream
- 6 squares (1 ounce *each*) bittersweet chocolate, chopped
- 2 tablespoons butter, softened
- 3 tablespoons sugar

1 In a small bowl, combine the water, coffee and 1 teaspoon cinnamon; set aside. In a small saucepan, bring cream just to a boil. Remove from heat; whisk in chocolate and butter until smooth. Stir in the coffee mixture. Press plastic wrap onto surface. Refrigerate for 1 hour or until easy to handle.

2 In a small bowl, combine sugar and remaining cinnamon. Shape chocolate into 1-in. balls; roll in cinnamon-sugar. Refrigerate for at least 2 hours or until firm.

Yield: 1-1/2 dozen.

CHERRY PEANUT BUTTER BALLS

leora muellerleile, turtle lake, wisconsin

Years ago, I saved this festive recipe and made it only at Christmastime. But my grandkids loved the sweet blend of peanut butter, chocolate and cherries so much that now I mix up a batch any time they ask or visit!

         1/2 cup butter, softened
           1 cup peanut butter
           1 teaspoon vanilla extract
           2 cups confectioners' sugar
          24 to 26 maraschino cherries with stems
Additional confectioners' sugar
           2 cups (12 ounces) semisweet chocolate chips
         1/4 cup shortening

1 In a small bowl, beat the butter and peanut butter until smooth. Beat in vanilla. Gradually add the confectioners' sugar and mix well. Cover and refrigerate for at least 1 hour.

2 Pat cherries dry with paper towel. Dust hands with additional confectioners' sugar. Wrap each cherry with a rounded tablespoon full of peanut butter mixture; shape into a ball. (Peanut butter mixture may need to be refrigerated occasionally while rolling cherries.) Cover and refrigerate for at least 1 hour.

3 In a microwave, melt chocolate chips and shortening; stir until smooth. Dip peanut butter balls in chocolate; allow excess to drip off. Place on waxed paper. Refrigerate for at least 1 hour or until set.

Yield: about 2 dozen.

Editor's Note: Reduced-fat or generic brands of peanut butter are not recommended for this recipe.

CINNAMON ALMOND STRIPS

fred grover, lake havasu city, arizona

These buttery cookies are tasty proof that sometimes the simplest combination of ingredients can result in the most delicious foods.

      1-1/2 cups butter, softened
           1 cup sugar
           3 eggs, *separated*
           3 cups all-purpose flour
TOPPING:
      1-1/2 cups sugar
           1 cup finely chopped almonds
      1-1/2 teaspoons ground cinnamon

1 In a large bowl, cream butter and sugar until light and fluffy. Beat in egg yolks. Gradually add flour and mix well.

2 Using a cookie press fitted with a bar disk, press dough 1 in. apart into long strips onto ungreased baking sheets. In a small bowl, beat egg whites until stiff peaks form; brush over dough.

3 Combine topping ingredients; sprinkle over strips. Cut each strip into 2-in. pieces (there is no need to separate the pieces).

4 Bake at 350° for 8-10 minutes or until the edges are firm (do not brown). Cut into pieces again if necessary. Remove to wire racks to cool.

Yield: about 10 dozen.

Separating Eggs

Place an egg separator over a custard cup; crack egg into the separator. As each egg is separated, place yolk in another bowl and empty egg whites into a mixing bowl. It's easier to separate eggs when they are cold.—Taste of Home Test Kitchen

OLD-FASHIONED CARAMELS

jan batman, oskaloosa, iowa
Before I was married, my future father-in-law would fix these creamy caramels at Christmas and send me some. The recipe has been in my husband's family for decades. When we got married, I learned to make them, too.

  1 tablespoon plus 1 cup butter, *divided*
  2 cups sugar
1-3/4 cups light corn syrup
  2 cups half-and-half cream
  1 teaspoon vanilla extract
  1 cup chopped pecans, optional

1 Line an 11-in. x 7-in. pan with foil; grease with 1 tablespoon butter and set aside.

2 In a large heavy saucepan over medium heat, combine the sugar, corn syrup and remaining butter. Bring to a boil, stirring constantly; boil gently for 4 minutes without stirring. Remove from the heat; stir in cream. Reduce heat to medium-low and cook until a candy thermometer reads 238° (soft-ball stage), stirring constantly. Remove from the heat; stir in vanilla and pecans if desired.

3 Pour into prepared pan; cool. Remove from pan and cut into 1-in. squares.

Yield: about 6 dozen.

Editor's Note: We recommend that you test your candy thermometer before each use by bringing water to a boil; the thermometer should read 212°. Adjust your recipe temperature up or down based on your test.

CHOCOLATE PEPPERMINT PINWHEELS

ellen johnson, hampton, virginia
My cookie-loving family is never satisfied with just one batch of these minty pinwheels, so I automatically double the recipe each time I bake them.

    1 cup shortening
1-1/2 cups sugar
    2 eggs
    2 tablespoons milk
    2 teaspoons peppermint extract
2-1/2 cups all-purpose flour
  1/2 teaspoon salt
  1/2 teaspoon baking powder
    2 squares (1 ounce *each*) unsweetened chocolate, melted

1 In a large bowl, cream the shortening and sugar until light and fluffy. Add eggs, milk and extract; mix well. Combine flour, salt and baking powder; gradually add to creamed mixture. Divide dough in half. Add chocolate to one portion; mix well.

2 Roll each portion between waxed paper into a 16-in. x 7-in. rectangle, about 1/4 in. thick. Remove the top sheet of waxed paper; place plain dough over chocolate dough. Roll up jelly-roll style, starting with a long side. Wrap in plastic wrap; refrigerate for 2 hours or until firm.

3 Unwrap dough and cut into 1/4-in. slices. Place 2 in. apart on greased baking sheets. Bake at 375° for 8-10 minutes or until lightly browned. Remove to wire racks to cool.

Yield: 4 dozen.

ORANGE COCONUT CREAMS

julie fornshell, bismark, north dakota

Originally a gift from our neighbors, this candy has become one of our own favorites to make and give at the holidays.

- 1 can (14 ounces) sweetened condensed milk
- 1/2 cup butter, cubed
- 1 package (2 pounds) confectioners' sugar
- 1 cup flaked coconut
- 1-1/2 teaspoons orange extract
- 2 cups (12 ounces) semisweet chocolate chips
- 2 packages (4 ounces *each*) German sweet chocolate, chopped
- 2 tablespoons shortening

1 In a small saucepan, combine milk and butter. Cook and stir over low heat until the butter is melted. Place the confectioners' sugar in a large bowl. Add milk mixture; beat until smooth. Add the coconut and orange extract; mix well. Roll into 1-in. balls; place on waxed paper-lined baking sheets. Refrigerate until firm, about 1 hour.

2 In a microwave, melt the chips, chocolate and shortening; stir until smooth. Dip balls into chocolate; allow excess to drip off. Place on waxed paper; let stand until set.

Yield: 9 dozen.

RAINBOW BUTTER COOKIES

anette tate, sandy, utah

We can't get through the holidays without these fun, colorful cookies. They come out of my oven by the dozens!

- 1/2 cup plus 2 tablespoons butter, softened
- 1/2 cup packed brown sugar
- 1/4 cup sugar
- 1 egg
- 1 teaspoon vanilla extract
- 2 cups all-purpose flour
- 1/2 teaspoon baking powder
- 1/2 teaspoon salt
- 1/8 teaspoon baking soda

Green, red and yellow food coloring
Milk

1 In a large bowl, cream butter and sugars until light and fluffy. Add egg and vanilla. Combine the flour, baking powder, salt and baking soda; gradually add to creamed mixture and mix well.

2 Divide the dough into three portions; tint each a different color. Roll each portion of dough on waxed paper into a 9-in. x 5-in. rectangle. Freeze for 10 minutes.

3 Cut each rectangle in half lengthwise. Lightly brush top of one rectangle with milk. Top with another colored dough. Remove waxed paper; brush top with milk. Repeat with remaining dough, alternating colors to make six layers. Press together lightly; cut in half lengthwise. Wrap each with plastic wrap. Refrigerate for several hours or overnight.

4 Unwrap dough; cut into 1/8-in. slices. Place 2 in. apart on ungreased baking sheets. Bake at 350° for 8-10 minutes. Cool for 1-2 minutes before removing from pans to wire racks to cool completely.

Yield: about 4 dozen.

Simple Slicing

To easily slice refrigerator cookies, slide a piece of dental floss (about 1 foot long) under the roll of dough, crisscross the ends above the dough and pull until you've cut through the dough.—G.W., Fairport, New York

ALMOND CRUNCH TOFFEE

anna ginsberg, austin, texas

This recipe has been my claim to fame since I was 14 years old. One bite and you won't be able to stop eating it!

1-1/2 teaspoons plus 1 cup butter, softened, *divided*
    1 cup sugar
  1/2 cup water
  1/4 teaspoon salt
    1 cup sliced almonds
  1/2 teaspoon baking soda
    8 ounces dark chocolate candy bars, chopped
    1 cup chopped pecans, toasted
  1/4 cup dry roasted peanuts, chopped
    3 tablespoons chocolate-covered coffee beans, halved
    4 squares (1 ounce *each*) white baking chocolate, chopped

1 Line a 13-in. x 9-in. pan with foil. Grease the foil with 1-1/2 teaspoons butter; set aside. In a heavy 3-qt. saucepan, melt the remaining butter. Stir in the sugar, water and salt. Cook over medium heat until a candy thermometer reads 240° (soft-ball stage), stirring occasionally.

2 Stir in almonds. Cook until candy thermometer reads 295° (hard-crack stage), stirring occasionally. Remove from the heat; stir in baking soda. Pour into prepared pan. Sprinkle with chocolate; let stand for 5 minutes. Carefully spread chocolate; sprinkle with pecans and peanuts. Cool on a wire rack for 30 minutes.

3 Sprinkle with coffee beans; press down lightly. Chill for 1 hour or until chocolate is firm.

4 In a microwave, melt the white chocolate at 70% power for 1 minute; stir. Microwave at additional 10 to 20-second intervals, stirring until smooth. Drizzle over the candy. Chill 30 minutes longer or until firm.

5 Using foil, lift candy out of pan; discard foil. Break candy into pieces. Store in an airtight container.

Yield: about 2 pounds.

CHOCOLATE-FILLED SPRITZ

theresa ryan, white river junction, vermont

I found this delicious cookie recipe years ago. Over time, I decided to liven them up with a smooth chocolate filling.

    1 cup butter, softened
  2/3 cup sugar
    1 egg
  1/2 teaspoon vanilla extract
  1/2 teaspoon lemon *or* orange extract
2-1/4 cups all-purpose flour
  1/4 teaspoon baking powder
  1/4 teaspoon salt
    4 squares (1 ounce *each*) semisweet chocolate

1 In a large mixing bowl, cream butter and sugar until light and fluffy. Beat in egg and extracts. Combine dry ingredients; gradually add to the creamed mixture and mix well.

2 Using a cookie press fitted with the disk of your choice, press dough 2 in. apart onto ungreased baking sheets. Bake at 350° for 10-12 minutes or until set (do not brown). Remove to wire racks to cool.

3 In a microwave, melt the chocolate; stir until smooth. Spread over the bottom of half of the cookies; top with remaining cookies.

Yield: about 3 dozen.

FROSTED BUTTER CUTOUTS

sandy nace, greensburg, kansas

I have fond memories of baking and frosting these cutout cookies with my mom. Now I carry on the tradition with my kids. It's a messy but fun day!

- 1 cup butter, softened
- 2 cups sugar
- 2 eggs
- 1 cup buttermilk
- 1 teaspoon vanilla extract
- 1/2 teaspoon almond extract
- 5 cups all-purpose flour
- 2 teaspoons baking powder
- 1 teaspoon baking soda
- 1/4 teaspoon salt

FROSTING:

- 1/4 cup butter, softened
- 2 cups confectioners' sugar
- 1/2 teaspoon almond extract
- 2 to 3 tablespoons heavy whipping cream

Green and red food coloring, optional

Red-hot candies, colored sugar, Cake Mate snowflake decors and colored sprinkles

1 In a large bowl, cream butter and sugar until light and fluffy. Add eggs, one at a time, beating well after each addition. Beat in the buttermilk and extracts. Combine the flour, baking powder, baking soda and salt; gradually add to creamed mixture and mix well. Cover and refrigerate overnight or until easy to handle.

2 On a lightly floured surface, roll out the dough to 1/4-in. thickness. Cut with floured 2-1/2-in. cookie cutters. Place 1 in. apart on greased baking sheets.

3 Bake at 350° for 6-7 minutes or until lightly browned. Remove to wire racks to cool.

4 For frosting, in a small bowl, combine the butter, confectioners' sugar, extract and enough cream to achieve spreading consistency. Add food coloring if desired. Decorate as desired with frosting and candies.

Yield: about 8-1/2 dozen.

PINK ICE

phyllis scheuer, wenona, illinois

You'll love the creamy goodness of this minty candy. Its festive pink color looks lovely on a treat tray.

- 10 ounces white candy coating
- 2 tablespoons crushed peppermint candies (about 7 candies)
- 1/4 teaspoon peppermint extract
- 2 drops red food coloring

1 In a microwave, melt the candy coating at 70% power for 1 minute; stir. Microwave at additional 10- to 20-second intervals, stirring until smooth.

2 Stir in the candies, peppermint extract and food coloring. Spread onto waxed paper to cool completely. Break into small pieces; store in an airtight container.

Yield: 10 ounces.

Leftover Mint Candies

I crush leftover peppermint candies or candy canes and add them to chocolate chip cookie dough to create minty chocolate chip treats. I also grind the candy in the food processor or blender until they become a fine powder, which I use to sweeten hot tea instead of sugar.—Joy K., Mukwonago, Wisconsin

RASPBERRY SANDWICH SPRITZ

joan o'brien, punta gorda, florida

I started baking these Christmas classics when I was a sophomore in high school...and I am still making them now for my grown children and grandkids. The combination of jam, buttery shortbread, chocolate and sprinkles adds up to a fancy and festive treat.

- 1   cup butter, softened
- 3/4 cup sugar
- 1   egg
- 1   teaspoon vanilla extract
- 2-1/4 cups all-purpose flour
- 1/2 teaspoon salt
- 1/4 teaspoon baking powder
- 1   cup seedless raspberry jam
- 1   cup (6 ounces) semisweet chocolate chips

Chocolate sprinkles

1   In a large bowl, cream butter and sugar until light and fluffy. Beat in egg and vanilla. Combine the flour, salt and baking powder; gradually add to creamed mixture and mix well.

2   Using a cookie press fitted with a ribbon disk, form dough into long strips on ungreased baking sheets. Cut each strip into 2-in. pieces (do not separate). Bake at 375° for 12-15 minutes or until edges are golden brown. Cut again if necessary. Remove to wire racks to cool.

3   Spread the bottom of half of the cookies with jam; top with remaining cookies. In a microwave, melt chocolate chips; stir until smooth. Place chocolate sprinkles on a bowl. Dip each end of cookies in melted chocolate, then in sprinkles. Place on waxed paper; let stand until firm.

Yield: 2 dozen.

SUGARED CHERRY JEWELS

jennifer branum, o'fallon, illinois

The texture and crunch of the sugar coating make these chewy cookies extra special. I love the bright cherry center and the fact that they look lovely in a holiday gift box or tin.

- 1   cup butter, softened
- 1/2 cup sugar
- 1/3 cup light corn syrup
- 2   egg yolks
- 1/2 teaspoon vanilla extract
- 2-1/2 cups all-purpose flour

Additional sugar

- 1   jar (10 ounces) maraschino cherries, drained and halved

1   In a large bowl, cream butter and sugar until light and fluffy. Beat in the corn syrup, egg yolks and vanilla. Gradually add the flour and mix well. Cover and refrigerate for 1 hour or until easy to handle.

2   Roll into 1-in. balls; roll each ball in additional sugar. Place 2 in. apart on ungreased baking sheets. Using the end of a wooden spoon handle, make an indentation in the center of each. Press a cherry half in the center.

3   Bake at 325° for 14-16 minutes or until lightly browned. Remove to wire racks to cool.

Yield: about 5 dozen.

TWO-TONE CHRISTMAS COOKIES

marie capobianco, portsmouth, rhode island

I dreamed up this recipe using two of my favorite flavors—pistachio and raspberry. These pink and green cookies are tasty and eye-catching, too. They're perfect for formal or informal gatherings, and everybody likes them.

- 1 cup butter, softened
- 1-1/2 cups sugar
- 2 egg yolks
- 2 teaspoons vanilla extract
- 1 teaspoon almond extract
- 3-1/2 cups all-purpose flour
- 1 teaspoon salt
- 1 teaspoon baking powder
- 1/2 teaspoon baking soda
- 9 drops green food coloring
- 1 tablespoon milk
- 1/3 cup finely chopped pistachios
- 9 drops red food coloring
- 3 tablespoons seedless raspberry preserves
- 2 cups (12 ounces) semisweet chocolate chips, melted

Additional chopped pistachios, optional

1 In a large bowl, cream butter and sugar until light and fluffy. Beat in egg yolks and extracts. Combine the flour, salt, baking powder and baking soda; gradually add to creamed mixture. Divide dough in half. Stir green food coloring, milk and nuts into one portion; mix well. Add red food coloring and jam to the other half.

2 Shape each portion between two pieces of waxed paper into an 8-in. x 6-in. rectangle. Cut in half lengthwise. Place one green rectangle on a piece of plastic wrap. Top with pink rectangle; press together lightly. Repeat. Wrap each in plastic wrap and refrigerate overnight.

3 Unwrap the dough and cut in half lengthwise. Return one of the rectangles to the refrigerator. Cut the remaining rectangle into 1/8-in. slices. Place 1 in. apart on ungreased baking sheets. Bake at 375° for 7-9 minutes or until set. Remove to wire racks to cool. Repeat with the remaining dough.

4 Drizzle cooled cookies with melted chocolate. Sprinkle with additional pistachios if desired.

Yield: 6-1/2 dozen.

SANTA CLAUS COOKIES

mary kaufenberg, shakopee, minnesota

I need just six ingredients to create these cute Kris Kringle confections. Store-bought peanut butter sandwich cookies turn jolly with white chocolate, colored sugar, mini chips and Red-Hots.

- 2 packages (6 ounces *each*) white baking chocolate, chopped
- 1 package (1 pound) Nutter Butter sandwich cookies

Red colored sugar

- 32 vanilla *or* white chips
- 64 miniature semisweet chocolate chips
- 32 red-hot candies

1 In a microwave, melt the white chocolate at 70% power for 1 minute; stir. Microwave at additional 10- to 20-second intervals, stirring until smooth.

2 Dip one end of each cookie into melted chocolate, allowing excess to drip off. Place on wire racks. For Santa's hat, sprinkle red sugar on top part of chocolate. Press one vanilla chip off-center on hat for pom-pom; let stand until set.

3 Dip other end of each cookie into melted chocolate for beard, leaving center of cookie uncovered. Place on wire racks. With a dab of melted chocolate, attach semisweet chips for eyes and a Red-Hot for nose. Place on waxed paper until set.

Yield: 32 cookies.

MAPLE GINGER FUDGE

steve westphal, milwaukee, wisconsin

I combine two fall favorites—maple and ginger—in this sweet, smooth fudge. One piece just isn't enough!

> 2 teaspoons plus 2 tablespoons butter, *divided*
> 2 cups sugar
> 2/3 cup heavy whipping cream
> 2 tablespoons light corn syrup
> 1/4 teaspoon ground ginger
> 1/2 teaspoon maple flavoring
> 1/2 cup chopped walnuts

1 Line a 9-in. x 5-in. loaf pan with foil and grease the foil with 1 teaspoon butter; set aside. Butter the sides of a small heavy saucepan with 1 teaspoon butter; add sugar, cream, corn syrup and ginger. Bring to a boil over medium heat, stirring constantly. Reduce heat; cook until a candy thermometer reads 238° (soft-ball stage), stirring occasionally.

2 Remove from the heat. Add maple flavoring and remaining butter (do not stir). Cool to 110° without stirring, about 1 hour. With a portable mixer, beat on low speed for 1-2 minutes or until fudge begins to thicken. With a clean dry wooden spoon, stir in walnuts until fudge begins to lose its gloss, about 5 minutes.

3 Spread into prepared pan. Refrigerate until firm, about 30 minutes. Using foil, lift fudge out of pan. Discard foil; cut fudge into 1-in. squares. Store in an airtight container in the refrigerator.

Yield: 1-1/4 pounds.

Editor's Note: We recommend that you test your candy thermometer before each use by bringing water to a boil; the thermometer should read 212°. Adjust your recipe temperature up or down based on your test.

HARD MAPLE CANDY

dorothea bohrer, silver spring, maryland

During the war, the women at my grandmother's church would donate sugar rations throughout the year to make candy as a fund-raiser at Christmas. I'm lucky enough to have inherited this tried-and-true recipe.

> 1-1/2 teaspoons butter, softened
> 3-1/2 cups sugar
> 1 cup light corn syrup
> 1 cup water
> 3 tablespoons maple flavoring

1 Grease a 15-in. x 10-in. x 1-in. pan with butter; set aside. In a large heavy saucepan, combine the sugar, corn syrup and water. Cook over medium-high heat until a candy thermometer reads 300° (hard-crack stage), stirring occasionally.

2 Remove from the heat; stir in maple flavoring. Immediately pour into prepared pan; cool. Break into pieces. Store in an airtight container.

Yield: 1-3/4 pounds.

Editor's Note: We recommend that you test your candy thermometer before each use by bringing water to a boil; the thermometer should read 212°. Adjust your recipe temperature up or down based on your test.

ENVELOPES OF FUDGE

donna nowicki, center city, minnesota

Sealed inside a golden crust is a delicious special delivery—a fudgy walnut filling that's almost like a brownie. These cookies are like two treats in one.

- 1/2 **cup butter, softened**
- 1 **package (3 ounces) cream cheese, softened**
- 1-1/4 **cups all-purpose flour**

FILLING:

- 1/2 **cup sugar**
- 1/3 **cup baking cocoa**
- 1/4 **cup butter, softened**
- 1 **egg yolk**
- 1/2 **teaspoon vanilla extract**
- 1/8 **teaspoon salt**
- 1/2 **cup finely chopped walnuts**

1 In a large bowl, beat the butter and cream cheese until smooth. Gradually add flour. On a lightly floured surface, knead until smooth, about 3 minutes. Cover and refrigerate for 1-2 hours or until easy to handle.

2 For filling, combine the sugar, cocoa, butter, yolk, vanilla and salt. Stir in walnuts; set filling aside. On a lightly floured surface, roll the dough into a 12-1/2-in. square; cut into 2-1/2-in. squares.

3 Place a rounded teaspoonful of filling in center of each square. Bring the two opposite corners to center. Moisten the edges with water and pinch together. Place 1 in. apart on lightly greased baking sheets.

4 Bake at 350° for 18-22 minutes or until lightly browned. Remove to wire racks to cool.

Yield: 25 cookies.

CHOCOLATE ZEBRA CLUSTERS

paige scott, murfreesboro, tennessee

Just one bite and chocolate lovers will melt over these yummy clusters filled with salted nuts, rice cereal and marshmallows! They're so pretty, no one can believe how easy they are.

- 2 **cups (12 ounces) semisweet chocolate chips**
- 12 **ounces white candy coating,** *divided*
- 1-1/4 **cups salted peanuts**
- 1-1/4 **cups crisp rice cereal**
- 2-1/4 **cups miniature marshmallows**
- 1 **teaspoon shortening**

1 Line two baking sheets with waxed paper; set aside. In a microwave, melt chips and 7 oz. white candy coating at 70% power; stir until smooth. Stir in peanuts and cereal. Cool slightly; fold in marshmallows. Drop by rounded tablespoonfuls onto prepared baking sheets.

2 In microwave, melt shortening and remaining candy coating; stir until smooth. Transfer to a pastry or plastic bag; cut a small hole in the corner of bag. Drizzle over clusters. Refrigerate for 5 minutes or until set. Store in an airtight container.

Yield: 2-1/2 dozen.

Quick Chocolate Candy

Chop eight 1-ounce squares of semisweet chocolate. Melt chocolate and 1 teaspoon shortening in a microwave or heavy saucepan; stir until smooth. Dip fresh or dried fruit, nuts, pretzels or cookies in chocolate; let excess chocolate drip off. Place on waxed paper until set. Or stir chopped nuts, flaked coconut, raisins or chow mein noodles into the melted chocolate. Drop by spoonfuls onto waxed paper and let stand until set. Store the chocolate candies in an airtight container.—Taste of Home Test Kitchen

ORANGE CAPPUCCINO CREAMS

lucile cline, wichita, kansas
As holiday gifts, these mocha-orange morsels are sure to be a success. The delighted response they get is well worth the kitchen time it takes to make them.

- 12 squares (1 ounce *each*) white baking chocolate, chopped
- 6 tablespoons heavy whipping cream, *divided*
- 1-1/2 teaspoons orange juice
- 1/2 teaspoon orange extract
- 1-1/2 teaspoons finely grated orange peel
- 1/4 cup finely chopped walnuts
- 2 teaspoons instant coffee granules
- 4 squares (1 ounces *each*) semisweet chocolate, chopped

1 In a small heavy saucepan over low heat, melt white chocolate with 1/4 cup cream, orange juice, extract and peel. Stir until chocolate is melted. Remove from the heat; stir in walnuts. Cool for 10-12 minutes.

2 Using a small spoon, fill 1-in. foil or paper candy cups about two-thirds full. Chill for 30 minutes. Meanwhile, in a small saucepan, combine coffee granules and remaining cream. Cook and stir over low heat until coffee is dissolved. Add semisweet chocolate; cook and stir until the chocolate is melted.

3 Spoon about 1/2 teaspoon over white chocolate in each cup. Store in an airtight container at room temperature.

Yield: about 4 dozen.

NOEL COOKIE GEMS

patsy noel, exeter, california
I found these cookies when my husband and I were dating. Since our last name is Noel, I whip up a batch every Christmas. They're a cinch to assemble and freeze, saving time during the holiday rush, and can be filled with other jams for variety.

- 1/4 cup butter, softened
- 1/4 cup shortening
- 3/4 cup sugar
- 1 egg
- 1 teaspoon vanilla extract
- 2-2/3 cups all-purpose flour
- 1/2 teaspoon salt
- 1/4 teaspoon baking powder
- 1/4 teaspoon baking soda
- 1/2 cup sour cream
- 3/4 cup finely chopped nuts
- 1/3 cup seedless strawberry jam

1 In a large bowl, cream the butter, shortening and sugar until light and fluffy. Beat in egg and vanilla. Combine the flour, salt, baking powder and baking soda; gradually add to creamed mixture alternately with sour cream, beating well after each addition. Shape into 1-1/4-in. balls; roll in nuts.

2 Place 2 in. apart on greased baking sheets. Using the end of a wooden spoon handle, make a 3/8- to 1/2-in.-deep indentation in the center of each ball. Fill with jam.

3 Bake at 350° for 10-12 minutes or until lightly browned. Remove to wire racks.

Yield: 3 dozen.

GINGER CRANBERRY BARS

lynn newman, gainesville, florida

These beautiful bars were among the winners of a cranberry festival bake-off. They're tangy, crunchy and subtly sweet.

- 1 cup butter, softened
- 1/2 cup sugar
- 2 teaspoons almond extract, *divided*
- 2 cups all-purpose flour
- 2 cans (16 ounces *each*) whole-berry cranberry sauce
- 2 tablespoons candied *or* crystallized ginger, chopped
- 3 egg whites
- 1/2 cup confectioners' sugar
- 1/2 cup sliced almonds

1 In a large bowl, cream butter and sugar until light and fluffy. Stir in 1-1/2 teaspoons almond extract. Beat in flour until crumbly.

2 Press into a greased 13-in. x 9-in. x 2-in. baking dish. Bake at 350° for 25-28 minutes or until golden brown.

3 Meanwhile, in a small saucepan, heat cranberry sauce and ginger. In a small bowl, beat egg whites on medium speed until soft peaks form. Gradually beat in confectioners' sugar, 1 tablespoon at a time, and remaining extract on high until stiff glossy peaks form. Spread cranberry mixture over crust. Spread meringue over cranberry layer; sprinkle with almonds.

4 Increase heat to 400°. Bake for 14-15 minutes or until lightly browned. Cool completely before cutting. Refrigerate leftovers.

Yield: 2 dozen.

DIPPED SPICE COOKIES

taste of home test kitchen

A hint of orange and a sprinkling of spices lend old-fashioned goodness to these delightful treats. The logs are dipped in melted chocolate and sprinkled with nuts for a special look that never fails to impress.

- 1/2 tube refrigerated sugar cookie dough, softened
- 1/2 cup all-purpose flour
- 1/4 cup packed brown sugar
- 1 tablespoon orange juice
- 3/4 teaspoon ground cinnamon
- 1/2 teaspoon ground ginger
- 1/2 teaspoon grated orange peel
- 1/2 cup semisweet chocolate chips
- 4 teaspoons shortening
- 1/4 cup finely chopped walnuts

1 In a large bowl, beat the cookie dough, flour, brown sugar, orange juice, cinnamon, ginger and orange peel until combined. Shape teaspoonfuls of dough into 2-in. logs. Place 2 in. apart on ungreased baking sheets.

2 Bake at 350° for 8-10 minutes or until edges are golden brown. Remove to wire racks to cool.

3 In a microwave-safe bowl, melt chocolate chips and shortening; stir until smooth. Dip one end of each cookie into melted chocolate, allowing excess to drip off; sprinkle with walnuts. Place on waxed paper; let stand until set.

Yield: about 3-1/2 dozen.

SWEET SHOPPE CARAMEL APPLES

mary bilyeu, ann arbor, michigan

My hand-dipped apples are as beautiful as the ones you'll find at fancy candy counters, only they're fresher, better-tasting and cost a lot less. Make some for your next special occasion.

- 6 large McIntosh apples
- 6 Popsicle sticks
- 2 cups sugar
- 2 cups half-and-half cream
- 1 cup light corn syrup
- 1/2 cup butter, cubed
- 1-1/4 cups English toffee bits *or* almond brickle chips
- 1 cup semisweet chocolate chips
- 1 cup vanilla or white chips

1 Line a baking sheet with waxed paper and grease the paper; set aside. Wash and thoroughly dry apples. Insert a Popsicle stick into each; place on prepared pan. Chill.

2 In a heavy 3-qt. saucepan, combine the sugar, cream, corn syrup and butter; bring to a boil over medium-high heat. Cook and stir until a candy thermometer reads 245°, about 1 hour.

3 Remove from the heat. Working quickly, dip each apple into hot caramel mixture to completely coat, then dip the bottom into toffee bits. Return to baking sheet; chill.

4 In a small microwave-safe bowl, microwave chocolate chips at 50% power for 1-2 minutes or until melted; stir until smooth. Transfer to a small heavy-duty resealable plastic bag; cut a small hole in a corner of bag. Drizzle over apples.

5 Repeat with vanilla chips. Chill until set. Remove from the refrigerator 5 minutes before serving.

Yield: 6 servings.

Editor's Note: We recommend that you test your candy thermometer before each use by bringing water to a boil; the thermometer should read 212°. Adjust your recipe temperature up or down based on your test.

FROSTED PEANUT BUTTER COOKIES

taste of home test kitchen

Are you looking for a quick way to dress up an ordinary cookie mix? Try this trick from our Test Kitchen. The frosting can be used on a variety of cookies, including sugar and chocolate chip.

- 1 package (17-1/2 ounces) peanut butter cookie mix
- 2 cups confectioners' sugar
- 1/4 cup baking cocoa
- 1/4 cup hot water
- 1 teaspoon vanilla extract

Sliced almonds or pecan halves

1 In a large bowl, prepare cookie dough according to package directions. Shape into 1-in. balls. Place 2 in. apart on ungreased baking sheets.

2 Bake at 375° for 8-10 minutes or until edges are golden brown. Cool for 1 minute before removing to wire racks.

3 For frosting, in a bowl, combine the confectioners' sugar, cocoa, water and vanilla. Spread over cookies; top with nuts.

Yield: about 2 dozen.

TOFFEE PEANUT CLUSTERS

joy dulaney, highland village, texas

These are a favorite among my family and friends. The clusters come together quickly, and the toffee adds a nice unique twist.

- 1-1/2 pounds milk chocolate candy coating, chopped
- 1 jar (16 ounces) dry roasted peanuts
- 1 package (8 ounces) milk chocolate English toffee bits

1 In a microwave, melt candy coating; stir until smooth. Stir in peanuts and toffee bits. Drop by rounded tablespoonfuls onto waxed paper-lined baking sheets. Let stand until set. Store in an airtight container.

Yield: 5 dozen.

CHUNKY FRUIT 'N' NUT FUDGE

allene bary-cooper, ramona, oklahoma

Variations on this fudge are endless, but this recipe is my favorite. Besides five types of chips, it includes everything from dried fruit to nuts. Every bite is packed with flavor and crunch.

- 1 package (11 ounces) dried cherries
- 1 cup dried cranberries
- 1-1/2 teaspoons plus 3/4 cup butter, softened, *divided*
- 1 can (14 ounces) sweetened condensed milk
- 1 package (12 ounces) miniature semisweet chocolate chips
- 1 package (11-1/2 ounces) milk chocolate chips
- 1 package (10 to 11 ounces) butterscotch chips
- 1 package (10 ounces) peanut butter chips
- 3 tablespoons heavy whipping cream
- 1 jar (7 ounces) marshmallow creme
- 1/2 teaspoon almond *or* rum extract
- 1-1/2 cups unsalted cashew halves
- 1 package (11-1/2 ounces) semisweet chocolate chunks

1 In a large bowl, combine cherries and cranberries. Add enough warm water to cover; set aside. Line a 15-in. x 10-in. x 1-in. pan with foil and grease the foil with 1-1/2 teaspoons butter; set aside.

2 In a large heavy saucepan, melt remaining butter. Stir in the milk, chips and cream. Cook and stir over low heat for 15-20 minutes or until chips are melted and mixture is smooth and blended (mixture will first appear separated, but continue stirring until fully blended). Remove from the heat; stir in marshmallow creme and extract.

3 Drain cherries and cranberries; pat dry with paper towels. Stir the fruit, cashews and chocolate chunks into chocolate mixture. Spread into prepared pan. Let stand at room temperature until set.

4 Using foil, lift fudge out of pan. Discard foil; cut fudge into 1-in. squares.

Yield: 6-3/4 pounds.

CARAMEL CHOCOLATE COOKIES

joan williams, eatontown, new jersey

I'm noted for my Christmas cookies, and this recipe is my all-time favorite to make and eat.

- 1/2 cup butter, softened
- 1 cup sugar
- 1 egg
- 1/3 cup milk
- 2 squares (1 ounce *each*) unsweetened chocolate, melted and cooled
- 1 teaspoon vanilla extract
- 2 cups all-purpose flour
- 1/2 teaspoon baking powder
- 1/2 teaspoon salt
- 12 caramels, quartered

FROSTING:
- 1-1/2 cups confectioners' sugar
- 1 square (1 ounce) unsweetened chocolate, melted and cooled
- 2 tablespoons light corn syrup
- 2 to 3 tablespoons hot water

Chopped pecans, optional

1 In a large mixing bowl, cream butter and sugar until light and fluffy. Beat in egg, milk, chocolate and vanilla. Combine the flour, baking powder and salt; gradually add to creamed mixture. Cover and refrigerate overnight or until easy to handle.

2 Shape rounded tablespoonfuls of dough around caramel pieces. Place 2 in. apart on ungreased baking sheets. Bake at 400° for 6-8 minutes or until set. Remove to wire racks to cool.

3 In a mixing bowl, combine confectioners' sugar, chocolate, corn syrup and enough water to achieve desired spreading consistency. Frost cookies. Sprinkle with pecans if desired.

Yield: 4 dozen.

RASPBERRY ALMOND STRIPS

taste of home test kitchen

Get ready to pour yourself a cup of tea, because you won't be able to resist sampling one of these. Almonds add taste and texture to the simple strips that are dressed up with raspberry pie filling.

- 1/2 tube refrigerated sugar cookie dough, softened
- 1/3 cup all-purpose flour
- 1/4 cup finely chopped almonds
- 3 tablespoons raspberry filling
- 1/4 cup confectioners' sugar
- 1-1/2 teaspoons milk
- 1/8 teaspoon almond extract

1 In a small bowl, beat the cookie dough, flour and almonds until combined. Roll into a 13-1/2-in. x 2-in. rectangle on an ungreased baking sheet.

2 Using the end of a wooden spoon handle, make a 1/4-in.-deep indentation lengthwise down the center of rectangle. Bake at 350° for 5 minutes.

3 Spoon raspberry filling into indentation. Bake 8-10 minutes longer or until lightly browned. Cool for 2 minutes. Remove to a cutting board; cut into 3/4-in. slices. Place on a wire rack.

4 In a small bowl, combine the confectioners' sugar, milk and extract until smooth. Drizzle over warm cookies.

Yield: 16 cookies.

CRANBERRY PECAN SANDIES

teresa jarrell, danville, west virginia
I am proud to share these delightfully delicate, crisp treats with pecans, cranberry and a hint of orange.

- 1 package (15.6 ounces) cranberry-orange quick bread mix
- 1/2 cup butter, melted
- 1 egg
- 2 tablespoons orange juice
- 3/4 cup chopped pecans
- 30 to 36 pecan halves

ORANGE GLAZE:
- 1 cup confectioners' sugar
- 3 to 4 teaspoons orange juice

1 In a large bowl, combine the bread mix, butter, egg and orange juice. Stir in chopped pecans. Roll into 1-in. balls. Place 2 in. apart on ungreased baking sheets. Flatten with the bottom of a glass coated with cooking spray. Press a pecan half into center of each cookie.

2 Bake at 350° for 12-14 minutes or until lightly browned. Cool for 1 minute before removing to wire racks. In a small bowl, whisk glaze ingredients. Drizzle over cookies.

Yield: 2-1/2 to 3 dozen.

FROSTED MAPLE PYRAMIDS

wanda goodell, kent, washington
The cute shape of these delights makes them a splendid sight on a Christmas cookie tray. You could use star-shaped cutters in place of the round ones.

- 1/2 cup shortening
- 1/3 cup packed brown sugar
- 1 egg
- 1 teaspoon vanilla extract
- 1/4 teaspoon maple flavoring
- 1-1/4 cups all-purpose flour
- 1/4 teaspoon salt
- 1/4 teaspoon baking powder

FROSTING:
- 1/4 cup butter, softened
- 3/4 cup confectioners' sugar
- 1 teaspoon vanilla extract
Red candied cherries, halved

1 In a large bowl, cream shortening and brown sugar until light and fluffy. Beat in the egg, vanilla and maple flavoring. Combine the flour, salt and baking powder; gradually add to the creamed mixture and mix well. Cover and refrigerate for 2 hours or until easy to handle.

2 On a lightly floured surface, roll out dough to 1/8-in. thickness. With floured 2-in. round cookie cutters, cut out 18 circles. Repeat with 1-1/2-in. and 1-in. round cookie cutters. Place 1 in. apart on greased baking sheets.

3 Bake at 375° for 7-9 minutes or until lightly browned. Remove to wire racks to cool.

4 In a small bowl, cream butter and confectioners' sugar until light and fluffy. Beat in vanilla. To assemble cookies, place a 2-in. cookie on waxed paper. Spread with 1 teaspoon frosting. Top with a 1-1/2-in. cookie; frost. Top with a 1-inch cookie; frost. Garnish with candied cherries.

Yield: 1-1/2 dozen.

WHITE CHOCOLATE CRANBERRY BLONDIES

erika busz, kent, washington

This recipe is often requested for wedding receptions. For a fancier presentation, cut the bars into triangle shapes and drizzle white chocolate over each one individually.

- 3/4 **cup butter, cubed**
- 1-1/2 **cups packed light brown sugar**
- 2 **eggs**
- 3/4 **teaspoon vanilla extract**
- 2-1/4 **cups all-purpose flour**
- 1-1/2 **teaspoons baking powder**
- 1/4 **teaspoon salt**
- 1/8 **teaspoon ground cinnamon**
- 1/2 **cup dried cranberries**
- 6 **squares (1 ounce *each*) white baking chocolate, coarsely chopped**

FROSTING:

- 1 **package (8 ounces) cream cheese, softened**
- 1 **cup confectioners' sugar**
- 1 **tablespoon grated orange peel, optional**
- 6 **squares (1 ounce *each*) white baking chocolate, melted**
- 1/2 **cup dried cranberries, chopped**

1 In microwave-safe bowl, melt butter; stir in brown sugar. Transfer to a large bowl; cool to room temperature. Beat in the eggs and vanilla. Combine the flour, baking powder, salt and cinnamon; gradually add to butter mixture. Stir in cranberries and chopped chocolate (batter will be thick).

2 Spread into a greased 13-in. x 9-in. x 2-in. baking dish. Bake at 350° for 18-21 minutes or until

a toothpick inserted near the center comes out clean (do not overbake). Cool on a wire rack.

3 For frosting, in a large bowl, beat the cream cheese, confectioners' sugar and orange peel if desired until blended. Gradually add half of the melted chocolate; beat until blended. Frost brownies. Sprinkle with cranberries. Drizzle with remaining melted chocolate. Cut into bars. Store in the refrigerator.

Yield: 2-1/2 dozen.

MIXED NUT BARS

bobbi brown, waupaca, wisconsin

One pan of these bars goes a long way. They get a nice flavor from butterscotch chips.

- 1-1/2 **cups all-purpose flour**
- 3/4 **cup packed brown sugar**
- 1/4 **teaspoon salt**
- 1/2 **cup plus 2 tablespoons cold butter, *divided***
- 1 **can (11-1/2 ounces) mixed nuts**
- 1 **cup butterscotch chips**
- 1/2 **cup light corn syrup**

1 In a small bowl, combine flour, sugar and salt. Cut in 1/2 cup butter until mixture resembles coarse crumbs. Press into a greased 13-in. x 9-in. x 2-in. baking pan. Bake at 350° for 10 minutes.

2 Sprinkle with nuts. In a microwave, melt butterscotch chips and remaining butter over 30% power; stir until smooth. Add corn syrup; mix well. Pour over nuts. Bake for 10 minutes or until set. Cool in pan on a wire rack.

Yield: about 3-1/2 dozen.

FRUIT-FILLED DAINTIES

taste of home test kitchen
Refrigerated cookie dough can be shaped into cookies or tarts in this recipe. Use one filling or make them both.

CRAN-ORANGE FILLING:
- 2 cups orange-flavored dried cranberries
- 9 tablespoons orange marmalade

APRICOT-ORANGE FILLING:
- 9 tablespoons orange marmalade
- 4-1/2 teaspoons water
- 2-1/4 cups chopped dried apricots

DOUGH:
- 1 tube (18 ounces) refrigerated sugar cookie dough, softened
- 1/4 cup all-purpose flour

Confectioners' sugar

1. Prepare either cran-orange or apricot-orange filling. For cran-orange filling, combine cranberries and marmalade in a food processor; cover and process until finely chopped. For apricot-orange filling, combine the marmalade, water and apricots in a food processor; cover and process until finely chopped.

2. In a large bowl, beat cookie dough and flour until smooth. Divide into thirds. Work with one portion at a time and keep remaining dough covered.

3. **To prepare cookies:** On a floured surface, roll out one portion of dough to 1/8-in. thickness. Cut into 2-1/2-in. squares or cut with a 2-1/2-in. round cookie cutter. Place 1 in. apart on ungreased baking sheets. Repeat with remaining dough.

4. Place a slightly rounded teaspoon of filling in the center of each square or circle. Shape by folding two opposite points of squares over one

another or by folding edges of circles together; press to seal. Bake at 350° for 9-12 minutes or until lightly browned. Cool for 2 minutes before removing to wire racks. Dust with confectioners' sugar.

5. **To prepare tarts:** Shape one portion of dough into twelve 1-in. balls. Press onto the bottom and up the sides of ungreased miniature muffin cups. Repeat with remaining dough. Bake at 350° for 10-12 minutes or until lightly browned.

6. Using the end of a wooden spoon handle, gently make a 3/8- to 1/2-in.-deep indentation in the center of each tart. Cool for 10 minutes before removing from pans to wire racks. Dust with confectioners' sugar. Spoon about a tablespoon of filling into each tart.

Yield: 3 dozen.

Editor's Note: Each type of filling makes enough to fill the entire batch of cookies. If you would like to use both fillings, make two batches of the dough.

ALMOND APRICOT DIPS

cathy childs, freeland, michigan
My family makes these candied apricots every Christmas. We sometimes dip half of the fruit in white candy coating and the other half in chocolate coating.

- 1 package (6 ounces) dried pitted Mediterranean apricots
- 24 whole almonds, toasted
- 4 ounces white candy coating

1. Stuff each apricot with an almond. In a microwave, melt candy coating over 70% power; stir until smooth. Dip each apricot halfway in coating, allowing excess to drip off. Place on a waxed paper-lined baking sheet; refrigerate for 15 minutes or until set. Store in the refrigerator.

Yield: 2 dozen.

BROWN SUGAR CUTOUTS

norma mueller, wauwatosa, wisconsin

I bake so many cookies for the holidays that I have one recipe box just for cookies alone! But of all of them, these simple cutouts are among my husband's most requested.

- 1 cup butter, softened
- 2 cups packed brown sugar
- 3 eggs
- 2 teaspoons grated lemon peel
- 3 cups all-purpose flour
- 1 teaspoon baking soda
- 1 teaspoon ground ginger

FROSTING:

- 1-1/2 cups confectioners' sugar
- 1/2 teaspoon vanilla extract
- 2 to 3 tablespoons half-and-half cream

Green food coloring, optional

1 In a large bowl, cream butter and brown sugar until light and fluffy. Beat in eggs and lemon peel. Combine the flour, baking soda and ginger; gradually add to the creamed mixture and mix well. Cover and refrigerate for 2 hours or until easy to handle.

2 On a floured surface, roll out dough to 1/8-in. thickness. Cut with lightly floured 2-in. cookie cutters. Place 2 in. apart on ungreased baking sheets. Bake at 350° for 8-10 minutes or until golden brown. Remove to wire racks to cool.

3 For frosting, in a small bowl, combine the confectioners' sugar, vanilla and enough cream to achieve spreading consistency. Add food coloring if desired to some or all of the frosting. Decorate the cookies.

Yield: About 6 dozen.

PEPPERMINT TWIST KISSES

traci wynne, falls church, delaware

As rosy as Santa's cheeks, these merry morsels with the chocolate kisses on top are a delightful Yuletide favorite and one of my best recipes.

- 1/2 cup butter, softened
- 1/3 cup sugar
- 1 egg yolk
- 1/2 teaspoon peppermint extract
- 1/2 teaspoon vanilla extract
- 1-1/4 cups all-purpose flour
- 1/4 teaspoon salt
- 4 to 8 drops red food coloring
- 36 chocolate kisses

1 In a large bowl, cream butter and sugar until light and fluffy. Beat in the egg yolk and extracts. Combine flour and salt; gradually add to creamed mixture and mix well. Divide dough in half; tint one portion red. Divide each into four portions. Cover and refrigerate for 1 hour.

2 Shape each portion into a 9-in. log. Place one red log next to one white log; twist gently to create one swirled roll. Roll gently until roll becomes one log. Repeat with remaining dough.

3 Cut each log into nine slices; roll each into a ball. Place 1 in. apart on ungreased baking sheets. Flatten slightly with a glass.

4 Bake at 350° for 10-12 minutes until edges are lightly browned. Press chocolate kisses into the center of warm cookies. Remove cookies to wire racks to cool.

Yield: 3 dozen.

SITTIN PRETTY PEANUT COOKIES

gloria hurl, galloway, ohio

For fun cookies that look as good as they taste, try this easy recipe. They have lots of peanut flavor, fluffy frosting middles and holiday-colored peanut M&M's on top.

- 1/2 cup butter, softened
- 1/4 cup packed brown sugar
- 1 egg, *separated*
- 1/2 teaspoon vanilla extract
- 1 cup all-purpose flour
- 1/4 teaspoon salt
- 1 cup finely chopped peanuts, toasted
- 1/2 cup vanilla frosting
  Peanut M&M's

1 In a mixing bowl, cream butter and brown sugar until light and fluffy. Beat in egg yolk and vanilla. Combine flour and salt; gradually add to creamed mixture. Cover and refrigerate for 2 hours. Roll into 1-in. balls. In a small bowl, beat egg white. Dip balls in egg white, then roll in peanuts. Place 2 in. apart on ungreased baking sheets.

2 Bake at 350° for 5 minutes. Remove from oven; using the end of a wooden spoon handle, make an indentation in the center of each. Bake 7-9 minutes longer or until firm. Remove to wire racks to cool. Fill centers with vanilla frosting and top with M&M's.

Yield: about 2 dozen.

ALOHA BRITTLE

marylyn richardson, windermere, british columbia

A vacation to Hawaii inspired me to create this mouth-watering brittle. Coconuts, macadamia nuts and pecans make my tropical-tasting recipe deliciously different.

- 2 teaspoons butter, *divided*
- 1/2 cup flaked coconut
- 1 cup sugar
- 1/2 cup light corn syrup
- 1 jar (3-1/4 ounces) macadamia nuts
- 1/2 cup chopped pecans
- 1 teaspoon baking soda
- 1 teaspoon water
- 1 teaspoon vanilla extract

1 Butter a large baking sheet with 1 teaspoon butter. Sprinkle coconut in a 12-in. circle on the prepared pan. In a large heavy saucepan, combine sugar and corn syrup. Cook over medium heat until a candy thermometer reads 240° (soft-ball stage), stirring constantly. Stir in the macadamia nuts, pecans and remaining butter; cook and stir until the mixture reads 300° (hard-crack stage).

2 Combine the baking soda, water and vanilla. Remove saucepan from the heat; stir in the baking soda mixture. Quickly pour over the coconut. Cool before breaking into pieces. Store in an airtight container with waxed paper between layers.

Yield: 1 pound.

Editor's Note: We recommend that you test your candy thermometer before each use by bringing water to a boil; the thermometer should read 212°. Adjust your recipe temperature up or down based on your test.

BUTTER BRICKLE BISCOTTI

darlene brenden, salem, oregon

These twice-baked toffee cookies are a must with coffee at Christmastime. They also make great gifts from the kitchen.

- 1/2   cup butter, softened
- 1/2   cup sugar
- 1/4   cup packed brown sugar
-   3   eggs
-   2   teaspoons vanilla extract
-   3   cups all-purpose flour
-   2   teaspoons baking powder
- 1/4   teaspoon salt
-   1   package (7-1/2 or 8 ounces) English toffee bits or almond brickle chips

1   In a large bowl, cream butter and sugars until light and fluffy. Add eggs, one at a time, beating well after each addition. Beat in vanilla. Combine the flour, baking powder and salt; gradually add to creamed mixture and mix well. Stir in toffee bits.

2   Divide dough in half. On a parchment paper-lined baking sheet, shape each portion into a 10-in. x 2-1/2-in. rectangle. Cover and refrigerate for 30 minutes.

3   Bake at 350° for 30-35 minutes or until golden brown. Cool for 10 minutes. Transfer to a cutting board; cut diagonally with a serrated knife into 1/2-in. slices.

4   Place slices cut side down on ungreased baking sheets. Bake for 20-24 minutes or until golden brown, turning once. Remove to wire racks to cool. Store in an airtight container.

Yield: about 2-1/2 dozen.

OATMEAL KISS COOKIES

anna mary knier, mount joy, pennsylvania

This is a nice change from the usual peanut butter cookie. Children really enjoy placing the kisses on top.

- 1/2   cup butter, softened
- 1/2   cup shortening
-   1   cup sugar
-   1   cup packed brown sugar
-   2   eggs
-   2   cups all-purpose flour
-   1   teaspoon baking soda
-   1   teaspoon salt
- 2-1/4 cups quick-cooking oats
-   1   cup chopped nuts
- 72   milk chocolate kisses

1   In a large bowl, cream the butter, shortening and sugars until light and fluffy. Add eggs, one at a time, beating well after each addition. Combine the flour, baking soda and salt; gradually add to creamed mixture and mix well. Stir in oats and nuts. Roll into 1-in. balls. Place 2 in. apart on un-greased baking sheets.

2   Bake at 375° for 10-12 minutes or until lightly browned. Immediately press a chocolate kiss in the center of each cookie. Remove to wire racks.

Yield: 6 dozen.

MOCHA COOKIE PRETZELS

taste of home test kitchen
Looking for a little something special to bake up for the holidays? Try these elegant mocha-frosted cookies our Test Kitchen created. They're wonderful with coffee and make an eye-catching addition to any cookie platter.

- 1/2 cup butter, softened
- 1/2 cup sugar
- 1 egg
- 2 squares (1 ounce *each*) unsweetened chocolate, melted and cooled
- 1 teaspoon vanilla extract
- 2 cups cake flour
- 1/4 teaspoon salt

GLAZE:
- 1 cup (6 ounces) semisweet chocolate chips
- 1 teaspoon shortening
- 1 teaspoon light corn syrup
- 1 cup confectioners' sugar
- 3 to 5 tablespoons hot brewed coffee
- 2 squares (1 ounce *each*) white baking chocolate, chopped

Green colored sugar, optional

1 In a large bowl, cream butter and sugar until light and fluffy. Beat in egg. Beat in melted chocolate and vanilla. Combine flour and salt; gradually add to the creamed mixture and mix well. Cover and refrigerate for 1 hour or until dough is easy to handle.

2 Divide dough into fourths; divide each portion into 12 pieces. Shape each piece into a 6-in. rope; twist into a pretzel shape. Place 1 in. apart onto lightly greased baking sheets.

3 Bake at 400° for 7-9 minutes or until set. Remove to wire racks to cool.

4 For glaze, in a microwave, melt the semisweet chips, shortening and corn syrup; stir until smooth. Stir in confectioners' sugar and enough coffee to achieve a glaze consistency. Dip cookies in glaze; allow excess to drip off. Place on waxed paper until set.

5 In a microwave, melt white chocolate over 30% power; stir until smooth. Drizzle over cookies. Decorate with red or green sprinkles if desired; let stand until set.

Yield: 4 dozen.

COCONUT CRANBERRY BARS

dolly mcdonald, edmonton, alberta
I begged a neighbor for the recipe after tasting these yummy bars at a get-together she hosted. The colors make them real eye-pleasers, too!

- 1-1/2 cups graham cracker crumbs (about 24 squares)
- 1/2 cup butter, melted
- 1-1/2 cups vanilla *or* white chips
- 1-1/2 cups dried cranberries
- 1 can (14 ounces) sweetened condensed milk
- 1 cup flaked coconut
- 1 cup pecan halves

1 In a small bowl, combine the cracker crumbs and butter until crumbly; press into a greased 13-in. x 9-in. x 2-in. baking pan. In a large bowl, combine the remaining ingredients.

2 Gently spread over crust. Bake at 350° for 25-28 minutes or until edges are golden brown. Cool on a wire rack. Cut into bars.

Yield: 3 dozen.

OLD-FASHIONED MOLASSES CANDY

laurie pester, colstrip, montana

This hard candy was always the first thing to sell out at fund-raisers we held back when I was in high school. I still make the melt-in-your-mouth morsels every Christmas, and they're much appreciated.

    3 tablespoons butter, softened, *divided*
    1 cup sugar
 3/4 cup light corn syrup
    2 teaspoons cider vinegar
 3/4 cup molasses
 1/4 teaspoon baking soda

1 Grease a 15-in. x 10-in. x 1-in. pan with 1 table-spoon butter; set aside. In a heavy saucepan, combine sugar, corn syrup and vinegar. Cook over low heat until sugar is dissolved, stirring frequently. Increase heat to medium; cook until a candy thermometer reads 245° (firm-ball stage), stirring occasionally. Add molasses and remaining butter. Cook, uncovered, until a candy thermometer reads 260° (hard-ball stage), stirring occasionally. Remove from the heat. Add the baking soda; beat well.

2 Pour into prepared pan. Let stand for 5 minutes or until cool enough to handle. Butter fingers; quickly pull candy until firm but pliable (color will be light tan). When candy is ready for cutting, pull into a 1/2-in. rope. Cut into 1-in. pieces. Wrap each in waxed paper or colored candy wrappers.

Yield: 1-1/2 pounds.

Editor's Note: We recommend that you test your candy thermometer before each use by bringing water to a boil; the thermometer should read 212°. Adjust your recipe temperature up or down based on your test.

PUMPKIN PECAN TASSIES

pat habiger, spearville, kansas

These delicious mini tarts are lovely for Christmas or to serve at a tea. They're worth the extra time it takes to make them.

 1/2 cup butter, softened
    1 package (3 ounces) cream cheese, softened
    1 cup all-purpose flour
FILLING:
 3/4 cup packed brown sugar, *divided*
 1/4 cup canned pumpkin
    4 teaspoons plus 1 tablespoon butter, melted, *divided*
    1 egg yolk
    1 tablespoon half-and-half cream
    1 teaspoon vanilla extract
 1/4 teaspoon rum extract
 1/8 teaspoon ground cinnamon
 1/8 teaspoon ground nutmeg
 1/2 cup chopped pecans

1 In a small mixing bowl, cream butter and cream cheese. Beat in flour. Shape into 24 balls. With floured fingers, press onto the bottom and up the sides of greased miniature muffin cups.

2 Bake at 325° for 8-10 minutes or until edges are lightly browned.

3 Meanwhile, in a bowl, combine 1/2 cup brown sugar, pumpkin, 4 teaspoons butter, egg yolk, cream, extracts, cinnamon and nutmeg. Spoon into warm cups. Combine the pecans and remaining brown sugar and butter; sprinkle over filling.

4 Bake 23-27 minutes longer or until set and edges are golden brown. Cool for 10 minutes before removing from pans to wire racks.

Yield: 2 dozen.

GINGERBREAD BOY COOKIES

donna sasser hinds, milwaukie, oregon

Mom always used the same round-headed cookie cutter to make her "boys." They always came out of the oven soft and chewy with plenty of traditional molasses-ginger flavor.

- 1/2 cup butter, cubed
- 1/2 cup sugar
- 1/2 cup molasses
-   2 teaspoons white vinegar
-   1 egg, lightly beaten
-   3 cups all-purpose flour
- 1/2 teaspoon baking soda
- 1/2 teaspoon ground ginger
- 1/2 teaspoon ground cinnamon
- 1/4 teaspoon salt

1 In a saucepan, combine the butter, sugar, molasses and vinegar; bring to a boil, stirring constantly. Remove from the heat; cool to lukewarm. Stir in egg. Combine the flour, baking soda, ginger, cinnamon and salt; stir into molasses mixture to form a soft dough.

2 Divide dough into thirds. Shape each portion into a disk; wrap in plastic wrap. Refrigerate for at least 2 hours or until easy to handle.

3 On a lightly floured surface, roll dough to 1/4-in. thickness. Cut with a floured 3-in. gingerbread boy cookie cutter. Place on greased baking sheets. Bake at 375° for 7-9 minutes or until edges are firm. Remove to wire racks.

Yield: 3-4 dozen.

PEANUT BUTTER PINWHEELS

kandy dick, junction, texas

These doubly delightful pinwheel cookies are very easy to prepare. They feature the classic combination of peanut butter and chocolate in an attractive swirl.

- 1/2 cup shortening
- 1/2 cup creamy peanut butter
-   1 cup sugar
-   1 egg
-   2 tablespoons milk
- 1-1/4 cups all-purpose flour
- 1/2 teaspoon baking soda
- 1/2 teaspoon salt
-   1 cup (6 ounces) semisweet chocolate chips

1 In a mixing bowl, cream shortening, peanut butter and sugar. Beat in egg and milk. Combine the flour, baking soda and salt; gradually add to creamed mixture.

2 Roll out between waxed paper into a 12-in. x 10-in. rectangle. Melt chocolate chips; cool slightly. Spread over dough to within 1/2 in. of edges. Roll up tightly, jelly-roll style, starting with a long side; wrap in plastic wrap. Refrigerate for 20-30 minutes or until easy to handle.

3 Unwrap dough and cut into 1/2-in. slices. Place 1 in. apart on greased baking sheets. Bake at 375° for 10-12 minutes or until edges are lightly browned. Remove to wire racks to cool.

Yield: about 4 dozen.

CARAMEL PRETZEL STICKS

mary bown, evanston, wyoming

Homemade caramel, smooth almond bark and chopped nuts make these pretzel rods sinfully delicious. They're always a huge hit at holiday parties. People think you spent all day in the kitchen!

- 2 cups sugar
- 1 cup light corn syrup
- 1 cup butter, cubed
- 1 can (14 ounces) sweetened condensed milk
- 1 package (10 ounces) pretzel rods
- 6 to 12 ounces white candy coating
- 6 to 12 ounces milk chocolate candy coating
- 3/4 cup finely chopped walnuts, optional

1 In a large heavy saucepan, combine the sugar, corn syrup and butter. Bring just to a boil over medium heat, stirring constantly. Continue boiling, without stirring, at a moderate-steady rate for 4 minutes. Remove from the heat; stir in milk. Return to the heat. Reduce to medium-low; cook and stir until a candy thermometer reads 245° (firm-ball stage). Keep warm.

2 Pour 2 cups caramel mixture into a 2-cup glass measuring cup. Quickly dip each pretzel halfway into caramel. Allow excess to drip off. Place on well-buttered baking sheets; let stand until hardened.

3 In a microwave-safe bowl or measuring cup, melt white candy coating. Dip half of the caramel coated pretzels into coating. Melt milk chocolate coating; dip remaining pretzels. Drizzle white coated pretzels with milk chocolate coating; drizzle milk chocolate-coated pretzels with white coating. Sprinkle with walnuts if desired. Store in an airtight container.

Yield: about 2-1/2 dozen.

Editor's Note: We recommend that you test your candy thermometer before each use by bringing water to a boil; the thermometer should read 212°. Adjust your recipe temperature up or down based on your test. Any remaining caramel mixture may be poured into a well-buttered 8-in. x 4-in. x 2-in. loaf pan. Cool to room temperature before cutting into squares and wrapping in waxed paper.

COLORFUL CANDY BAR COOKIES

taste of home test kitchen

No one will guess these sweet treats with the candy bar center start with store-bought dough. Roll them in colored sugar, or just dip the tops for even faster assembly.

- 1/2 tube refrigerated sugar cookie dough, softened
- 1/4 cup all-purpose flour
- 24 miniature Snickers candy bars

Red and green colored sugar

1 In a small bowl, beat cookie dough and flour until combined. Shape 1-1/2 teaspoonfuls of dough around each candy bar. Roll in colored sugar.

2 Place 2 in. apart on parchment paper-lined baking sheets. Bake at 350° for 10-12 minutes or until edges are golden brown. Remove cookies to wire racks.

Yield: 2 dozen.

EVERGREEN SANDWICH COOKIES

evelyn moll, tulsa, oklahoma
A fluffy vanilla filling makes these cookies a big holiday favorite at our house. My family also likes their rich shortbread flavor.

- 1 cup butter, softened
- 2 cups all-purpose flour
- 1/3 cup milk
- 1/4 teaspoon salt

FILLING:
- 1/4 cup shortening
- 1/4 cup butter, softened
- 2 cups confectioners' sugar
- 4-1/2 teaspoons milk
- 1/2 teaspoon vanilla extract
- Green paste food coloring

GLAZE:
- 1-1/3 cups confectioners' sugar
- 4 teaspoons milk
- Green paste food coloring
- Green colored sugar

1 In a large mixing bowl, combine the butter, flour, milk and salt. Cover and refrigerate for 1-1/2 hours or until easy to handle.

2 Divide dough into thirds. On a floured surface, roll out each portion to 1/8-in. thickness. Cut with a 3-3/4-in. Christmas tree cookie cutter. Place on ungreased baking sheets. Prick each with a fork several times. Bake at 375° for 8-11 minutes or until set. Remove to wire racks.

3 For filling, in a small mixing bowl, cream the shortening, butter and confectioners' sugar. Add milk and vanilla. Tint with food coloring. Spread about a tablespoon each over half of the cookies; top with remaining cookies.

4 For glaze, combine confectioners' sugar and milk until smooth; set aside 1/4 cup. Stir food coloring into remaining glaze; spread a thin layer over cooled cookies. If desired, sprinkle tops of half of the cookies with colored sugar. Let stand until set. Pipe garland onto half of the cookies with reserved glaze. Let stand until set.

Yield: about 2 dozen.

CHERRY ALMOND BARS

ruth ann stelfox, raymond, alberta
A sweet Japanese lady I used to work for gave me this recipe. It is so easy to make and so festive-looking—and wonderfully delicious.

- 2 cups all-purpose flour
- 1/2 cup packed brown sugar
- 1 cup cold butter
- 1 cup golden raisins
- 1 cup chopped red and/or green maraschino cherries
- 1 cup sliced almonds
- 1 can (14 ounces) sweetened condensed milk

1 In a large bowl, combine flour and brown sugar; cut in butter until crumbly. Press into an ungreased 15-in. x 10-in. x 1-in. baking pan. Bake at 325° for 12-14 minutes or until lightly browned.

2 Sprinkle with raisins, cherries and almonds; drizzle with milk. Bake 25-30 minutes longer or until golden brown. Cool on a wire rack. Cut into squares.

Yield: 4 dozen.

TRIPLE-NUT CANDY

ardis gatons olson, brookings, south dakota

I've been making homemade candy for years. Family and friends look forward to this caramel and nut sweet treat each Christmas.

- 1 cup walnut halves
- 1 cup pecan halves
- 1 cup Brazil nuts, halved
- 1 teaspoon butter
- 1-1/2 cups sugar
- 1 cup heavy whipping cream
- 1/2 cup light corn syrup

1 Place the walnuts, pecans and Brazil nuts in a single layer on a baking sheet. Bake at 350° for 4-8 minutes or until toasted and golden brown, stirring once. Cool on a wire rack. Line an 8-in. square pan with foil; grease the foil with butter and set aside.

2 In a large heavy saucepan, combine the sugar, cream and corn syrup. Bring to a boil over medium heat, stirring constantly. Stir in the toasted nuts. Cook, without stirring, until a candy thermometer reads 238° (soft-ball stage).

3 Remove from the heat. Stir with a wooden spoon until creamy and thickened. Quickly spread into prepared pan; cool. Cover and refrigerate for 8 hours or overnight.

4 Using foil, lift candy out of pan; discard foil. Cut candy into squares. Store in an airtight container in the refrigerator.

Yield: 2 pounds.

Editor's Note: We recommend that you test your candy thermometer before each use by bringing water to a boil; the thermometer should read 212°. Adjust your recipe temperature up or down based on your test.

FRUIT-AND-CHEESE BARS

tina hagen, emo, ontario

One pan of these rich bars goes a long way. Colorful candied fruit makes it especially festive.

- 1/2 cup butter, softened
- 1/2 cup packed brown sugar
- 1 cup all-purpose flour
- 1 package (8 ounces) cream cheese, softened
- 1/4 cup sugar
- 1 egg
- 1 tablespoon lemon juice
- 1/2 cup chopped mixed candied fruit

1 In a small bowl, cream butter and brown sugar until light and fluffy. Add flour; beat until crumbly. Set aside 1/2 cup for topping.

2 Press remaining crumb mixture into a greased 8-in. square baking dish. Bake at 350° for 10-12 minutes or until lightly browned.

3 Meanwhile, in a large bowl, beat cream cheese and sugar until smooth. Beat in the egg and lemon juice. Stir in candied fruit. Spread over crust; sprinkle with reserved crumb mixture.

4 Bake 18-20 minutes longer or until firm. Cool on a wire rack. Store in the refrigerator.

Yield: About 2-1/2 dozen.

PECAN CHOCOLATE PUDDLES

joyce kutzler, clinton, minnesota

Since my grandchildren like frosted cookies, I came up with this chocolate-topped version that satisfies them and is almost fuss-free for me. I have used the recipe for years and now make them for my great-grandchildren.

- 1/2 cup butter, softened
- 1 cup packed brown sugar
- 1 egg
- 1 teaspoon vanilla extract
- 1 cup all-purpose flour
- 1/2 cup quick-cooking oats
- 1/2 teaspoon salt
- 1/2 teaspoon baking powder
- 1 cup chopped pecans
- 1 cup (6 ounces) miniature semisweet chocolate chips

FILLING:

- 1 cup (6 ounces) semisweet chocolate chips
- 1/2 cup sweetened condensed milk
- 48 pecan halves

1 In a mixing bowl, cream butter and brown sugar until light and fluffy. Beat in egg and vanilla. Combine the flour, oats, salt and baking powder; gradually add to creamed mixture. Stir in chopped pecans and miniature chocolate chips. In a saucepan, melt chocolate chips with milk; stir until smooth. Roll dough into 1-in. balls. Place 2 in. apart on ungreased baking sheets.

2 Using the end of a wooden spoon handle, make an indentation in the center of each ball. Fill with a rounded teaspoonful of melted chocolate; top with a pecan half. Bake at 350° for 14-16 minutes or until the edges are lightly browned. Remove to wire racks to cool.

Yield: 4 dozen.

CHERRY BONBON COOKIES

pat habiger, spearville, kansas

This is a very old recipe from my grandma. The cherry filling surprises folks trying them for the first time.

- 1/2 cup butter, softened
- 3/4 cup confectioners' sugar
- 2 tablespoons milk
- 1 teaspoon vanilla extract
- 1-1/2 cups all-purpose flour
- 1/8 teaspoon salt
- 24 maraschino cherries

GLAZE:

- 1 cup confectioners' sugar
- 1 tablespoon butter, melted
- 2 tablespoons maraschino cherry juice

Additional confectioners' sugar

1 In a large mixing bowl, cream butter and sugar until light and fluffy. Add milk and vanilla. Combine the flour and salt; gradually add to the creamed mixture.

2 Divide dough into 24 portions; shape each portion around a cherry, forming a ball. Place on ungreased baking sheets. Bake at 350° for 18-20 minutes or until lightly browned. Remove to wire racks to cool.

3 For glaze, combine the sugar, butter and cherry juice until smooth. Drizzle over cookies. Dust with confectioners' sugar.

Yield: 2 dozen.

CHERRY BROWNIE CUPS

rebecca brown, cumberland, maryland

I like to lavish the chocolate lovers on my gift list with small Christmas tins of these cheery, cherry-topped treats.

- 3/4 **cup butter, cubed**
- 2 **squares (1 ounce *each*) unsweetened chocolate, chopped**
- 2 **cups sugar**
- 4 **eggs**
- 1 **teaspoon vanilla extract**
- 1 **cup all-purpose flour**

FUDGE FILLING:

- 1 **package (3 ounces) cream cheese, softened**
- 1 **teaspoon vanilla extract**
- 1/4 **cup corn syrup**
- 1-1/2 **squares (1.5 ounces) unsweetened chocolate, melted and cooled**
- 1 **cup confectioners' sugar**
- 1 **jar (10 ounces) maraschino cherries with stems, drained and patted dry**

1 In a microwave, melt butter and chocolate until melted. Stir in sugar until dissolved. Transfer to a large bowl. Add eggs, one at a time, beating well after each addition. Beat in vanilla. Gradually stir in flour and mix well.

2 Fill paper-lined miniature muffin cups two-thirds full. Bake at 350° for 20-22 minutes or until a toothpick comes out clean. Cool for 5 minutes.

3 With the end of a wooden spoon handle, make a 1/2-in. indentation in the top of each brownie; remove from pans to wire racks to cool completely.

4 For filling, in a large bowl, beat cream cheese and vanilla until smooth. Beat in corn syrup and melted chocolate until well blended. Add confectioners' sugar and beat until smooth. Spoon 1 teaspoon of filling in the center of each brownie. Top with a cherry. Store in the refrigerator.

Yield: 5 dozen.

MINT SANDWICH COOKIES

taste of home test kitchen

Chocolate-covered mint candies are the filling in these doctored-up sugar cookies from our Test Kitchen. You can use different colors of sugar to suit the season.

- 1 **tube (18 ounces) refrigerated sugar cookie dough, softened**
- 1/4 **cup all-purpose flour**
- 1/8 **teaspoon peppermint extract**

Coarse sugar

- 40 **chocolate-covered thin mints**

1 In a large bowl, beat the cookie dough, flour and extract until blended. Roll into 1/2-in. balls.

2 Place 2 in. apart on greased baking sheets. Coat the bottom of a glass with cooking spray, then dip in coarse sugar. Flatten balls with prepared glass to 1/4-in. thickness, dipping in additional sugar as needed.

3 Bake at 350° for 7-9 minutes or until set. Carefully remove one cookie from baking sheet. Immediately turn cookie over and place a mint on the bottom of the cookie; top with another cookie, pressing lightly. Repeat with remaining cookies and mints. Cool on wire racks.

Yield: 40 cookies.

FUDGE-FILLED TOFFEE COOKIES

karen barto, churchville, virginia

I combined three recipes to come up with these crisp cookies topped with a sweet chocolate center. They're a nice addition to a holiday cookie tray.

- 1/2 cup butter, softened
- 1/2 cup sugar
- 1/2 cup confectioners' sugar
- 1/2 cup canola oil
- 1 egg
- 1/2 teaspoon almond extract
- 1/4 teaspoon coconut extract
- 1-3/4 cups all-purpose flour
- 1/2 cup whole wheat flour
- 1/2 teaspoon salt
- 1/2 teaspoon baking soda
- 1/2 teaspoon cream of tartar
- 3/4 cup English toffee bits *or* almond brickle chips
- 2/3 cup chopped pecans
- 2/3 cup flaked coconut

Additional sugar

FILLING:

- 1-1/2 cups semisweet chocolate chips, melted
- 3/4 cup sweetened condensed milk
- 1-1/2 teaspoons vanilla extract
- 1-1/4 cups pecan halves

1 In a large bowl, cream butter and sugars until light and fluffy. Beat in the oil, egg and extracts. Combine the flours, salt, baking soda and cream of tartar; gradually add to the creamed mixture and mix well. Stir in the toffee bits, pecans and coconut. Cover and refrigerate for 1 hour or until easy to handle.

2 Shape dough into 1-in. balls; roll in sugar. Place 2 in. apart on ungreased baking sheets. Using the end of a wooden spoon handle, make an indentation in the center of each.

3 In a large bowl, combine melted chocolate, milk and vanilla until smooth. Spoon 1 teaspoon into the center of each cookie. Top with a pecan half.

4 Bake at 350° for 12-14 minutes or until lightly browned. Remove to wire racks to cool.

Yield: 5-1/2 dozen.

PISTACHIO CRANBERRY BARK

susan wacek, pleasanton, california

This bark is divine! I was quick to ask for the recipe after tasting it at a holiday cookie candy exchange. For a lovely gift, fill a plate or cup with bark, gather up clear cellophane around it and tie with red and green satin ribbons. Friends and family will appreciate your thoughtfulness.

- 2 cups (12 ounces) semisweet chocolate chips
- 5 ounces white candy coating, chopped
- 1 cup chopped pistachios, toasted, *divided*
- 3/4 cup dried cranberries, *divided*

1 In a microwave-safe bowl, melt chocolate chips; stir until smooth. Repeat with candy coating. Stir 3/4 cup pistachios and half of the cranberries into semisweet chocolate. Thinly spread onto a waxed paper-lined baking sheet.

2 Drizzle with candy coating. Cut through with a knife to swirl. Sprinkle with remaining pistachios and cranberries. Chill until firm. Break into pieces. Store in an airtight container in the refrigerator.

Yield: about 1 pound.

APRICOT WHITE FUDGE

debbie purdue, westland, michigan

This fudge has become a family favorite because of the luscious blending of flavors. I often make it for gifts at Christmastime. Use a candy thermometer to be sure the mixture reaches soft-ball stage; then chill until set.

- 1-1/2 teaspoons plus 1/2 cup butter, *divided*
-     2 cups sugar
-   3/4 cup sour cream
-    12 squares (1 ounce *each*) white baking chocolate, chopped
-     1 jar (7 ounces) marshmallow creme
-   3/4 cup chopped dried apricots
-   3/4 cup chopped walnuts

1   Line a 9-in. square pan with foil and grease with 1-1/2 teaspoons butter; set aside. In a heavy saucepan, combine sugar, sour cream and remaining butter. Bring to a boil over medium heat, stirring constantly. Cook and stir until a candy thermometer reads 234° (soft-ball stage), about 5-1/2 minutes.

2   Remove from the heat. Stir in chocolate until melted. Stir in marshmallow creme until blended. Fold in apricots and walnuts. Pour into prepared pan. Cover and refrigerate overnight. Using foil, lift fudge out of pan. Discard foil; cut fudge into 1-in. squares.

Yield: about 2 pounds.

Editor's Note: We recommend that you test your candy thermometer before each use by bringing water to a boil; the thermometer should read 212°. Adjust your recipe temperature up or down based on your test.

CHERRY ICEBOX COOKIES

patty courtney, jonesboro, texas

The maraschino cherries add colorful flecks to these slice-and-bake cookies.

-     1 cup butter, softened
-     1 cup sugar
-   1/4 cup packed brown sugar
-     1 egg
-     1 teaspoon vanilla extract
- 3-1/4 cups all-purpose flour
-   1/2 teaspoon baking soda
-   1/2 teaspoon ground cinnamon
-   1/4 teaspoon cream of tartar
-   1/4 cup maraschino cherry juice
- 4-1/2 teaspoons lemon juice
-   1/2 cup chopped walnuts
-   1/2 cup chopped maraschino cherries

1   In a large bowl, cream butter and sugars until light and fluffy. Beat in egg and vanilla. Combine dry ingredients; gradually add to creamed mixture and mix well. Beat in cherry and lemon juices. Stir in nuts and the cherries.

2   Shape into four 12-in. rolls; wrap each in plastic wrap. Refrigerate for 4 hours or until firm.

3   Unwrap and cut into 1/4-in. slices. Place 2 in. apart on ungreased baking sheets. Bake at 375° for 8-10 minutes or until the edges begin to brown. Remove to wire racks to cool.

Yield: about 6 dozen.

CHOCOLATE PECAN BARS

carole fraser, north york, ontario

These chewy, chocolaty bars are a hit at Thanksgiving or Christmas...and always enjoyed by everyone. They're easy to prepare and yield a big batch. We find them simply irresistible!

- 2/3 cup butter, softened
- 1/3 cup sugar
- 2 cups all-purpose flour

FILLING:

- 6 squares (1 ounce *each*) semisweet chocolate
- 1-1/4 cups light corn syrup
- 1-1/4 cups sugar
- 4 eggs, lightly beaten
- 1-1/4 teaspoons vanilla extract
- 2-1/4 cups chopped pecans

GLAZE:

- 4 squares (1 ounce *each*) semisweet chocolate
- 1-1/4 teaspoons shortening

1. In a small bowl, cream butter and sugar until light and fluffy. Beat in flour. Press into a greased 15-in. x 10-in. x 1-in. baking pan. Bake at 350° for 12-15 minutes or until golden brown.

2. Meanwhile, in a large saucepan, melt chocolate with corn syrup over low heat; stir until smooth. Remove from the heat. Stir in the sugar, eggs and vanilla. Add pecans.

3. Spread evenly over hot crust. Bake for 25-30 minutes or until firm around the edges. Cool on a wire rack.

4. In a microwave, melt chocolate and shortening; stir until smooth. Drizzle over bars.

Yield: 4 dozen.

FAVORITE SUGAR COOKIES

judith scholovich, waukesha, wisconsin

I've been delighting my children and grandchildren for years with this special recipe. These cookies are good throughout the year.

- 1 cup butter, softened
- 1 cup confectioners' sugar
- 1 egg
- 1-1/2 teaspoons almond extract
- 1 teaspoon vanilla extract
- 2-1/2 cups all-purpose flour
- 1 teaspoon salt

FROSTING:

- 6 tablespoons butter, softened
- 3 cups confectioners' sugar
- 1 teaspoon vanilla extract
- 2 to 4 tablespoons milk

Food coloring of your choice, optional

Colored sugar of your choice, optional

1. In a large bowl, cream butter and confectioners' sugar until light and fluffy. Beat in egg and extracts. Combine flour and salt; add to creamed mixture and mix well. Chill for 1-2 hours.

2. On a lightly floured surface, roll dough to 1/8-in. thickness. Cut with 2-1/2-in. cookie cutters. Place on greased baking sheets. Bake at 375° for 7-9 minutes or until lightly browned. Remove to wire racks to cool.

3. For frosting, in a small bowl, combine the butter, sugar, vanilla and enough milk to achieve a spreading consistency. Tint with food coloring if desired. Frost cookies; sprinkle with colored sugar if desired.

Yield: 6-7 dozen.

LAYERED MINT FUDGE

denise hanson, anoka, minnesota

I make this festive fudge year-round, but especially at Christmastime. I've brought it to many different occasions, and I am asked for the recipe every time. I also entered it in our local fair and won the coveted blue ribbon!

1-1/2 teaspoons butter, softened
   2 cups (12 ounces) semisweet chocolate chips
   1 can (14 ounces) sweetened condensed milk, *divided*
   2 teaspoons vanilla extract
   1 cup vanilla or white chips
   3 teaspoons peppermint extract
   1 to 2 drops green food coloring

1 Line a 9-in. square pan with foil; grease the foil with butter and set aside. In a heavy saucepan, melt chocolate chips and 1 cup milk over low heat; cook and stir for 5-6 minutes or until smooth. Remove from the heat. Add vanilla; stir for 3-4 minutes or until creamy. Spread half of the mixture into the prepared pan. Refrigerate for 10 minutes or until firm. Set the remaining chocolate mixture aside.

2 In a heavy saucepan, melt vanilla chips and remaining milk over low heat; cook and stir for 5-6 minutes or until smooth (mixture will be thick). Remove from the heat. Add peppermint extract and food coloring; stir for 3-4 minutes or until creamy. Spread evenly over chocolate layer. Refrigerate for 10 minutes or until firm.

3 Heat reserved chocolate mixture over low heat until mixture achieves spreading consistency; spread over mint layer. Cover and refrigerate overnight or until firm.

4 Using foil, lift fudge out of pan. Gently peel off foil; cut fudge into 1-in. squares. Store in the refrigerator.

Yield: 1-3/4 pounds.

CHOCOLATE PEANUT BUTTER GRAHAMS

geraldine sliwa, elgin, illinois

Because so many people seem to love the combination of chocolate and peanut butter, I came up with this no-bake cookie recipe.

   1 jar (18 ounces) peanut butter
   1 package (14.3 ounces) graham crackers, broken into rectangles
1-1/2 pounds milk chocolate candy coating

1 Spread a rounded teaspoonful of peanut butter on one side of half of the graham crackers. Top with remaining crackers.

2 In a microwave, melt candy coating; stir until smooth. Dip cookies in coating to completely cover; allow excess to drip off.

3 Place on waxed paper-lined baking sheets; let stand until set. Store in an airtight container in a cool dry place.

Yield: 5 dozen.

CARAMEL MARSHMALLOW TREATS

tamara holschen, anchor point, alaska

I created this candy by combining my husband's favorite cookie recipe and my mom's caramel dip. These sweets really appeal to kids. Plus, they can help make them.

    5 cups crisp rice cereal, coarsely crushed
    1 can (14 ounces) sweetened condensed milk
    1 package (14 ounces) caramels
    1 cup butter, cubed
    1 teaspoon ground cinnamon
 1/2 teaspoon vanilla extract
    1 package (16 ounces) large marshmallows

1 Line two baking sheets with waxed paper; set aside. Place cereal in a shallow bowl. In a large saucepan, cook and stir the milk, caramels and butter over low heat until melted and smooth. Remove from heat; stir in cinnamon and vanilla.

2 With a toothpick, dip each marshmallow into warm caramel mixture; turn to coat. Press marshmallow bottoms in cereal; place on prepared pans. Let stand until set.

Yield: 5 dozen.

COCONUT CRUNCH COOKIES

maria regakis, somerville, massachusetts

These sweet drop cookies are loaded with coconut and chocolate chips. Their crisp edges and soft centers add up to a perfect cookie.

    1 cup butter, softened
 3/4 cup sugar
 3/4 cup packed brown sugar
    2 eggs
    2 teaspoons vanilla extract
    1 teaspoon almond extract
    2 cups all-purpose flour
    1 teaspoon baking soda
 3/4 teaspoon salt
    2 cups flaked coconut
    1 package (11-1/2 ounces) milk chocolate chips
1-1/2 cups finely chopped almonds

1 In a large bowl, cream butter and sugars until light and fluffy. Beat in eggs and extracts. Combine the flour, baking soda and salt; gradually add to creamed mixture and mix well. Stir in the coconut, chocolate chips and almonds.

2 Drop by rounded teaspoonfuls 2 in. apart onto ungreased baking sheets. Bake at 375° for 9-11 minutes or until lightly browned. Cool for 1 minute before removing from pans to wire racks.

Yield: about 4-1/2 dozen.

CRANBERRY GUMDROPS

elaine thu, graettinger, iowa

This unique treat combines two holiday favorites—the tangy flavor of cranberry and a sweet chewy candy. I've made them for years. They're popular with all ages.

- 2 envelopes unflavored gelatin
- 1/2 cup cold water
- 1 can (16 ounces) jellied cranberry sauce
- 2 cups sugar, *divided*
- 3 packages (3 ounces *each*) raspberry gelatin

Additional sugar, optional

1 In a saucepan, sprinkle unflavored gelatin over water; let stand for 2 minutes to soften. Add cranberry sauce and 1 cup of sugar; cook over low heat until sauce is melted and sugar is dissolved, about 10 minutes. Whisk until smooth.

2 Remove from the heat and add raspberry gelatin; stir until completely dissolved, about 3 minutes. Pour into an 8-in. square dish coated with cooking spray. Cover and let stand at room temperature for 12 hours or overnight (do not refrigerate).

3 Cut into 1-in. squares; roll in remaining sugar. Place on baking sheets; let stand at room temperature for 3 hours. Turn pieces over and let stand 3 hours longer. Roll in additional sugar if desired. Store in an airtight container at room temperature.

Yield: about 5 dozen.

BUTTER BALL CHIFFONS

myla harvey, stanton, michigan

The combination of lemon pudding and toffee candy bars sets these crisp cookies apart from all others. Keep the ingredients on hand for when you need a treat in a hurry.

- 1 cup butter, softened
- 1/4 cup confectioners' sugar
- 1 package (3.4 ounces) instant lemon pudding mix
- 2 teaspoons water
- 1 teaspoon vanilla extract
- 2 cups all-purpose flour
- 1 cup chopped pecans *or* walnuts
- 2 Heath candy bars (1.4 ounces *each*), chopped

1 In a small bowl, cream butter and confectioners' sugar until light and fluffy. Beat in the pudding mix, water and vanilla. Gradually add flour. Stir in nuts and chopped candy bars.

2 Roll into 1-in. balls. Place 2 in. apart on ungreased baking sheets. Bake at 325° for 12-15 minutes or until lightly browned. Cool for 3 minutes before removing to wire racks.

Yield: 5 dozen.

Editor's Note: This recipe does not use eggs.

FESTIVE SHORTBREAD LOGS

michele fenner, girard, pennsylvania

I first made these rich and tender cookies as a teenager and now make them for my husband and our two sons. The smiles on their faces are well worth the time and effort.

        1 cup butter, softened
    1/2 cup confectioners' sugar
        1 teaspoon vanilla extract
        2 cups all-purpose flour
    1-1/2 cups semisweet chocolate chips
        4 teaspoons shortening
    3/4 cup ground walnuts

1   In a large bowl, cream butter and confectioners' sugar until light and fluffy. Add vanilla. Gradually add flour and mix well.

2   With lightly floured hands, shape tablespoonfuls into 2-in. logs. Place 2 in. apart on ungreased baking sheets. Bake at 350° for 9-11 minutes or until edges and bottom are lightly browned. Cool cookies for 2-3 minutes before removing to wire racks.

3   In a microwave, melt chocolate chips and shortening; stir until smooth. Drizzle chocolate over half of the cookies. Dip one end of remaining cookies into chocolate; allow excess to drip off. Sprinkle with walnuts. Place on waxed paper; let stand until set.

Yield: 4 dozen.

PEPPERMINT FUDGE

connie denmark, macon, illinois

Three of the season's best flavors—nuts, chocolate and peppermint—combine in a delightful manner in this scrumptious fudge. The two distinct layers are eye-catching, which is another reason why this candy makes a great holiday gift.

    1-1/2 teaspoons butter, softened
        2 ounces cream cheese, softened
        2 cups confectioners' sugar
        3 tablespoons baking cocoa
        1 teaspoon milk
    1/2 teaspoon vanilla extract
    1/4 cup chopped nuts

PEPPERMINT LAYER:

        2 ounces cream cheese, softened
        2 cups confectioners' sugar
    1-1/2 teaspoons milk
    1/2 teaspoon peppermint extract
    1/4 cup crushed peppermint candy

1   Line bottom and sides of an 8-in. x 4-in. loaf pan with foil. Grease foil with 1-1/2 teaspoons butter; set aside.

2   In a small bowl, beat cream cheese until creamy. Gradually beat in the confectioners' sugar, cocoa, milk and vanilla until smooth. Stir in nuts. Spread into prepared pan. Chill for 1 hour or until firm.

3   For peppermint layer, beat cream cheese in a small bowl until creamy. Gradually beat in confectioners' sugar, milk and extract until smooth. Stir in peppermint candy. Spread evenly over chocolate layer. Chill for 1 hour or until firm.

4   Using foil, lift fudge from pan. Gently peel off foil. Cut into squares.

Yield: 1-1/4 pounds.

CHOCOLATE-GLAZED ALMOND BARS

robin hart, north brunswick, new jersey

With a moist almond filling and a flaky golden crust, these bars are sure to be the perfect dessert for a Yuletide get-together.

- 2 cups all-purpose flour
- 1/2 cup packed brown sugar
- 1/2 teaspoon salt
- 3/4 cup cold butter
- 3 egg whites
- 1 cup sugar
- 1 can (12-1/2 ounces) almond cake and pastry filling
- 2 cups sliced almonds
- 4 squares (1 ounce *each*) bittersweet chocolate, melted

1 In a large bowl, combine the flour, brown sugar and salt. Cut in butter until mixture resembles coarse crumbs. Pat into a 13-in. x 9-in. baking pan coated with cooking spray. Bake at 350° for 18-22 minutes or until edges are lightly browned.

2 Meanwhile, in a large bowl, whisk the egg whites, sugar and almond filling until blended. Stir in almonds. Pour over crust. Bake for 20-25 minutes or until set. Cool completely on a wire rack.

3 Drizzle with chocolate. Cut into bars. Store in an airtight container in the refrigerator.

Yield: 40 bars.

Editor's Note: This recipe was tested with Solo brand cake and pastry filling. Look for it in the baking aisle.

PEPPERMINT MELTAWAYS

denise wheeler, newaygo, michigan

This recipe is very pretty and festive-looking on a cookie platter. I often cover a plate of these meltaways with red or green plastic wrap and a bright holiday bow in one corner. And yes, they really do melt in your mouth!

- 1 cup butter, softened
- 1/2 cup confectioners' sugar
- 1/2 teaspoon peppermint extract
- 1-1/4 cups all-purpose flour
- 1/2 cup cornstarch

FROSTING:

- 2 tablespoons butter, softened
- 1-1/2 cups confectioners' sugar
- 2 tablespoons milk
- 1/4 teaspoon peppermint extract
- 2 to 3 drops red food coloring, optional
- 1/2 cup crushed peppermint candies

1 In a small bowl, cream butter and confectioners' sugar until light and fluffy. Beat in extract. Combine flour and cornstarch; gradually add to creamed mixture and mix well.

2 Shape into 1-in. balls. Place 2 in. apart on ungreased baking sheets. Bake at 350° for 10-12 minutes or until bottoms are lightly browned. Remove to wire racks to cool.

3 In a small bowl, beat butter until fluffy. Add the confectioners' sugar, milk, extract and food coloring if desired; beat until smooth. Spread over the cooled cookies; sprinkle with the crushed candies. Store in an airtight container.

Yield: 3-1/2 dozen.

BUTTERSCOTCH HARD CANDY

edna hoffman, hebron, indiana

The old-fashioned flavor of these butterscotch candies appeals to kids of all ages. My family can't stop eating them!

        1   teaspoon plus 1/2 cup butter, softened, *divided*
        2   cups sugar
      1/4   cup light corn syrup
        2   tablespoons water
        2   tablespoons white vinegar

1   Line a 15-in. x 10-in. x 1-in. pan with foil. Grease the foil with 1 teaspoon butter; set aside.

2   In a heavy saucepan, combine the sugar, corn syrup, water, vinegar and remaining butter. Bring to a boil over medium heat, stirring occasionally. Cover and cook for 3 minutes to dissolve any sugar crystals.

3   Uncover; cook, without stirring, until a candy thermometer reads 300° (hard-crack stage). Remove from the heat. Pour into prepared pan without scraping the saucepan; do not spread mixture.

4   Cool for 1-2 minutes or until candy is almost set. Using a sharp knife, score into 1/2-in. squares; cool completely. Break squares apart. Store in an airtight container.

Yield: 1 pound.

Editor's Note: We recommend that you test your candy thermometer before each use by bringing water to a boil; the thermomeer should read 212°. Adjust your recipe temperature up or down based on your test.

JELLY-TOPPED SUGAR COOKIES

june quinn, kalamazoo, michigan

On busy days, I appreciate this fast-to-fix drop sugar cookie. Top each cookie with your favorite variety of jam or jelly.

      3/4   cup sugar
      3/4   cup canola oil
        2   eggs
        2   teaspoons vanilla extract
        1   teaspoon lemon extract
        1   teaspoon grated lemon peel
        2   cups all-purpose flour
        2   teaspoons baking powder
      1/2   teaspoon salt
    Additional sugar
      1/2   cup jam *or* jelly

1   In a large bowl, beat sugar and oil until blended. Beat in eggs, extracts and lemon peel. Combine the flour, baking powder, and salt; gradually add to sugar mixture and mix well.

2   Drop by rounded tablespoonfuls 2 in. apart onto ungreased baking sheets. Coat bottom of a glass with cooking spray, then dip in sugar. Flatten cookies with prepared glass, redipping in sugar as needed.

3   Place 1/4 teaspoon jelly in the center of each cookie. Bake at 400° for 8-10 minutes or until set. Remove to wire racks to cool.

Yield: about 3-1/2 dozen.

TERRIFIC TOFFEE

carol gillespie, chambersburg, pennsylvania

This buttery toffee is one of those must-make items my family requests for the holidays. You can also try substituting hazelnuts for the almonds.

1-1/2 teaspoons plus 1 cup butter, *divided*
   1 cup semisweet chocolate chips
   1 cup milk chocolate chips
   1 cup sugar
   3 tablespoons water
   2 cups coarsely chopped almonds, toasted, *divided*

1 Butter a large baking sheet with 1-1/2 teaspoons butter; set aside. In a small bowl, combine semisweet and milk chocolate chips; set aside.

2 In a heavy saucepan, combine the sugar, water and remaining butter. Cook and stir over medium heat until a candy thermometer reaches 290° (soft-crack stage). Remove from the heat; stir in 1 cup almonds. Immediately pour onto prepared baking sheet.

3 Sprinkle with chocolate chips; spread with a knife when melted. Sprinkle with remaining almonds.

Let stand until set, about 1 hour. Break into 2-in. pieces. Store in an airtight container.

Yield: about 2 pounds.

Editor's Note: We recommend that you test your candy thermometer before each use by bringing water to a boil; the thermometer should read 212°. Adjust your recipe temperature up or down based on your test.

RAISIN CASHEW DROPS

cheryl butler, lake placid, florida

At Christmas, I serve these bite-size chocolates in festive paper cups decorated with snowmen or Santas. They're easy to make, and my family loves the combination of salty and sweet.

   2 cups (12 ounces) semisweet chocolate chips
   1 can (14 ounces) sweetened condensed milk
   1 tablespoon light corn syrup
   1 teaspoon vanilla extract
   2 cups coarsely chopped cashews
   2 cups raisins

1 In a heavy saucepan over low heat, melt chocolate chips with milk and corn syrup for 10-12 minutes, stirring occasionally. Remove from the heat; stir in vanilla until blended. Stir in cashews and raisins.

2 Drop by teaspoonfuls onto waxed paper-lined baking sheets. Refrigerate for 3 hours or until firm. Store in the refrigerator.

Yield: 2-1/2 pounds.

SNOWMEN COOKIES

sherri johnson, burns, tennessee

These cute snowmen cookies make great treats for children's parties. Kids are always willing to chip in and help decorate them.

> 1 package (16 ounces) Nutter Butter cookies
> 1-1/4 pounds white candy coating, melted
> Miniature chocolate chips
> M&M's miniature baking bits
> Pretzel sticks, halved
> Orange and red decorating gel *or* frosting

1 Using tongs, dip cookies in candy coating; allow excess to drip off. Place on waxed paper. Place two chocolate chips on one end of cookies for eyes. Place baking bits down middle for buttons.

2 For arms, dip ends of two pretzel stick halves into coating; attach one to each side. Let stand until set. Pipe nose and scarf with gel or frosting.

Yield: 32 cookies.

SNOWCAPPED GINGERBREAD BISCOTTI

trisha kruse, eagle, idaho

These cookies are one of my favorites to add to the holiday cookie trays I prepare. They blend the great flavor of gingerbread and texture of biscotti.

> 1/3 cup butter, softened
> 1 cup packed brown sugar
> 1/4 cup molasses
> 3 eggs
> 3-1/4 cups all-purpose flour
> 3 teaspoons ground cinnamon
> 1 teaspoon ground nutmeg
> 1/2 teaspoon *each* baking powder and salt
> 1/2 teaspoon ground allspice
> 1/2 teaspoon ground cloves
> 1 cup hazelnuts, toasted and chopped
> 1/4 cup candied *or* crystallized ginger, finely chopped
> 1 cup butterscotch chips, melted
> 1 cup vanilla or white chips, melted

1 In a large mixing bowl, cream butter and brown sugar until light and fluffy. Beat in molasses. Add eggs, one at a time, beating well after each addition. Combine the flour, cinnamon, nutmeg, baking powder, salt, allspice and cloves; gradually add to creamed mixture and mix well. Stir in hazelnuts and ginger.

2 Divide dough in half. Cover and refrigerate for 30 minutes.

3 On a lightly floured surface, shape dough into two 10-in. x 3-in. logs. Transfer to greased baking sheets. Bake at 350° for 20-25 minutes or until lightly browned and firm to the touch.

4 Transfer to a cutting board; cut diagonally with a sharp knife into 1/2-in. slices. Place cut side down on greased baking sheets. Bake for 7-9 minutes on each side or until lightly browned. Remove to wire racks to cool.

5 Dip biscotti halfway into melted butterscotch chips; shake off excess. Place on waxed paper until set. Dip butterscotch-coated ends partially into melted vanilla chips; shake off excess. Place on waxed paper until set. Store biscotti in an airtight container.

Yield: 2-1/2 dozen.

POLKA-DOT MACAROONS

janice lass, dorr, michigan

These chewy cookies are really easy to mix up in a hurry, and they're a favorite with both adults and kids. I've been baking for 35 years, and believe me, these never last long.

> 5 cups flaked coconut
> 1 can (14 ounces) sweetened condensed milk
> 1/2 cup all-purpose flour
> 1-1/2 cups M&M's miniature baking bits

1 In a large bowl, combine the coconut, milk and flour. Stir in baking bits.

2 Drop by rounded tablespoonfuls 2 in. apart onto baking sheets coated with cooking spray. Bake at 350° for 8-10 minutes or until edges are lightly browned. Remove to wire racks.

Yield: about 4-1/2 dozen.

MACADAMIA NUT FUDGE

kristine sokowski, tremont, illinois

Family and friends look forward to this creamy treat every holiday season. The macadamia nuts make it extra special.

> 1 tablespoon plus 1 cup butter, *divided*
> 4-1/2 cups sugar
> 1 cup milk

> 36 large marshmallows
> 2 squares (1 ounce *each*) unsweetened chocolate, melted
> 4 cups (24 ounces) semisweet chocolate chips
> 1-1/2 cups chopped macadamia nuts
> 1 teaspoon vanilla extract

Vanilla frosting

Red and green paste food coloring

M&M's miniature baking bits

1 Line a 15-in. x 10-in. x 1-in. pan with foil. Grease the foil and 3-in. cookie cutters with 1 tablespoon butter. Place cookie cutters in pan; set pan aside.

2 In a large heavy saucepan, combine the sugar, milk and remaining butter. Cook and stir over medium heat until mixture comes to a full rolling boil. Remove from the heat; stir in marshmallows until melted. Add unsweetened chocolate and chocolate chips; stir until chips are melted. Stir in nuts and vanilla.

3 Spoon warm fudge into the prepared cookie cutters, filling to the top. Cool until set. To remove, gently push fudge out of cookie cutters. Tint frosting red and green; decorate fudge with frosting and candies.

Yield: about 5-1/2 pounds.

Editor's Note: Instead of using cookie cutters, fudge can be prepared in a foil-lined buttered 13-in. x 9-in. x 2-in. baking pan and cut into squares.

CHERRY CHOCOLATE BARK

udith batiuk, san luis obispo, california

This recipe from my daughter caught my eye because it reminded me of a candy bar I liked as a child. I love the fudge-like texture.

- 1 tablespoon plus 1/2 cup butter, softened, *divided*
- 2 cups sugar
- 12 large marshmallows
- 1 can (5 ounces) evaporated milk

Dash salt

- 1 cup vanilla or white chips
- 1-1/2 teaspoons cherry extract
- 1 teaspoon vanilla extract
- 1 cup semisweet chocolate chips
- 1/3 cup creamy peanut butter
- 1/4 cup finely chopped dry roasted peanuts

1. Line a 15-in. x 10-in. x 1-in. pan with foil. Grease the foil with 1 tablespoon butter; set aside. In a large heavy saucepan, combine the sugar, marshmallows, milk, salt and remaining butter. Bring to a boil; cook and stir for 5 minutes. Remove from the heat. Stir in vanilla chips and extracts until smooth. Pour into prepared pan.

2. In a microwave-safe bowl, melt chocolate chips; stir until smooth. Stir in peanut butter and peanuts. Drop by tablespoonfuls over first layer; cut through with a knife to swirl. Chill until firm.

3. Using foil, lift candy out of pan. Discard foil. Break candy into pieces. Store in an airtight container in the refrigerator.

Yield: about 2 pounds.

RASPBERRY NUT PINWHEELS

pat habiger, spearville, kansas

I won first prize in a recipe contest with these yummy swirl cookies a number of years ago. The taste of raspberries and walnuts really comes through in each bite, and they're so much fun to make!

- 1/2 cup butter, softened
- 1 cup sugar
- 1 egg
- 1 teaspoon vanilla extract
- 2 cups all-purpose flour
- 1 teaspoon baking powder
- 1/4 cup seedless raspberry jam
- 3/4 cup finely chopped walnuts

1. In a large bowl, cream butter and sugar until light and fluffy. Beat in egg and vanilla. Combine flour and baking powder; gradually add to creamed mixture and mix well.

2. Roll out dough between waxed paper into a 12-in. square. Remove top piece of waxed paper. Spread dough with jam and sprinkle with nuts. Roll up tightly jelly-roll style; wrap in plastic wrap. Refrigerate for 2 hours or until firm.

3. Unwrap dough and cut into 1/4-in. slices. Place 2 in. apart on ungreased baking sheets. Bake at 375° for 9-12 minutes or until edges are lightly browned. Remove to wire racks to cool.

Yield: about 3-1/2 dozen.

4. Meanwhile, in a microwave, melt chocolate chips and shortening; stir until smooth. Dip bottoms of cones into chocolate; allow excess to drip off. Return to waxed paper to harden. Store in an airtight container in the refrigerator.

Yield: about 3 dozen.

CARDAMOM COOKIES

mary steiner, west bend, wisconsin

Cardamom, almond extract and walnuts enhance the charm of these delicious cookies.

- 2 cups butter, softened
- 2-1/2 cups confectioners' sugar, *divided*
- 1-1/2 teaspoons almond extract
- 3-3/4 cups all-purpose flour
- 1 teaspoon ground cardamom
- 1/8 teaspoon salt
- 1 cup finely chopped walnuts

1. In a large bowl, cream butter and 1-1/2 cups confectioners' sugar until smooth. Beat in extract. Combine the flour, cardamom and salt; gradually add to the creamed mixture. Stir in walnuts.

2. Roll dough into 1-in. balls. Place 2 in. apart on ungreased baking sheets. Bake at 350° for 15-17 minutes or until edges are golden.

3. Roll warm cookies in remaining confectioners' sugar. Cool on wire racks.

Yield: 6 dozen.

COCONUT PEAKS

patricia shinn, fruitland park, florida

I found this gem on a slip of paper in a cookbook I got at a yard sale. The candies get great flavor from browned butter. I've received many requests for this recipe over the years.

- 1/4 cup butter
- 3 cups flaked coconut
- 2 cups confectioners' sugar
- 1/4 cup half-and-half cream
- 1 cup (6 ounces) semisweet chocolate chips
- 2 teaspoons shortening

1. Line a baking sheet with waxed paper; set aside. In a large saucepan, cook butter over medium-low heat until golden brown, about 5 minutes. Remove from the heat; stir in the coconut, sugar and cream.

2. Drop by rounded teaspoonfuls onto prepared baking sheet. Refrigerate until easy to handle, about 25 minutes.

3. Roll mixture into balls, then shape each into a cone. Return to baking sheet; refrigerate for 15 minutes.

CHINESE ALMOND COOKIES

jane garing, talladega, alabama

Each Christmas, my mother made lots of these cookies and stored them in clean coffee cans. When she passed away, I started giving our kids a can of these sentimental sweets.

- 1 cup butter, softened
- 1 cup sugar
- 1 egg
- 1 teaspoon almond extract
- 3 cups all-purpose flour
- 1 teaspoon baking soda
- 1/2 teaspoon salt
- 1/4 cup sliced almonds
- 1 egg white
- 1/2 teaspoon water

1 In a large bowl, cream butter and sugar. Beat in egg and extract. Combine the flour, baking soda and salt; gradually add to creamed mixture.

2 Roll into 1-in. balls. Place 2 in. apart on ungreased baking sheets. Flatten with a fork. Sprinkle with the almonds.

3 In a small bowl, beat egg white and water. Brush over cookies. Bake at 325° for 14-16 minutes or until the edges and bottoms are lightly browned. Cool for 2 minutes before removing from pans to wire racks.

Yield: about 5 dozen.

FENNEL TEA COOKIES

susan beck, napa, california

These tender cookies have a lovely fennel flavor and add a touch of elegance to any holiday cookie tray. Rolled in confectioners' sugar, they look like snowballs!

- 1 tablespoon fennel seed, crushed
- 2 tablespoons boiling water
- 3/4 cup butter, softened
- 2/3 cup packed brown sugar
- 1 egg
- 2 cups all-purpose flour
- 1/2 teaspoon baking soda

Confectioners' sugar

1 In a small bowl, soak fennel seed in boiling water; set aside. In a large bowl, cream butter and brown sugar until light and fluffy. Beat in egg. Drain the fennel seed. Combine the flour, baking soda and fennel seed; gradually add to creamed mixture and mix well.

2 Roll dough into 1-in. balls; place 2 in. apart on ungreased baking sheets. Bake at 350° for 10-12 minutes or until lightly browned. Roll warm cookies in confectioners' sugar. Cool on wire racks.

Yield: 3 dozen.

WHITE CHOCOLATE PUMPKIN DREAMS

jean kleckner, seattle, washington

If you like pumpkin pie, you'll love these delicious cookies dotted with white chocolate chips and chopped pecans. Spread with a brown sugar icing, they're irresistible.

- 1 cup butter, softened
- 1/2 cup *each* sugar and packed brown sugar
- 1 egg
- 2 teaspoons vanilla extract
- 1 cup canned pumpkin
- 2 cups all-purpose flour
- 3-1/2 teaspoons pumpkin pie spice
- 1 teaspoon *each* baking powder and baking soda
- 1/4 teaspoon salt
- 1 package (11 ounces) vanilla *or* white chips
- 1 cup chopped pecans

PENUCHE FROSTING:

- 1/2 cup packed brown sugar
- 3 tablespoons butter
- 1/4 cup milk
- 1-1/2 to 2 cups confectioners' sugar

1 In a large bowl, cream the butter and sugars until light and fluffy. Beat in the egg, vanilla and the pumpkin. Combine dry ingredients; gradually add to the creamed mixture and mix well. Stir in chips and pecans.

2 Drop by rounded teaspoonfuls 2 in. apart onto ungreased baking sheets. Bake at 350° for 12-14 minutes or until firm. Remove to wire racks to cool.

3 For frosting, combine brown sugar and butter in a small saucepan. Bring to a boil; cook over medium heat for 1 minute or until slightly thickened. Cool for 10 minutes. Add milk; beat until smooth. Beat in enough confectioners' sugar to reach desired consistency. Spread over cooled cookies.

Yield: about 4-1/2 dozen.

PEANUT BUTTER PRETZEL BITES

lois farmer, logan, west virginia

During the holidays, I was making candy with my daughter and we came up with this recipe. Bite into these special sweets to discover luscious peanut flavor and a salty pretzel crunch.

- 1 package (14 ounces) caramels
- 1/4 cup butter, cubed
- 2 tablespoons water
- 5 cups miniature pretzels
- 1 jar (18 ounces) chunky peanut butter
- 26 ounces milk chocolate candy coating

1 In a microwave-safe bowl, melt caramels with butter and water; stir until smooth. Spread one side of each pretzel with 1 teaspoon peanut butter; top with 1/2 teaspoon caramel mixture. Place on waxed paper-lined baking sheets. Refrigerate until set.

2 In a microwave, melt candy coating; stir until smooth. Using a small fork, dip each pretzel into coating until completely covered; shake off excess. Place on waxed paper. Let stand until set. Store in an airtight container in a cool dry place.

Yield: 8-1/2 dozen.

Editor's Note: This recipe was tested in a 1,100-watt microwave.

Slow-Cooked Chocolate

When I melt bulk chocolate or almond bark to coat candies, fruit or pretzels, I like to use my slow cooker. It keeps the chocolate warm for repeated dips.
—C.M. H., Walker, Minnesota

GIFTS FROM THE KITCHEN

HIDDEN
MINT
MORSELS
P. 276

CHOCOLATE-DIPPED ORANGE COOKIES

linda call, falun, kansas

These tender cookies are pretty to look at, and the combination of cream cheese, orange, chocolate and almonds makes them almost irresistible.

- 1 cup butter, softened
- 1 package (8 ounces) cream cheese, softened
- 1 cup sugar
- 1/2 teaspoon vanilla extract
- 2 tablespoons grated orange peel
- 2-1/2 cups all-purpose flour
- 1/2 teaspoon salt
- 1 cup finely chopped blanched almonds

GLAZE:

- 5 squares (1 ounce *each*) semisweet chocolate
- 3 tablespoons butter
- 1/4 cup finely chopped blanched almonds

1 In a large bowl, cream butter, cream cheese and sugar until light and fluffy. Beat in vanilla and orange peel. Combine flour and salt; gradually add to creamed mixture and mix well. Stir in almonds.

2 Roll into 1-in. balls. Place 2 in. apart on ungreased baking sheets. Flatten with a glass dipped in sugar. Bake at 325° for 20-25 minutes or until firm. Remove to wire racks to cool.

3 For glaze, in a microwave, melt chocolate and butter; stir until smooth. Dip each cookie halfway into chocolate; shake off excess. Immediately sprinkle with almonds. Place on waxed paper until set.

Yield: 6 dozen.

Flatten Cookies

I use a meat tenderizer dipped in sugar to flatten shaped cookie dough. This saves time and makes a nice round cookie with a decorative impression on the top.—Harriet H., La Porte City, Iowa

COCONUT CHOCOLATE-COVERED CHERRIES

sylvia chiappone, san ardo, california

A friend gave me this recipe because she knew how much I like chocolate-covered cherries. Coconut and nuts make this version absolutely divine.

- 1/2 cup butter, softened
- 3-3/4 cups confectioners' sugar
- 1/2 cup sweetened condensed milk
- 1 teaspoon vanilla extract
- 2 cups flaked coconut
- 2 cups finely chopped walnuts
- 2 jars (16 ounces *each*) maraschino cherries with stems, well drained and patted dry
- 2 packages (11-1/2 ounces *each*) milk chocolate chips
- 1 tablespoon shortening

1 In a large bowl, beat butter and confectioners' sugar until smooth. Beat in milk and vanilla until well blended and mixture looks like softened butter. Fold in the coconut and walnuts.

2 With moist hands, shape 2 teaspoonfuls of coconut mixture around each cherry, forming a ball. Place on a waxed paper-lined baking sheet. Cover and refrigerate for 1 hour or until chilled.

3 In a microwave, melt chocolate chips and shortening; stir until smooth. Dip coated cherries into chocolate. Place on waxed paper; let stand until set. Store in an airtight container at room temperature for up to 1 month.

Yield: about 5 dozen.

HIDDEN MINT MORSELS

adina skilbred, prairie du sac, wisconsin

Is it a cookie or a candy? No matter which answer folks choose, they find these minty morsels yummy. The recipe makes so much that you can whip up dozens of gifts at once.

- **1/3 cup *each* shortening and butter, softened**
- **3/4 cup sugar**
- **1 egg**
- **1 tablespoon milk**
- **1 teaspoon vanilla extract**
- **1-3/4 cups all-purpose flour**
- **1/3 cup baking cocoa**
- **1-1/2 teaspoons baking powder**
- **1/4 teaspoon salt**
- **1/8 teaspoon ground cinnamon**

PEPPERMINT LAYER:

- **4 cups confectioners' sugar**
- **6 tablespoons light corn syrup**
- **6 tablespoons butter, melted**
- **2 to 3 teaspoons peppermint extract**

CHOCOLATE COATING:

- **2 packages (11-1/2 ounces *each*) milk chocolate chips**
- **1/4 cup shortening**

1 In a large bowl, cream the shortening, butter and sugar until light and fluffy. Beat in the egg, milk and vanilla. Combine the flour, cocoa, baking powder, salt and cinnamon; gradually add to the creamed mixture. Cover and refrigerate for 8 hours or overnight.

2 On a lightly floured surface, roll dough to 1/8-in. thickness. Cut with a lightly floured 1/2-in. round cookie cutter; place on ungreased baking sheets.

3 Bake at 375° for 6-8 minutes or until set. Cool for 2 minutes before removing to wire racks to cool completely.

4 In a large bowl, combine all the peppermint layer ingredients. Knead for 1 minute or until smooth. Shape into 120 balls, 1/2 in. each. Place a ball on each cookie and flatten to cover cookie. Place on waxed paper-lined baking sheets; refrigerate for 30 minutes.

5 In a microwave, melt chips and shortening; stir until smooth. Spread about 1 teaspoonful over each cookie. Chill until firm.

Yield: about 10 dozen.

MIXED NUT-CORNFLAKE BRITTLE

rosemary lorentz, stratford, ontario

This five-ingredient brittle is one of the best I've made. The recipe is so easy to follow and can be completed in about 30 minutes. Friends ask me for the recipe all the time.

- **3/4 cup sugar**
- **1/2 cup light corn syrup**
- **1/4 cup butter**
- **6 cups cornflakes**
- **1-1/2 cups mixed nuts**

1 Line a 15-in. x 10-in. x 1-in. baking pan with foil and heavily grease the foil; set aside. In a large heavy saucepan, combine the sugar, corn syrup and butter. Cook and stir over medium-high heat until sugar is dissolved and mixture begins to a boil. Remove from the heat. Stir in cornflakes and nuts.

2 Spread into prepared pan. Bake at 300° for 25 minutes. Cool on a wire rack. Break into pieces. Store at room temperature in an airtight container.

Yield: about 1-1/4 pounds.

WHITE CHOCOLATE PEANUT BUTTER SQUARES

gloria jarrett, loveland, ohio

People regularly request the recipe once they try my peanut butter fudge dipped in melted white chocolate. It's a nice contrast to typical chocolates on a candy platter.

    1   tablespoon plus 3/4 cup butter, *divided*
    3   cups sugar
  2/3   cup evaporated milk
    1   package (10 ounces) peanut butter chips
    1   jar (7 ounces) marshmallow creme
    1   cup chopped nuts
    1   tablespoon vanilla extract
1-1/2   pounds white candy coating
  1/2   cup semisweet chocolate chips, optional
    1   teaspoon shortening, optional

1   Line a 13-in. x 9-in. pan with foil. Grease the foil with 1 tablespoon butter; set aside. In a heavy saucepan, combine the sugar, evaporated milk and remaining butter. Bring to a boil over medium heat; cook and stir for 5 minutes. Remove from the heat; stir in the peanut butter chips until melted. Add the marshmallow creme, nuts and vanilla; stir until blended. Pour into prepared pan. Cool.

2   Remove from pan and cut into 1-in. squares. Place on waxed paper-lined baking sheets; freeze or refrigerate until firm.

3   In a microwave, melt candy coating; stir until smooth. Dip the squares into the coating; place on waxed paper-lined baking sheets until set.

4   In a microwave, melt chocolate chips and shortening if desired; stir until smooth. Drizzle over the squares. Store in an airtight container.

Yield: 3-1/4 pounds (about 9-1/2 dozen).

BANANA NUT FRUITCAKE

brenda williams, silsbee, texas

Combining two popular baked goods—banana bread and fruitcake—yielded this treat. Even people who don't care for fruitcake will like this version!

1-1/2   cups sugar
  3/4   cup canola oil
    2   eggs, lightly beaten
    1   teaspoon vanilla extract
1-1/2   cups mashed ripe bananas (about 3 medium)
    3   cups all-purpose flour
    1   teaspoon salt
    1   teaspoon baking soda
1-1/2   cups chopped pecans
    1   cup chopped candied cherries
  1/2   cup chopped candied pineapple

1   In a large bowl, beat the sugar and oil. Beat in eggs and vanilla. Add bananas. Combine the flour, salt and baking soda; add to banana mixture just until blended. Fold in the pecans, cherries and pineapple.

2   Pour into two greased 8-in. x 4-in. loaf pans. Bake at 350° for 50-60 minutes or until golden brown and a toothpick inserted near the center comes out clean. Cool for 10 minutes before removing from pans to wire racks.

Yield: 2 loaves (16 slices each).

PINWHEEL MINTS

marilou roth, milford, nebraska

Both my grandmother and my mom used to make these eye-catching confections as a replacement for ordinary mints at Christmas. When I offer them at parties, guests tell me the mints are wonderful, and then ask how I created the pretty swirl pattern.

> 1 package (8 ounces) cream cheese, softened
> 1/2 to 1 teaspoon mint extract
> 7-1/2 to 8-1/2 cups confectioners' sugar

Red and green food coloring

Additional confectioners' sugar

1 In a large bowl, beat the cream cheese and mint extract until smooth. Gradually beat in as much confectioners' sugar as possible; knead in remaining confectioners' sugar until a firm mixture is achieved. Divide mixture in half; with food coloring, tint half pink and the other light green.

2 On waxed paper, lightly sprinkle remaining confectioners' sugar into a 12-in. x 5-in. rectangle. Divide pink portion in half; shape each portion into a 10-in. log. Place one log on sugared waxed paper and flatten slightly. Cover with waxed paper; roll into a 12-in. x 5-in. rectangle. Repeat with remaining pink portion; set aside. Repeat with light green portion.

3 Remove top piece of waxed paper from one pink and one green rectangle. Place one over the other. Roll up jelly-roll style, starting with a long side. Wrap in waxed paper; twist ends. Repeat. Chill overnight.

4 To serve, cut into 1/2-in. slices. Store in an airtight container in the refrigerator for up to 1 week.

Yield: about 3 dozen.

FROSTED CARROT MINI MUFFINS

taste of home test kitchen

These delicate muffins feature the sweet goodness of carrots and coconut topped with rich, citrusy frosting. Young and old alike will love them and definitely ask for seconds...and thirds!

> 1/4 cup *each* butter, softened and shortening
> 6 tablespoons sugar
> 1 egg
> 1/2 cup mashed cooked carrots
> 1/2 teaspoon vanilla extract
> 1 cup all-purpose flour
> 1 teaspoon baking powder
> 1/4 teaspoon salt
> 6 tablespoons flaked coconut, chopped

FROSTING:

> 2 tablespoons butter, softened
> 1 cup confectioners' sugar
> 1 teaspoon grated orange peel
> 1/2 teaspoon orange juice
> 1 to 2 teaspoons milk

1 In a large bowl, cream the butter, shortening and sugar until light and fluffy. Beat in the egg, carrots and vanilla. Combine the flour, baking powder and salt; gradually add to creamed mixture just until combined. Stir in coconut.

2 Fill greased or paper-lined miniature muffin cups three-fourths full. Bake at 400° for 12-14 minutes or until a toothpick comes out clean. Cool for 5 minutes before removing from pans to wire racks to cool completely.

3 For frosting, in a small bowl, cream the butter, confectioners' sugar, orange peel and juice until light and fluffy; add enough milk to achieve the desired consistency. Frost muffins.

Yield: 2-1/2 dozen.

COUNTRY CHRISTMAS CUTOUT MIX

eneatha attig secrest, mattoon, illinois

I have relied on the mix for these light sugar cookies for years, even selling it at bazaars. I package it in a plastic bag tied with pretty ribbon and attach a cookie cutter and copy of the recipe.

- 5 cups all-purpose flour
- 3 cups confectioners' sugar
- 2 teaspoons *each* baking soda and cream of tartar

ADDITIONAL INGREDIENTS:

- 1 cup butter, softened
- 1 egg
- 1 teaspoon vanilla extract
- 1/2 teaspoon almond extract

FROSTING:

- 3 tablespoons butter, softened
- 4 cups confectioners' sugar
- 1 teaspoon vanilla extract
- 2-1/2 to 3 tablespoons milk

Liquid *or* paste food coloring, optional

1 In a large bowl, combine first four ingredients. Store in an airtight container in a cool dry place for up to 6 months.

Yield: 2 batches (8 cups total).

2 **To prepare cookies (for one batch):** Contents of mix may settle during storage. When preparing recipe, spoon mix into measuring cup. In a large bowl, cream the butter until light and fluffy. Beat in egg and extracts. Gradually add 4 cups cookie mix; mix well. Cover and chill for 2-3 hours or overnight.

3 On lightly floured surface, roll out the dough to 1/8-in. thickness. Cut with a lightly floured 2-1/2-in. cookie cutter. Place 1 in. apart on ungreased baking sheets.

4 Bake at 375° for 7-9 minutes or until the edges are lightly browned. Remove from pans to cool on wire racks.

5 **For frosting:** In a small bowl, beat the butter, confectioners' sugar and vanilla until smooth. Gradually add milk until desired consistency is achieved. Add food coloring to some of the frosting if desired. Frost and decorate cookies.

Yield: about 4 dozen per batch.

PEPPERMINT HARD CANDY

lois ostenson, aneta, north dakota

This easy-to-make clear hard candy has a mint flavor from the combination of peppermint and vanilla extracts. Plus, the eye-catching sweets won't stick to your teeth.

- 1 tablespoon butter
- 2 cups sugar
- 1 cup light corn syrup
- 1 to 1-1/2 teaspoons peppermint extract
- 1 teaspoon vanilla extract
- 6 to 8 drops green food coloring, optional

1 Line a 13-in. x 9-in. pan with foil. Grease the foil with 1 tablespoon butter; set aside. In a large heavy saucepan, combine sugar and corn syrup. Bring to a boil over medium heat, stirring occasionally. Cover and cook for 3 minutes to dissolve sugar crystals. Uncover; cook over medium-high heat, without stirring, until a candy thermometer reads 300° (hard-crack stage).

2 Remove from the heat; stir in extracts and food coloring. Pour into prepared pan. Cool; break into pieces. Store in airtight containers.

Yield: about 1-1/4 pounds.

Editor's Note: We recommend that you test your candy thermometer before each use by bringing water to a boil; the thermometer should read 212°. Adjust your recipe temperature up or down based on your test.

CHOCOLATE CHIP NOUGAT

sandi friest, paynesville, minnesota
This sweet, chewy nougat adds a holiday blush to Yuletide gatherings. It takes a little extra effort to make, but candy this festive is worth it!

- 1 teaspoon plus 1/4 cup butter, softened, *divided*
- 3 cups sugar, *divided*
- 2/3 cup plus 1-1/4 cups light corn syrup, *divided*
- 2 tablespoons water
- 2 egg whites
- 2 cups chopped walnuts, toasted
- 2 teaspoons vanilla extract
- 1 cup (6 ounces) miniature semisweet chocolate chips
- 2 to 3 drops *each* red *and/or* green food coloring, optional

1 Line a 9-in. square pan with foil; grease foil with 1 teaspoon butter and set aside. In a small heavy saucepan, combine 1 cup sugar, 2/3 cup corn syrup and water. Bring to a boil over medium heat, stirring constantly. Reduce heat to medium-low. Cook, without stirring, until a candy thermometer reads 250°-266° (hard-ball stage).

2 Meanwhile, beat egg whites in a heat-proof large bowl until stiff peaks form. With mixer running on high speed, carefully add hot syrup in a slow steady stream, beating constantly at high speed until thickened; cover and set aside.

3 In a large heavy saucepan, combine remaining sugar and corn syrup. Bring to a boil over medium heat, stirring constantly. Reduce heat to medium-low; cook, without stirring, until a candy thermometer reads 275° (soft-crack stage).

4 Meanwhile, melt remaining butter. Pour hot syrup into reserved egg white mixture; stir with a wooden spoon. Stir in the walnuts, vanilla and melted butter.

5 Pour half of nougat mixture into prepared pan; press evenly. Sprinkle with chocolate chips. Tint remaining nougat mixture with red and/or green food coloring if desired; spread over chocolate chips. Press down evenly with buttered fingers. Let stand for several hours until set.

6 Using a knife coated with cooking spray, cut nougat into 1-in. squares. Wrap in plastic wrap or waxed paper if desired. Store at room temperature.

Yield: 2-1/2 pounds.

Editor's Note: We recommend that you test your candy thermometer before each use by bringing water to a boil; the thermometer should read 212°. Adjust your recipe temperature up or down based on your test.

CHOCOLATE-COATED PRETZELS

virginia chronic, robinson, illinois
These pretty pretzels are simple to make and are great presents any time of year.

- 1 to 1-1/4 pounds white *and/or* milk chocolate candy coating
- 1 package (8 ounces) miniature pretzels

Nonpareils, colored jimmies and colored sugar, optional

1 In a microwave, melt half of candy coating at a time. Dip pretzels in candy coating; allow excess to drip off. Place on waxed paper; let stand until almost set. Garnish as desired; let stand until set.

Yield: 5-6 dozen.

CINNAMON WALNUT BRITTLE

julie radcliffe, butte, montana

Seasoned with cinnamon, this spicy brittle is a great gift or family snack to munch while watching Christmas movies. Best of all, it goes together quick as a wink in the microwave.

- 1 cup sugar
- 1/2 cup light corn syrup
- 1 cup chopped walnuts
- 1 teaspoon butter
- 1/2 teaspoon ground cinnamon
- 1 teaspoon baking soda
- 1 teaspoon vanilla extract

1 Butter a baking sheet; set aside. In a 2-qt. microwave-safe bowl, combine sugar and corn syrup. Microwave, uncovered, on high for 3 minutes; stir. Cook, uncovered, on high 2-1/2 minutes longer. Stir in the walnuts, butter and cinnamon.

2 Microwave, uncovered, on high for 2 minutes longer or until mixture turns a light amber color (mixture will be very hot).

3 Quickly stir in baking soda and vanilla until light and foamy. Immediately pour onto prepared pan; spread with a metal spatula. Cool; break into pieces.

Yield: 3/4 pound.

Editor's Note: This recipe was tested in a 1,100-watt microwave.

HEARTY PASTA SOUP MIX

taste of home test kitchen

Warm up loved ones on frosty winter nights with a gift of this stick-to-the-ribs soup mix. Layered in pretty bow-tied jars, it looks just as good as it tastes! Be sure to include preparation instructions and a list of any additional ingredients needed with your gift card.

- 1/2 cup dried split peas
- 2 tablespoons chicken bouillon granules
- 1/2 cup dried lentils
- 2 tablespoons dried minced onion
- 1 teaspoon dried basil
- 1 teaspoon dried parsley flakes
- 1 envelope savory herb with garlic soup mix *or* vegetable soup mix
- 2 cups uncooked tricolor spiral pasta

ADDITIONAL INGREDIENTS:

- 10 cups water
- 3 cups cubed cooked chicken
- 1 can (28 ounces) diced tomatoes, undrained

1 In a 1-qt. glass container, layer first seven ingredients in the order listed. Place the pasta in a 1-qt. resealable plastic bag; add to the jar. Seal tightly.

Yield: 1 batch (4 cups).

2 **To prepare soup:** Remove pasta from top of jar and set aside. Place water in a Dutch oven; stir in soup mix. Bring to a boil. Reduce heat; cover and simmer for 45 minutes. Add the chicken, tomatoes and pasta. Cover and simmer for 15-20 minutes longer or until pasta, peas and lentils are tender.

Yield: 14 servings (3-1/2 quarts).

LEMON PEPPER BISCOTTI

dorothy smith, el dorado, arkansas

Flavored with a zesty combination of black pepper, garlic, lemon and Parmesan cheese, these crisp, savory cookies—a fun variation on the sweet version—are great for dipping or solo snacking.

- 1/2 cup butter, softened
- 2 tablespoons sugar
- 1 garlic clove, minced
- 2 eggs
- 2-1/4 cups all-purpose flour
- 1/2 cup grated Parmesan cheese
- 2 tablespoons minced fresh parsley
- 4 teaspoons grated lemon peel
- 1-1/2 teaspoons baking powder
- 1 to 2 teaspoons coarsely ground pepper
- 1/2 teaspoon salt

1 In a large bowl, cream the butter, sugar and garlic until fluffy. Add eggs, one at a time, beating well after each addition. Combine the flour, Parmesan cheese, parsley, lemon peel, baking powder, pepper and salt; gradually add to creamed mixture, beating until blended (dough will be stiff).

2 Divide dough in half. On an ungreased baking sheet, roll each portion into a 12-in. log. Bake at 350° for 25-30 minutes or until golden brown. Carefully transfer to a wire rack; cool for 15 minutes.

3 Transfer to a cutting board; cut diagonally with a sharp knife into 1/2-in. slices. Place cut side down on ungreased baking sheets. Bake for 10 minutes on each side or until golden brown and firm. Remove to wire racks to cool. Store in an airtight container.

Yield: 2 dozen.

HOLIDAY DIVINITY

helen white, kerrville, texas

I've been whipping up this Christmasy treat—with its jolly red and green candied cherries and scrumptious chopped nuts—for over fifty years. It's so light it melts in your mouth.

- 2 cups sugar
- 1/2 cup water
- 1/3 cup light corn syrup
- 2 egg whites
- 1 teaspoon vanilla extract
- 1/8 teaspoon salt
- 1 cup chopped walnuts, toasted
- 1/4 cup diced candied cherries
- 1/4 cup diced candied pineapple

1 In a heavy saucepan, combine the sugar, water and corn syrup; cook and stir until sugar is dissolved and mixture comes to a boil. Cook over medium heat, without stirring, until a candy thermometer reads 250°-266° (hard-ball stage). Remove from the heat.

2 Meanwhile, in a stand mixer, beat the egg whites until stiff peaks form. With mixer running on high speed, carefully pour hot syrup in a slow, steady stream into the mixing bowl. Add vanilla and salt. Beat on high speed just until candy loses its gloss and holds its shape, about 10 minutes. Stir in nuts and fruit.

3 Drop by teaspoonfuls onto waxed paper. Store in airtight containers.

Yield: 1-1/4 pounds.

SPICY OATMEAL COOKIE MIX

taste of home test kitchen

Brown sugar and spice and everything nice—like cinnamon, coconut, oats and chips—are layered together in pretty jars of yummy, ready-to-bake cookies. It's a quick and easy gift idea that's appreciated any time of year. Remember to include preparation instructions and a list of any additional ingredients needed with your gift tag.

- 1 cup all-purpose flour
- 1 teaspoon ground cinnamon
- 3/4 teaspoon baking soda
- 1/4 teaspoon salt
- 1/8 teaspoon ground nutmeg
- 1/2 cup *each* packed brown sugar and sugar
- 1 cup old-fashioned oats
- 1 cup swirled milk chocolate and caramel chips
- 1/2 cup flaked coconut

ADDITIONAL INGREDIENTS:

- 1/2 cup butter, softened
- 1 egg
- 3/4 teaspoon vanilla extract

1　In a small bowl, combine the first five ingredients. In a 1-qt. glass jar, layer the flour mixture, brown sugar, sugar, oats, chips and coconut, packing well between each layer. Cover and store in a cool, dry place for up to 6 months.

Yield: 1 batch (4 cups).

2　**To prepare cookies:** In a large bowl, beat the butter, egg and vanilla. Add the cookie mix and mix well. Drop by rounded teaspoonfuls 2 in. apart onto ungreased baking sheets. Bake at 350° for 9-11 minutes or until golden brown. Cool for 2 minutes before removing to wire racks.

Yield: about 3-1/2 dozen.

BUTTER ALMOND CRUNCH

judy hamilton, charleston, west virginia

I always draw rave reviews for this buttery, melt-in-your-mouth candy. From the coconut bottom layer to the chocolate drizzled on top, it's a winner all year-round.

- 1-1/2 teaspoons plus 1/2 cup butter, *divided*
- 3/4 cup flaked coconut
- 1-1/2 cups sugar
- 3 tablespoons water
- 1 tablespoon light corn syrup
- 3/4 cup sliced almonds
- 1/2 cup semisweet chocolate chips

1　Line a 13-in. x 9-in. pan with foil. Grease the foil with 1-1/2 teaspoons butter. Spread coconut evenly into prepared pan; set aside.

2　In a heavy saucepan, combine the sugar, water and corn syrup. Bring to a boil over medium heat, stirring occasionally. Add remaining butter; cook and stir until butter is melted. Continue cooking, without stirring, until a candy thermometer reads 300° (hard-crack stage). Remove from the heat. Stir in almonds. Pour over coconut. Cool.

3　In a microwave, melt chocolate chips; stir until smooth. Drizzle over the candy; cool until firm. Remove from foil and break into pieces. Store in airtight containers.

Yield: about 1-1/4 pounds.

RAISIN BRAN MUFFIN MIX

darlene brenden, salem, oregon

My husband likes to take muffins to work. And with this mix in my pantry, I can have muffins ready in mere minutes.

- 2 cups all-purpose flour
- 1-1/4 cups sugar
- 1 cup nonfat dry milk powder
- 6 teaspoons baking powder
- 1 teaspoon salt
- 1/2 teaspoon ground cinnamon
- 1 cup shortening
- 1-1/2 cups raisin bran cereal
- 1 cup chopped almonds

ADDITIONAL INGREDIENTS (for each batch):

- 1 egg
- 1 cup water

1 In a large bowl, combine the first six ingredients. Cut in shortening until crumbly. Stir in cereal and nuts. Store in an airtight container in a cool dry place or in the freezer for up to 2 months.

Yield: 2 batches (8 cups total).

2 **To prepare muffins:** Place 4 cups of muffin mix in a bowl. Beat egg and water; stir into mix just until moistened. Fill greased muffin cups two-thirds full. Bake at 400° for 15-17 minutes or until a toothpick comes out clean. Cool for 5 minutes before removing from pan to a wire rack.

Yield: 1 dozen.

FLAVORED MOCHA DRINK MIX

edna hoffman, hebron, indiana

I rely on extracts to get three great flavors from one hot beverage mix. At Christmastime, you can package these fun mixes in pretty jars, decorative tins or holiday mugs to make great-tasting gifts.

- 1-1/2 cups powdered nondairy creamer
- 1 cup sugar
- 1/2 cup instant coffee granules
- 1/2 cup baking cocoa

Dash salt

FOR ALMOND MOCHA DRINK:

- 1/4 teaspoon vanilla extract
- 1/4 teaspoon almond extract

FOR MINT MOCHA DRINK:

- 1/4 teaspoon vanilla extract
- 1/4 teaspoon mint extract

FOR ORANGE MOCHA DRINK:

- 1/4 teaspoon vanilla extract
- 1/4 teaspoon orange extract

ADDITIONAL INGREDIENTS (FOR EACH SERVING):

- 3/4 cup boiling water

Whipped cream, optional

1 In a bowl, combine the first five ingredients. Add vanilla, almond, mint or orange extract; mix well. Store in an airtight container in a cool dry place for up to 1 year.

Yield: 14-16 batches, about 3 cups total.

2 **To prepare beverage:** Dissolve about 3 tablespoons mix in water; stir well. Top with whipped cream if desired.

Yield: 1 serving per batch.

FRIENDSHIP SOUP MIX

wendy taylor, mason city, iowa

I layer this pretty, delicious soup mix in glass jars to give as gifts. It's always well received.

- 1/2 cup dried green split peas
- 1/3 cup beef bouillon granules
- 1/4 cup medium pearl barley
- 1/2 cup dried lentils, rinsed and well dried
- 1/4 cup dried minced onion
- 2 teaspoons Italian seasoning
- 1/2 cup uncooked long grain rice
- 1/2 cup uncooked alphabet pasta *or* other small pasta

ADDITIONAL INGREDIENTS:

- 1 pound ground beef
- 3 quarts water
- 1 can (28 ounces) diced tomatoes, undrained

1 In a 1-1/2-pint jar, layer the first seven ingredients in the order listed. Wrap pasta in a small sheet of plastic wrap; add to jar. Seal tightly. Store in a cool dry place for up to 3 months.

2 **To prepare soup:** Remove pasta from jar and set aside. In a Dutch oven over medium heat, cook the beef until no longer pink; drain. Add the water, tomatoes and soup mix; bring to a boil. Reduce heat; cover and simmer for 45 minutes. Stir in the reserved pasta; cover and simmer for 15-20 minutes or until the pasta, peas, barley and lentils are tender.

Yield: 16 servings (4 quarts) per batch.

POPPY SEED BREAD MIX

laurie marini, newport, north carolina

I'm always on the lookout for recipes that are quick, easy and use ingredients I normally have on hand. This simple seeded loaf is delicious alone or spread with cream cheese or jam. It freezes well, too.

- 10 cups all-purpose flour
- 4 cups sugar
- 1 cup poppy seeds
- 1/4 cup plus 2 teaspoons baking powder
- 4 teaspoons salt

ADDITIONAL INGREDIENTS:

- 1 egg
- 1-1/4 cups milk
- 1/3 cup canola oil
- 1 teaspoon vanilla extract

1 In a large bowl, combine the first five ingredients. Store in an airtight container in a cool dry place for up to 6 months.

Yield: 4 batches (16 cups total).

2 **To prepare one loaf:** In a large mixing bowl, combine the egg, milk, oil and vanilla. Add 4 cups bread mix; stir just until moistened.

3 Pour into a greased 9-in. x 5-in. x 3-in. loaf pan. Bake at 350° for 55-60 minutes or until a toothpick inserted near the center comes out clean. Cool for 10 minutes; remove the loaf from the pan to a wire rack.

Yield: 1 loaf per batch.

STRAWBERRY COFFEE CAKE

caroline roggenbuck, pullman, washington

I came across this winning recipe when helping my mom organize her extensive recipe collection.

    1 tablespoon cornstarch
    1 package (10 ounces) frozen sweetened sliced strawberries
 1/4 teaspoon ground cinnamon
 1/4 teaspoon almond extract
2-1/3 cups all-purpose flour
 3/4 cup sugar
 3/4 cup cold butter
 1/2 teaspoon baking powder
 1/2 teaspoon baking soda
 1/8 teaspoon salt
 3/4 cup buttermilk
    1 egg, lightly beaten

1 In a large saucepan, combine cornstarch and strawberries until blended. Bring to a boil over medium heat or until thickened. Remove from the heat. Stir in cinnamon and extract; set aside.

2 In a large bowl, combine flour and sugar. Cut in butter until mixture is crumbly. Set aside 1/2 cup for topping. Add baking powder, baking soda and salt to the remaining flour mixture. Stir in buttermilk and egg until moistened.

3 Spread 1-1/2 cups batter into a greased 8-in. square baking dish. Carefully spread with strawberry

mixture. Drop remaining batter by tablespoonfuls over strawberry mixture. Sprinkle with reserved crumb mixture. Bake at 350° for 35-40 minutes or until golden brown. Cool on a wire rack.

Yield: 9 servings.

HERBED POPCORN

(PICTURED ON NEXT PAGE)

donna gonda, north canton, ohio

This savory popcorn is a nice break from the usual sweet snack mixes and is a great hostess gift.

    8 cups popped popcorn
    2 cups potato sticks
    1 cup mixed nuts
 1/3 cup butter, melted
    1 teaspoon dill weed
    1 teaspoon lemon-pepper seasoning
    1 teaspoon Worcestershire sauce
 1/2 teaspoon onion powder
 1/2 teaspoon garlic powder

1 In a large bowl, combine the popcorn, potato sticks and nuts. In a small bowl, combine the remaining ingredients. Drizzle over popcorn mixture and toss to coat.

2 Spread into two ungreased 15-in. x 10-in. x 1-in. baking pans. Bake, uncovered, at 250° for 25-30 minutes or until lightly browned, stirring twice. Cool on a wire rack. Store the popcorn in an airtight container.

Yield: 9 cups.

GLAZED MACADAMIA NUTS

(PICTURED ON NEXT PAGE)

sandy frano, polo, illinois

I started using this recipe years ago, and it's been a hit ever since. Family and friends can't stop nibbling on the sweet coated nuts.

    3 cups macadamia nuts
 1/2 cup sugar, *divided*
    3 tablespoons light corn syrup
    2 teaspoons canola oil
 1/8 teaspoon salt
    3 tablespoons butter

1 Spread macadamia nuts in a single layer in a greased 15-in. x 10-in. x 1-in. baking pan. Bake at 250° for 5 minutes; set aside.

2 In a heavy saucepan, combine 6 tablespoons sugar, corn syrup, oil and salt; bring to a boil,

stirring constantly. Boil without stirring until a candy thermometer reads 238° (soft-ball stage).

3 Remove from the heat; stir in butter until melted. Pour over the nuts; stir to coat. Bake for 50-55 minutes or until lightly browned, stirring occasionally. Sprinkle with remaining sugar; toss to coat. Spread on foil to cool. Break apart and store in an airtight container.

Yield: 5 cups.

Editor's Note: We recommend that you test your candy thermometer before each use by bringing water to a boil; the thermometer should read 212°. Adjust your recipe temperature up or down based on your test.

SWEET 'N' CRUNCHY SNACK MIX

(PICTURED BELOW)

susan grummert, plymouth, nebraska

A combination of sweet and savory ingredients gives this treat a fun look and fabulous flavor. The recipe makes a big batch so there's plenty to share...if you can stop your family from eating it!

3 cups Cocoa Puffs
3 cups Rice Chex
1-1/2 cups pretzel twists
1 cup dry roasted peanuts
1 cup packed brown sugar
1/2 cup butter, cubed
1/4 cup light corn syrup
1/4 teaspoon cream of tartar
1/4 teaspoon baking soda
1/2 teaspoon vanilla extract

1 In a roasting pan, combine the cereals, pretzels and peanuts; set aside. In a heavy saucepan, combine the brown sugar, butter and corn syrup. Cook and stir over low heat until sugar is dissolved. Boil slowly for 4 minutes without stirring.

2 Remove from the heat; stir in the cream of tartar and baking soda. Stir in the vanilla. Pour over the cereal mixture and stir gently to coat. Bake at 300° for 30 minutes, stirring once. Spread on foil to cool. Store the mix in an airtight container.

Yield: 12 cups.

COOKIE ORNAMENTS

patricia slater, baldwin, ontario

What a welcome gift these fun frosted ornaments will make. But beware...the ginger-flavored cookies are so appetizing, they might never make it to the tree!

1/3 cup butter, softened
1/3 cup shortening
3/4 cup sugar
1 egg
1 teaspoon vanilla extract
2 cups all-purpose flour
1-1/2 teaspoons baking powder
1 teaspoon ground ginger
1/4 teaspoon salt
1/8 teaspoon ground cloves
FROSTING:
1-1/2 cups confectioners' sugar
3 tablespoons butter, softened
1/2 teaspoon vanilla extract
1 to 2 tablespoons milk
Food coloring and colored sprinkles, optional

1 In a mixing bowl, cream the butter, shortening and sugar until light and fluffy. Beat in egg and vanilla. Combine the flour, baking powder, ginger, salt and cloves; gradually add to creamed mixture. Cover and refrigerate the dough for 1 hour or until easy to handle.

2 Divide dough in half. On a lightly floured surface, roll out each portion to 1/8-in. thickness. Cut with floured 2-1/2-in. cookie cutters. Using a floured spatula, place cookies 1 in. apart on ungreased baking sheets. With a straw, make a hole about 1/2 in. from the top of each cookie. Bake at 375° for 7-9 minutes or until edges are lightly browned. Remove to wire racks to cool.

3 In a small mixing bowl, combine confectioners' sugar, butter, vanilla and enough milk to achieve frosting consistency. Frost cookies. Decorate with tinted frosting and colored sprinkles if desired. Let dry completely. Thread ribbon or string through holes.

Yield: about 4 dozen.

HOT RASPBERRY-LEMONADE DRINK MIX

taste of home test kitchen

To accompany the warm wishes you send in a gift basket, include this fruity blend. The combination of powdered mixes for lemonade, raspberry drink and tea is one folks can enjoy by simply stirring in hot water.

1-1/2 cups powdered lemonade mix with sugar
1 carton (1.3 ounces) raspberry soft drink mix
1 cup instant tea mix
Boiling water

1 In a bowl, combine the first three ingredients. Store in an airtight container in a cool dry place for up to 3 months.

Yield: 3 cups mix.

2 **To prepare one serving:** Dissolve 1 teaspoon of mix in 1 cup of boiling water.

Yield: 1 serving.

COCONUT CHOCOLATE CREAMS

kelly-ann gibbons, prince george, british columbia

My mom gave me the recipe for these tempting truffle-like candies. They make any occasion special for my family. I love to impress dinner guests by setting out a pretty plate of these treats at the end of the meal.

> 2-1/2 cups flaked coconut
> 1 cup (6 ounces) semisweet chocolate chips
> 1/2 cup evaporated milk
> 2-1/2 cups confectioners' sugar
> 1/3 cup chopped pecans
> 1/3 cup chopped maraschino cherries

1 Place coconut in a blender or food processor; cover and process until finely chopped. In a microwave or heavy saucepan, melt chocolate chips and milk. Remove from the heat; stir in confectioners' sugar, 1-1/4 cups coconut, pecans and cherries. Cover and refrigerate for hours or until firm. Set remaining coconut aside.

2 Shape chocolate mixture into 1-in. balls; roll in reserved coconut. Place on waxed paper-lined baking sheets. Refrigerate for 2 hours or until firm. Store in an airtight container in the refrigerator.

Yield: about 3 dozen.

APPLE-CINNAMON OATMEAL MIX

lynne van wagenen, salt lake city, utah

Oatmeal is a breakfast staple at our house. It's a warm, nutritious start to the day that keeps us going all morning. We used to buy the oatmeal mixes, but we think our homemade version tastes much better! Feel free to substitute raisins or other dried fruit for the apples.

> 6 cups quick-cooking oats
> 1-1/3 cups nonfat dry milk powder
> 1 cup dried apples, diced
> 1/4 cup sugar
> 1/4 cup packed brown sugar
> 1 tablespoon ground cinnamon
> 1 teaspoon salt
> 1/4 teaspoon ground cloves

ADDITIONAL INGREDIENT (for each serving):

> 1/2 cup water

1 In a large bowl, combine the first eight ingredients. Store in an airtight container in a cool dry place for up to 6 months.

Yield: 8 cups total.

2 **To prepare oatmeal:** Shake the mix well. In a small saucepan, bring water to a boil; slowly stir in 1/2 cup mix. Cook and stir over medium heat for 1 minute. Remove from the heat. Cover and let stand for 1 minute or until oatmeal reaches desired consistency.

Yield: 1 serving.

BANANA FRUIT MINI LOAVES

jean engle, pella, iowa
Plenty of goodies come in these little breads. The recipe is from my aunt, who always baked homemade treats for my sister and me when we visited her. Several of her recipes remain favorites of mine today.

          2 eggs
        2/3 cup sugar
          1 cup mashed bananas (about 2 medium)
      1-3/4 cups all-purpose flour
          3 teaspoons baking powder
        1/2 teaspoon salt
          1 cup mixed candied fruit
        1/2 cup raisins
        1/2 cup chopped walnuts

1   In a mixing bowl, beat the eggs and sugar. Add bananas; mix well. Combine the flour, baking powder and salt; gradually add to egg mixture. Fold in fruit, raisins and walnuts.

2   Transfer to three greased 5-3/4-in. x 3-in. x 2-in. loaf pans. Bake at 350° for 30-35 minutes or until a toothpick comes out clean. Cool for 10 minutes before removing from pans to wire racks to cool completely.

Yield: 3 mini loaves.

FRIENDSHIP BROWNIES

travis burkholder, middleburg, pennsylvania
Layered in a jar, this brownie mix is the perfect gift to give to loved ones during the holiday season.

BROWNIE MIX:
          1 cup plus 2 tablespoons all-purpose flour
        2/3 cup packed brown sugar
        3/4 teaspoon salt
        2/3 cup sugar
          1 teaspoon baking powder
        1/3 cup baking cocoa
        1/2 cup semisweet chocolate chips
        1/2 cup chopped walnuts
ADDITIONAL INGREDIENTS:
          3 eggs
        2/3 cup canola oil
          1 teaspoon vanilla extract

1   Pour the flour into a 1-qt. glass container with a tight-fitting lid. Layer with the brown sugar, salt, sugar, baking powder, cocoa, chocolate chips and nuts (do not mix). Cover and store in a cool dry place for up to 6 months.

2   **To prepare brownies:** In a large bowl, beat the eggs, oil and vanilla. Stir in the brownie mix until well combined.

3   Spread into a greased 9-in. square baking pan. Bake at 350° for 34-38 minutes or until a toothpick inserted near the center comes out clean. Cool on a wire rack.

Yield: 16 brownies.

HOMEMADE CREAM-STYLE SOUP MIX

deann alleva, worthington, ohio
This easy soup mix is a wonderful substitute for canned cream soup in a recipe. It's great to have on hand for those nights when you need to whip up supper in a hurry.

- 2 cups nonfat dry milk powder
- 1/2 cup plus 2 tablespoons cornstarch
- 1/2 cup mashed potato flakes
- 1/4 cup chicken bouillon granules
- 2 teaspoons dried parsley flakes
- 2 teaspoons dried minced onion
- 1 teaspoon dried celery flakes
- 1 teaspoon dried minced garlic
- 1 teaspoon onion powder
- 1/2 teaspoon dried marjoram
- 1/4 teaspoon garlic powder
- 1/8 teaspoon white pepper

1 In a small bowl, combine all ingredients. Store in an airtight container in a cool dry place for up to 1 year.

2 Use as a substitute for half of a 10-3/4-oz. can of condensed cream of chicken, mushroom or celery soup.

3 In a microwave-safe bowl, whisk 2/3 cup water and 3 tablespoons soup mix. Microwave, uncovered, on high for 2 to 2-1/2 minutes or until thickened and bubbly, whisking occasionally.

4 For mushroom soup, add 1/4 to 1/2 cup sauteed sliced mushrooms. For celery soup, add 1/8 teaspoon celery salt or one sauteed sliced or chopped celery rib.

Yield: 3 cups (16 batches).

PISTACHIO CRANBERRY COOKIES

arlene kroll, vero beach, florida
I came up with these one year when looking for a cookie that had a little red and green in it. The combination of cranberries and pistachios is delicious.

- 1/2 cup butter, softened
- 1/2 cup canola oil
- 1/2 cup sugar
- 1/2 cup packed brown sugar
- 1 egg
- 1 teaspoon vanilla extract
- 1-3/4 cups all-purpose flour
- 1/2 teaspoon salt
- 1/2 teaspoon baking powder
- 1/2 teaspoon baking soda
- 1 cup crisp rice cereal
- 1/2 cup old-fashioned oats
- 1/2 cup dried cranberries
- 1/2 cup chopped pistachios

1 In a large bowl, cream the butter, oil and sugars until light and fluffy. Beat in the egg and vanilla. Combine flour, salt, baking powder and baking soda; gradually add to the creamed mixture and mix well. Stir in the cereal, oats, cranberries and pistachios.

2 Drop by tablespoonfuls 2 in. apart onto ungreased baking sheets. Bake at 350° for 10-12 minutes or until lightly browned. Remove to wire racks to cool.

Yield: 5 dozen.

CURRIED RICE MIX

pat kelly, worthington, west virginia

Giving containers filled with homemade goodies is my merry habit. This zesty rice side dish is a particular favorite.

- 2 cups uncooked long grain rice
- 1 cup chopped dried mixed fruit
- 1 cup slivered almonds
- 1/2 cup golden raisins
- 2 tablespoons dried minced onion
- 4 teaspoons beef bouillon granules
- 4 teaspoons curry powder
- 1 teaspoon salt

ADDITIONAL INGREDIENTS FOR RICE:
- 2-1/2 cups water
- 2 tablespoons butter

1 In a large bowl, combine the first eight ingredients. Store in an airtight container in a cool dry place for up to 3 months.

Yield: 2 batches.

2 **To prepare rice:** Combine water and butter in a saucepan; bring to a boil. Add 2 cups rice mix; reduce heat. Cover and simmer for 20 minutes or until liquid is absorbed.

Yield: 4-6 servings per batch.

CHOCOLATE PEPPERMINT PINWHEELS

ellen johnson, hampton, virginia

My cookie-loving family is never satisfied with just one batch of these minty pinwheels, so I automatically double the recipe each time I bake them.

- 1 cup shortening
- 1-1/2 cups sugar
- 2 eggs
- 2 tablespoons milk
- 2 teaspoons peppermint extract
- 2-1/2 cups all-purpose flour
- 1/2 teaspoon salt
- 1/2 teaspoon baking powder
- 2 squares (1 ounce *each*) unsweetened chocolate, melted

1 In a large mixing bowl, cream shortening and sugar until light and fluffy. Add eggs, milk and extract; mix well. Combine the flour, salt and baking powder; gradually add to creamed mixture. Divide dough in half. Add the chocolate to one portion; mix well.

2 Roll each portion between waxed paper into a 16-in. x 7-in. rectangle, about 1/4 in. thick. Remove top sheet of waxed paper; place plain dough over chocolate dough. Roll up jelly-roll style, starting with a long side. Wrap in plastic wrap; refrigerate for 2 hours or until firm.

3 Unwrap dough and cut into 1/4-in. slices. Place 2 in. apart on greased baking sheets. Bake at 375° for 8-10 minutes or until lightly browned. Remove to wire racks to cool.

Yield: 4 dozen.

GENERAL RECIPE INDEX

BEVERAGES *(continued)*

HOT
Cinnamon Mocha Coffee 7
Cinnamon Orange Cider 29
Eggnog Coffee 19
Flavored Mocha Drink Mix 284
Hot Buttered Rum Mix 9
Hot Raspberry-Lemonade Drink
  Mix 288
Mulled Pomegranate Sipper 15
Warm Chocolate Eggnog 26
Warm Percolator Punch 5
Winter's Warmth Hot Chocolate 16

BLUEBERRIES
Blueberry-Stuffed French Toast 127

BREADS & ROLLS *(also see Coffee Cakes; Muffins; Scones; Stollen)*
Banana Fruit Mini Loaves 290
Banana Wheat Bread 176
Blender Yeast Rolls 149
Braided Wreath Bread 174
Celebration Braid 181
Cherry Nut Bread 160
Chocolate Chip Caramel Rolls 163
Chocolate Chip Cinnamon Rolls 149
Chocolate-Filled Crescents 151
Chocolate-Pecan Sticky Buns 153
Chocolate Pumpkin Bread 178
Christmas Banana Bread 169
Christmas Cranberry Rolls 172
Christmas Morning Croissants 179
Christmas Tree Sweet Rolls 172
Cranberry Corn Bread 163
Cranberry-Nut Poppy Seed Bread 151
Cranberry Swirl Loaf 170
Creamy Chocolate Crescents 169
Crunchy Onion Sticks 24
Dilly Onion Dinner Rolls 177
Easy-Does-It Fruitcake 173
Feather Whole Wheat Rolls 165
Featherlight Rolls 179
Freezer Crescent Rolls 175
Gigantic Cinnamon Rolls 144
Gingerbread Loaf 182
Herb Potato Rolls 164
Holiday Braids 153
Holiday Cranberry Yeast Bread 167
Maple-Oat Dinner Rolls 156
Maple Pecan Coffee Twist 170
Maraschino Cherry Mini Loaves 154
Orange Cranberry Bread 162
Orange-Hazelnut Spiral Rolls 168
Peachy Rolls 180
Pistachio Pumpkin Bread 157
Poppy Seed Bread Mix 285
Poppy Seed Sweet Rolls 150
Pretzel Wreaths 161
Scrambled Egg Brunch Bread 125
Sun-Dried Tomato 'n' Basil
  Wreath 154
Swedish Pastry Rings 155
Walnut-Crusted Wheat Loaves 159

White Chocolate Cranberry
  Bread 165
Yummy Yeast Rolls 168

BROCCOLI
ABC Salad 94
Broccoli Potato Supreme 73
Broccoli Quiche Crepe Cups 120
Triple-Cheese Broccoli Puff 78

BRUSSELS SPROUTS
Buttery Carrots & Brussels Sprouts 58
Creamy Brussels Sprouts Bake 68

CABBAGE
Sweet-and-Sour Red Cabbage 82

CAKES *(also see Tortes)*
Apple-Raisin Bundt Cake 216
Caramel Chocolate Cake 190
Chocolate Ganache Cake 210
Chocolate Hazelnut Gateau 202
Chocolate Mint Cake Roll 198
Gift-Wrapped Chocolate Cake 204
Ginger Peach Upside-Down Cake 212
Old-Fashioned Jam Cake 224
Peppermint Cake Log 192
Yuletide Pound Cake 190

CANDY
Almond Apricot Dips 247
Almond Crunch Toffee 234
Aloha Brittle 249
Apricot White Fudge 260
Bavarian Mint Fudge 226
Butter Almond Crunch 283
Butter Ball Chiffons 264
Butterscotch Hard Candy 267
Cappuccino Truffles 230
Caramel Marshmallow Treats 263
Caramel Pretzel Sticks 254
Cherry Chocolate Bark 271
Cherry Peanut Butter Balls 231
Chocolate Caramel Candy 225
Chocolate Caramel Thumbprints 227
Chocolate Chip Nougat 280
Chocolate-Coated Pretzels 280
Chocolate Zebra Clusters 239
Cinnamon Walnut Brittle 281
Coconut Chocolate-Covered
  Cherries 275
Coconut Chocolate Creams 289
Coconut Peaks 272
Cranberry Almond Bark 227
Cranberry Gumdrops 264
Crunchy Chocolate Cups 228
Hard Maple Candy 238
Holiday Divinity 282
Layered Mint Fudge 262
Macadamia Nut Fudge 270
Maple Ginger Fudge 238
Mixed Nut-Cornflake Brittle 276
Old-Fashioned Caramels 232
Old-Fashioned Molasses Candy 252

Orange Cappuccino Creams 240
Orange Coconut Creams 233
Peanut Butter Pretzel Bites 274
Peppermint Fudge 265
Peppermint Hard Candy 279
Peppermint Lollipops 226
Pink Ice 235
Pinwheel Mints 278
Pistachio Cranberry Bark 259
Raisin Cashew Drops 268
Terrific Toffee 268
Toffee Peanut Clusters 243
Triple-Nut Candy 256
White Chocolate Peanut Butter
  Squares 277
White Chocolate Peppermint
  Fudge 230

CARROTS
Baked Shredded Carrots 71
Buttery Carrots & Brussels Sprouts 58
Frosted Carrot Mini Muffins 278
Honey-Glazed Carrots 80
Maple-Glazed Carrots 77
Red Pepper Carrot Soup 99
Whipped Carrots with Cranberries 72

CAULIFLOWER
Baked Cauliflower 69
Roasted Peppers 'n' Cauliflower 57
Swiss-Topped Cauliflower Soup 95

CHEESE

APPETIZERS
Bake Brie with Roasted Garlic 12
Black Forest Ham Pinwheels 17
Cajun Canapes 26
Cranberry Camembert Pizza 14
Feta Artichoke Bites 6
Fruit and Caramel Brie 16
Jalapeno Cheese Spread 22
Mozzarella Marinara 23
Pimiento-Olive Cheese Log 21
Ranch-Sausage Wonton Cups 27
Salsa Cheesecake 8
Savory Ham Cheesecake 19
Shrimp Toast Cups 29
Sweet Cheese Ball 27
Tangy Cheese Bites 30

BREADS
Strawberry Cheesecake Muffins 160

DESSERTS *(also see Cheesecakes)*
Cheese-Filled Shortbread Tartlets 203
Cream Puff Dessert 208
Fruit-and-Cheese Bars 256
Ricotta Nut Torte 201

ENTREES
Artichoke Spinach Lasagna 35
Aspargus Cheese Quiche 142
Asparagus Pie 148
Asparagus Veal Cordon Bleu 41
Chicken 'n' Ham Frittata 143
Chicken Saltimbocca 44

SALADS & SALAD DRESSING
(continued)

GELATIN SALADS

SAUSAGE

APPETIZERS

SEAFOOD & FISH

APPETIZERS

SCONES

SIDE DISHES

SNACK MIXES

SOUPS

SPINACH

SQUASH & ZUCCHINI

ALPHABETICAL INDEX